International Capital Flows in Calm and Turbulent Times

Development and Inequality in the Market Economy

The purpose of this series is to encourage and foster analytical and policy-oriented work on market-based reform in developing and postsocialist countries. Special attention will be devoted in the series to exploring the effects of free market policies on social inequality and sustainable growth and development.

Titles in the Series:

Andrés Solimano, Editor. *Road Maps to Prosperity: Essays on Growth and Development*

Andrés Solimano, Editor. *Social Inequality: Values, Growth, and the State*

Lance Taylor, Editor. *After Neoliberalism: What Next for Latin America?*

Andrés Solimano, Eduardo Aninat, and Nancy Birdsall, Editors. *Distributive Justice and Economic Development: The Case of Chile and Developing Countries*

Jaime Ros. *Development Theory and the Economics of Growth*

Felipe Larraín B., Editor. *Capital Flows, Capital Controls, and Currency Crises: Latin America in the 1990s*

Mitchell A. Orenstein. *Out of the Red: Building Capitalism and Democracy in Postcommunist Europe*

Ricardo Ffrench-Davis. *Economic Reforms in Chile: From Dictatorship to Democracy*

Stephany Griffith-Jones, Ricardo Gottschalk, and Jacques Cailloux, Editors. *International Capital Flows in Calm and Turbulent Times: The Need for New International Architecture*

Carol Wise. *Reinventing the State: Economic Strategy and Institutional Change in Peru*

International Capital Flows in Calm and Turbulent Times

The Need for New International Architecture

Edited by Stephany Griffith-Jones, Ricardo Gottschalk, and Jacques Cailloux

The University of Michigan Press
Ann Arbor

Published in the United States of America by
The University of Michigan Press
Manufactured in the United States of America
∞ Printed on acid-free paper

2006 2005 2004 2003 4 3 2 1

A CIP catalog record for this book is available from the British Library.

Library of Congress Cataloging-in-Publication Data

International capital flows in calm and turbulent times : the need for new international architecture / edited by Stephany Griffith-Jones, Ricardo Gottschalk, and Jacques Cailloux.
p. cm. — (Development and inequality in the market economy)
Includes bibliographical references and index.
ISBN 0-472-11309-7 (cloth : alk. paper)
1. Capital movements. 2. Financial crises. 3. International finance. 4. Capital movements—Developing countries. 5. Financial crises—Developing countries. I. Griffith-Jones, Stephany. II. Gottschalk, Ricardo, 1964– III. Cailloux, Jacques. IV. Series.
HG3891.I559 2002
332' .042—dc21 2002013304

Contents

List of Figures

List of Tables

Preface

The frequency, severity, and high development cost of currency and financial crises—which hit mainly developing countries during the 1990s—posed a key challenge, both to those who support the spreading and deepening of the market economy through globalization and to those concerned with reducing poverty worldwide. For the first group, it became evident that, though markets and their liberalization worldwide have very important overall benefits (in aspects such as trade and technological dissemination), financial liberalization—especially in its international dimension—seemed to pose the risk of very high costs; naturally, capital flows—especially long-term ones—also have important benefits such as facilitating technology transfer, helping deepen domestic financial markets, and complementing domestic savings. However, particularly in certain phases, there seemed to be net costs to extreme capital account liberalization. This threatened the overall net benefits (real and perceived) of globalization. Those concerned with development rightly saw costly crises as posing the threat of interrupting—and, worse, possibly undermining—growth and development, with very negative effects on poverty reduction. This was particularly dramatic in East Asia, where major achievements during the preceding three decades in both growth and poverty reduction were not only interrupted but for a time reversed due to financial and currency crises. It was also very disturbing that "new-style" crises were particularly damaging in economies that had been very successful. Given the importance of the issue, a large academic literature emerged in an attempt to understand why these crises happened and why they were so frequent (during a third of the 1990s, major financial crises were taking place). Furthermore, a major debate began—among both policymakers and academics—over what changes should be introduced, both nationally and especially internationally, to make crises less likely and less costly when they do occur. This book's aim is to make a contribution, both to the analysis of crises and to the policy discussion of a new international financial architecture. Our particular focus is on both the empirical and the policy aspects related to the supply side of capital flows, an aspect somewhat understudied in depth in the recent literature.

It is important to note that a worrying asymmetry has emerged in the international discussion of recent crises. Much of the analysis—for example, Stiglitz 1998,[1] Radelet and Sachs (1998),[2] Bhagwati (1998),[3] and IMF 1998[4]—rightly stressed the importance of imperfections in international capital markets such as asymmetries of information and herding as one of the main causes of these "new-style" capital-account-led crises.

Whereas some of the analysis stressed the fact that imperfections in international capital markets were the dominant cause, others emphasized far more the role of domestic factors of both a structural and a policy nature. However, most of the literature gave great causal importance to the behavior of international capital flows and their imperfections (for a list of plausible relevant market failures, see Eichengreen, Tobin, and Wyplosz 1995).[5] As Wyplosz (2001)[6] points out, the literature on the econometric analysis of crises explains fairly little (typically less than 50 percent) of the determinants of crises.[7] This leads Wyplocz to the "inescapable conclusion" that our knowledge of the determinants of crises is still limited.[8] He suggests that to date the best hypothesis is that crises are often of a self-fulfilling nature and that such unexplained self-fulfilling crises are likely to reflect failures of international capital markets.

However, the international policy discussion has increasingly focused only on national measures to be adopted by emerging markets, with serious neglect of necessary international measures to better curb or manage international capital market imperfections. This book aims to contribute to filling this important gap and helping analysts overcome this serious asymmetry both by deepening the empirical understanding of the supply aspect of crises (especially by examining the role of different market actors) and by emphasizing international policy measures—such as better regulation of global capital flows—that have been largely neglected, particularly in their implementation. Naturally, we agree that appropriate domestic policies in emerging countries need to play an important role in crisis avoidance and that the significant progress made in implementing them is valuable. But we believe they should be complemented by measures at the international level. At this global level, fairly large changes are clearly required if we are to deal with a world substantially different from that for which the existing international financial architecture was created in the mid-1940s. This new world is characterized by far larger and more volatile private capital flows than existed at the time the Bretton Woods institutions were created. In the nineteenth century, institutions emerged nationally, after private credit and capital markets grew, to help prevent and better manage crises; a similar institutional response is urgently required internationally so as to regulate flows, to help prevent crises, and manage them better by providing appropriate liquidity in times of distress as well as creating mechanisms for orderly debt workouts. Although some steps have been taken in this direction, unfortunately, from our perspective, they have been insufficient (see chap. 11).

At the level of national policies, the early 1990s were marked by a growing consensus on the value of full capital account liberalization in developing countries. Indeed, many emerging market economies opened up their capital accounts very quickly during the 1990s. There is growing evidence (including that provided in the country studies in this book), however, that speedy capital account liberalization pursued in a context of the abundant availability of international capital, even though it can have important positive effects, clearly contributed to the serious macroeconomic management problems associated with massive capital inflows. Permitting these flows to move freely into and out of these countries very quickly contributed to very costly developmental crises. The literature on the link between capital account, as well as financial, liberalization and financial crises is abundant and quickly growing (for a valuable survey, see Eichengreen and Mussa 1998,[9] Rossi 1999,[10] Williamson and Mahar 1998,[11] Kaminsky and Reinhart 1999,[12] and Wyplocz 2001). Overall, the evidence seems to be converging to the view that liberalization contributes to both banking and currency crises. As a result, mainstream policy advice on capital account liberalization has been shifting.

Indeed, the very high initial costs of deep capital account liberalization clearly suggest that the traditional conventional wisdom of the 1970s and early 1980s, which advocated a cautious approach to capital account opening, is indeed the most appropriate one for developing countries and that those countries that have already considerably liberalized their capital accounts should seriously consider the reintroduction of some regulatory mechanisms. Furthermore, the country-based evidence gathered in this book suggests that countries can reduce the risks of capital account liberalization by pursuing a liberalization path that is suitable to its specific characteristics and circumstances. Thus, although the main focus of the book is on international regulatory measures, it also points to the need for these to be complemented with regulatory measures at the national level, including the area of the capital account, as well as regulation of the domestic financial sector. There are a number of important domestic policy issues—such as the exchange rate policy—that we do not discuss in detail here, as they have been amply discussed, though not resolved, in the literature

The book begins with an analysis of the supply side, in an attempt to answer among others, the following questions. What determines or triggers massive changes in the perceptions and sentiments of different investors and lenders? Does one type of investor or lender play a more important role in financial crises, either by taking the lead or by deepening the crisis by withdrawing massively or are different actors important in different crises? To what extent does contagion spread not just among countries but between actors? What are the policy implications of this analysis?

In chapter 1, we try to help fill an empirical gap by providing systematic evidence, based on primary data, on the size, composition, and maturity of capital flows to crisis countries during the 1990s. We draw attention to the type of lenders and investors that triggered and deepened the crises, focusing particularly on bank lending, portfolio flows, and foreign direct investment. We examine the "hierarchy of volatility" of such flows based on a novel methodological approach, thus confronting other important, related contributions (e.g., Claessens, Dooley, and Warner 1995)[13] or supporting them (e.g., Sarno and Taylor 1999).[14] Based on such analyses, as well as the buildup of some vulnerability indices inferred from crisis experiences in the 1990s, we offer a number of policy conclusions and suggestions.

Then we examine in detail the role of institutional investors (chap. 2) and banks (chap. 3); in the latter, we provide for the first time evidence based on the balance sheets of individual international banks in the recent crisis episodes. In both chapters, we draw policy implications. Our analysis draws from the literature on herdlike behavior and imperfect information as well as from interviews with market participants. This analysis has also greatly benefited from discussions with our London-based private-public-sector discussion group, which was established as part of the project in which this book originated.

In chapters 4 through 9, we provide in-depth analysis—carried out by country experts—of the countries most severely affected by the 1997–98 East Asian crisis (Indonesia, South Korea, Malaysia, and Thailand) as well as the Czech Republic and Brazil, which were also hit when the crisis spread beyond East Asia.

Finally, the book provides a summary of the main findings and policy lessons, from both the country analysis in the case studies and the empirical analysis of capital flows (chap. 10), and concludes (chap. 11) with an analysis of the asymmetries we see in financial architecture discussions and implementation as well as our policy proposals. The latter focus on the field of international financial regulation, which we feel has been understudied in recent debates and actions.

We would like to thank the Swedish aid agency SIDA, the Danish aid agency DANIDA, Oxfam UK, and the United Nations Development Programme (UNDP) for providing essential financial support for the research project that led to this book. Within these institutions, many were helpful not just in arranging financial support but in providing valuable intellectual inputs; among these, we would especially like to thank Dag Ehrenpreis, Mario Zejan, Ole Molgaard, Siddo Deva, and Inge Kaul.

We are also very grateful to all those who contributed to making this book possible. We thank particularly our chapter authors, the members of our London-based private-public-sector study group, and especially Robert Gray for his enthusiastic and valuable support. We also wish to thank those who presented additional papers or acted as insightful commentators on our work at the September 1999 workshop on this study at Sussex. These include especially Sergio Schmukler, Helmut Reisen, Andy Haldane, Colin Miles, and Mahmood Pradhan.

Notes

1. J. Stiglitz, *More instruments and broader goals: Moving toward the post-Washington consensus* (Helsinki: WIDER, 1998).

2. S. Radelet and J. Sachs, "The onset of the East Asian crisis," mimeo, Harvard University, 1998.

3. J. Bhagwati, "The capital myth," *Foreign Affairs* 77, no. 3 (May-June 1998): 7–12.

4. International Monetary Fund, *Toward a framework for financial stability* (Washington, DC: IMF, 1998).

5. B. Eichengreen, J. Tobin, and C. Wyplosz, "Two cases for sand in the wheels of international finance," *Economic Journal* 105 (1995): 162–72.

6. C. Wyplosz, "How risky is financial liberalization in the developing countries?" paper presented at the Seventh Dubrovnik Conference on Current Issues in Emerging Market Economies, Dubrovnik, June 28–29, 2001.

7. However, Goldstein, Kaminsky, and Reinhart (2000), based on their empirical analysis of early warning systems, make the point that fundamentals seem to explain a good many of the crises.

8. The limited explanatory results of econometric analyses of crises should also lead economists to a sense of humility and some tentativeness in offering policy prescriptions, features that unfortunately are rather rare in our profession!

9. B. Eichengreen and M. Mussa, "Capital account liberalization: Theoretical and empirical aspects," IMF Occasional Papers, no. 172, International Monetary Fund, 1998.

10. M. Rossi, "Financial fragility and economic performance in developing countries: Do capital controls, prudential regulation, and supervision matter?" IMF Working Paper WP/99/66, International Monetary Fund, 1999.

11. J. Williamson and M. Mahar, "A survey of financial liberalization," Essays in International Finance, no. 211, 1998.

12. G. Kaminsky and C. Reinhart, "The twin crises: The causes of banking and balance-of-payments problems," *American Economic Review* 89, no. 3 (1999): 473–500.

13. S. Claessens, M. P. Dooley, and A. Warner, "Portfolio capital flows: Hot or cold?" *World Bank Economic Review* 9, no. 1 (January 1995): 153–74.

14. L. Sarno and M. Taylor, "Hot money, accounting labels, and the permanence of capital flows to developing countries: An empirical investigation," *Journal of Development Economics* 59 (1999): 337–64.

CHAPTER 1

Global Capital Flows to East Asia: Surges and Reversals

Jacques Cailloux and Stephany Griffith-Jones

Recent major currency crises in developing countries (and particularly those in Mexico in 1994–95 and East Asia in 1997–98) had three main characteristics. First, they were very sudden and very large, as measured by the scale of the capital flow reversal, by the size of the devaluation, and by the initial cost in terms of decreases in output and increases in unemployment and poverty. Second, particularly in relation to financial variables—such as capital flows, levels of stock prices, and so on—but also on the whole with regard to output, these crises lasted for relatively short periods and were followed by surprisingly large recoveries of both capital flows and growth. A third feature was that the crises themselves, as well as their massive scale and the resulting contagion to other countries, were largely unexpected.[1]

A central feature of the recent currency crises is the sudden and major reversal of capital flows that these economies experience. Such reversals are either mainly in bank loans (East Asia) or in debt portfolio flows (Mexico, Brazil, Russia). Clearly, these reversals are the immediate cause of such crises. This chapter explores in detail the features of the capital surges that preceded these crises and of the massive reversals that accompanied the crises. We focus on four Asian countries hit by the East Asian crisis (Thailand, Malaysia, South Korea, and Indonesia), although we make some comparisons with Latin America.

Given the large scale and suddenness of reversals of capital flows from countries that were previously regarded as highly successful, we hypothesize that an important—though clearly not the only—cause of such reversals is imperfections in international capital markets.

These imperfections contribute to excess volatility and large reversals in capital flows. They have almost always featured in the financial panics of earlier times, but their impact has increased significantly due to a number of factors, including the speed with which markets can react in today's global economy with its highly sophisticated information technology (Griffith-Jones

1998). Paradoxically, this impact sometimes appears to be strongest in economies that either were or were perceived to be in the process of becoming highly successful. It should be recognized that even though the East Asian countries had very strong fundamentals, especially in the macroeconomic sphere, they also had a number of structural weaknesses, particularly in their financial sectors and their regulation. Furthermore, policy mistakes were made in the East Asian economies—including the establishment of the Bangkok International Banking Facility (BIBF) in Thailand and freeing offshore bank borrowing in South Korea in the very early stages of its financial liberalization—that artificially favored short-term flows and thus made these countries more vulnerable to large reversals of capital flows. Clearly, it was the interaction of structural and policy weaknesses in the countries with imperfections in international capital markets that caused the 1997–98 crises. Indeed, Demirguc-Kunt and Detragiache (1998), Edwards (2000), and others have argued that it is the interaction between liberalization and poor institutions, such as, for example, lack of proper bank regulation and supervision that contributes to crises. This seems to reinforce the message that full liberalization should be postponed until a proper infrastructure is in place domestically. Although we agree with these insights, the main concern of this book is with the role of international capital flows and their imperfections in contributing to crises. Capital and financial markets are special in that, although they generally function well, they are prone to important imperfections. Asymmetric information and adverse selection play an important role in explaining these imperfections, as financial markets are particularly information intensive. Furthermore, there are strong incentives for "herding" (i.e., an investor trying to mimic another investor's investment decision).[2]

It is evident that surges and crises in emerging markets have been more frequent than in the past. It can be hypothesized that technological and institutional developments—which may reflect secular trends—can explain the increase in the volatility of capital flows experienced during the 1990s. Clearly, the development of information technology has increased the speed with which capital can flow in and out of countries and more generally the speed and ease with which financial transactions can be made and reversed. Furthermore, it has been argued that the growing importance of institutional investors and increased international diversification of their assets, the risk and reward structures of delegated portfolio fund managers, and the resulting growing appetite for liquid, transferable securities that can be easily sold may further contribute to the volatility of capital flows to developing countries.

A second factor is the massive scale of institutional investors' assets, which surpass $40 trillion, (see, e.g., Griffith-Jones 1998 and World Bank, 1997).

This contrasts with the relatively small size of many recipient markets. This asymmetry highlights the potential for volatility, as marginal portfolio adjustments by institutional investors can lead to massive changes in the volume of capital flows to individual countries.

A third factor is linked to the risk and reward structures of fund managers and in particular to the frequent (every three or even every one month) evaluation of fund managers' investment performances with reference to market benchmarks and peer performance. As a result, fund managers fear underperformance because it can imply loss of business and therefore lower fees. This discourages positions that differ from benchmarks or peer averages. There is evidence that these incentives contribute to herding and therefore to high volatility of capital flows.

A fourth, broader factor may be linked to the fact that capital market financing is more rapidly affected by changes in market sentiment, as securities investors have looser relationships with borrowers and are more easily influenced by daily price movements—as they mark to market their assets—than commercial banks are (BIS 1999). This would help explain why fund managers seemed to withdraw earlier than commercial banks in East Asia (see chap. 2). However, the evidence on this point is not totally clear-cut, as various types of intermediaries—especially large ones—have adopted similar risk management systems. Indeed, the fact that different actors (e.g., banks, pension funds, and mutual funds) have increasingly highly correlated strategies may contribute to an aggravation of capital flow volatility and of the scale of asset price movements. This is an area in which further research is needed, which is at present beginning to be carried out. Combined with the asymmetries of scale—between total assets globally and the size of emerging market economies—this raises the possibility that in the future high capital flow volatility will remain or even increase, particularly if effective measures are not taken nationally and internationally to counteract it.

This chapter attempts to bring out the key features of private capital flows and their reversal, with special reference to the most affected economies in Asia, namely, Indonesia, Malaysia, South Korea, and Thailand (the Asian-4). Indeed, the project on which this book is based was initially about the East Asian crisis; this is why we focused this chapter on capital flows to and from the four East Asian countries hit by 1997–98 crises. In the middle of the project, a currency crisis hit Brazil. For the sake of completeness, we added a case study of Brazil (which incorporates detailed analysis of the flows); for an additional comparative perspective, we also added the Czech minicrisis. Section 1 reviews the inflow and outflow periods before and during the crisis, with special attention to the volume, maturity, and composition of flows. The key role of accumulated stocks or external liabilities is highlighted. Each of the four countries is studied, assessing similarities and differences. Section 2 contributes to the discussion of the so-called hierarchy of volatility by providing new measurements of the volatility of capital flows that are linked to the stock of foreign investment held by recipient countries. Section 3 studies the reversals experienced by crisis countries in an attempt to identify patterns across time and countries. Section 4 presents our conclusions and discusses policy implications. Finally, the appendix at the end of the chapter presents some graphic comparisons of foreign investments in Indonesia, Korea, and Thailand and in Argentina, Brazil, and Mexico.

1. SURGES AND REVERSALS IN EAST ASIA FROM 1989 TO 1998

In this section, we present key stylized facts concerning the inflow (1989–96) and outflow (1997–98) periods in East Asia,[3] with some comparisons with Latin American countries. Our analysis is restricted in several respects by data availability, even though we made a great effort to compile all the existing data. For example, we would have liked to examine empirically the role of highly leveraged institutions (HLIs). Unfortunately, not enough systematic data are available on HLI positions to do a full empirical analysis. One of our conclusions is that significantly improved data on international capital markets are essential, not just for research but for policymakers as well.

Surges of capital flows to Asia and Latin America have been studied with respect to the first half of the 1990s, a period that has been described as "the return of private finance" to emerging markets.[4] The picture that emerges from this literature is, first, that both Asia and Latin America experienced surges, though at different periods of time, and Asia received large capital flows earlier than Latin America did. Second, the composition of the flows between Asia and Latin America was quite different until the mid-1990s, though, as we shall see, the composition became more similar later.

1.1. THE BUILDUP OF EXTERNAL FRAGILITY IN ASIA: A TWO-SURGE STORY

Between 1989 and 1996, the Asian-4 received very high and sustained levels of private capital flows, amounting on average to 7.6 percent of gross domestic product (GDP) per year (see table 1.1). This compares to an average of 3.4 percent in the case of the three largest Latin American countries (the LA-3). The seven-year period of high inflows can be divided into two subperiods, 1989–94 and 1995–96, which correspond to the pre and post-Mexican crisis.

During the first period (1989–94), the Asian-4 were already experiencing very high levels of inflows as a proportion of GDP. Annual average inflows amounted to 7.1 percent of GDP compared to 3.3 percent in Latin America; the flows to East Asia were even higher (though only slightly so) than the 6.7 percent of GDP of capital inflows experienced by Mexico in its 1989–94 precrisis period. It is worth stressing that, although the East Asian region experienced very high levels of inflows during that period together with large current account deficits, it did not undergo any major financial crisis at that time. This can be explained partly by the very high levels of GDP and export growth (especially the latter) achieved. The structure of external financing did not explain the resilience of the Asian economies. Indeed, although the composition of flows to Asia seemed to be more stable than those to other regions because of the very large foreign direct investment (FDI) inflows (as was highlighted in the literature up to the mid-1990s), it was China and Singapore that attracted the bulk of these flows and not the Asian-4. Thus, the latter was already receiving in the 1989–94 period a very significant share of potentially reversible financial flows.

It is very interesting to note that in the aftermath of the peso crisis (1995–96) the Asian-4 received even larger inflows than in the 1989–94 period, with an average of 9.2 percent of GDP. This very high level of inflows was two and a half times higher than inflows to Argentina, Brazil, and Mexico at the time. The Asian-4 thus experienced a second surge just before the crisis.

Over that period, GDP growth was still very high, but current account

TABLE 1.1. Total Net Private Flows to East Asia, as a Percentage of GDP

	Average Annual Inflow				
	1989–96	1989–94	1995–96	1997–98	Maximum Annual Flow
Indonesia	4.2	3.9	5.3	−3.5[b]	1995: 5.4
South Korea	4.7	3.2	9.1	−0.9	1996:10.0
Thailand	12.2	12.0	12.5	−9.5	1995:15.3
Malaysia	9.3	9.2	9.7	3.8[a]	1993:20.0
Asian-4	7.6	7.1	9.2	−2.5	12.7
Argentina	3.5	3.0	5.1	4.4[a]	1991: 7.3
Brazil	1.4	0.3	4.7	3.4[a]	1995: 4.9
Mexico	5.3	6.7	1.3	3.1[a]	1993:10.0
LA-3	3.4	3.3	3.7	3.6	7.4

Source: IFS 1999; authors' calculations.

[a]1997 only.

[b]First semester of 1998.

deficits grew substantially, increasing the external vulnerability of the region. Furthermore, the rapidly growing stock of external liabilities, with a high proportion of them easily reversible, made these economies increasingly vulnerable to changes in investors' and lenders' perceptions.

The very steep increase of private flows in 1989–94 can be explained by means of two main driving forces. The first is the deepening of the liberalization process of capital accounts in Asia, with Korea being the most notable example (see chap. 10). The second driving force can be found in the increased share of international investments and loans allocated to emerging markets by institutional investors and banks as well as a broader trend toward the globalization of finance. As for the 1995–96 period, it is likely that as a response to the Mexican peso crisis international investors reallocated a higher share of their emerging market portfolios to Asia.

Compared to that of Latin America, the Asian surge lasted longer (seven years versus four or five in Latin America) and amounted to significantly larger annual amounts as a proportion of GDP. This contributed to much higher accumulated stocks of external liabilities in Asia, which may have contributed to the greater severity of the Asian crisis than that of Mexico.

As far as the composition of capital flows is concerned, and as can be seen in tables 1.2 and 1.3, between 1989 and 1996 the Asian-4 received, on average, 66 percent of flows in the form of foreign portfolio investments (FPI) and other investments (OI) (representing mainly credits). They respectively accounted for 15 and 51 percent of total inflows. Thus, credits were by far the

TABLE 1.2. Global Net Flows to the Asian-4 in Billions of 1990 U.S. Dollars

		1989	1990	1991	1992	1993	1994	1995	1996	1997	1998
Indonesia	FDI	0.7	1.1	1.4	1.7	1.8	1.9	3.7	5.2	3.8	−0.1
	FPI	−0.2	−0.1	0.0	−0.1	1.6	3.4	3.5	4.2	−2.1	−1.4
	OI	2.5	3.5	4.1	4.1	2.0	−1.4	2.1	0.2	−2.0	−3.3
South Korea	FDI	1.2	0.8	1.1	0.7	0.5	0.7	1.5	1.9	2.3	4.1
	FPI	0.0	0.2	2.2	4.6	9.5	7.2	11.9	17.6	10.0	−0.2
	OI	−1.5	5.5	6.7	4.6	−1.3	12.0	18.4	20.5	−6.7	−12.4
Thailand	FDI	1.9	2.4	1.9	2.0	1.6	1.2	1.8	1.9	3.0	5.7
	FPI	1.6	0.0	−0.1	0.9	4.9	2.2	3.5	3.0	3.9	0.2
	OI	3.9	7.0	9.3	6.0	6.1	8.7	16.6	9.9	−18.0	−14.9
Malaysia	FDI	1.7	2.3	3.8	4.8	4.5	3.8	3.6	4.2	4.1	
	FPI	−0.1	−0.2	0.2	−1.0	−0.6	−1.4	−0.4	−0.2	−0.2	
	OI	−0.3	−0.1	0.5	2.9	6.7	−1.7	4.0	3.8	−0.9	
Asian-4	FDI	5.5	6.6	8.2	9.2	8.4	7.6	10.6	13.2	13.2	9.7
	FPI	1.3	−0.1	1.9	4.4	15.4	11.4	18.5	24.6	11.6	−1.4
	OI	4.6	15.9	20.6	17.6	13.5	17.6	41.1	34.4	−27.6	−30.6

Source: IFS 1999; WDI 1999.

main source of external financing. It is important to stress that as early as 1992, as shown in figure 1.1, most bank loans already had a maturity date of less than one year. This high ratio of short-term to total borrowing was consistently higher than in Latin America throughout the 1990s.

The FDI share was relatively small (34 percent) compared to the emerging market average of 50 percent and declined, for the Asian-4, from 37 percent in the period 1989–94 to 25 percent in 1995–96. This decline was mainly compensated for by an increase in the share of FPI, which rose from 12 to 22 percent, though credits also rose a bit (see table 1.3). As a consequence, the share of flows that were more easily reversible increased in the 1995–96 period.

When looking at individual countries, there are differences in terms of levels, particularly in the composition of flows.

Between 1989 and 1996, Thailand, the largest recipient of net private flows among the Asian-4, had an annual average inflow of 12.2 percent of GDP, while Malaysia, Korea, and Indonesia received 9.3, 4.7, and 4.2 percent, respectively (see table 1.1).

During the first period (1989–94), while Korea and Indonesia did not receive very large amounts of inflows, Thailand and Malaysia experienced surges, with levels significantly higher than those witnessed by Latin American

TABLE 1.3. Composition of Flows as a Percentage of Total Flows

		Composition of Cumulated Positive Flows				Composition of Cumulated Negative Flows			
		1989–96	1989–94	1995–96	1997–98	1989–96	1989–94	1995–96	1997–98
Indonesia	FDI	36	29	47	100	0	0	0	7
	FPI	26	17	41	0	21	21	0	93
	OI	38	54	12	0	79	79	0	0
South Korea	FDI	7	9	5	39	0	0	0	0
	FPI	41	41	41	61	0	0	0	1
	OI	52	50	54	0	100	100	0	99
Thailand	FDI	15	18	10	68	0	0	0	0
	FPI	16	15	18	32	100	100	0	0
	OI	69	67	72	0	0	0	0	100
Malaysia	FDI	61	67	100	100	0	0	0	0
	FPI	0	1	0	0	67	100	100	20
	OI	38	32	0	0	33	0	0	80
Asian-4[a]	FDI	21	25	17	62	0	0	0	1
	FPI	25	21	31	38	42	49	100	7
	OI	53	53	53	0	58	51	0	92

Source: Same source as table 1.2.

Note: The percentages of net inflows (outflows) are calculated as the sum of all annual positive (negative) flows over the period for one type of flow divided by the sum of positive (negative) flows of all types. This is to avoid inconsistent percentages due to negative flows. Data for Malaysia cover only 1997.

[a]The percentages for the Asian-4 are calculated as the ratio of the sum of all inflows (outflows) for all countries divided by total inflows (outflows) over a given period.

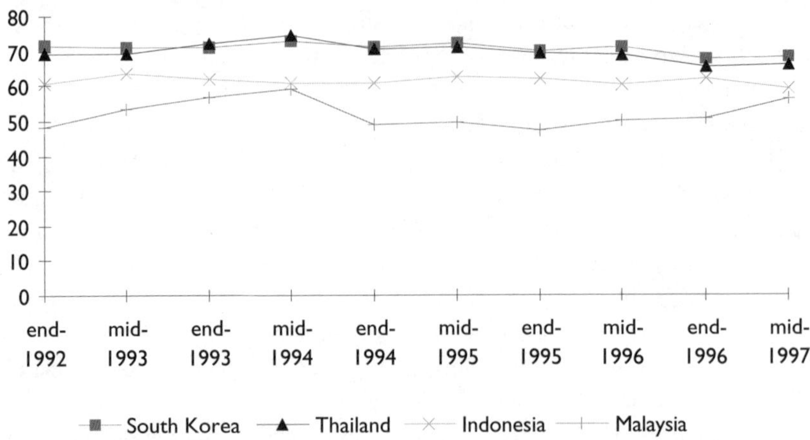

Fig. 1.1. Share of bank claims with maturity of up to and including one year, in % of total claims. (Data from BIS, various issues.)

countries, with, on average, 12.0 and 9.2 percent of GDP. During 1995 and 1996, further increases in total inflows brought the relative size of net private capital flows to new heights, with Thailand and Malaysia (in that order) again having the largest flows (see table 1.1). South Korea's net inflows almost tripled while Indonesia's inflows increased by far less. As a result, three out of the four East Asian countries experienced their largest yearly inflow in the 1995–96 period, with a peak in Thailand in 1995 of about 15 percent of GDP. Malaysia's inflows had peaked in the previous period, with an inflow as high as 20 percent of GDP in 1993 (see table 1.1).

As far as the composition of flows is concerned, and as can be seen in table 1.3, the bulk of private capital flows to South Korea took the form of loans; between 1989 and 1996, 52 percent of inflows were bank loans. Korea's inflows of FDI only accounted for 7 percent of its overall external private financing. This was mainly due to the deliberate policy of restricting FDI to avoid other countries' firms controlling South Korea's assets. Similarly, the Thai economy was mainly financed with bank loans. The two countries also shared a similar structure of maturity of their external debt, with more than 65 percent being short term.

On the other hand, Malaysia's inflows were more than 60 percent via FDI, a ratio far higher than the average for emerging markets. The remaining source of international finance was bank loans. Portfolio flows were negative during most of the period covered. The maturity structure of the external debt was the most long term of the Asian-4 (with 50 percent of the debt maturing within a period of one year), reflecting, among other things, the more prudent regulation of foreign borrowing by local firms (see chap. 5).

Finally, Indonesia's share of FDI inflows in total private flows followed a trend opposite that of the other East Asian countries: it rose sharply with time, from an average of 29 percent in 1989–94 to an average of 47 percent in 1995–96. It is worth underlining that FPI to Indonesia rose even more sharply, reaching 41 percent of total inflows in 1995–96. The substitution in Indonesia of credits for FPI and FDI can be attributed to the policy response to the surge in international credits experienced during the first half of the 1990s, such as ceilings on foreign borrowing (see Nasution 1997). Indonesia's share of short-term debt remained stable over that period at around 60 percent.

1.2. OUTFLOWS DURING THE 1997–98 CRISIS

The composition of outflows in table 1.3 shows that in 1997–98 these were dominated by outflows in bank credit, *with 92 percent of outflows in the form of credits.* As can be seen in table 1.2, the Asian-4 experienced successively outflows in bank credit of 27.6 and 30.6 billion U.S. dollars in 1997 and 1998, that is, outflows of a magnitude of 18.6 and 26.6 percent of GDP, respectively.

As can be seen in figure 1.2, the three countries experienced dramatic outflows, mainly, although not only, in the form of bank credit. The most striking case is clearly Thailand, which faced a very large outflow of bank credit from the second quarter of 1997 onward. The outflow reached a peak in the fourth quarter with −7.3 billion U.S. dollars. Although portfolio flows did not flow out of the country, inflows remained very low. South Korea also experienced very large outflows of credit but slightly later, from the third quarter of 1997 onward. These were accompanied with small outflows of FPI in both bonds and equities. Indonesia faced a different situation, as it was exposed to outflows in the three categories, that is, FDI, FPI, and loans, during two quarters (the fourth quarter of 1997 and the first quarter of 1998). The very large outflow of FPI was only in equity. The outflow of FDI is unique to the Indonesian case and might thus reflect the deeper nature of both the economic and the political crises in that country. Nasution (1999) has shown that FDI flows were still negative early in 1999.

To summarize, first, the high level and share of foreign capital inflows as a proportion of GDP were not a new feature of the external financial position of the Asian-4; indeed, this had begun at the end of the 1980s and remained very high over most of the following decade.

Second, the composition and maturity of inflows to East Asia do not seem to have changed greatly through time; however, the share of portfolio flows grew in the mid-1990s, and so did the stock of accumulated short-

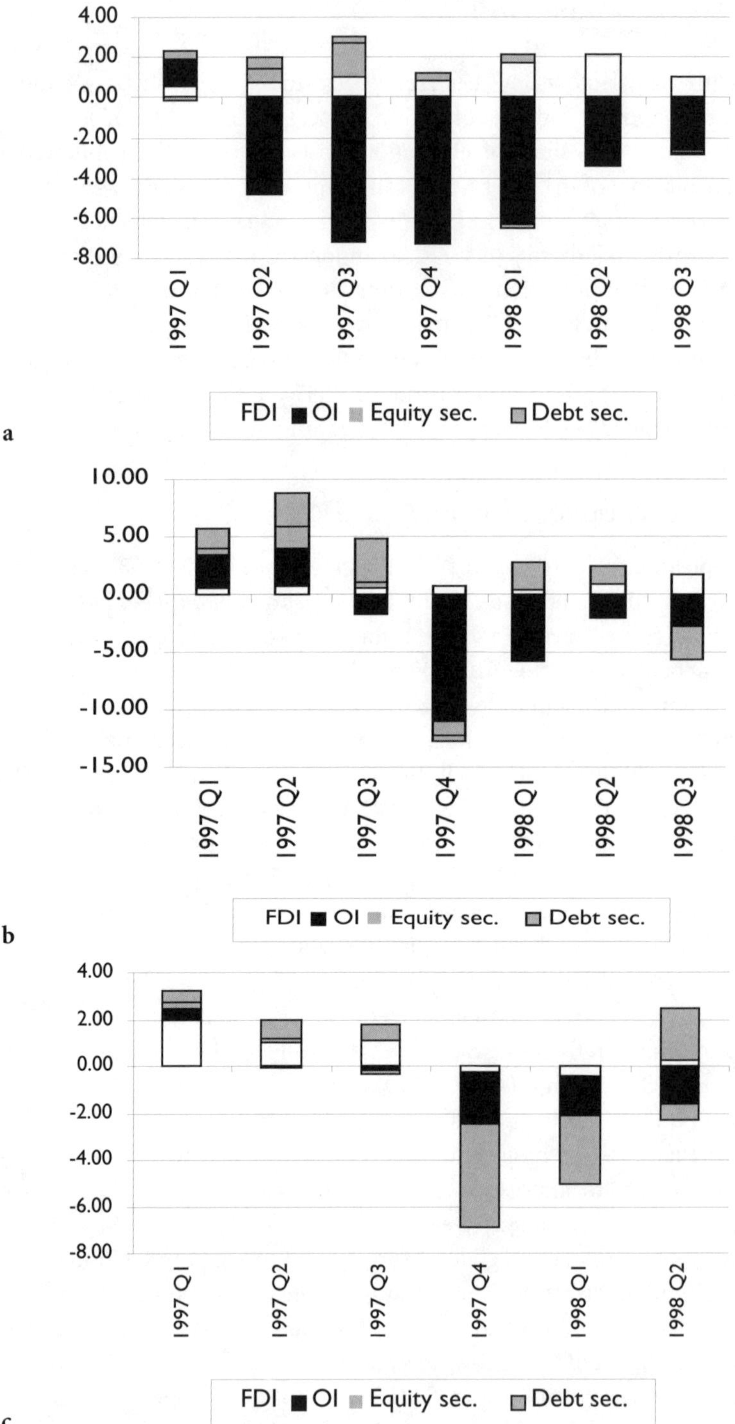

Fig. 1.2. Composition of capital flows in billions of U.S. dollars, 1997–98: *a*, to Thailand; *b*, to South Korea; *c*, to Indonesia. (Data from IFS data base.)

term debt. Indeed, the Asian-4 accumulated, over eight years, about half of their external liability in the form of debt, that is, 173.4 billion U.S. dollars or 22 percent of total GDP in the region, the majority of which was shorter than a year. The Asian-4 have thus been financed, since the end of the 1980s, mostly by potentially reversible flows that contributed to greater vulnerability than in Latin America, which had not experienced large inflows for such a long period of time. This large accumulated stock of potentially reversible external liabilities contributed to making East Asia particularly vulnerable to a major change in sentiment. It also helps explain the severity of the Asian crisis.

Third, the pattern of foreign private flows to East Asia and the differences between countries can mainly be explained by the deep financial liberalization process undertaken by recipient countries and their different responses to surges and reversals. Interestingly, the Asian-4 have taken, over time, different approaches to capital account liberalization, all quite different from what conventional wisdom would dictate.

The following section attempts to contribute to the empirical literature on the volatility of capital flows.

2. MEASURES OF VOLATILITY

There are two related issues in the study of movements of capital flows. One is the assessment of volatility levels through statistical analysis of the time-series properties (using simple indicators such as the standard deviation or more sophisticated econometric analysis such as vector auto-regressive [VAR] modeling). These studies are very important because a prerequisite for formulating appropriate policies to prevent crises is the assessment of whether capital flows can be distinguished by their volatility characteristics. If they can be, a differentiated treatment of inflows by the host country may be in order.

The second issue refers to shocks or sudden and large fluctuations that are highly disruptive but whose frequency of occurrence is typically relatively low. These shocks have been recently characterized as "sudden stops" (see Reisen 1999 and Calvo 1999). The reversals experienced by Mexico in 1994 and by the Asian-4, Russia, and Brazil in 1998 and 1999 clearly belong to this category and are of utmost importance to policymakers, particularly but not only in host countries. They are studied in greater depth in the next section.

Measures of volatility are particularly important if flows that are more volatile are also more prone to large reversals as a percentage of the stock of liabilities.

In this section, we contribute to the ongoing debate on the hierarchy of volatility by providing a new indicator, which has the advantage of being more reliable and robust than the traditional indicator of volatility while not requiring extensive data processing.

As has been underlined in previous studies, the measurement of the volatility of capital flows is difficult and the indicators used can sometimes be misleading. The main limits are related to the low frequency of the data, which reduces the range of tools such as time-series econometric models, which are commonly used to gauge stock market volatility. Another limit is related to the data on capital flows, which are often published as net flows.

Most studies, which present simple and readily usable indicators of volatility of capital flows, rely mainly on the coefficient of variation, that is, the ratio of the standard deviation of flows over their mean (see Tesar and Werner 1995, Claessens et al. 1995, World Bank 1997, and UNCTAD 1999). Although this indicator can be informative, we argue that it can sometimes be largely misleading because it is calculated on the basis of *net flows.* This is particularly problematic because the denominator of the coefficient is the mean of net flows and because, as seen earlier, capital flows exhibit a pattern of cyclical behavior and/or of surges rapidly followed by large outflows, which can result in very low means over a given period. The ratio is thus extremely sensitive to the chosen period and is meaningless when the mean is close to zero. Indeed, if the chosen period corresponds to an equal amount of inflows and outflows, the coefficient of variation equals infinity. This poses an acute problem for measurement of the volatility of both portfolio flows and bank loans, which often fluctuate between positive and negative values.[5] Interestingly, Turner (1991) has raised the issue, but no simple alternative measurement has been proposed since then.

As an example, the coefficient of variation of bank credits to Argentina between the *first quarter* of 1990 and the last quarter of 1995 is equal to about 300. When measured between the *second quarter* of 1990 and the last quarter of 1995, the coefficient falls to −10. This shows how sensitive the measurement can be to small changes in the period covered. In this example, it is explained by the fact that the mean is very close to zero in the first case.

In order to avoid the limitations of the coefficient of variation, we propose a new indicator (which we call coefficient of volatility), which departs from the coefficient of variation in the extent to which the mean of net flows is replaced by the capital stock and in that the standard deviation applies to the ratio of the flow over the stock. More formally, the proposed ratio is the standard deviation of the flow of investment at time m divided by the moving average of total cumulated flows.

It can be written as follows :

$$\frac{\sum_{m=5}^{N}[X_m - \bar{X}_m]^2}{(N-5)-1} \quad \text{with } X_m = \frac{I_m}{\frac{1}{4}\sum_{j=m-1}^{m-4}\sum_{1}^{j} I_i},$$

where I_m is the flow of investment at time m and X_m is the flow normalized by the moving average of cumulated flows. The moving average is calculated over the four quarters preceding the inflow in order to make the indicator less sensitive to large shocks occurring just before the net flow. We compute cumulated flows as a proxy for stocks due to the lack of data on the latter. The cumulated flows are calculated from the earliest period in which data are available, that is, from the beginning of the 1970s for most countries. They are then compared to published data on stocks and adjusted when necessary.

The indicator does not suffer from the time period selected. Furthermore, it is consistent with standard portfolio allocation models, which evaluate the share of a given portfolio invested in risky assets (see Calvo 1998 for a theoretical model). Indeed, it measures the volatility of the risky asset (in this case, the investment made in an emerging market) normalized by the stock of foreign liabilities. It is thus preferable to analyze the behavior of investors with respect to their investment strategies toward emerging markets rather than the coefficient of variation.

We report the results in tables 1.4 and 1.5 for a set of eight countries using quarterly data from 1980 to 1997. As mentioned earlier, cumulated flows are calculated as the sum of net flows from 1974 and are adjusted to match current stocks.[6]

A number of interesting results emerges. First, the hierarchy of volatility appears very clearly. As can be seen in tables 1.4 and 1.5, FPI flows are the most volatile in any country over the 1990–97 period (see also table 1 in appendix 5 in Cailloux and Griffith-Jones 1999). Bank credits are much less volatile than portfolio flows, especially during the second period. Finally, FDI is the least volatile source of financing for any given country (see table 1.5), with the exception of India, whose loans are more stable (this is confirmed by data published by the BIS on the maturity of international loans to India).

On average, FPI is almost eight times as volatile as FDI per unit of stock while loans are only two times as volatile. This result is counterintuitive, as one would expect a higher degree of volatility in bank loans, especially for the three Asian countries in the sample, as they accounted for the bulk of the reversals in the Asian crisis. This can be explained by the very large stocks of foreign bank debt accumulated in the region. Although volatility per unit of stock is lower for bank loans than portfolio flows, reversals are larger due to the large amount of accumulated bank debt stocks.

Second, the volatility of flows to Latin America is much higher than that of flows to Asia, for any type of flow or country and both in the 1980s and 1990s (with the exception of FPI to Asia in the 1980s). Furthermore, Latin America experienced a huge increase in the volatility of FPI in the 1990s (almost tripling) as compared to the 1980s. This increase primarily corresponds to the very large fluctuations in portfolio flows experienced during the first half of the 1990s, including the 1994 episode in Mexico and its contagion effect on both Argentina and Brazil.

In Cailloux and Griffith-Jones 1999, we examined the time-series behavior of the coefficient of volatility between the first quarter of 1990 and the second quarter of 1998. It is interesting that bank loans exhibit a significant change in the value of their coefficient of volatility from the first quarter of 1997 onward for Thailand and from the third quarter for Indonesia and Korea. This captures very well the increase in volatility at the onset of the Asian crisis. A similar trend is noticeable in the case of portfolio flows for Indonesia and in FDI for Thailand and Indonesia, though to a lesser extent in the latter country. There is an increase in the coefficient of volatility in FDI for Thailand that corresponds to what has been referred to as "fire sales" (see Krugman 1998b); it is associated with large inflows.

TABLE 1.4. Volatility of Capital Flows to Selected Emerging Markets, in Percentages

	Foreign Direct Investment		Portfolio Investments		Other Investments	
	1980–89	1990–97	1980–89	1990–97	1980–89	1990–97
Indonesia	0.2	1.0		21.1	4.7	1.6
South Korea	2.3	1.6	23.0	9.3	2.7	3.7
Thailand	3.7	2.4	8.9	9.2	2.8	4.3
Average	2.1	1.7	15.9	13.2	3.4	3.2
Argentina	5.7	3.4	2.2	14.7	3.9	6.4
Brazil	0.6	1.5	2.7	14.8	2.6	3.4
Mexico	5.8	1.4	12.4	18.7	11.1	2.9
Average	4.0	2.1	5.8	16.1	5.9	4.2
South Africa	1.4	2.3	16.9	21.4	15.0	5.1
India		3.5			2.4	1.6
Average	1.4	2.9	16.9	21.4	8.7	3.3

Source: IFS 1999; author's calculations based on the preceding formula.

TABLE 1.5. Ratios of the Volatility of FPI and OI over FDI between 1990 and 1997

	FPI/FDI	OI/FDI
Indonesia	21.7	1.6
South Korea	5.9	2.4
Thailand	3.8	1.8
Average	7.9	1.9
Argentina	4.4	1.9
Brazil	10.2	2.4
Mexico	13.5	2.1
Average	7.8	2.0
South Africa	9.4	2.2
India		0.4
Average	7.4	1.1

Source: Calculated from table 1.3.

The results we find are broadly consistent with the ones found by Sarno and Taylor (1999a), who perform filtering techniques on U.S. private capital flows to Asia and Latin America between 1988 and 1997. The authors decompose the flows in temporary and permanent components and conclude that portfolio flows, both equity and debt, are the most volatile categories. Second are bank loans and then FDI flows. Again, bank loans do not exhibit the highest level of volatility, which is counterintuitive given the scale of the outflow of that category in the Asian crisis. Similarly, Sarno and Taylor (1999b) conduct the same analysis with special reference to the East Asian crisis but fail to identify discriminating characteristics in bank loans that could explain such a large and sudden stop. As mentioned earlier, although our static analysis of the coefficient also fails to identify bank loans, the dynamic one in Cailloux and Griffith-Jones 1999 does highlight an increase in the volatility of that type of investment.

3. THE EMPIRICS OF SUDDEN REVERSALS

The pattern of capital flows that has been witnessed in the recent financial crisis episodes tends to follow a boom and bust cycle, that is, as documented in section 1, large inflows of private capital followed by large and sudden outflows whose scale is not related to fluctuations in economic fundamentals. The other feature is the relatively low frequency of occurrence of such "accidents," which thus fails to be captured in the statistical analysis. In this section, we complement our analysis by trying to identify major disruptions faced by three Latin American countries (Argentina, Brazil, and Mexico) and three Asian countries (Indonesia, Korea, and Thailand) during the 1990s.[7]

In all six countries, we identify the boom and bust periods by means of visual inspection (see Cailloux and Griffith-Jones 1999b, appendix), and then retain reversals of more than 1 percent of GDP for each particular type of flow.[8] We conduct this exercise for the three types of flows: FDI, FPI, and bank loans. The reversals are reported in table 1.6.

We find twelve reversals that comply with these criteria, nine in FPI and four in bank loans. Five reversals are identified in Latin America, all in the form of FPI. Mexico and Brazil experienced reversals in both 1994 and 1997, while Argentina only faced a reversal in 1994–95. The remaining seven reversals (four in FPI and three in bank loans) occurred in Asia, most of them during the 1997–98 crisis, with the exception of Thailand, which was subject to a reversal in 1993–94. Although the reversals in bank loans are much less frequent (three occurrences over 12 reversals), their scale is much larger, from 3.7 to 13.6 percent, compared to reversals in FPI, which vary between 1.0 and 4.5 percent of GDP.

Five reversals are associated with financial crises (one is the Mexican crisis and four are Asian). Three took the form of FPI and two of bank loans. It is worth underlining that the size of the reversal in absolute terms or relative to GDP is not clearly linked to the occurrence of financial crises. For example, Thailand and Mexico experienced in 1993–94 and 1997, respectively, reversals of about 3 percent of GDP without facing a crisis. In Mexico, the reversal of FPI was compensated for with more positive trends in other flows. Thus, some flows might smooth the shock (countercyclical flows) while others might aggravate it (procyclical flows). On the contrary, South Korea in 1997 suffered a reversal in FPI of only 1.7 percent of GDP but also faced a reversal in bank loans of 4.5 percent of GDP in the same year, which put considerable pressure on the balance of payments, as no other flows compensated for it. The net aggregate behavior of the financial account is obviously the key variable, on which we now focus.

The relationship between the scale of the reversal in financial accounts and crises is more clear-cut. Indeed, as can be seen from table 1.6, the smallest reversal associated with a crisis amounts to 4.8 percent of GDP and the largest to 11.5 percent of GDP. On the other hand, financial accounts reversals not associated with financial crises are much smaller. They range from 0.1 to 3.1 percent of GDP. The behavior of the financial account rather than each particular flow thus seems better suited to drawing potential conclusions about the size of a sustainable reversal in the financial account. In light of the cases

TABLE 1.6. Reversals during the 1990s

Episodes of Financial Turmoil		Type of Flow Experiencing the Reversal	Inflow (bn U.S.$) (1)	Outflow (bn U.S.$) (2)	Total Reversal		Foreign Liabilities (bn U.S.$) (5)	Total Financial Account during the Reversal Period			
					bn U.S.$ (3)	% of GDP (4)		Balance Inflow Period (bn U.S.$) (6)	Balance Outflow Period (bn U.S.$) (7)	Reversal[a] bn U.S.$ (8)	Reversal[a] % GDP (9)
97Q3–97Q4[b]	Indonesia	FPI	0.5	−4.4	4.9	2.8	15.6	1.5	−6.9	8.4	4.8
98Q2–98Q3	South Korea	FPI	1.4	−3.0	4.4	1.2	69.9	−0.5	−3.0	2.5	0.7
97Q3–97Q4[b]		FPI	4.4	−1.7	6.1	1.7	68.1	0.6	−16.9	17.5	4.9
97Q2–97Q4[b]		OI	3.3	−1.7; −11.1	16.1	4.5	121.2	5.5	−16.9	22.4	10.2
93Q4–94Q1	Thailand	FPI	2.9	−0.6	3.5	3.1	10.4	2.4	1.9	0.5	0.4
97Q1–97Q3[b]		OI	1.4	−4.9; −7.2; −7.3	20.8	13.6	93.1	2.0	−3.2; −6.5; −6.0	17.7	11.5
96Q2–96Q3		OI	4.3	−1.0	5.3	3.7	90.6	4.9	3.0	1.9	1.3
97Q2–97Q3	Mexico	FPI	5.6	−2.6	8.2	3.0	72.8	1.9	4.7	−2.8	−1.0
94Q3–95Q1[b]		FPI	3.2	−4.8; −6.4	14.4	4.0	73.2	3.9	−3.1; −7.6	14.6	9.5
97Q3–97Q4	Brazil	FPI	5.1	−6.6	11.7	1.8	65.8	8.4	0.7	7.7	1.2
94Q4–95Q1[c]		FPI	2.4	−3.2	5.6	1.2	26.0	0.7	0.4	0.3	0.1
94Q4–95Q1[c]	Argentina	FPI	1.9	−0.5	2.4	1.0	25.5	3.3	−3.5	6.8	2.8

Source: IFS 1999; authors' calculations.

Note: Numbered column headings are as follows: (1) last positive flow before the outflow; (2) all outflows until the largest outflow—for example, in 1997 in Thailand the largest outflow occurred three quarters after the last inflow; (3) inflow minus the sum of outflows; (4) reversal of the flow as a share of GDP; (5) stock of foreign liabilities of the financial flow experiencing the reversal at the beginning of the reversal; (6) financial account balance during the last inflow; (7) financial account balance during the outflow period; (8) and (9) reversal experienced by the financial account.

[a]A minus corresponds to a financial account deficit.

[b]Episode with a financial crisis.

[c]Episode with intense pressure on the exchange rate and stock market but without a major financial crisis.

studied in the table, any country facing a reversal in the range of 5 percent of GDP would be bound to face a crisis.

Although the analysis of the financial account is informative, the assessment of a particular country's ability to cope with adverse external shocks obviously needs to integrate the overall balance of payments composition and more specifically the trade account and the level of international reserves (See Calvo 1998 and Calvo and Reinhart 1999).

The likely impact of a reversal of capital depends to an important extent on the current account balance and the level of international reserves at the time of the reversal. For example, in the case of a current account deficit and a pegged exchange rate regime the level of foreign exchange reserves is crucial. Indeed, it serves to temporarily smooth both the current account deficit and the outflow of capital (due to repayments of maturing bonds and credits not being rolled over). Table 1.7 provides additional important information during the reversal period. It includes the level of international reserves, the balance of the current account during the reversal, and three indicators of vulnerability. The first indicator is the ratio of the financial account reversal over the level of international reserves. It indicates the relative importance of the need for financing to the stock of foreign exchange. The need for financing is here equal to the reversal, reflecting both the drying out of external finance and the outflow of foreign capital. As can be seen from table 1.7, the ratio ranges from 50.6 to 100 percent for crisis countries (with an average of 72.2 percent) and from 0.9 to 15.9 percent for noncrisis countries (excluding Argentina, which has a ratio of 53.5 percent, and Mexico in 1997, as the financial account is in surplus). The second ratio is an indicator of the size of outflows relative to their stock. It is in the same spirit as the coefficient of volatility presented in the previous section. On average, outflows amount to 15.6 percent of the stocks for crisis countries and −5.5 for noncrisis countries. Indonesia has the highest ratio, as it had almost 30 percent of its stock of FPI flowing out in 1997.

The third indicator is similar to the first, as it reflects the need for financing drawn from international reserves at the time of a reversal but differs in the way the financing need is calculated. Indeed, we replace the financial account reversal with the sum of the balance of the current and financial accounts. Here the distinction between crisis and noncrisis countries appears quite clearly. The absolute value appears to be, on average, much higher for crisis than noncrisis countries (47.5 as opposed to 6.7 percent). Argentina has a high ratio, reflecting the spillover effect from Mexico.

If these ratios have more general validity for future potential crises, they can indicate the danger of accumulating large stocks of FPI or OI, as even a reversal equal to a small share of such a stock can provoke a crisis unless foreign

TABLE 1.7. **Reversals and Financial Crises, Selected Indicators**

			International Reserves, Beginning of Reversal (bn U.S.$)	Current Account		Reversal of Financial Accounts/ International Reserves (%)	Outflow Outflow Liabilities (%)	(Current Accounts + Financial Accounts)/ International Reserves (%)[a]
				Beginning of Reversal (bn U.S.$)	End of Reversal (bn U.S.$)			
97Q3–97Q4[b]	Indonesia	FPI	16.6	−1.1	−0.2	50.6	−28.2	−42.8
98Q2–98Q3	South Korea	FPI	32.8			7.6	−4.3	
97Q3–97Q4[b]		FPI	24.7	−1.7	3.2	70.9	−2.5	−55.5
97Q2–97Q4[b]		OI	27.8	−2.2	−1.7; 3.2	80.6	−10.6	−49.3
93Q4–94Q1	Thailand	FPI	22	−1.7	−1	2.3	−5.8	−7.3
97Q1–97Q3[b]		OI	30.5	−1.7	−2.6; −0.6; 2.4	58.0	−20.8	−23.3
96Q2–96Q3		OI	32.5	−4.1	−3	5.8	−1.1	0.0
97Q2–97Q3	Mexico	FPI	19.4	−0.9	−2.1	−14.4	−3.6	13.4
94Q3–95Q1[b]		FPI	14.5	−6.9	−6.6; −1.2	100.7	−15.3	−66.9
97Q3–97Q4	Brazil	FPI	49.3	−6.3	−8.9	15.6	−10.0	−16.6
94Q4–95Q1[c]		FPI	32.5	−4.6	−4.9	0.9	−12.3	−13.8
94Q4–95Q1[c]	Argentina	FPI	12.7	−2.3	−1.6	53.5	−2.0	−40.2

Source: IFS 1999; authors' calculations.

[a]Both current and financial account values correspond to the end of the reversal. When the reversal lasts for more than two quarters, the second quarter is retained.

[b]Episode with a financial crisis.

[c]Episode with intense pressure on the exchange rate and stock market but without a major financial crisis.

exchange reserves are extremely high and current account deficits are very small or current accounts have large surpluses.

One option for countries that wish to protect themselves from currency turmoil, if a massive reversal of foreign loans were to occur, is to maintain adequate levels of foreign exchange reserves (a mechanism we call "self-insurance"); indeed, the existence of high levels of such reserves may well discourage large reversals and especially speculative attacks on currencies. Countries like South Korea have in fact, since the East Asian crisis, accumulated very high levels of reserves, presumably mainly with this objective.

Our empirical analysis of reversals of different categories of capital flows in recent crises (especially in table 1.7) provides an empirical basis for estimating how large such foreign exchange reserves should be, assuming a similar pattern of reversals, in proportion to liabilities. Under these assumptions, if a country accumulated significant external liabilities, wanted to be more protected against a major currency crisis, and wished to rely mainly on its own reserves to prevent such a crisis, then it would need to have reserves equivalent to up to 30 percent of its portfolio liabilities plus approximately 20 percent of its bank liabilities to cover potential reversals in the two most reversible categories. We are being conservative with regard to foreign exchange reserve requirements in the sense that we are assuming that FDI will behave in the future the same way as it did in the 1990s, that is, it will broadly follow a sustained growth trend. Such an estimate would also risk being conservative in that it would not require reserves for potential residents' capital flight. Potential capital flight seems harder to estimate, as the historical figures are not precise and the trends seem very different in different contexts, for example, in Latin America versus East Asia (UNCTAD 1999). Further research is clearly required. In the context of this chapter, we can estimate that potential capital flight could be half the level of the potential reversal of bank loans and portfolio flows; therefore, we will assume that a country would need to have extra reserves on that order to avoid potential capital flight.

Additionally, such a country should have reserves that cover at least three months of imports to finance the current account deficit (using traditional definitions of foreign reserve requirements that are relevant when shocks come mainly from the trade account).

In table 1.8, we present estimates for desirable levels of net foreign exchange reserves (calculated in 1990 U.S. dollars) for mid-1997 for Indonesia, South Korea, Thailand, and Brazil, which according to our preliminary calculations (based on the analysis and assumptions described earlier) would have hopefully made their currency crises far less likely to happen. We can see that the levels (estimated in 1990 U.S. dollars) for South Korea ($89.4 billion) and Thailand ($46.0 billion) were extremely high.

TABLE 1.8. Estimated Required Level of Net Reserves (U.S.$ billions at 1990 prices) for Crisis Avoidance in Mid-1997

	Indonesia	South Korea	Thailand	Brazil
30% of FPI	4.5	19.1	6.2	18.2
20% of OI	12.0	24.2	17.7	13.9
50% of 1 + 2 (capital flight)	8.3	21.7	12.0	16.1
3 months of imports	7.5	24.4	10.1	10.2
Total	32.3	89.4	46.0	58.4

Source: Authors' calculations, based on previous tables and data, plus IMF data for imports.

Although a high level of international reserves, along the lines we have suggested, could clearly be beneficial in terms of crisis avoidance, for countries highly integrated into the international financial system it is clearly not without cost. Indeed, high net foreign reserves accumulated as a result of foreign borrowing tend to have a return well below the cost of the foreign borrowing. Furthermore, the cost of sterilizing private borrowing falls on the central bank, leading to significant quasi-fiscal deficits (see, e.g., Akyuz and Cornford 1999 and UNCTAD 1999). We discuss the implications of this in the following, concluding section.

CONCLUSIONS AND POLICY IMPLICATIONS

Capital flows into East Asia in the last 10 years are a two-surge story. It is noteworthy that the first surge, with particularly high levels of flows into Thailand and Malaysia (1989–94) did not lead to any major financial or currency crisis in that region. A second surge occurred in the 1995 period, with Thailand and Malaysia again having the largest flows (at levels that continued to be far higher than those of the major Latin American economies) and with South Korea's net inflows tripling.

Thus, the surge of flows to Asia was higher (as a proportion of GDP) than for Latin America and lasted longer. As a result, accumulated stocks of external liabilities were higher in Asia than in Latin America. The composition changed in East Asia between the first and second surge, with an important increase in the level and share of portfolio flows. The level and share of credits (of which a high proportion was short term) also grew during the surge. The high level of the stock of external liabilities, and the very high share within that of easily reversible flows, helps explain why East Asia was so vulnerable to a change of sentiment. It also helps explain the severity of the Asian crisis.

A clear, though perhaps not totally new, lesson is that not only the level of flows is an indicator of vulnerability but so is the stock of accumulated external liabilities and their structure. These variables (and their relation to foreign exchange reserves, GDP, and other indicators) need to be very carefully monitored.

An important cause of the increased and high flows was naturally capital account liberalization. This seems, for example, particularly clear for South Korea and least clear for Indonesia. It is interesting that the four countries undertook liberalization in different ways. However, all four had a crisis (which to an important extent may also be explained by contagion). The policy lessons seem to relate to the desirability of liberalization under certain conditions, such as high debt to equity ratios in a context of weak banking systems, as well as the sequencing, with South Korea's emphasis on liberalizing bank credit so quickly and the establishment in Thailand of the BIBF being the least appropriate aspects of this liberalization. It is also interesting that the policy response to the crisis in this aspect has been so different, with Malaysia, for example, radically tightening controls on outflows while South Korea accelerated liberalization. What is striking is that both countries seem to have recovered from the crisis fairly well and rather quickly, though South Korea's resurgence is particularly impressive. Further research will be required to assess whether these different policy responses lead to differences in the *quality* of recovery.

We have measured in detail short-term volatility and the empirics of sudden reversals. We conclude that large accumulated stocks of potentially reversible flows are always and particularly dangerous, as even if a fairly small proportion of that total stock leaves the country the scale of the outflow will be such that it is likely to provoke a crisis; this likelihood naturally increases if foreign exchange reserves are relatively small and current account deficits are large. Put in another way, as capital flows are likely to be as prone to reversals as they were in the 1990s, countries may need to choose one of the policy options if they do not wish to have a fairly high risk of major currency crises: (1) countries must not allow large foreign liabilities of potentially reversible flows to accumulate; or (2), if they do accumulate large external liabilities, countries must keep very high levels of net foreign exchange reserves to protect them from the risk of large and costly reversals. The problem of the latter option is naturally its high cost (as investments in reserves typically yield less than the cost of borrowing). Furthermore, we must ask whether there is a point, from a country's perspective, to accepting such large inflows if they cannot sustain a large current account deficit—and thus higher investment and imports—and they need to maintain such costly and high reserves.

If recipient countries and the international institutions feel that such extremely high reserves are not desirable, then it becomes essential for: (1) countries to curb both large current account deficits and above all large capital inflows to avoid the accumulation of foreign liabilities; for (2) large contingency credit lines, from both the International Monetary Fund (IMF) and the private sector, to be fairly easily available to all countries with large inflows and large liabilities of foreign capital so as to reduce the need for countries' own reserves in these situations; and/or for (3) mechanisms to be available internationally for orderly debt workouts and standstills to reduce the level of outflows when these become excessive. This returns us to the now familiar and important, but as yet unresolved, policy discussion of liberalization of the capital account, of selective measures to discourage excessive surges of capital, and of a new international financial architecture. The latter is discussed in the last chapter of this book, by Griffith-Jones and Ocampo, where we offer our perspective on necessary measures to be taken as well as mentioning other perspectives.

Our analysis has been based on country experiences. However, the importance of contagion poses difficult challenges for analysis and policymakers. Criteria for indicators of vulnerability, as well as existing and proposed responses to prevent or managing crises, tend to be based on national indicators. However, if a country can become more crisis prone due to events in other countries or developments in the international economy, account needs to be taken of those possibilities. As these may be hard to predict (though indicators could perhaps be devised), extra cushions need to be introduced in boom times so that such indicators can take account of such unpredictable external events.

APPENDIX

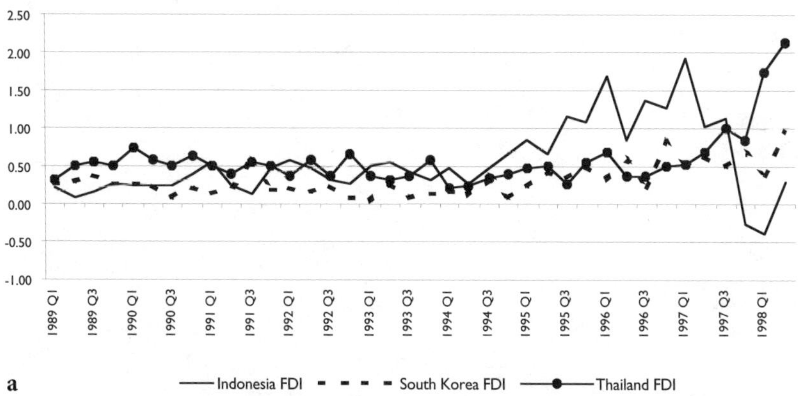

Fig. A1.1. Foreign investments to Indonesia, Korea, and Thailand, in 1990 $bn: *a,* direct investments; *b,* portfolio investments; *c,* other investments

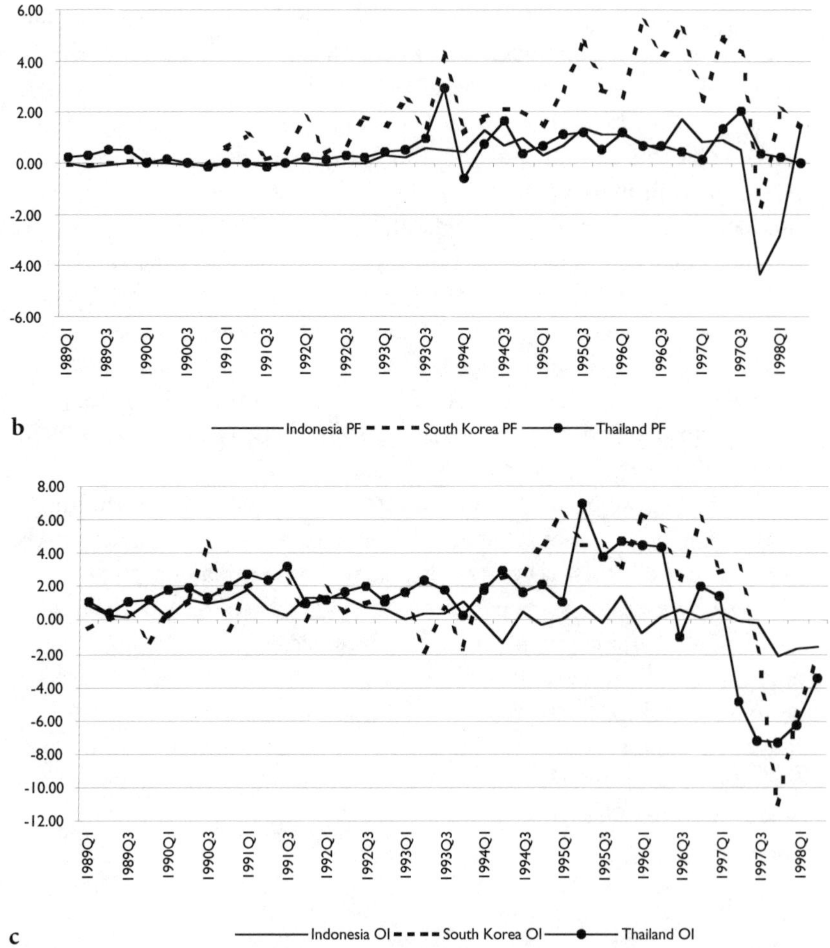

Fig. A1.1. Continued

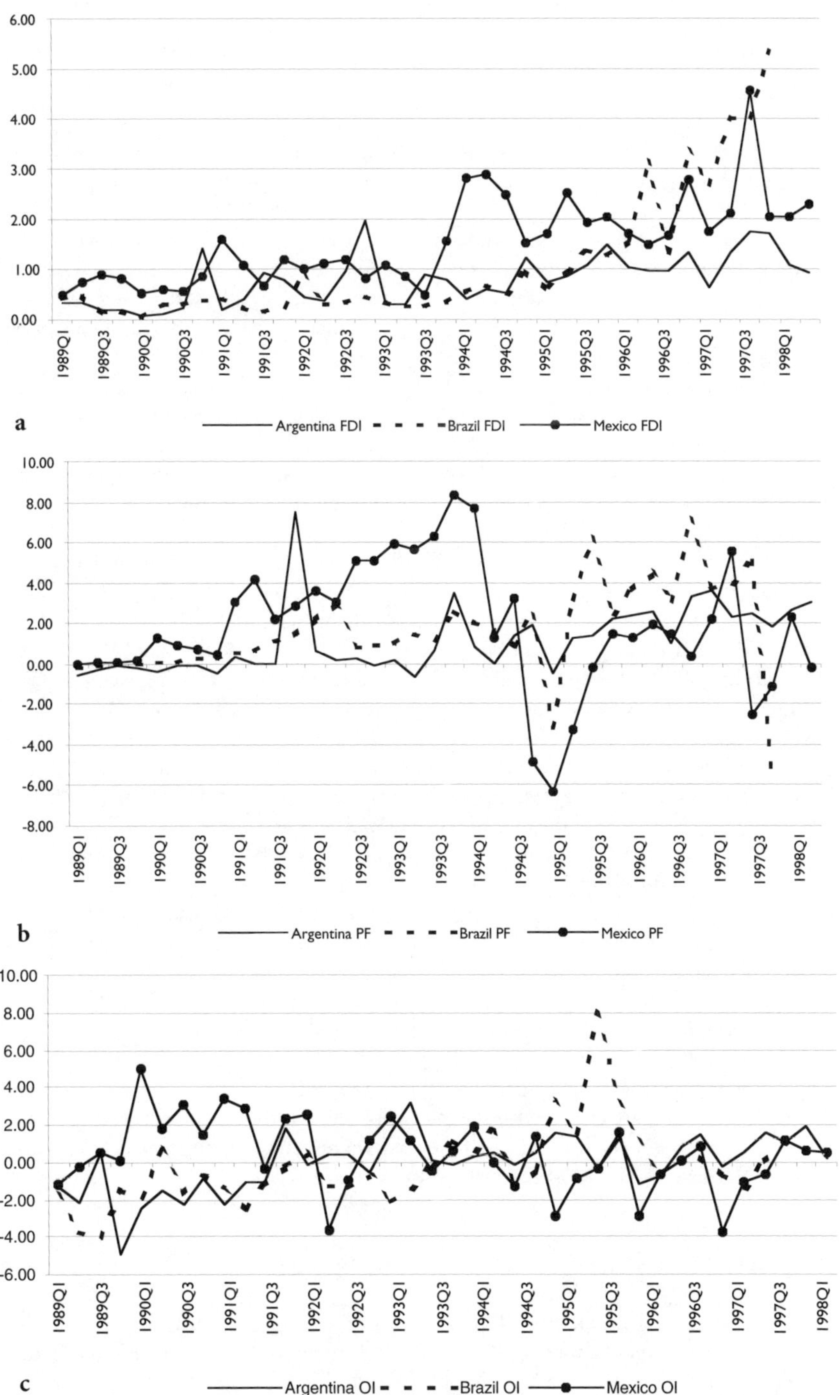

Fig. A1.2. Foreign investments to Argentina, Brazil, and Mexico, in 1990 $bn: *a,* direct investments; *b,* portfolio investments; *c,* other investments

NOTES

We thank Helmut Reisen, as well as other participants of the September 1999 Institute of Development Studies (IDS) workshop Global Capital Flows, for very helpful comments.

1. *Contagion* refers to the phenomenon of market disturbances spreading from one country to another. More narrowly, it takes the form of comovement in variables such as exchange rates and stock prices across different countries. At least two forms of contagion have been identified in the literature: "fundamentals-based contagion," in which contagion is explained in terms of trade and/or financial links between the countries; and "true contagion," which refers to comovements caused by financial panic and herd behavior rather than to fundamentals (Dornbush, Park, and Claessens 2000; Frankel and Schmukler 1998).

2. A market participant sees herding as the tendency of banks and investors "to buy what others are buying, sell what others are selling and own what others own" (Persaud 2000, 4).

3. The data on private flows have been retrieved from the International Financial Statistics CD-Rom and deflated by the U.S. Consumer Price Index (CPI). Three categories of net private flows have been defined in the fifth edition of the Manual of Balance of Payments: Foreign Direct Investments, Portfolio Flows (Debt and Equity), and Other Investments, which are mainly international credits. The data on Malaysia are less comparable, as the Bank of Negara still publishes data on the capital account using the fourth edition. Nominal GDP data come from the 1999 edition of the World Development Indicators (WDI) and have also been deflated by the U.S. CPI. Some data for 1998 have either been given by the IMF Statistics Department or been retrieved directly from national data bases. This is the case for South Korea and Indonesia.

4. See, for example, Ffrench-Davis and Griffith-Jones 1995, Fernandez-Arias and Montiel 1995, and Park and Song 1997.

5. Flows of FDI, on the other hand, have been increasing steadily for some time and thus have a mean significantly different from zero in most cases and whatever the chosen period. In this case, the coefficient of variation is relevant.

6. In cases in which major differences were found between the cumulated flows and the stocks, an initial stock of investment was added to the series (see Cailloux and Griffith-Jones 1999 for data on stocks).

7. We do not have reliable quarterly data for Malaysia.

8. The reversals are measured as the "distance" between the top of the boom (last inflow before reversal) and the bottom of the crisis (cumulating all outflows up to and including the largest one). Most reversals occur in two quarters.

REFERENCES

Akyuz, Y., and A. Cornford. 1999. "Capital flows to developing countries and the reform of the international financial system." Mimeo, United Nations Conference on Trade and Development (UNCTAD), Geneva.

BIS (Bank for International Settlements). 1999. *The BIS consolidated international banking statistics.* May.

Cailloux, J., and S. Griffith-Jones. 1999. "Encouraging the long term: Institutional investors and emerging markets." Office of Development Studies Discussion Papers, no. 16. New York: United Nations Development Programme (UNDP).

Calvo, G. 1998. "Capital flows and capital market crises: The simple economics of sudden stops." *Journal of Applied Economics* 1, no. 1 (November): 35–54.

———. 1999. "When capital flows come to a sudden stop: Consequences and policy options." Mimeo, University of Maryland, <http://www.bsos.umd.edu/econ/ciecalvo.htm>.

Calvo, G., and C. M. Reinhart. 1999. "Capital flow reversals, the exchange rate debate, and dollarization." *Finance and Development* 36, no. 3 (September): 13–15.

Claessens, S., M. P. Dooley, and A. Warner. 1995. "Portfolio capital flows: Hot or cold?" *World Bank Economic Review* 9, no. 1 (January): 153–74.

Demirguc-Kunt, A., and E. Detragiache. 1998. "The determinants of banking crises in developing and developed countries." *IMF Staff Papers* 45, no. 1:81–109.

Dornbush, R., Y. Park, and S. Claessens. 2000. "Contagion: How it spreads and how it can be stopped." *World Bank Research Observer* 15, no. 2 (August): 177–97.

Economic Commission for Latin America and the Caribbean (ECLAC). 1997. *La inversion extranjera en America Latina y el Caribe, Edicion 1997.* Santiago, Chile: United Nations.

———. 1998. *Foreign investment in Latin America and the Caribbean.* Santiago, Chile: United Nations.

Edwards, S. 2000. "Capital flows and economic performance." Manuscript, University of California, Los Angeles.

Frankel, J., and S. Schmukler. 1998. "Crisis, contagion, and country funds: Effects on East Asia and Latin America." In *Managing capital flows and exchange rates: Perspectives from the Pacific Basin,* ed. R. Glick. New York: Cambridge University Press.

Fernandez-Arias, E., and P. J. Montiel. 1995. "The surge in capital inflows to developing countries: Prospects and policy implications." Policy Research Working Paper, World Bank, Washington, DC.

Ffrench-Davis, R., and S. Griffith-Jones, eds. 1995. *Coping with capital surges: The return of finance to Latin America.* Ottawa: International Development Research Centre (IDRC).

Griffith-Jones, S. 1998. *Global capital flows: Should they be regulated?* Basingstoke: Macmillan

Griffith-Jones, S., J. A. Ocampo, and J. Cailloux. 1999. "The poorest countries and the emerging international financial architecture." Mimeo, Institute of Development Studies, Brighton. Available at <http://www.ids.ac.uk/ids/global/finance/ifpubs .html>.

Krugman, P. 1998a. "What happened to Asia?" Mimeo, Massachusetts Institute of Technology, January.

———. 1998b. "Fire sale FDI". Paper presented at the conference Capital Flows to Emerging Markets, National Bureau of Economic Research, Washington, DC, February 20–21.

Montes, M. 1997. "Short term policy responses to massive capital inflows." Paper presented at the conference Short Term Capital Movements and Balance of Payments Crises, Institute of Development Studies/World Institute for Development Economics Research (IDS/WIDER), IDS, Brighton, U.K., May.

Nasution, A. 1997. "Capital inflows and policy responses in Indonesia in the 1990's." Paper presented at the conference Global Capital Flows, IDS/WIDER, Sussex, England, September.

———. 1999. "Indonesia's responses to the recent economic crisis." Paper presented at the Workshop on Capital Flows, IDS, Sussex, England, September.

Park, Y. C., and C.-Y. Song. 1997. "Managing foreign capital flows: The experiences of Korea, Thailand, Malaysia, and Indonesia." In *International monetary and financial issues for the 1990s.* Research Papers for the Group of 24, no. 8. Geneva: United Nations Conference on Trade and Development.

Reisen, H. 1999. "After the great Asian slump: Towards a coherent approach to global capital flows." OECD Development Centre Policy Briefs, no. 16. Paris.

Sarno, L., and M. Taylor. 1999a. "Hot money, accounting labels, and the permanence of capital flows to developing countries: An empirical investigation." *Journal of Development Economics* 59:337–64.

———. 1999b. "Moral hazard, asset price bubbles, capital flows, and the East Asian crisis: A first test." *Journal of International Money and Finance* 18:637–57.

Tesar, L. L., and I. M. Werner. 1995. "US equity investment in emerging stock markets." *World Bank Economic Review* 9, no. 1 (January): 109–29.

Turner, P. 1991. "Capital flows in the 1980s: A survey of major trends." BIS Economic Papers, no. 30. April.

UNCTAD (United Nations Conference on Trade and Development). 1999. *Trade and development report, 1999.* Geneva: UNCTAD.

World Bank. 1997. *The road to financial integration.* Washington, DC: World Bank.

CHAPTER 2

The Role of Mutual Funds and Other International Investors in Currency Crises

Stephany Griffith-Jones

As we have seen in chapter 1, the key source of the reversals of capital flows that triggered the Asian crisis was bank loans. However, portfolio flows also played an important, if more secondary, role, representing 27 percent of the reversal of flows during the crisis, that is, between 1996 and 1998, according to International Monetary Fund (IMF) data (see table 1.2 in chap. 1). Furthermore, as we also saw in chapter 1, as a proportion of the total stock of liabilities of different categories of flows, portfolio flows are far more reversible than loans. Finally, it should be stressed that in the Mexican peso crisis, (see, e.g., Griffith-Jones 1996), portfolio flows were the main source of the reversal.

In this chapter, we wish to gather the empirical evidence available on the role that portfolio flows in general (sec. 1) and one major category of international institutional investors, mutual funds (sec. 2), have played, particularly in recent currency crises. Our review of the evidence will show that international mutual funds, in particular, did play a fairly important role in outflows from the four Asian countries most affected by the crisis; investments of mutual funds also were extremely volatile in Latin America during the Mexican, Asian, and Russian crises. In section 3, we review the evidence on the link between changes in investments by foreign institutional investors and market returns. Most of the existing literature has indeed focused on this aspect. However, even though this is an important channel for transmitting and magnifying crises (lower stock prices may affect the quality of banks' portfolios of loans and they may also indirectly encourage further capital outflows), it is clearly not the main channel, which is via the direct impact on capital flows. This will be discussed in sections 1 and 2. Whereas sections 1, 2, and 3 provide the empirical basis for regulating inflows by institutional investors, section 4 briefly reviews the theoretical case. It also emphasizes the growing importance of mutual funds, particularly in the U.S. financial sector, which further strengthens the case for some source country regulations of that sector. Section 5 concludes with some regulatory proposals.

1. THE ROLE OF PORTFOLIO FLOWS IN THE ASIAN CRISIS

As any serious analyst of capital flows knows only too well, data on these flows suffer from a number of problems. Furthermore, data from different sources show extremely large differences that are only partly explained by differences in methodology and coverage. This is particularly so for portfolio flows. We will nevertheless attempt to provide as precise an overview as possible.

We will begin with what seems to be the most reliable source of data, the IMF.[1] As can be seen in table 2.1, in the beginning of the 1990s portfolio flows to the Asian-4 were not very large, with the exception of South Korea, which received significant inflows as early as 1991, flows whose level grew very rapidly till 1996. Indonesia and Thailand became major recipients from 1993 onward. Malaysia experienced mainly outflows over the period. Interestingly, there is no evidence of an impact of the 1994 Mexican crisis on any of the four Asian countries. On the contrary, all four Asian economies experienced higher flows in 1995, suggesting that portfolio flows were somewhat diverted

TABLE 2.1. Portfolio Flows to the Four Most Affected Asian Economies (billions of current U.S.$)

	1990	1991	1992	1993	1994	1995	1996	1997	1998
Indonesia portfolio investment	−0.09	−0.01	−0.09	1.81	3.88	4.10	5.01	−2.63	−2.00[a]
Equity securities				1.81	1.90	1.49	1.82	−4.99	−4.50[a]
Debt securities	−0.09	−0.01	−0.09		1.98	2.61	3.19	2.36	2.49[a]
South Korea portfolio investment	0.22	2.34	4.95	10.55	8.15	13.87	21.18	12.29	−3.40[a]
Equity securities	0.38	0.20	2.48	6.62	3.61	4.22	5.95	2.53	2.70[b]
Debt securities	−0.16	2.14	2.47	3.94	4.53	9.66	15.23	9.76	−2.00[b]
Malaysia portfolio investment	−0.25	0.17	−1.12	−0.71	−1.65	−0.44	−0.27	−0.25	
Debt securities	−0.25	0.17	−1.12	−0.71	−1.65	−0.44	−0.27	−0.25	
Thailand portfolio investment	−0.04	−0.08	0.92	5.46	2.49	4.08	3.59	4.80	0.16[a]
Equity securities	0.44	0.04	0.46	2.68	−0.39	2.12	1.16	3.90	0.35[a]
Debt securities	−0.48	−0.12	0.47	2.78	2.87	1.96	2.42	0.90	−0.20[a]
Total portfolio investment	−0.16	2.42	4.67	17.12	12.85	21.62	29.50	14.21	−5.24[c]
Equity securities	0.82	0.24	2.94	11.11	5.12	7.83	8.93	1.44	
Debt securities	−0.98	2.18	1.73	6.01	7.73	13.79	20.57	12.77	

Source: IMF 1999; IFS 1999.
[a]Full year.
[b]First three quarters of 1998.
[c]Excludes Malaysia.

from Latin America to Asia. This remained the case in 1996 except for Thailand, which experienced a decline.

The Asian crisis seems to have had its greatest impact on Indonesia, which is the only country to have experienced a reversal of portfolio flows for the full year 1997. South Korea suffered a sharp decline in 1997 and a reversal in 1998, while Thailand saw an increase in flows. It is worth noting that these annual data hide the short-term volatility of flows, which was most striking in the second semester of 1997.

As far as the instruments are concerned, it is worth underlining that from 1994 onward bonds represent the main source of portfolio flows. This is true for all countries taken either as a group or individually. The share of debt securities in total portfolio flows rose steadily between 1994 and 1996 from 60 to 70 percent (see table 2.1). However, the percentage decline in equity flows between 1996 and 1997 was sharper than in bonds (an 84 percent decline in equity compared to 38 percent for bonds). Nevertheless, only in Indonesia did equity investment experience a reversal during the crisis. This is in sharp contrast to Thailand, where equity investments actually increased.

More detailed information can be found on portfolio equity flows, where three categories can be distinguished:

(1) Listed securities in local Asian markets

(2) Placements of Asian equities in international markets (mainly American Depository Receipts/General Depository Receipts [ADRs/GDRs] and private placements)

(3) Private equity funds

As Barth and Zhang (1999) point out, the latter two categories, which are often neglected in recent analyses, constitute the bulk of foreign portfolio flows to Asia between 1990 and 1998.

According to the data in table 2.2 (which differ quite widely from the IMF data presented in table 2.1), in the four most affected countries there were either very sharp declines of portfolio equity flows in 1997 (Indonesia and South Korea) or a reversal into negative figures (Malaysia and Thailand). Interestingly, according to the data in table 2.2, by 1998 portfolio equity flows had practically recovered their 1996 levels (in South Korea) and even exceeded them (in Thailand). On the other hand, Malaysia had a fairly insignificant recovery into positive territory while flows to Indonesia declined further. It is also interesting that China saw a different pattern of evolution, with portfolio equity flows actually increasing significantly in 1997 and falling only in 1998.

TABLE 2.2. Portfolio Equity Investments by Different Flows in Selected East Asian Countries (U.S.$ million; yearly data, 1990–98)

	1990	1991	1992	1993	1994	1995	1996	1997	1998
China	0	653	1,194	4,241	4,679	3,714	4,378	8,919	1,220
International placements	0	12	689	1,874	2,602	892	2,078	9,103	1,052
Listed	0	0	334	720	1,134	206	537	1,484	234
Unlisted	0	12	355	1,154	1,468	686	1,541	7,619	818
Local portfolio investment	0	641	505	1,944	1,313	1,915	1,388	−646	101
Private equity				423	764	907	912	462	67
Indonesia	586	110	119	2,510	3,795	5,046	3,230	472	250
International placements	586	110	119	345	1,322	1,473	1,234	935	
Listed	586	73	69	23	531	671	58	127	
Unlisted	0	36	50	322	791	802	1,175	808	
Local portfolio investment	0	0	0	2,107	2,350	3,400	1,865	−638	250
Private equity				58	123	173	131	174	
South Korea	387	200	2,154	5,903	2,392	3,452	5,513	1,521	4,557
International placements	387	200	252	328	1,168	1,310	1,151	630	150
Listed	304	131	252	226	330	300	323		
Unlisted	83	69	0	103	838	1,010	828	630	150
Local portfolio investment			1,902	5,391	1,025	1,803	3,968	456	3,574
Private equity				184	200	339	394	435	833
Malaysia	292	0	385	3,709	1,370	2,369	4,455	−408	604
International placements	0	0	385	0	0	569	600	424	162
Listed	0	0	134	0	0	0	44		
Unlisted	0	0	251	0	0	569	556	424	162
Local portfolio investment	292	0	0	3,700	1,320	1,730	3,753	−913	430
Private equity				9	50	70	102	81	12
Philippines	32	98	333	1,464	1,596	2,025	1,341	102	697
International placements	32	98	333	126	949	749	1001	265	375
Listed	8	98	195	82	0	0	142		
Unlisted	23	0	138	44	949	749	858	265	375
Local portfolio investment	0	0	0	1,319	458	1,212	332	−192	3
Private equity				19	189	64	8	29	319
Thailand	449	41	4	3,145	−513	2,175	1,583	−248	2,449
International placements	83	134	4	561	759	531	151	28	2,265
Listed	61	115	4	156	38	56	0		
Unlisted	21	19	0	405	721	476	151	28	2,265
Local portfolio investment	366	−93	0	2,556	−1,298	1,623	1,400	−336	167
Private equity				28	25	21	32	59	17
Total	1,746	1,102	2,286	15,581	12,294	16,978	16,532	9,902	6,203
International placements	1,087	554	1,781	3,234	6,800	5,524	6,215	11,386	4,004
Listed	960	418	987	1,206	2,032	1,232	1,105	1,611	234
Unlisted	127	136	794	2,028	4,767	4,292	5,110	9,775	3,770
Local portfolio investment	659	548	505	11,626	4,144	9,880	8,738	−2,725	951
Private equity		0	0	721	1,351	1,574	1,579	1,240	1,247

Source: Barth and Zhang 1999.

China's more stable evolution after the Asian crisis broke out seems to have been strongly related to the composition of its portfolio equity inflows, which in turn depended on the level of openness and maturity of capital markets. In countries with relatively tight capital controls and less well developed equity markets (such as China), international placements—via mechanisms such as ADRs and GDRs—and private equities account for a higher proportion of total portfolio flows than portfolio investment in local markets. In economies with more open and mature capital markets (such as those of Malaysia and Thailand at the time), foreign portfolio investment in local equity markets represents the primary form of foreign equity inflows. The latter seem clearly more easily reversible (see table 2.2).[2] As Barth and Zhang conclude, "Ironically, economies that relied most heavily on international placements and private equities were hurt less by the crisis than economies that attracted more direct portfolio equity investment in their markets" (1999, p. 9). It could be concluded that paradoxically the more equity markets are opened and developed the greater the share of foreign portfolio investment in local markets is (as a proportion of total portfolio flows), and the more reversible they are, and therefore they may become more vulnerable to crises.

More detailed empirical analysis of the components of portfolio equity flows for other countries would be desirable. However, a preliminary policy conclusion, based on the existing evidence for Asia, would seem to indicate the possible desirability of caution in indiscriminately opening local stock markets to foreign portfolio flows, with greatest emphasis placed on international placements and private equities. However, the possible disadvantages of excessive emphasis on international placements, via GDRs and ADRs, need to be carefully examined; these include a possible increase in the stocks at home price volatility (Domowitz, Glen, and Madhavan 1998) and loss of business for national brokers and others (interview material).

2. THE ROLE OF MUTUAL FUNDS

To analyze the role of mutual funds and other institutional investors in the East Asian crisis, we need first to put this discussion into the context of the size and foreign presence of Asian stock markets as well as the importance of the mutual fund industry within this foreign presence.

According to data from the International Finance Corporation (IFC) Emerging Markets Database, there was very rapid growth and volatility of East Asia's equity markets in the 1990s. Total market capitalization for Indonesia, South Korea, Malaysia, and Thailand, the four main victim countries of the crisis, reached $129 billion in the late 1980s. It increased more than fourfold to $637 billion in late 1996. By the end of 1997, market capitalization in these countries fell to $188 billion, a decline of around 70 percent.

In the context of this study, it is important to stress that 90 percent of total portfolio flows to emerging economies are estimated to be intermediated by fund managers (Howell 1998). Furthermore, by mid-1996 about 10 percent of international and global mutual funds' assets were invested in emerging markets, while assets of specialized emerging market funds (both closed and open end) were estimated to be as high as $131 billion (World Bank 1997).

As far as the size of total net asset value of emerging market mutual funds is concerned, Asia is the largest region, with more than $40 billion in assets from 1993 onward. Interestingly, this relatively high share of assets had been stable since 1993, following a period of dramatic increases between 1990 and 1993. During the first quarter of 1997, Asia was still experiencing a significant increase in assets, which brought the share of assets in this region to 50 percent of total assets of emerging market mutual funds. Latin America accounted for about 15 percent, and its share remained stable throughout the period (Cailloux and Griffith-Jones 1999).

Barth and Zhang (1999) estimate that assets of U.S. dedicated Asian mutual funds and U.S. mutual funds that have some exposure in Asia amounted to $85.1 billion by the end of 1996. Pension funds and hedge funds are estimated to have had far fewer assets by the end of 1996, $4.5 and $12.9 billion, respectively.

According to Cailloux and Griffith-Jones (1999), equity funds accounted for about 90 percent of emerging market funds, the remaining 10 percent being invested through bond funds. It is also worth noting that the largest increase in assets has been experienced by mutual funds investing in emerging markets not dedicated to any region in particular (especially between 1993 and beginning of 1997).

Barth and Zhang (1999) provide empirical evidence on foreign ownership in Asian markets but without distinguishing between types of investors. Table 2.3 reports the share of foreign ownership of local market capitalization. The share of foreign ownership of total market capitalization is rather small for the four Asian countries, with the notable exception of Malaysia, where foreigners accounted for half of all market capitalization in 1997.

Table 2.3 also provides data on the share of foreign ownership of "free float" (i.e., of stocks readily available for public ownership). This distinction is important, as in many countries a large share of quoted stocks are in the hands of a small number of owners, either the government or top families. Access to ownership by foreigners is thus limited to stocks not owned by this set of investors. The results are striking. Indonesia and Malaysia had the largest share of foreign ownership of free float, with levels as high as 76.3 and 69.4 percent, respectively. It reached 44.6 and 19.3 percent in Thailand and South Korea, respectively. The latter figure is due to the 20 percent ceiling on foreign equity investment that was still in place at the beginning of 1997. The likely impact of the reversal of foreign financial flows on the South Korean stock market thus seems to be limited. This is confirmed by our findings on outflows in South Korea during 1997–98, which are not significant (see table 1.3 in chap. 1) and by Park and Park (in chap. 7 of this volume), who find that foreign investors had a negligible effect on the domestic markets in 1997. However, for the other countries—and particularly for Indonesia and Malaysia—the presence of foreign investors in the free float was already dominant.

Since 1998 and 1999, with increased openness and the lowering of barriers to investment in most Asian countries, especially in South Korea, foreign ownership of free float has been increasing steadily. This increase will eventually raise the ratio of foreign ownership to total market capitalization, especially in cases such as South Korea, where there is still much room for an increase in foreign ownership of free float (about 80 percent was still available in 1997 due to capital controls) and where free float represents a significant share of total market capitalization (62 percent in the case of South Korea). Foreign equity investment is thus bound to increase and have a larger impact on domestic stock markets. This is particularly important when foreign capital flows exhibit large and unpredictable fluctuations. Although Barth and Zhang (1999) provide evidence that on average foreign investors tend to hold their securities for a longer period of time than local investors, the recent episode of large reversals documented in this chapter favors the hypothesis of destabilizing foreign capital flows.

We will now attempt to examine the role played by mutual funds during crises, looking first at the issue, understudied in the literature, of their impact

TABLE 2.3. Foreign Ownership in the Asian-4 in 1997, in Percentages

	Indonesia		Korea		Malaysia		Thailand	
	Foreign	Domestic	Foreign	Domestic	Foreign	Domestic	Foreign	Domestic
Ownership of total market cap	29.0	71.0	12.0	88.0	50.0	50.0	21.0	79.0
Foreign shares of trading	35.4	64.5	13.6	86.3	50.0	50.0	26.0	74.0
Free float over market cap	38.0		62.0		72.0		47.0	
Ownership of free float	76.3	23.6	19.3	80.6	69.4	30.5	44.6	55.3

Source: Barth and Zhang 1999.

on the balance of payments. Due to differences in data sources and coverage, there are again important differences in outcomes. However, overall it seems that mutual funds have played a very large role in capital outflows in Latin America and a significant (though somewhat smaller) role in East Asia.

Kaminsky, Lyons, and Schmukler (1999) carefully examine data for the majority of Latin American open-ended equity funds. As is shown clearly in figure 2.1, Latin American mutual funds had *extremely large* outflows, both during the Mexican peso crisis and during the Asian and Russian crises (the movements are expressed in beginning of quarter share prices so that the deflated declines would be somewhat smaller). In the Mexican crisis, mutual funds pulled out of Mexico and Argentina in a major way, contributing very significantly to the peso crisis (see Griffith-Jones 1996). However, funds did not pull out of more illiquid markets, like that of Colombia. During the Asian and Russian crises of 1997 and 1998, withdrawals by mutual funds from Latin America were more broadly based (with regard to countries) and more persistent (see fig. 2.1). During the latter crises, mutual funds' retreat from Latin America was more generalized, with heavy sales reaching even the most illiquid markets; the largest outflows were from Venezuela, Brazil, Peru. and Argentina.

Kaminsky, Lyons, and Schmukler (1999) therefore find very important outflows by mutual funds from Latin America during the recent major crises. Another paper (Froot, O'Connell, and Seasholes 1999), which looked at net equity flows by all institutional investors—thus including not just mutual funds but pension funds and hedge funds—finds fairly significant outflows from Latin America during the Russian and Long Term Capital Management (LTCM) crisis and fairly small outflows from Latin America during the Asian crisis (see fig. 2.2). A possible explanation of the difference between these and the previous results is that the other institutions included in Froot, O'Connell, and Seasholes (1999)—such as hedge funds and pension funds—may have bought Latin American shares at the time, counteracting the clear net selling by mutual funds.

Froot, O'Connell, and Seasholes (1999) report that at an aggregate level institutional investors temporarily sold emerging Asia shares (between August and November 1997); however, the scale of these sales, even if it is significant, was not very dramatic (see fig. 2.2). Focusing on mutual funds' assets in Asia (reported in the Lipper Inc. universe), Barth and Zhang (1999) report a decline in asset value of $7.5 billion in 1997 and almost $2 billion in 1998. Of these figures, value compression—due to drops in share prices—account for just over 50 percent in 1997. As a result, outflows would explain around $4.0 billion from all of Asia. Unfortunately, the data do not disaggregate for the four most affected countries. However, we can fairly safely

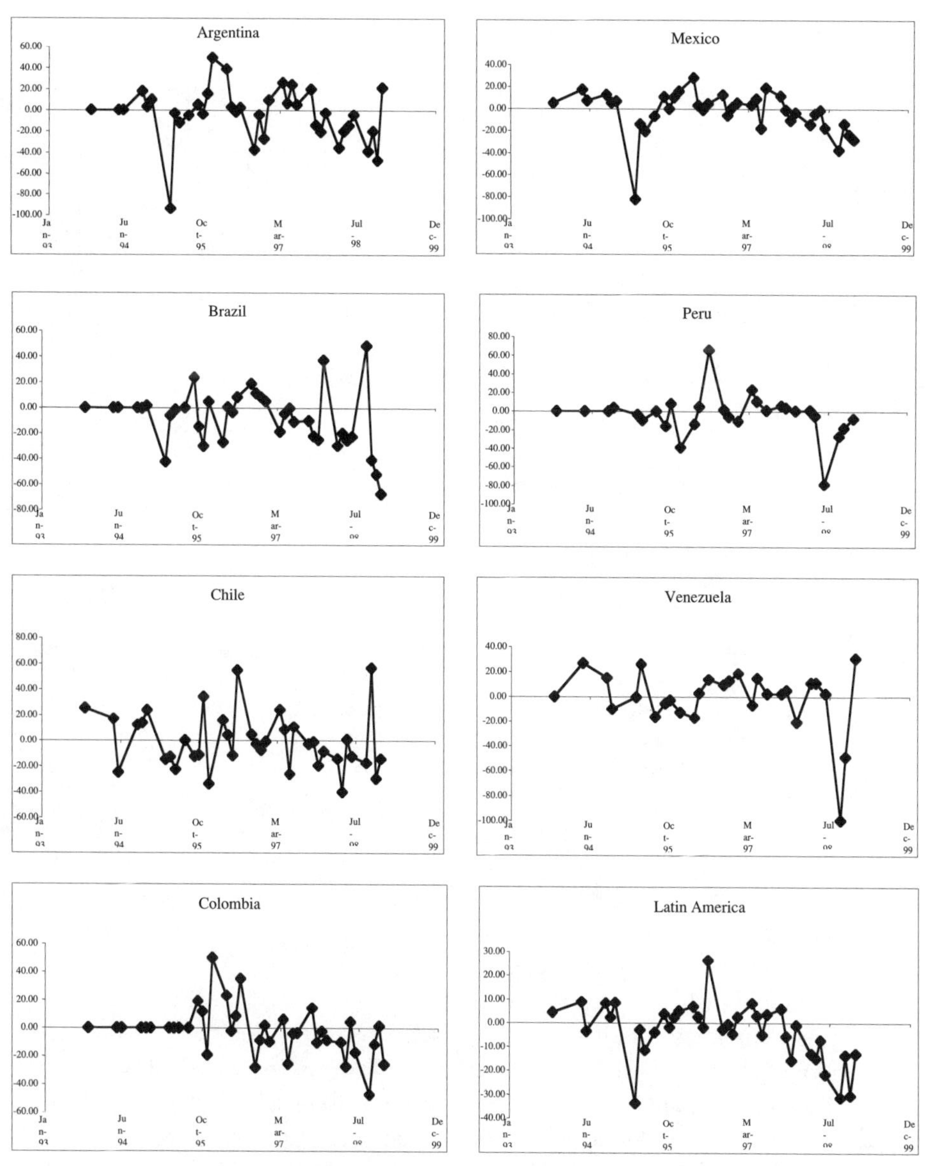

Fig. 2.1. Mutual funds' net buying/selling of stocks in Latin America. Net buying/selling is equal to the value-weighted percentage change in quarterly holdings of all funds in each country, where the value weighting uses the beginning-of-period share price. All figures are in percentages. (Data from Kaminsky, Lyons, and Schmukler 1999.)

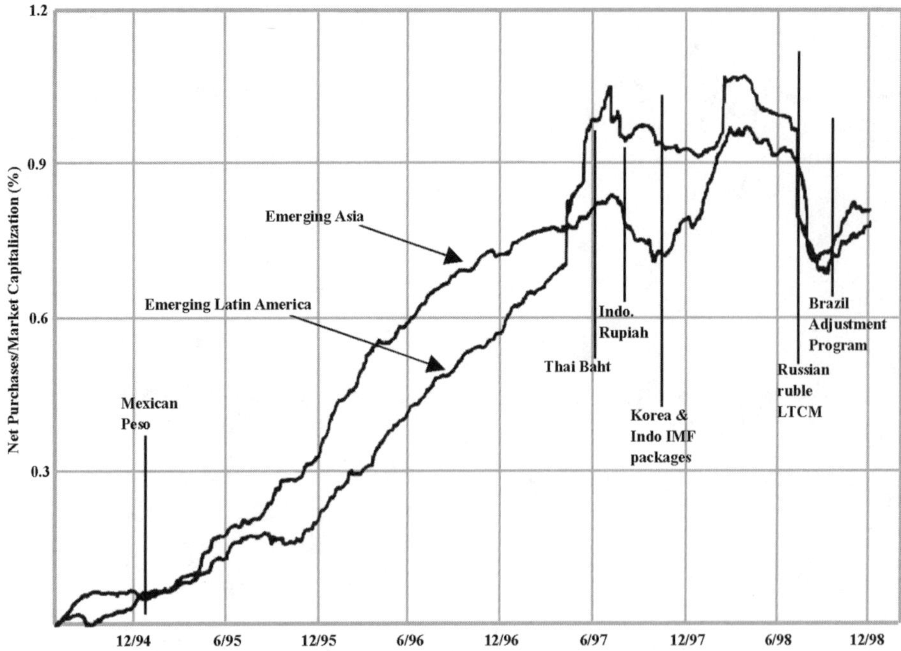

Fig. 2.2. Cumulative net equity flows into emerging Asia and Latin America, August 1994 to December 1998. (Data from Froot, O'Connell, and Seasholes 1999.)

assume that outflows from the four most affected countries in 1997 were larger than the $4.0 billion estimated earlier, as countries like China had large net inflows in 1997 (see table 2.2).

According to data and analysis in Post and Millar 1998, net new cash flows by shareholders in U.S. Asian emerging market equity funds exhibited a pattern of almost continuous net redemptions between late 1996 and late 1997. The largest monthly outflows for these funds were 4.8 percent of their investment stock in July 1997 and 4.1 percent in August 1997. Overall, in 1997 shareholders withdrew about 27 percent of their 1996 year-end investment in these funds, 10 percent prior to the beginning of the crisis (marked by the float of the Thai baht in July) and 17 percent thereafter. It is interesting that, according to data in Post and Millar 1998, U.S. emerging market equity fund managers who were invested in Asia only had net outflows mainly in the first half of 1997 (equivalent to around 7 percent of assets), with only small sales (of around 1 percent of assets) in November 1997 and reportedly net purchases of shares between July and October 1997. This trend is explained by the fact that, though Asia regional funds registered outflows in every month between June 1996 and September 1997 (reflecting large cash outflows from shareholders), Asian exposure in global funds was positive during most of that period. The sum of both trends gives the result reported earlier, of net outflows only during the first half of 1997 and in November 1997. If these data are accurate, it would appear that U.S. mutual funds in aggregate helped *trigger* the beginning of the East Asian crisis but did not deepen it.

Post and Millar (1998) also offer country by country analysis of portfolio managers' actions. According to these data, there were very significant net sales by U.S. emerging market equity mutual funds only in Malaysia—between March and October 1998—equivalent to around 20 percent of the total assets of those funds; there were also fairly large outflows by these mutual funds but only in October 1997 from South Korea, equivalent to around 6 percent of their total assets. According to Post and Millar, Indonesia, and particularly Thailand, had net inflows from U.S. emerging market equity funds during 1997.

It can be concluded that U.S. mutual funds did play some role in the East Asian crisis, particularly by helping to trigger it; they also contributed to the deepening of the crisis, especially in Malaysia. However, the size of portfolio outflows were clearly not as large as the reversal of bank loans in the East Asian crisis. Furthermore, in Latin America mutual funds' holdings have been extremely volatile, and their outflows have put significant pressure on currencies and stock market prices during recent crises. Further studies are required to determine more precisely the impact of inflows and outflows of different categories of institutional investors (and particularly mutual funds) on different emerging markets. A crucial precondition for this is the improvement of primary data, partly by providing wider access to existing data that are produced and controlled by private firms, and the improvement of statistics on these flows by international organizations such as the Bank for International Settlements (BIS) and IMF.

3. LINKS BETWEEN CHANGES IN THE ASSETS OF INTERNATIONAL INSTITUTIONAL INVESTORS AND MARKET RETURNS

Most of the literature on the potential impact of international institutional investors on countries in crisis somewhat surprisingly has not focused on the flows themselves, nor on their impact on the exchange rate and the balance of payments, but has focused on their effect on stock markets and in particular on the relationship between foreign flows and market returns. Three hypotheses are usually tested: first, whether returns lag behind foreign flows (foreign investors are market leaders) and inflows (or outflows) lead to an increase (or decrease) in prices; and, second, whether returns precede flows (foreign investors follow "positive feedback trading strategies," that is, they are trend chasers (past performance can predict future levels of flows). The third hypothesis that is sometimes tested is whether flows and returns are contemporaneous. Table 2.4 reports most of the major results.

Positive feedback strategies are interesting to study because they can inform us about the potential destabilizing impact of investors on stock market returns (see, e.g., De Long et al. 1990 or Lakonishok, Shleifer, and Vishny 1992 for an analysis of how rational feedback trading can be destabilizing). Nofsinger and Sias (1997) stress that these strategies are often associated with herding behavior.

Of all the studies reviewed here (see table 2.4), only one (Barth and Zhang 1999) does not find evidence of positive feedback trading. This could be due to, as underlined by the authors themselves, the less sophisticated econometric technique used by these authors, which might fail to uncover that type of behavior. The overwhelming result that emerges from all the other studies is that foreign investors on average buy stocks that have been performing well and sell stocks that have been performing badly.

This behavior is likely to exacerbate boom and bust cycles, as they accentuate stock market trends. However, positive feedback trading strategies are not always destabilizing, as is shown in some of the results reported in table 2.4. As a matter of fact, the impact on the stock market of foreign investors following this strategy largely depends on the share of their ownership of local stocks. That is why the analyses carried out on South Korea (whose foreign participation was between 6 percent (Park and Song 1998) and 12 percent (Barth and Zhang 1999) of trading, though they provide some evidence on potentially destabilizing strategies, do not find a significant impact on price fluctuations.

The impact of the opening of financial markets to foreign investors could well increase volatility. Indeed, some studies (e.g., Bekaert, Harvey, and Lumsdaine 1999), find that after liberalization equity capital flows increase significantly and impact domestic prices. The same is true for outflows. However, Park and Park (1999) find no impact of foreign investment movements on the South Korean stock market, even after the lifting of ceilings on foreign investments, after the crisis. This could still be due to the rather low level of foreign participation.

Borio, Chiancarini, and Tsatsoronis (1997) compute the likely impact of the reallocation of portfolio by institutional investors on local market capitalization. The results are quite striking, as can be seen from table 2.5. Indeed, a 1 percent reallocation in the portfolio of U.S. institutional investors is likely to have a 34.9 percent impact on Latin America's market capitalization and a 14.2 percent impact on Asia. This is in stark contrast to industrial countries, where the impact is bound to be on the order of less than 1 percent.

These conflicting results concerning the potential impact of foreign financial flows on domestic stock markets call for further research. One possible area of interest is the conduct of studies similar to those carried out on South Korea but applied to stock markets that have a larger proportion of foreign participation, such as Malaysia, for example, distinguishing between crisis and noncrisis times. Clearly, the lack of data is a problem.

From the evidence we have gathered, it is still difficult to form a clear picture of the impact of foreign investors and more particularly of foreign institutional investors. However, there is some consensus on two aspects. First, foreign investors follow, on average, positive feedback strategies that can sometimes be destabilizing. These strategies seem to be followed especially in times of crisis. Second, seemingly their behavior did not lead to large impacts on recipient countries' stock markets because of the rather small share of foreign ownership of local total market capitalization. As liberalization deepens, and the share of foreign investors rise, their impact on prices will most probably increase.

It should be noted that, though it makes an important contribution, the literature just reviewed only focuses on the link between foreign, as well as domestic, institutional investors' behavior and stock market prices. Important as this is, these analyses exclude the key area of the impact of institutional investors' behavior on capital flows, as changes in capital flows have a significant impact on key macroeconomic variables. We have attempted to make an initial contribution to this in sections 1 and 2.

4. THE CASE FOR REGULATING INSTITUTIONAL INVESTORS

The frequency of recent currency crises, and their harmful effects on recipient economies—as well as the large bailouts used to contain such crises—have posed a strong challenge to the view that international private financial intermediation is always and inherently efficient.

It is becoming increasingly accepted that the process of international financial intermediation is a second-best one in which welfare for both source and recipient countries can be increased by means of regulatory changes.

The current view is that it may be desirable to regulate excessive surges of potentially reversible capital flows in recipient countries. However, the experience of the 1990s, with a very large scale of international funds—compared

TABLE 2.4. Momentum Strategies of Foreign Investors

Source	Sample and Period Studied	Herding	Impact	Positive Feedback Trading, Returns Precede Flows (trend chasers)	Contemporaneous Effect	Returns Lag Flows, Market Leaders
Barth and Zhang 1999	Monthly and weekly foreign portfolio equity flows, Indonesia, Taiwan, Thailand; Oct 1992–Dec 1998			No	Not tested	Yes
Bekaert, Harvey, and Lumsdaine 1999	20 emerging markets, 20 years, bonds and equities		Movements of equity capital are much faster when they leave than when they enter, unexpected equity flows are associated with strong short-lived increases in returns but a reduction in dividend yields		Yes, equity flows have a strong positive contemporaneous effect on returns	Yes
Froot, O'Connell, and Seasholes 1998				Yes	Yes	
Froot, O'Connell, and Seasholes 1999	Daily international portfolio flows (equity and debt), 28 emerging markets and 16 developed markets; Aug 1994–Dec 1998		Strong persistence of "price pressure in emerging flows markets is substantial, so that a cessation on inflow can reduce emerging market prices"	Yes	Yes	Yes for emerging markets even after controlling for past flows, no for developed markets

Kaminsky, Lyons, and Schmukler 1999	Quarterly mutual fund holdings, 13 Latin American open-end equity funds; April 1993–Jan 1999		Evidence of contagion strategies	Yes, stronger during noncrisis times and on the buy side	Yes, stronger in periods of crises and on the sell side
Kim and Wei 1999a	Monthly positions of foreign investors (institutional and individual) in Korea, Dec. 1996–June 1998	Individual investors herd more than institutional investors, nonresident herd more than resident ones	Impact of herding not significant	Yes for nonresident institutional investors both before and during the crisis but stronger during the crisis	
Kim and Wei 1999b	End of 1996–June 1998, 77 offshore funds' domicile is in a tax haven, 783 funds in the U.S. and U.K., and 36 funds in Singapore/Hong Kong, the funds can be mutual funds, unit trusts or hedge funds	Both onshore and offshore funds herd the former more than the latter	Offshore funds trade "more aggressively" than onshore funds	No evidence that offshore funds engage in positive feedback trading, but strong evidence that U.S./U.K. do so	
Choe and Stulz 1998	Korean stock market, Dec 1996–Dec 1997	Yes	Small	Yes	
Park and Park 1999	Korean stock market, Dec 1996–April 1999, monthly data		No, but local investors yes	Yes during the crisis, negative feedback trading by local individual investors	

Source: Barth and Zhang 1999 data are from Jardine Fleming Securities. Froot, O'Connell, and Seasholes 1998 and 1999 data are from State Street Bank. Kaminsky, Lyons, and Schmukler 1999 data are from Morningstar. Kim and Wei 1999a and Park and Park 1999 data are from Korea Securities Computer Corporation (KOSCOM).

to the small size of developing country markets—leads to the question of whether measures intended to discourage excessive short-term flows by recipient countries are sufficient to deal with capital surges and the risk of their reversal. First, as the Thai experience showed, for example, some recipient countries may be unwilling to discourage short-term capital inflows and indeed may—intentionally or unintentionally—implement policies to encourage them. Second, even those recipient countries that have used a number of measures to discourage short-term flows have on occasion found them insufficient to stem very massive inflows (see chap. 10 on that point). Third, if major emerging countries experience large reversals and/or outflows of either loans or portfolio flows—leading to currency and financial crises—they will be forced to seek large amounts of official liquidity. To the extent that this official liquidity is granted, which may be essential to prevent the crisis from deepening and spreading, there will be an element of moral hazard. This moral hazard implies that in the previous phase lenders and investors had assumed excessive risks in the expectation that they would be bailed out if the situation became critical. Also, for this reason, there is a clear need for source country regulation to discourage the underpricing of risk that can lead to excessive capital inflows.

It is noteworthy that U.S. Federal Reserve chairman Alan Greenspan proposed—for the case of interbank lending—that it could be appropriate for either borrowing countries or lending ones to impose reserve requirements on excessive borrowing. In chapter 11, we provide a detailed analysis of the appropriateness of reserve requirements in both source and recipient countries. The chapter discusses a theoretical model developed by Aizenman and Turnovsky (1999) that shows that reserve requirements can be welfare enhancing, particularly in source countries. The model thus provides theoretical support for the view that in a second-best world welfare can be improved by appropriate regulatory changes.

TABLE 2.5. Impact of Institutional Investors' Reallocation of Portfolios on Local Market Capitalization (1 percent increase in portfolio allocation to equity as a percentage of stock market capitalization)

	Latin America				Asia				
	Pension Funds	Insurance Companies	Open-end Investment Companies	Total	Pension Funds	Insurance Companies	Open-end Investment Companies	Total	Industrial Countries Total
United States	16.4	8.25	10.25	34.9	6.66	3.35	4.16	14.18	0.58
Japan	5.90	6.67	1.97	14.54	2.40	2.71	0.80	5.91	0.24
Europe	5.32	9.17	6.29	20.78	2.15	3.79	2.55	8.49	0.43

Source: Borio, Chiancarini, and Tsatsaronis.

Note: Latin America includes Argentina, Brazil, Chile, Colombia, Mexico, Peru, and Venezuela; Asia includes China, South Korea, Philippines, Taiwan, India, Indonesia, Malaysia, Pakistan, Sri Lanka, and Thailand.

The broad welfare case for applying reserve requirements in both source and recipient countries can also be extended to institutional investors and in particular to mutual funds, which became increasingly important in relation to banks in the 1990s, particularly within the United States (see the more detailed discussion in chap. 11).

Not only have international investors gained more prominence in domestic economies and global financial markets, but the distinction between banks and securities institutions has become increasingly blurred. For example, some of the strategies used to promote public confidence in banks are beginning to be adapted to the needs of mutual funds; in the United States, the most important of these adaptations—which was contained in legislation enacted in 1991—not only gave securities markets explicit access to the lender of last resort via access to Federal Reserve Bank lending but also expanded the type of collateral against which the Federal Reserve can lend in an emergency to include corporate stocks and bonds (d'Arista and Griffith-Jones 2001).

The narrowing of differences between banks and institutional investors and the fact that securities markets also have access to the lender of last resort make the case for improving prudential standards for institutional investors such as mutual funds.

5. REGULATORY PROPOSALS

As pointed out earlier, institutional investors are becoming more prominent in international financial markets, forming a very large proportion of total deposits in the financial systems of developed economies; the flows that they channel to developing countries—mainly via portfolio flows—also represent a large proportion of total flows to those countries, including some of the most volatile ones. As a consequence of this, problems of moral hazard linked to possible needs for bailouts if crises threaten or occur are increasingly relevant to them. The case for appropriate regulation to counteract any potential moral hazard, and enhance welfare to investors and recipients alike, becomes then very strong.

With regard to portfolio flows to emerging economies, there is an important regulatory gap, as at present there is no regulatory framework internationally for taking account of market or credit risks on flows originating in institutional investors such as mutual funds (and more broadly for flows originating in nonbank institutions). This important regulatory gap needs to be filled, both to protect retail investors in developed countries and to protect developing countries from the negative effects of excessively large and potentially volatile portfolio flows.

A serious problem relates to the very liquid nature of the flows originating in institutional investors and therefore the role these flows play in contributing to currency crises. This problem could be best tackled by introducing regulation to discourage excessive surges of portfolio flows. This problem could be addressed by adopting a variable risk-weighted cash requirement for institutional investors so as to discourage excessive capital flows to developing countries. These cash requirements would be placed as interest-bearing deposits in commercial banks.

There would be guidelines for macroeconomic risk, which would determine the cash requirement; these guidelines would take into account such vulnerability variables as the ratio of a country's current account deficit (or surplus) to GDP, the level of its short-term external liabilities to foreign exchange reserves, the fragility of the banking system, and other relevant country risk factors. A sophisticated analysis would be required in the risk assessment exercise in order to avoid simplistic criteria that could harm countries unnecessarily. The level of required cash reserves would vary with the level of countries' perceived "macroeconomic risk," which would make it more profitable to invest more in countries with good fundamentals and less in countries with problematic fundamentals. The logic behind these reserve requirements is that if fundamentals in a country deteriorate portfolio flows to that country will gradually decline, thus forcing an early policy correction and a resumption of flows. Although the requirement for cash reserves on mutual fund assets invested in emerging markets could increase the cost of foreign capital somewhat, this would be compensated for by the benefit of a more stable supply of funds at a more stable cost. Furthermore, this countercyclical smoothing of flows would hopefully help discourage the massive and sudden reversal of flows that have helped spark major crises in emerging markets.

This proposal on cash requirements for institutional investors is discussed in more detail in chapter 11.

NOTES

1. The IMF defines portfolio investments and equity securities as follows. "Portfolio investment includes in addition to equity securities and debt securities in the form of bonds and notes, money market instruments and financial derivatives such as options. Excluded are any of the aforementioned instruments included in the categories of direct investment and reserves assets" (IMF 1993, 91). It continues: "Equity securities cover all instruments and records acknowledging after the claims of all creditors have been met, claims to the residual values on incorporated enterprises. Shares, stocks, participation or similar documents such as American Depository Receipts usually denote ownership of equity. Preferred stocks or shares which also provide for participation in

the distribution of an incorporated enterprise, are included. Mutual funds and investment trusts are also included" (91).

2. Some caution in interpretation should be exercised because an important part of the international placements occurred in the first half of 1997.

REFERENCES

Aizenman, J., and S. Turnovsky. 1999. "Reserve requirements on sovereign debt in the presence of moral hazard on debtors or creditors?" Mimeo, Dartmouth College.

Barth, M., and X. Zhang. 1999. "Foreign equity flows and the Asian financial crisis." Paper presented at the conference Preventing Crises in Emerging Markets, World Bank and Brookings Institution, Palisades, NY, March 26–27.

Bekaert, G., C. Harvey, and R. Lumsdaine. 1999. "Structural breaks in emerging market capital flows." NBER working paper 7219, July.

Borio, C., L. Chiancarini, and K. Tsatsaronis. 1997. "Institutional investors, asset management, and financial markets." Mimeo, BIS, December.

Cailloux, J., and S. Griffith-Jones. 1999. "Encouraging the long term: Institutional investors and emerging markets." Discussion paper 16, Office of Development Studies, UNDP.

Choe, Bong-Chan, and R. M. Stulz. 1998. "Do foreign investors destabilise stock markets? The Korean experience in 1997." NBER working paper 6661, June.

D'Arista, Jane, and Stephany Griffith-Jones. 2000. "The boom of portfolio flows to emerging markets and its regulatory implications." In *Short-Term Capital Flows and Economic Crises,* UNV/WIDER Studies in Development Economics, ed. S. Griffith-Jones, M. Montes, and A. Nasution. Oxford and New York: Oxford University Press.

De Long, J., A. Shleifer, L. H. Summers, and R. J. Waldmann. 1990. "Positive feedback investment strategies and destabilising rational speculation." *Journal of Finance* 45, no. 2 (June): 379–95.

Domowitz, I., J. Glen, and A. Madhavan. 1998. "International cross-listing, market quality, and foreign ownership rights: Evidence from an emerging market." *Journal of Finance* 53, no. 6 (December): 2001–27.

Froot, K. A., P. G. J. O'Connell, and M. Seasholes. 1998. "The portfolio flows of international investors, I." NBER working paper 6687, August.

———. 1999. "The portfolio flows of international investors, I." Mimeo, Harvard University, August.

Griffith-Jones, S. 1996. "Mexican peso crisis." *CEPAL Review* 60 (December): 155–76.

———. 1998. *Global capital flows: Should they be regulated?* London: Macmillan Press.

Howell, M. 1998. "Asia's 'Victorian' financial crisis." Paper presented at the East Asia Crisis Workshop, Institute of Development Studies, Sussex, England, July.

IMF (International Monetary Fund). 1993. *Balance of payments manual.* 5th ed. Washington, DC: IMF.

Kaminsky, G., R. Lyons, and S. Schmukler. 1999. "Managers, investors, and crises: Mutual fund strategy in emerging markets." Mimeo, World Bank.

Kim, W., and S. J. Wei. 1999a. "Foreign portfolio investors before and during a crisis." NBER working paper 6968, February.

———. 1999b. "Offshore investment funds: Monsters in emerging markets?" NBER working paper, 7133, May.

Lakonishok, J., A. Shleifer, and R. W. Vishny. 1992. "The impact of institutional trading on stock prices." *Journal of Financial Economics* 32, no. 1 (August): 339–79.

Nofsinger, J., and R. Sias. 1997. "Herding by institutional and individual investors." Manuscript, Washington State University, October.

Park, Y. C., and I. Park. 1998. "Who destabilised the Korean Stock Market?" Paper presented at the conference Global Capital Flows, Institute of Development Studies, Sussex, England, September.

Park, Y. C., and C.-Y. Song. 1998. "Managing foreign capital flows: The experiences of the Republic of Korea, Thailand, Malaysia, and Indonesia." In *International monetary and financial issues for the 1990s,* ed. G. K. Helleiner, 82–140. London: McMillan Press: In association with United Nations Conference on Trade and Development (UNCTAD).

Post, M., and K. Millar. 1998. "U.S. emerging market equity funds and the 1997 crisis in Asian financial markets." *Perspective* (Investment Company Institute) 4, no. 2 (June): 1–12.

World Bank. 1997. *The road to financial integration.* Washington, DC: World Bank.

CHAPTER 3

International Bank Lending and the East Asian Crisis

Jacques Cailloux and Stephany Griffith-Jones

> There is a structural fault in the nature of capital flows. Short-term debt flows, especially bank finance, are highly volatile. Unless the problem is tackled the potential for future crises will remain.
>
> —Mervyn King

> There is growing agreement that an excessive build-up of short-term debt was a proximate cause of the recent crises, particularly in East Asia.
>
> —Dani Rodrik and Andres Velasco

As was discussed in chapter 1, the proximate cause of the crises in East Asia was a sharp reversal in capital flows, and the dominant category in the reversal of these flows was bank credits, which represented 92 percent of the outflows in the four most affected countries during 1997 and 1998 and 72 percent of the reversals between 1996 and 1998 (see table 1.2 in chap. 1).

As we also highlighted, a particular feature of bank lending to East Asia was that a very high proportion of those loans was short term. This implied a large accumulated stock of short-term debt (particularly bank debt), which made the East Asian countries particularly prone to large reversals. We have noted that the higher the stocks of liabilities the higher the scale of potential outflows; this is particularly true for short-term bank debt, for which the potential for reversal is extremely high, as creditors have the simple option of not renewing loans. As the empirical analysis of Radelet and Sachs (1998) and particularly Rodrik and Velasco (1999) confirm, short-term debt (and especially short-term debt to banks) as a proportion of reserves is a strong predictor of both the likelihood and the severity of crises.

There has been surprisingly little detailed empirical analysis of the nature and causes of reversals of bank loans to the East Asian countries, for example, by nationality of banks and by individual banks (an exception is Kaminsky and Reinhart 1999). Given the importance of these flows and their reversal in

East Asia, we develop such a detailed empirical analysis here, which gives us a basis for a more in-depth examination of the causes of these large reversals.

In section 1, we present the broad picture of bank lending to East Asia, focusing on the main players. Section 2 then analyses the different reasons behind the rapid buildup of short-term external debt. Section 3, in turn, presents some explanations for the withdrawal of bank loans.

1. RECENT TRENDS IN BANK LENDING TO EAST ASIA

In this section, we analyze the maturity structure and sectoral distribution of bank loans and then examine the behavior by creditor banks' nationality. Our analysis focuses on the period between the end of June 1995 and the end of June 1999 and draws on data published by the Bank for International Settlements (BIS).

1.1. GLOBAL TRENDS TO EAST ASIA

As can be seen in table 3.1, international lending to East Asia (Indonesia, South Korea, Malaysia, and Thailand) rose sharply during the years just preceding the crisis. However, it is worth underlining that the stock of external debt at the beginning of the 1990s was fairly small in all four countries (with

TABLE 3.1. International Claims on the Asian-4 by Nationality of Reporting Banks (in billions of U.S.$ and percentages of total lending)

	Total	Japan		EU		U.S.		Local Subsidiaries
	Bn U.S.$	Bn U.S.$	%	Bn U.S.$	%	Bn U.S.$	%	%
End of June 99	160.6	53.4	33	66.5	41	12.4	8	18
End of Dec. 98	171.7	62.4	36	70.4	41	12.0	7	16
End of June 98	192.5	72.0	37	76.4	40	13.5	7	16
End of Dec. 97	239.0	84.0	35	88.1	37	18.8	8	20
End of June 97	261.1	95.1	36	92.0	35	20.9	8	20
End of Dec. 96	247.9	92.1	37	83.1	34	22.0	9	20
End of June 96	226.8	89.8	40	70.9	31	19.5	9	21
End of Dec. 95	201.7	86.6	43	59.8	30	16.0	8	19
End of June 95	180.2	80.1	44	57.8	32	13.6	8	16

Source: BIS, *The maturity and sectoral and nationality distribution of international bank lending,* various issues.

Note: The total in the first column also includes international claims of domestically owned banks in Switzerland, which are not shown separately in this table, as well as those of local subsidiaries and branches of banks that have their head offices outside the BIS reporting area. The last column is thus the share of bank lending mainly from local subsidiaries and branches of banks that have their head offices outside the BIS reporting area.

the exception of South Korea) but it had been increasing very rapidly throughout the period. For example, total lending to the region between December 1993 (the first period for which BIS data are available on the four countries) and June 1997 more than doubled (an increase of 133 percent).[1] By the end of 1996, to give an order of magnitude, total external debt amounted to roughly 25 percent of the region's gross domestic product (GDP), compared to a level of 13 percent of GDP in Latin America.[2]

From June 1997 onward, and as the crisis unfolded, total lending fell dramatically, reaching at the end of June 1999 a level below that of June 1995. The largest drop was experienced during the first semester of 1998, with a decline of almost 20 percent of total claims compared to a decline of 8 percent during the previous semester. The reduction in exposure continued throughout 1998 and the first half of 1999, with successive drops of 11 and 6 percent. Between June 1997 and June 1999, the exposure of international banks to East Asia had fallen by 38 percent!

As far as source countries are concerned, although Japan is the main source of bank lending to the region at the beginning of the period, its share actually declines fairly rapidly over time in favor of European lenders (see table 3.1). Indeed, while between June 1995 and June 1997 Japanese debt only increased by 18.6 percent, European debt rose by 61.4 percent. As a result of the very rapid increase in European lending, by the time of the onset of the crisis Europe had caught up with Japan in terms of exposure to the region, with $92 billion (compared to $95 billion for Japan) by June 1997. During and after the crisis, Japanese claims contracted quicker than those of European banks, so that by the end of June 1999 the share of Japanese claims on the Asian-4 was significantly smaller than that of Europeans (see table 3.1). Interestingly, the share of U.S. banks was both stable and relatively small throughout the period.

We now study in turn each of the four most affected countries.

1.2. SOUTH KOREA

As of December 1996, South Korea had accumulated about $100 billion of debt with international lenders, that is, 40 percent of the four East Asian countries' total claims. South Korea was thus the main recipient of international bank lending to the region, although its claims only accounted for 20 percent of its GDP, the smallest share of the four countries.

Table 3.2 provides data on bank lending to South Korea by nationality. In June 1997, Japan represented 23 percent of total bank lending, the European Union (EU) 36 percent (of which France and Germany represented 10 percent each), and the United States 10 percent.

With regard to total declines since the crisis broke out, all the big creditor countries' banks see very large declines of similar magnitude. Thus, from their peak to June 1999, Japanese and U.S. banks' exposure falls by 37 and 36 percent, respectively. German, French, and British banks also fall significantly, though somewhat less, by 30, 19, and 23 percent, respectively. This seems to provide some evidence of herding between big players. It is interesting that some of the smaller creditor country banks' claims fall much more, with Belgium declining by 85 percent from the peak and Finland by 88 percent, while banks of two creditor nationalities (Netherlands and Canada) behave in a somewhat countercyclical manner, actually increasing their lending during the crisis period or its immediate aftermath.

Finally, an important feature to highlight is that bank exposure to South Korea not only fell sharply during the crisis period but continued to do so until June 1999. This trend also holds for the major creditor countries, except for the United States and France, where lending recovered somewhat from the end of December 1998.

An important feature of the buildup and reversal of bank loans to South Korea worth highlighting is that approximately 60 percent of the increase of bank lending between June 1995 and the peak in June 1997 and around 90 percent of the decline in bank lending between June 1997 and June 1999 can be explained by lending of up to one year.

Similarly, around 60 percent of the increase in bank lending (between June 1995 and the peak in June 1997) and around 80 percent of the outflow were accounted for by interbank lending. Therefore, we can clearly see that in South Korea a very significant proportion of the reversal of capital flows can

TABLE 3.2. International Claims on South Korea by Nationality of Banks (in billions of U.S.$ and as a share of grand total)

	Total	Japan		EU		U.S.		Local Subsidiaries
	Bn U.S.$	Bn U.S.$	%	Bn U.S.$	%	Bn U.S.$	%	%
End of June 99	63.5	15.0	24	24.9	39	6.4	10	27
End of Dec. 98	65.3	16.9	26	26.2	40	6.3	10	24
End of June 98	72.4	18.9	26	28.1	39	7.4	10	25
End of Dec. 97	94.2	20.3	22	33.7	36	9.5	10	33
End of June 97	104.1	23.7	23	37.0	36	10.0	10	32
End of Dec. 96	100.0	24.3	24	33.8	34	9.4	9	32
End of June 96	88.0	22.5	26	26.9	31	9.6	11	33
End of Dec. 95	77.6	21.4	28	23.6	30	7.6	10	32
End of June 95	71.4	20.9	29	24.5	34	7.1	10	27

Source: See table 3.1.
Note: See table 3.1.

be explained by a very sharp reversal of short-term interbank loans, which had previously increased very sharply.

Bank loans to the nonbank private sector increased and fell quite significantly in the same period but accounted for a clearly smaller proportion of the outflows. Curiously, bank lending to the public sector was countercyclical, falling between December 1995 and December 1997 and increasing until June 1999.

1.3. THAILAND

Thailand is the second-largest borrower of the region, following South Korea, with a share in total claims of 28 percent (compared to 40 percent for South Korea). At the end of December 1996, total claims on Thailand amounted to about $70 billion or 37 percent of its GDP (which is a very high level).

Thailand is the only country among the Asian-4 to experience a reversal in total lending, though on a small scale, as early as the first semester of 1997. This is mainly due to U.S. and U.K. banks, which lowered their total claims by about 20 and 10 percent, respectively, during that period.

As can be seen from table 3.3, in June 1997 European claims accounted for 29 percent of total claims while the United States' and Japan's shares amounted to 6 and 54 percent, respectively. Total claims on Thailand fell by 50 percent between June 1997 and June 1999. The sharpest decline was experienced by claims on U.S. banks, with a decline of 70 percent, followed by Japan with 51 percent. European banks also sharply reduced their exposure to Thailand and to a greater extent than in other countries. Indeed, U.K.

TABLE 3.3. International Claims on Thailand by Nationality of Banks (in billions of U.S.$ and as a share of grand total)

	Total	Japan		EU		U.S.		Local Subsidiaries
	Bn U.S.$	Bn U.S.$	%	Bn U.S.$	%	Bn U.S.$	%	%
End of June 99	34.7	18.3	53	12.2	35	1.2	4	9
End of Dec. 98	40.7	22.4	55	14.1	35	1.4	3	7
End of June 98	46.8	26.1	56	15.4	33	1.8	4	8
End of Dec. 97	58.9	33.1	56	17.2	29	2.5	4	10
End of June 97	69.4	37.7	54	19.8	29	4.0	6	11
End of Dec. 96	70.1	37.5	53	19.1	27	5.1	7	12
End of June 96	69.4	37.6	54	18.1	26	4.4	6	13
End of Dec. 95	62.8	36.8	59	14.9	24	4.1	7	11
End of June 95	53.6	32.6	61	13.3	25	3.1	6	8

Source: See table 3.1.
Note: See table 3.1.

claims fell by 48 percent while French and German claims fell by 43 and 39 percent, respectively.

As of June 1997, 66 percent of total lending was of maturity shorter than one year. About 76 percent of the decline in total claims can be explained by the reduction in short-term debt.

As opposed to South Korea, but in a similar way to Indonesia, foreign bank lending was mainly to the corporate sector. It accounted, in June 1997, for 60 percent of the external debt. However, it is the decline in interbank lending that explains most of the decline in total lending (about 55 percent) in a similar way to South Korea.

It is worth underlining that all major lenders were still reducing their exposure during the first semester of 1999.

1.4. MALAYSIA

Malaysia experienced a peak in external indebtedness in June 1997. Total debt almost doubled between June 1995 and June 1997 to reach about $29 billion. By the end of December 1996, Malaysia's claims represented only 9 percent of the region's total external claims and accounted for about 22 percent of its GDP, a share just above that of South Korea. Total claims then declined by 35 percent between June 1997 and June 1999.

As in the other countries, short-term debt played an important role in both the buildup and the reversal of foreign loans. Indeed, the increase in short-term debt explains more than 60 percent of the total debt growth and more than 80 percent of the decline. Loans to both local banks and the cor-

TABLE 3.4. International Claims on Malaysia by Nationality of Banks (in billions of U.S.$ and as a share of grand total)

	Total	Japan		EU		U.S.		Local Subsidiaries
	Bn U.S.$	Bn U.S.$	%	Bn U.S.$	%	Bn U.S.$	%	%
End of June 99	18.6	6.1	33	8.7	46	1.1	6	15
End of Dec. 98	20.8	6.6	32	10.6	51	0.9	4	13
End of June 98	23.0	7.9	34	10.9	47	1.1	5	13
End of Dec. 97	27.5	8.6	31	14.0	51	1.8	6	12
End of June 97	28.8	10.5	36	12.7	44	2.4	8	11
End of Dec. 96	22.2	8.2	37	9.2	41	2.3	11	11
End of June 96	20.1	8.1	40	7.9	39	1.9	9	11
End of Dec. 95	16.8	7.3	44	6.2	37	1.5	9	10
End of June 95	14.7	6.1	41	6.5	44	1.1	7	7

Source: See table 3.1.
Note: See table 3.1.

porate sector sharply increased during the boom period, but it is largely interbank lending that fell dramatically (by more than 60 percent).

As far as source countries are concerned, in the same fashion as the other countries, Europe accounted in June 1997 for the bulk of Malaysian external debt, with a share of 44 percent, while the United States and Japan accounted for 8 and 36 percent (see table 3.4).

1.5. INDONESIA

Like the other three countries, Indonesia enjoyed a sharp rise in total claims during the period preceding the crisis. Between June 1995 and June 1997, they increased by 45 percent. Most of the increase can be explained by additional EU lending. As of December 1996, total claims accounted for 25 percent of Indonesia's GDP and 22 percent of the region's liabilities.

At the onset of the crisis, the share of Japanese and European claims were almost the same (about 40 percent each). However, there are clear differences in the way they pulled out. Indeed, the data in table 3.5 show that European bank lending exhibited a much more stable trend with a drop of only 8 percent between June 1997 and June 1999 compared to a drop of 39 percent for Japanese lending. Within Europe, according to the breakdown provided by the BIS data set, the large creditor countries (Germany, France, and the United Kingdom) reduced their exposure by about 20 percent, slightly less than their U.S. counterparts (−24 percent).

About half of the increase in total claims was due to short-term loans, while 86 percent of the decline was caused by a reduction in short-term lending. The vast majority of debt was held by the private sector (about 70

TABLE 3.5. International Claims on Indonesia by Nationality of Banks (in billions of U.S.$ and as a share of grand total)

	Total	Japan		EU		U.S.		Local Subsidiaries
	Bn U.S.$	Bn U.S.$	%	Bn U.S.$	%	Bn U.S.$	%	%
End of June 99	43.8	14.4	32	20.8	47	3.7	9	12
End of Dec. 98	44.8	16.4	37	19.5	44	3.5	8	12
End of June 98	50.3	19.0	38	22.0	44	3.2	6	12
End of Dec. 97	58.4	22.0	38	23.3	40	4.9	8	14
End of June 97	58.7	23.2	39	22.5	38	4.6	8	14
End of Dec. 96	55.5	22.0	40	21.0	38	5.8	10	13
End of June 96	49.3	21.6	44	18.1	37	3.6	7	12
End of Dec. 95	44.5	21.0	47	15.0	34	2.8	6	13
End of June 95	40.4	20.5	51	13.5	33	2.3	6	10

Source: See table 3.1.
Note: See table 3.1.

percent). However, the reversal was experienced in both the banking sector and the nonbank private sector, which explained, respectively, 53 and 45 percent of the total decline. Interestingly, and as in the other three countries, lending to the public sector was countercyclical.

As a conclusion, the analysis on individual countries that we have carried out shows that all four countries experienced similar trends both before and during the crisis. Japan was the largest lender to the region in the mid-1990s but at a similar level to Europe taken as a whole. Following the mid-1990s, the share of Japanese exposure fell, both before, during, and after the crisis, while that of European banks grew. Within Europe, the largest lender countries are France and Germany, with similar levels of exposure, and then the United Kingdom. The United States represents only 10 percent or less of total claims.

Short-term bank lending represented the majority of total claims in all countries. This can be explained by the fluctuations in total lending. However, it played a more important role in the reduction of exposure by foreign lenders than in the buildup. Indeed, it accounted on average for about 60 percent of the increase and 80 percent of the decline in bank lending to the region.

Similarities were also found in terms of the allocation of foreign debt at the sectoral level. With the exception of South Korea, where interbank lending was dominant, in the three other countries it is the nonbank private sector that was the largest borrower.

In the next section, we analyze the explanatory factors behind the very rapid buildup of short-term debt.

2. WHY DID BANKS LEND SO MUCH AND SO SHORT TERM?

As we saw in the previous section, all four Asian countries experienced a very rapid increase in their external commercial debt, a large part of which was of a short-term nature. A number of factors have been widely discussed as being clearly important in the buildup of external debt. As Radelet and Sachs (1998) rightly stress, the excellent growth record and wide-ranging financial deregulations clearly contributed to strengthening banks' willingness to lend. It is clear that these countries were seen and saw themselves as very creditworthy and thus did not worry about borrowing short-term, as they thought they could roll over the loans very easily (in the same way Mexico did before the 1994 crisis). In this section, we focus our analysis on other, complementary explanations. We analyze in turn the role of moral hazard in its international dimension, the impact of the 1988 capital asset ratio implemented by the BIS, and the role of Japanese banks.

2.1. THE MORAL HAZARD HYPOTHESIS

In some of the literature that emerged in the aftermath of the Asian crisis, the moral hazard argument played a relatively important role in explaining the size and to some extent the maturity of international lending to the most affected economies. For example, Corsetti, Pensenti, and Roubini (1998) and Krugman (1998) argue that moral hazard, in the form of implicit guarantees by governments, contributed to excess borrowing from abroad. This was seen as particularly true for Thailand and South Korea, where most of the financial institutions had guaranteed liabilities at the beginning of the crisis (Krugman 1998). According to this analysis, it is thus the international dimension of moral hazard that had an impact on the behavior of international banks. Indeed, these institutions based their lending decisions on the assumption that local governments would guarantee those loans or, if not, that institutions such as the IMF would bail out borrowers. Following this line of analysis, moral hazard led to excessive risk taking with less monitoring of projects' quality, which in turn led to financial collapse.

The argument of implicit guarantee has also been stressed by McKinnon and Pill (1996, 1998), who argue that, even with a clear intention by the authorities—national or international—not to bail out, the impact of financial crises can be so costly that these institutions will ultimately have to bail out the financial system.

The authors then argue that, in the context of a badly regulated financial system, that is, one in which the financial authorities are unable to monitor the moral hazard problem, implicit guarantees lead to overborrowing and increased instability. Interestingly, the authors argue that good supervision and regulation of the financial system might not be sufficient, as exemplified by the financial crises that occurred in developed countries. The authors propose that monetary authorities should also monitor the composition of bank credit expansion as well as the aggregate lending levels of property, construction, and personal consumption. These levels should be limited in order to prevent speculative borrowing, which can have a destabilizing impact on the economy. As for the international dimension of moral hazard, McKinnon and Pill propose that "direct and indirect measures to restrain inflows of foreign financial capital may be necessary" (1998, 352).

However, it is worth stressing that the moral hazard hypothesis has been challenged more recently from both an empirical and a theoretical point of view, including by Krugman himself. At a theoretical level, Krugman (1999) argues that, if implicit guarantees were the main causal factor in the East Asian crisis, one should have observed a decline in investments that had no guarantee at all (such as equity investment) in favor of other forms of loans, which were assumed to have some form of guarantee either explicit or implicit. This pattern clearly was not witnessed in the case of East Asia. Krugman adds that if the moral hazard argument had played an important role it would have led to a substantial number of bad loans earlier in the most affected economies. However, it has been recognized that most of the bad loans were in fact a result of the sharp recessions and depreciations and not the other way around.

On the empirical side, two recent studies find conflicting evidence. On the one hand, the Institute for International Finance (IIF) (1999ab) analyzes the impact of the Mexican bailout in 1995 on the large flows of bank lending toward emerging markets that took place between 1996 and mid-1997 at low spreads. The findings do not support the moral hazard hypothesis; on the contrary, declines in emerging market spreads are mainly explained by the sharp increase in international liquidity conditions.

Sarno and Taylor (1999), on the other hand, do find evidence in favor of the moral hazard hypothesis. The study finds evidence of asset price bubbles in all affected countries and a high degree of reversibility in capital flows to East Asia. According to the authors, these two findings are consistent and are necessary conditions for the moral hazard interpretation to hold. However, this analysis is problematic. First, although moral hazard might lead to a sharp increase in the demand for speculative and risky assets itself, leading to an asset price bubble, the latter can have other causal factors. This is all the more true in that the bubbles that are tested are stock market bubbles. Indeed, as we have noted, the stock market does not typically have any insurance guarantee. Second, Sarno and Taylor do not provide a clear theoretical explanation of the relationship between a high degree of reversibility and moral hazard. Furthermore, they find a high reversible component in portfolio flows (consistent, according to the authors, with the moral hazard hypothesis) while bank credits have a relatively higher permanent component. This is a rather disturbing result, as one would expect that bank credits rather than portfolio flows should confirm the moral hazard hypothesis.

2.2. A REGULATORY BIAS IN THE BIS CAPITAL ACCORD?

There is still no definitive explanation for the large ratio of short-term to total debt accumulated by the Asian-4. One argument has focused on a potential distortion in the Basle Capital Accord, which would make short-term lending more profitable for creditor banks. Indeed, interbank lending to non-OECD (Organization for Economic Cooperation and Development) countries of a residual maturity of up to one year has a weighting of only 20 percent for capital adequacy purposes, while loans of more than one year require a 100 percent weighting.[3] Short-term lending to non-OECD countries thus only requires a 1.6 percent capital cover as opposed to 8 percent for medium- to long-term lending. The underlying rationale of these weightings is that the shorter the loan maturity the higher the probability that the lender will recover it. However, from a debtor country standpoint, these weightings could shift the overall maturity structure of the country's external balance sheet toward short term.

It is worth underlining that the weighting structure could have an impact not only on the maturity but also on the relative amount of interbank lending compared to that of the corporate sector. This issue was addressed by a working group established by the Basle Committee on Banking Supervision as part of a broader review of the current banking supervisory framework and the lessons that could be drawn from the Asian crisis (see Basle Committee on Banking Supervision 1999). Four studies were conducted in an attempt to assess these potential distortions in terms of both volume and maturity.

The first study analyzes the changes in the *overall lending maturity* of countries following their membership in the OECD. These countries are Mexico, South Korea, the Czech Republic, and Hungary (although Poland joined in 1996, it was not included in the sample as it was still affected by past rescheduling). In the case of Mexico and South Korea, there was some evidence that their change in status from non-OECD to OECD members reduced the proportion of short-term to total debt. However, the lack of observations and the fact that Mexico and South Korea suffered a financial crisis just after joining the OECD somewhat weakened the robustness of the results.

The second study assesses the impact of joining the OECD on the *size of interbank lending.* A significant rise in the proportion of interbank to total lending was observed in three countries out of four following their accession to the OECD. But this increase, as underlined by the study, could also partly have been a result of the liberalization measures undertaken under the OECD codes.

Third, the maturity structure of OECD countries was compared to non-OECD countries that have the same ratings. It was found that for relatively highly rated countries, the share of short-term debt was higher in non-OECD countries, confirming the hypothesis of a short-term bias for non-OECD countries. This relationship was not as clear in the case of lower ratings.

Finally, the report assessed whether the lower weights applied to interbank lending lead to *more lending being channeled to banks rather than the corporate sector.* The study was conducted both within the OECD, where the bias was expected to be the strongest (because interbank lending requires a small risk weight for short-term as well as for long-term lending), and outside it. No evidence was found that the capital accord significantly impacted upon lending composition.

Further work could compare the trends in total short-term lending to non-OECD countries with the trends in lending to the banking and corporate sectors. This analysis could reduce the data limitation due to the non-availability of data on the maturity of interbank lending. Indeed, a higher correlation between short-term lending and lending to the corporate sector would confirm the hypothesis of a short-term bias.

Reisen (1999) adds that new OECD members benefited from cheaper borrowing through lower interest rates due to the lowering of risk weights.

There is thus some evidence that the Basle Capital Accord has encouraged more short-term lending to non-OECD countries, though the evidence is somewhat constrained by data limitations (see Cornford 2000). It is worth underlining that the new Basle proposal has suggested amending the current system, especially as a response to the criticisms that arose after the Asian crisis. A discussion of the proposal is provided in chapter 11.

2.3. THE ROLE OF JAPANESE BANKS

As was pointed out in the first section, Japan is the largest lender to each Asian-4 country.[4] In June 1997, Japanese banks had a slightly higher exposure to the Asian-4 than Europe did. Part of the explanation behind the rapid growth of international credit to these four countries must thus lie in the behavior of Japanese banks. Interestingly, in 1997 the position of Japan in the region was quite unique compared to that of other countries. Indeed, while all other countries had their greatest exposure in South Korea, followed by Thailand, Indonesia, and Malaysia (with the exception of the United States, where Indonesia was second in exposure), Japan's greatest exposure was in Thailand ($16.1 bn), followed by Indonesia ($10.9 bn), South Korea ($9.5 bn), and Malaysia ($4.6 bn).

The international expansion of Japanese banks needs to be placed within the broader context of the so-called Main Bank and its role within the industrial group with which it has cross holdings. Indeed, as underlined by Peek and Rosengren (1998), the wave of Japanese foreign direct investment (FDI) in the United States during the 1980s was associated with a sharp increase in Japanese lending, most of which was initially made to Japanese affiliates. The Main Bank, which provides most of the financing to group members, thus tends to behave similarly domestically and internationally. However, Japanese banks later diversified their portfolios and expanded their loans to a wider U.S. customer base that included many nonaffiliates. During the first half of the 1990s, Japanese FDI shifted to Asia. Ito (1999) underlines that between 1990 and 1996 the Asian-4 experienced increases of Japanese FDI on a scale ranging from twofold to fourfold. As mentioned earlier, Japanese lending to

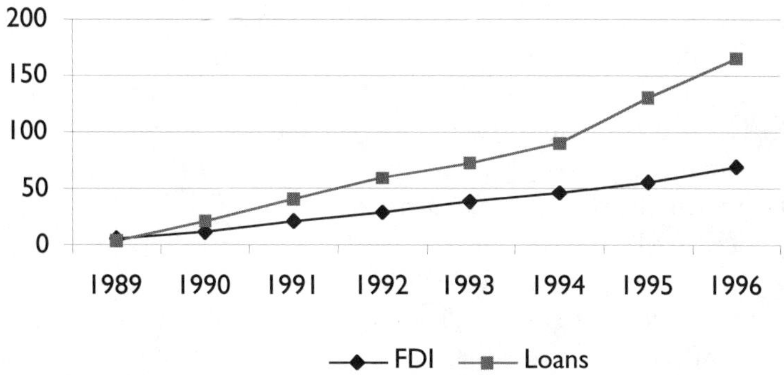

Fig. 3.1. Global cumulative inflows of FDI and bank loans to the Asian-4 countries, 1989–96. (Data from chap. 1, table 1.2.)

the region also increased during that period. This is confirmed by figure 3.1, which compares the cumulative inflows of FDI and bank loans to the Asian-4 between 1989 and 1996.[5]

Interestingly and paradoxically, the financial turmoil that began in Japan in late 1990 and early 1991 barely affected that trend. This is in sharp contrast with the decline of Japanese lending to the United States observed during the first half of the 1990s. At that time, the fall was mainly explained by the need for Japanese banks to rebalance their loans in favor of domestic companies so as to avoid a major credit crunch in Japan (see Peek and Rosengren 1997). The sharp increase in Japanese lending to East Asia was thus mainly led by the wave of FDI to the region and the banks' strategies to strengthen their position in the region (to facilitate both production and distribution). These new loans were typically issued with guarantees from the parent company. This is particularly true for Malaysia, Thailand, and Indonesia but less true for South Korea due to its relatively high barriers to FDI.

Peek and Rosengren (1998) note two other important driving forces behind the rapid increase in Japanese lending that must have been particularly important in the years just preceding the crisis. First, East Asia enjoyed much higher yields than other regions and financial centers. The authors show that Japanese banks abandoned most of the low margin wholesale markets, especially in Hong Kong and Singapore, in favor of more profitable markets. Second, Japanese banks developed customer relationships with nonaffiliates, as these retail operations also proved to be more profitable. In sum, Japanese banks decreased their international exposure due to the drop in asset prices in Japan but kept a strong position in Asia as that region enjoyed relatively higher yields than other regions in the world, especially higher than Japan, where interest rates were low. The fixed or quasi-fixed exchange rate regimes adopted by most of the countries in the region also significantly increased the confidence of Japanese lenders.

The fact that Japanese banks may behave similarly abroad and domestically could also explain why so much of lending was short term. Indeed, short-term lending to group affiliates is common practice, as loans are routinely rolled over, thereby ensuring long-term finance (see, e.g., Aoki and Patrick 1994). Furthermore, under Japanese law, commercial banks which provide the vast majority of lending both domestically and internationally, can only lend short term (less than a year). Long-term lending is provided by the long-term credit banks.

Another factor that may have also played a role is the incentive for Japanese banks facing low capital-asset ratios to lend short term. This was particularly true at the beginning of the 1990s because their capital adequacy ratio was so close to 8 percent (see Reisen 1999).

McCauley and Yeaple (1994) stress that the Basle Accord did have an impact on Japanese banks' lending, at least in the interbank market, but not in the way one would expect. Although the weighting for interbank lending is only 20 percent, Japanese banks still reduced their exposure to that market because the yields were not high enough. Indeed, the low weights were not sufficient to promote interbank lending, as this market's profitability was too low.

In conclusion, we have shown that the rapid buildup of short-term foreign debt in the East Asian region can be explained by a mix of factors. Apart from the high growth and very good rating records of the four countries, which was clearly a major factor, we have analyzed the relative importance of moral hazard, the bias in the BIS capital accord, and the behavior of Japanese banks. Interestingly, the latter factor, which has received least attention in the literature, seems to have counted for a great deal. However, more research needs to be conducted in that area.

3. WHY DID EAST ASIA EXPERIENCE SUCH LARGE REVERSALS?

In this section, we try to identify the reasons behind the large reversals in bank lending to the region starting with recent work that has been done in an attempt to shed new light on the rationale behind the large reversals. Following a brief review of the common lender channel literature (sec. 3.1), we provide new evidence, based on data from individual banks, on the driving forces underlying the reversals in bank loans.

We do not analyze in depth the more widely discussed causes that have been highlighted in the literature and are now accepted as having played an important role.[6] These factors are clearly important. For example, the factor that has gained the most support in the literature is certainly the financial panic argument. This was put most forcefully by Radelet and Sachs (1998) and Krugman (1999) and was formalized most notably by Chang and Velasco (1998). According to Chang and Velasco, the scale of the reversal experienced by the East Asian countries cannot be attributed solely to changes in economic fundamentals. Indeed, in a bank-run-style panic taking place at the international level, short-term creditors can precipitate a financial crisis by withdrawing their loans. The economy then moves from a good to a bad equilibrium because of a very sharp loss in investor confidence. It is now widely accepted that the most seriously affected East Asian countries suffered from a run by international banks and investors.

3.1. THE COMMON LENDER HYPOTHESIS

Recent studies argue that Japanese banks, in a fashion similar to U.S. banks in the 1980s in the case of Latin America, due to their dominant position in East Asia, played an important role in aggravating the crisis (see, e.g., Kaminsky and Reinhart 1999). Kaminsky and Reinhart's hypothesis is that if a country enters a crisis the lender will need to pull out of other borrowing countries in order to rebalance its portfolio and meet capital adequacy requirements. Thus, all countries that have a common lender are exposed to a crisis should it occur in any one country. The literature on the common lender channel argues further that the explanation of a decline across countries is a response to an almost "mechanical" readjustment (see Van Rijckeghern and Weder 1999).

Table 3.6 clearly shows the dominant position of Japan in the region, although, as was shown in section 1, it has been decreasing over the period.

Van Rijckeghern and Weder (1999) also test for the common lender hypothesis and find results similar to those of Kaminsky and Reinhart (1999): the hypothesis is confirmed in the cases of both Mexico and Asia.[7]

The results are quite robust and convincing. Evidently, and as shown in

TABLE 3.6. Share of Japanese Liabilities in Total Liabilities

	As of June 1994 (%)	As of June 1997 (%)	As of June 1999 (%)
Indonesia	54	39	32
South Korea	29	23	24
Malaysia	40	36	33
Thailand	57	54	53

Source: Kaminsky and Reinhart 1999; table 3.1.

section 1, aggregate data on countries' exposure to East Asia show that Japanese loans reversed in all four countries at the time of the crisis. However, if the common lender channel were to hold, this trend would also be reflected at the level of individual banks: banks should withdraw on the same scale in countries to which they are exposed following difficulties experienced by one of their main borrowers. We analyze this hypothesis in the next section.

3.2. NEW EVIDENCE FROM INDIVIDUAL BANKS

We have gathered data on selected individual banks' exposure to East Asia during 1997 and 1998. The data were collected from the annual reports of banks that devoted a special section to their exposure to East Asia. Although we do not include all banks involved in Asia, we believe the sample provides a satisfying overall picture.

Table 3.7 reports international banks' exposure to Asia at the end of 1997 and in 1998. Due to the lack of data, we focus on France, the United Kingdom, Japan, and the United States. The United States is the least representative, as we did not find data on many banks. A number of caveats in the data need to be underlined, especially in the case of Japan. First, in some cases the data include on and off balance sheet exposure. Second, the data on Japanese banks report their positions at the end of the 1997 and 1998 fiscal years, that is, at the end of March 1998 and the end of March 1999, and thus do not exactly cover the crisis. Third, the data were available either directly in U.S. dollars or in yen. But Japanese banks' exposure includes loans in both foreign currencies (mainly in dollars) and local currencies. There is thus a potential bias due to exchange rate problems (this could also be true for other countries). Fourth, the definition of the exposure varies from one bank to another and might thus limit comparisons between banks and countries. Bearing in mind these words of caution, and the fact that better data would be necessary for a more in-depth analysis, we believe that the data set still represents a valuable contribution and allows for a better understanding of the microeconomic behavior of banks during the crisis.

In order to assess how representative the sample is, we compare total exposure by country to other sources of data. As can be seen in table 3.7, we find an outflow from the four countries of $32 billion during 1998. The IIF (1999ab) finds an outflow of $36.1 billion after including the Philippines. However, the BIS reports an outflow for the four countries of $67.3 billion. At the country level, we find similar exposures to those reported by the BIS for France ($25.3 bn compared to $23.3 bn) and the United Kingdom ($14.1 bn compared to $15.7 bn). For Japan, the difference is bigger, as we find a total exposure of $41.1 bn as opposed to the $88.7 bn reported by the BIS. We can thus conclude that, although the coverage is not fully comprehensive, the data gathered are still representative enough to draw some conclusions about the behavior of individual banks by country.

As can be seen from table 3.7, French, British, and American banks behave as expected. All banks diminish their exposure to all countries significantly. However, the scale of the declines varies between banks and borrowing countries. For example, while Barclays reduced its exposure to the four Asian countries by 40 percent, Hong Kong and Shanghai Bank Corporations' (HSBC) exposure declined by far less (−16 percent). The declines do not seem to be related to the stock of claims, as, although HSBC had a position six times larger than Barclays, other banks with a similar exposure (Chase Manhattan, Société Générale) also pulled out very significantly.

The fact that HSBC is largely based in the region and is characterized by long-standing ties with local customers could be a plausible explanation for the smaller decline. Furthermore, as was pointed out by an economist from a London bank, the fact that HSBC has balance sheets in East Asia has led it to assess its risk exposure differently. Indeed, it is more likely that during a crisis a bank, such as HSBC, with a local physical presence will adopt a more long term strategy and reduce its exposure to a lesser extent than other banks if the crisis is viewed as a cyclical phenomenom.[8]

Apart from HSBC and Banque Nationale de Paris (BNP), all European and U.S. banks reduced their exposure on a large scale across the four countries (between 26 and 62 percent of their claims).

The case of Japan is much more striking. Contrary to the behavior of European and U.S. banks, Japanese banks do not behave similarly. Three out of the seven banks studied reduced their exposure by 15 percent or less while the remaining four cut their exposure by more than 20 percent (up to 30 percent in the case of the Tokai Bank). The Bank of Tokyo-Mitsubishi is the largest lender to the region compared to both other Japanese and international banks. It is also the Japanese bank that reduced the most its exposure. This is duc to the different historical background of the Bank of Tokyo-Mitsubishi. Indeed, it has the longest presence of any Japanese bank at the international level because of its role in the promotion of exports of national industries.[9] More differences appear when we look at each of the four borrowers. Five out of the seven banks actually increased or maintained their exposure in one or more borrowing countries.[10]

Surprisingly, we find an increase in total Japanese lending to South Korea, which is not reflected in the BIS data. This is due to a significant increase in exposure by three Japanese banks, the Dai Ichi Kangyo Bank (DKB), Sanwa, and Fuji. According to an economist from a Japanese bank based in Tokyo, this can be explained by the negotiations held in January 1998 between the

TABLE 3.7. **Exposure of Individual International Banks to the Four Most Affected Countries, 1997–98 (in billions of U.S.$)**

		South Korea			Indonesia			Malaysia			Thailand			Total		
		End 1997	End 1998	Change	End 1997	End 1998	Change	End 1997	End 1998	Change	End 1997	End 1998	Change	End 1997	End 1998	Change
France	BNP	1.7	1.6	−6%	1.0	0.8	−20%	0.6	0.5	−17%	1.0	0.7	−30%	4.3	3.6	−16%
	Crédit Agricole	1.9	1	−47%	0.7	0.5	−29%	0.2	0.1	−50%	1.1	0.6	−45%	3.9	2.2	−44%
	Crédit Lyonnais	3.7	2.4	−35%	1.3	1.0	−23%	0.3	0.2	−33%	0.6	0.5	−17%	5.9	4.1	−31%
	Paribas	1.5	1.0	−33%	0.4	0.4	0%	0.3	0.3	0%	0.4	0.3	−25%	2.6	2.0	−23%
	Société Générale	4.5	2.7	−40%	0.8	0.6	−25%	0.9	0.6	−33%	2.4	1.8	−25%	8.6	5.7	−34%
Total France		13.3	8.7	−35%	4.2	3.3	−21%	2.3	1.7	−26%	5.5	3.9	−29%	25.3	17.6	−30%
U.K.	Barclays	1.0	0.8	−20%	0.5	0.2	−60%				0.5	0.2	−60%	2.0	1.2	−40%
	Natwest	1.8	1.3	−28%	0.4	0.3	−25%				0.4	0.2	−50%	2.6	1.8	−31%
	HSBC	4.1	3.6	−12%	1.8	1.4	−22%				2.8	2.3	−18%	8.7	7.3	−16%
	Lloyds TSB		0.5											0.8		
	Abbey National												0.8			
Total U.K.		6.9	6.2	−10%	2.7	1.9	−30%				3.7	2.7	−27%	14.1	11.1	−21%

Japan	Bank of Tokyo-Mitsubishi	3.4	2.7	−21%	2.6	1.2	−54%	1.3	1.1	−15%	4.5	2.7	−40%	11.8	7.7	−35%
	Dai Ichi Kangyo	1.6	1.7	6%	1.4	1.0	−29%	0.4	0.4	0%	1.8	1.6	−11%	5.2	4.7	−10%
	Sanwa	0.9	2.0	122%	2.3	0.9	−61%	0.8	0.7	−13%	2.2	1.7	−23%	6.2	5.3	−15%
	Fuji	0.9	1.2	33%	1.4	0.8	−43%	0.6	0.5	−17%	1.8	1.1	−39%	4.7	3.6	−23%
	Sumitomo	1.6	1.2	−25%	1.2	0.9	−25%	0.6	0.6	−0%	2.0	1.4	−30%	5.4	4.1	−24%
	Tokai	0.4	0.3	−25%	0.6	0.5	−17%	0.6	0.5	−17%	1.4	0.8	−43%	3.0	2.1	−30%
	Sakura	0.7	1.0	−43%	1.4	1.4	0%	0.3	0.3	0%	2.4	1.5	−38%	4.8	4.2	−13%
Total Japan		9.5	10.1	6%	10.9	6.7	−39%	4.6	4.1	−11%	16.1	10.8	−33%	41.1	31.7	−23%
U.S.	Chase Manhattan	5.3	2.4	−55%	2.2	1.2	−45%	0.9	0.6	−33%	1.4	0.9	−36%	9.8	5.1	−48%
	Citicorp	2.6	<0.8		0.6			0.7			0.3			3.5		
	J. P. Morgan	3.4	1.7	−50%	0.8	0.2	−75%	0.4			1.2	0.2	−83%	5.8	2.1	−64%
Total U.S.[a]		11.3	4.1	−64%	3.6	1.4	−61%	2	0.6	−70%	2.9	1.1	−62%	19.1	7.2	−62%
Grand Total		41.0	29.1	−29%	21.4	13.3	−38%	8.9	6.4	−28%	28.2	18.5	−34%	99.6	67.6	−32%

Note: Exchange rate: 31/12/97, 1 ECU = 1.10 USD, 1 FRF = 0.17 USD; 1 GDP = 1.65 USD; 31/12/98, 1 EURO = 1.17 USD; 1 GDP = 1.66 USD; 1 FRF = 0.18 USD 31/03/98, 1 JPY = 0.007524 USD; 30/09/98, 1 JPY = 0.007369 USD; 31/03/99, 1 JPY = 0.008396 USD. Some banks include their on and off balance sheets credit exposure while others do not. Data exclude for most banks sovereign risk, trade credit risk, and export credit agency guarantees.

[a]The total for the United States needs to be interpreted with care due to lack of data.

South Korean government and private creditors, which resulted in the exchange of $24 billion of short-term debt for government-guaranteed loans. Under this agreement, South Korean banks exchanged their short-term nontrade credit for new loans with longer maturities. Sanwa was one of the 13 international banks that negotiated the deal.[11]

The differences in behavior among Japanese banks can be explained by several factors.

First, it is quite likely that lending decisions in times of crisis might differ depending on whether the borrower is a group affiliate or not. Indeed, as stated in the annual report of the Bank of Tokyo-Mitsubishi, much lower provisions were made for bad loans that had been given to group affiliates: "From a credit perspective, we regard affiliates of Japanese corporations differently from other types of borrowers since, in many cases, we obtain some kind of guaranty or other form of assurance of support from the affiliated Japanese corporations" (Bank of Tokyo-Mitsubishi 1999). Table 3.8 reports on the exposure of DKB to the Asian-4 between the end of March 1998 and the end of March 1999.

The data show that DKB reduced its exposure to Japanese affiliates to a lesser extent than to nonaffiliates with the exception of South Korea. Malaysia is a striking example in which lending to affiliates actually increased (by more than 21 percent) while it was cut by more than half to nonaffiliates (−58 percent). DKB's 1998 annual report, like that of the Bank of Tokyo-Mitsubishi, differentiates between affiliates and nonaffiliates: "Many Japanese corporations have operations in the region and will continue to require financial services. For these reasons, the Bank continues to regard Asia as an important area in its international activities and will continue to promote its operations there" (DKB 1998, 25). As far as South Korea is concerned, and as mentioned earlier, the increase in loans to non-Japanese affiliates (mostly banks) reflects the deal reached between the South Korean government and private creditors in January 1998.

Another factor that might explain these differences is that the banking crisis in Japan has not affected Japanese banks equally. Healthier banks might thus behave differently from more fragile ones, as they do not face the same capital asset constraints.

Another question worth investigating is why loans would be renewed during a crisis. Although the answer to that question is not clear-cut, at least two reasons can be identified apart from the rescheduling of agreements. First, as underlined by Hoshi, Kashyap, and Scharfstein (1990, 1991), one feature of the main bank system is that in times of crisis it is likely to continue providing finance to its customers. This is due to the more long term perspective it adopts. Second, Peek and Rosengren (1998) point out that some banks might be

TABLE 3.8. Dai Ichi Kangyo Bank's Loans Outstanding in Asia by Location of Borrowers (millions of U.S.$)

	Japanese Affiliates			Non-Japanese			Public			Total		
	1997	1998	Change 1997–98	1997	1998	Change 1997–98	1997	1998	Change 1997–98	1997	1998	Change 1997–98
Thailand	829.4	788.4	−4%	948.9	734.7	−14%	56.0	41.1	−2%	1,834.3	1,565.0	−15%
Indonesia	430.0	339.2	−10%	914.0	597.0	−30%	77.8	107.5	9%	1,421.8	1,045.3	−26%
Malaysia	95.0	152.8	21%	271.5	48.7	−58%	18.6	179.7	105%	385.1	382.9	−1%
South Korea	54.4	47.0	−1%	1,290.3	1,660.7	21%	263.8	26.9	−504%	1,608.5	1,736.3	8%

Source: DKB 1998, 1999.

rolling over loans to help borrowers in difficulty meet their repayments so that the lending bank does not have to report an increase in its bad loans. It is worth noting that this particular behavior is not unique to the Japanese case.

Why then did they pull out? The banks that pulled out did so mainly because they needed to improve their balance sheets and profitability. The deterioration in their balance sheets was caused by at least three factors. The first two are specific to the Japanese economy.

First, it is important to underline that Japan experienced the worst of its crisis in the first half of 1997. This was highlighted by the failure of major commercial banks and later, in November 1997, by the collapse of four major stockbroking firms. The deepening of the Japanese banking crisis led the financial authorities to call for the restructuring of banks' balance sheets.[12] This led to a massive reorganization of international portfolios through the reduction of overseas operations in Asia (see the decline in the second half of 1997 in table 3.1), Europe, and the United States. In 1998, new legislation adopted by the financial authorities formally called for the restructuring of balance sheets, which led to further withdrawals of loans. According to an economist from a Japanese bank based in London, during the second half of 1997 and first half of 1998, nonaffiliates were the primary targets of the reductions in exposure. According to this economist, the end of the fiscal year (March 1998) and interim reports (September 1997 and September 1998) were used as benchmarks for the reallocation of portfolios due to publication requirements and thus played an important role in the timing of the reversals.

Second, Kwan (1999) points out that the weakening of the yen directly impacted the capital adequacy ratios of Japanese banks, as 80 percent of overseas lending is denominated in dollars. Indeed, a decline in the yen reduces the capital adequacy ratio by raising the value of risky assets in yen terms.

The third factor, which is not so specific to Japanese banks, is the increasing amounts of bad loans. As a matter of fact, the devaluation of local currencies in the Asian-4 increased the debt burden of local borrowers and thus decreased their ability to repay. Repayments were all the more threatened because of the loss of access to refinancing and because of monetary policy tightening.

These three factors led some Japanese and other international banks to pull out. This was accompanied by a loss of confidence among international banks, mainly European and American.

In sum, we have shown that the reversal in bank loans from international banks during the Asian crisis has several causes. They are both bank and country specific. We have found clear differences between European and Japanese banks. The behavior of the former seems to confirm the common lender channel and the panic hypothesis. Indeed, bank loans fall similarly between banks and across borrowers with the exception of the HSBC and BNP.

As for Japanese banks, the story appears to be more complex than just a common lender channel, as we do not find any clear similarities in their behavior. We have proposed a number of explanations. First, Japanese banks have long-term relationships with their customers—both affiliated or nonaffiliated with the group. These long-term relations provide, in normal times, a guarantee for long-term finance. However, in times of crises one needs to take into consideration the likelihood of repayment on the side of the borrower and the capital asset ratio on the side of the lender. Japanese banks usually treat bad loans differently depending on whether they originate from affiliates or nonaffiliates, as in the first case they are backed by their parent companies. However, as the crisis unfolded the impact of the devaluation on the level of bad loans might have interrupted the rolling over of loans even to affiliates. On the supply side, the Japanese banking system crisis worsened the capital asset ratios of many banks. This was aggravated by the declining yen. As a result, banks were forced to reduce their exposure. However, and as pointed out earlier, the fact that some banks are healthier than others is another reason for the differences between banks.

Figure 3.2 sums up the different scenarios and their potential impact on lending decisions in the case of Japanese banks. The figure shows that a combined deterioration in both supply side (capital asset ratios) and demand side (increasing numbers of bad loans) factors eventually leads to the nonrenewal

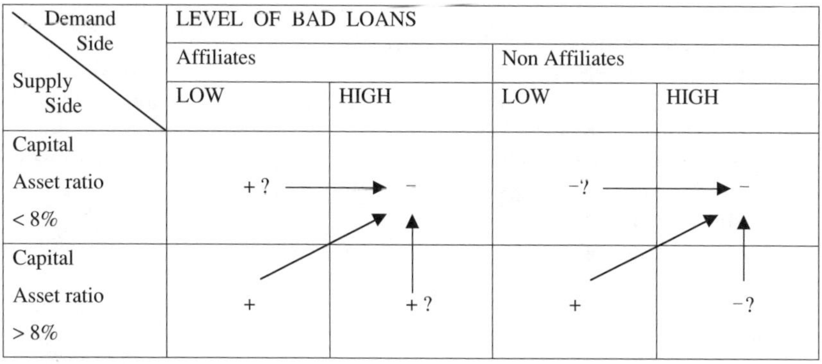

Demand Side / Supply Side	LEVEL OF BAD LOANS			
	Affiliates		Non Affiliates	
	LOW	HIGH	LOW	HIGH
Capital Asset ratio < 8%	+ ?	–	–?	–
Capital Asset ratio > 8%	+	+ ?	+	–?

Fig. 3.2. Impact of the level of the capital asset ratio and bad loans on lending decisions. In the matrix, + means that banks roll over their loans, – means that banks do not roll over, – ? means that the impact on decisions is unclear but the tendency is for the bank to pull out, + ? means the impact on decisions is unclear but the tendency is for the bank to roll over the loans, and the arrows indicate changes in decisions as the crisis unfolds.

of existing loans. Although there are differences in treatment between affiliates and nonaffiliates, these differences seem to fade away as the crisis deepens.

As we have discussed, the Basle Capital Accord may have played a role in the buildup of the large volumes of credit lending to Asia. We discuss in some detail in chapter 11 the recent proposal by the BIS for the reform of the accord as well as its implications for credit flows to developing countries.

NOTES

We would like to thank Stephen Spratt for helping us gather the data. The Mervyn King quotation at the beginning of the chapter is from King 1999. The Dani Rodrik and Andres Velasco quotation is from Rodrik and Velasco 1999.

1. See BIS 1993 and table 3.1.
2. Only three Latin American countries, Mexico, Argentina, and Brazil, have been selected here. The percentages are calculated as the proportion of total claims from BIS-reporting banks to the countries' GDP.
3. Interbank lending by the OECD receives a 20 percent weighting irrespective of its maturity.
4. This is not true if Europe is taken as a whole.
5. Due to the lack of data, we use global flows from the IFS data base rather than Japanese flows.
6. For our analyses of these factors, see Griffith-Jones, Cailloux, and Pfaffenzeller 1998.
7. In order to test the importance of the common lender channel, the authors measure the impact of a crisis occurring in one country on the country's lenders' exposure in other countries.
8. Interview material.
9. Interview material.
10. It is also worth noting that the scale of the declines in exposure to different countries for a single bank varies widely. For example, the Bank of Tokyo-Mitsubishi reduced its exposure in Indonesia by 54 percent, that is, more than twice the reduction in South Korea (−21 percent) and Malaysia (−15 percent).
11. Interview material.
12. Interview material.

REFERENCES

Aoki, M., and H. Patrick. 1994. *The Japanese main bank system: Its relevance for developing and transforming economies.* Oxford: Oxford University Press.

Bank of Tokyo-Mitsubishi. 1999. *Annual report.* Tokyo: Bank of Tokyo-Mitsubishi.

Basle Committee on Banking Supervision. 1999. "Supervisory lessons to be drawn from the Asian Crisis." Working Paper 2, June. Available at <www.bis.org>.

BIS (Bank for International Settlements). 1993. *The BIS consolidated international banking statistics.* Basel, Switzerland: BIS.

———. 1999. "A new capital adequacy framework." Consultative paper, Basle Committee on Banking Supervision, June.

Chang, R., and A. Velasco. 1998. "Financial crises in emerging markets: A canonical model." Working Paper 98–10, Federal Reserve Bank of Atlanta, July.

Cornford, A. 2000. "The Basle committee's proposals for revised capital standards: Rationale, design, and possible incidence." Paper presented at a meeting of the Technical Committee of the Intergovernmental Group of 24, Lima, Peru, March 1–3.

Corsetti, G., P. Pensenti, and N. Roubini. 1998. "What caused the Asian currency and financial crisis?" Mimeo, Stern University.

DKB (Dai Ichi Kangyo Bank). 1998. *Annual report.* Tokyo: DKB.

Griffith-Jones, S., with J. Cailloux and S. Pfaffenzeller. 1998. "The East Asian financial crisis: A reflection on its causes, consequences, and policy implications." Discussion Paper 367, IDS.

Hoshi, T., A. Kashyap, and D. Scharfstein. 1990. "The role of banks in reducing the costs of financial distress in Japan." *Journal of Financial Economics* 27, no. 1 (September): 67–88.

———. 1991. "Corporate structure, liquidity, and investment: Evidence from Japanese industrial groups." *Quarterly Journal of Economics* 106, no. 1 (February): 33–60.

IIF. 1999a. "Capital flows to emerging market economies." Institute for International Finance (IIF), Washington, DC, April.

———. "Testing for moral hazard in emerging market lending." Research Paper 99–1, IIF.

Ito, T. 1999. "Capital flows in Asia." Working Paper 7134, NBER, May.

Jackson, P. 1999. "Capital requirements and bank behaviour: The impact of the Basle Accord." Working Paper 1, Basle Committee on Banking Supervision, April.

Kaminski, G. L., and C. M. Reinhart. 1999. "The twin crises: The causes of banking and balance-of-payments problems." *American Economic Review* 89, no. 3 (June): 473–500.

King, Mervyn. 1999. "Reforming the international financial system: The middle way." Speech delivered to a session of the Money Marketeers at the Federal Reserve Bank of New York, September 9, 1999. This speech was published in the November 1999 issue of the *Financial Stability Review.*

Krugman, P. 1989. "Private capital flows to problem debtors," in Sachs, J. (ed), *Developing country debt and economic performance,* NBER, Vol. 1.

———. 1998. "What happened to Asia." Mimeo, Harvard University.

———. 1999. "Balance sheets, the transfer problem, and financial crises." Mimeo, Massachusetts Institute of Technology.

Kwan, C. H. 1999. "Sayonara dollar peg." Paper presented at a meeting of the T5, Royal Institute of International Affairs, October.

McCauley, R., and S. Yeaple. 1994. "How lower Japanese asset prices affect Pacific financial markets." *Federal Reserve Bank of New York Quarterly Review* (spring): 19–33.

McKinnon, R. I., and H. Pill. 1996. "Credible liberalization and international capital flows: The overborrowing syndrome." In *Financial deregulation and integration in East Asia,* ed. T. Ito and A. O. Krueger. Chicago: University of Chicago Press.

———. 1998. "International overborrowing: A decomposition of credit and currency risks." *World Development* 26, no. 7 (June): 1267–82.

Peek, J., and E. Rosengren. 1997. "The international transmission of financial shocks: The case of Japan." *American Economic Review* 87 (September): 495–505.

———. 1998. "Japanese banking problems: Implications for Southeast Asia." Paper presented at the second annual conference Banking, Financial Integration, and Macroeconomic Stability, Central Bank of Chile, Santiago, September 3–4.

Radelet, S., and J. Sachs. 1998. "The onset of the East Asian crisis." Mimeo, Harvard University.

Reisen, H. 1999. "Revisions of the Basle Accord and sovereign ratings." Mimeo, OECD Development Centre, Paris.

Rodrik, D., and A. Velasco. 1999. "Short-term capital flows." Working Paper 7364, NBER.

Sarno, L., and M. Taylor. 1999. "Hot money, accounting labels, and the permanence of capital flows to developing countries: An empirical investigation." *Journal of Development Economics* 59:337–64.

Van Rijckeghem, C., and B. Weder. 1999. "Sources of contagion: Finance or trade." IMF Working Paper WP/99/146, October.

CHAPTER 4

Foreign Capital Flows to Thailand: Determinants and Impact

Ammar Siamwalla, Yos Vajragupta, and Pakorn Vichyanond

1. CHRONOLOGY

Before 1997, relatively low yields in industrial countries together with impressive economic growth and attractive returns in developing economies motivated Western investors to relocate their funds to money and capital markets in the East. This corresponded well with the trend toward trade globalization, international financial linkages, and expansion of production bases overseas. That was why the aggregate volume of net capital inflows to developing countries surged from U.S.$100.8 billion in 1990 to U.S.$338.1 billion in 1997. However, these net inflows plunged to U.S.$275 billion in 1998 after the world was shaken by widespread financial crises.

Thailand benefited a great deal from the Plaza Accord in 1985 because gluts of capital inflows from Japan in the form of foreign direct investment, as a result of the surging value of the yen, spurred up both investment and export activities. Concurrently, the Thai government was successful in achieving several consecutive years of cash balance surplus. The central authority believed that resource inflows represented a key driving force for continual economic expansion. After committing to the obligations under Article VIII of the International Monetary Fund (IMF), the Thai government in 1991 decided to start dismantling its exchange controls and liberalizing the activities of financial institutions, but it left its pegged exchange rate unchanged. Consequently, Thailand's net capital inflows grew rapidly from U.S.$10.9 billion in 1990 to U.S.$18.2 billion in 1996. However, once the market began to question Thailand's micro- as well as macroeconomic situation and the ability of the government to maintain stability, both creditors and investors rapidly withdrew their funds. The scenario was exacerbated by debtors' (p)repayments and speculators' hedging (table 4.1). The resulting capital outflows forced the Thai government to float the baht exchange rate in July 1997, sparking a series of financial crises in East Asia and other regions later on.

TABLE 4.1. Net Flows of Private Financial Accounts into Thailand (millions of U.S.$)

										1997				1998			
	1990	1991	1992	1993	1994	1995	1996	1997	1998	Quarter 1	Quarter 2	Quarter 3	Quarter 4	Quarter 1	Quarter 2	Quarter 3	Quarter 4
Bank	1,594	−259	1,933	3,599	13,925	11,236	5,007	−6,442	−13,944	2,369	36	−5,799	−3,048	−1,472	−3,883	−4,394	−4,195
Commercial bank	1,594	−259	1,933	−4,039	3,837	3,103	428	−4,735	−4,310	1,515	−273	−4,459	−1,518	623	−1,756	−2,459	−718
BIBF	0	0	0	7,638	10,087	8,133	4,579	−1,707	−9,634	855	309	−1,340	−1,531	−2,095	−2,127	−1,935	−3,478
Nonbank	9,333	10,544	7,415	6,717	−1,910	9,561	13,183	−1,916	−2,024	−585	−905	−953	527	−2,788	1,716	1,252	−2,203
Direct investment	2,391	1,848	1,979	1,439	902	1,168	1,454	3,205	4,688	528	568	1,147	961	1,016	1,481	1,218	973
Foreign direct investment	2,531	2,016	2,116	1,732	1,323	2,004	2,270	3,645	4,810	654	780	1,211	999	1,019	1,492	1,248	1,052
Thai direct investment	−140	−168	−136	−293	−421	−837	−816	−441	−123	−126	−212	−64	−39	−3	−11	−30	−79
Other loans	4,495	5,638	2,725	−2,420	−5,838	1,530	5,451	−3,786	−4,279	−115	−846	−858	−1,968	−2,052	−808	−737	−682
Portfolio investment	450	151	556	4,848	1,095	3,283	3,485	4,501	539	511	1,228	2,375	387	447	47	−17	62
Equity securities	450	36	454	2,682	−409	2,120	1,123	3,875	354	416	882	2,081	496	449	−142	−77	123
Debt securities	0	115	102	2,166	1,504	1,164	2,362	626	185	95	346	294	−109	−3	190	60	−62
Nonresident baht account	1,342	2,057	1,754	2,682	2,036	3,381	2,913	−5,850	−2,715	−1,694	−1,800	−3,861	1,505	−2,186	1,139	789	−2,457
Trade credits	655	745	307	539	456	256	−146	−242	−494	252	−68	13	−439	−185	−92	−160	−57
Other	0	105	92	−370	−560	−58	25	257	237	−67	13	230	81	172	−52	160	−42
Total private capital (net)	10,927	10,284	9,348	10,316	12,014	20,797	18,190	−8,358	−15,968	1,785	−869	−6,753	−2,521	−4,261	−2,167	−3,142	−6,398

Source: Bank of Thailand.

Private capital inflows to Thailand are hereby separated into two categories, bank and nonbank. The banking sector began to play an active role from 1993 onward after the Bangkok International Banking Facilities (BIBF) went into effect. The nonbank sector consists of foreign direct investment (FDI), loans, portfolio investment (PI), and nonresident baht accounts (NRB).

1.1. 1990–92

As early as 1984, the Thai baht was tied to a basket of currencies, with considerable weight (roughly 84 percent) given to the U.S. dollar. In effect, the baht value was practically pegged to the U.S. dollar, engendering negligible exchange risks upon dollar-denominated foreign borrowings. Substantially higher domestic interest rates, together with the small exchange risks mentioned earlier, induced the Thai nonbank sector to tap funds from abroad, especially under the categories of loans and NRB.

Large portions of net loan inflows went to financial institutions, trade, industry (especially electrical appliances), and real estate (table 4.2). A majority of these funds came from Hong Kong and Singapore.

1.2. 1993–96

Since borrowings via BIBF enjoyed several distinct tax privileges, private Thai businesses shifted their foreign borrowings from loans to BIBF. Moreover, some FDI inflows, especially the Japanese ones, were rebooked under the BIBF category so as to gain access to tax privileges and satisfy BIBF requirements. Overall, BIBF increased the share of banks' net inflows from 21 percent in 1992 to 58 percent in 1993–96. Meanwhile, the loan category saw some outflows in 1993–94.

TABLE 4.2. Net Flows of Foreign Direct Loans Classified by Sectors (millions of U.S.$)

	1990	1991	1992	1993	1994	1995	1996	1997
Financial institutions	383	488	965	874	538	1,993	834	−2,129
Trade	829	638	158	−22	−536	426	866	−333
Construction	135	95	2	17	−30	−16	191	−39
Mining and quarrying	−10	25	−14	−34	−31	1	19	−44
Agriculture	72	2	24	−27	−11	15	−11	−1
Industry	1,843	3,032	1,466	1,043	−66	2,234	2,269	−583
Services	99	71	59	−4	33	326	332	165
Investment	0	210	−152	87	−55	738	795	−93
Real estate	752	1,012	220	−180	407	445	977	−855
Other	392	65	−3	1	99	−19	−47	−20
Total	4,495	5,638	2,725	1,755	348	6,145	6,223	−3,933

Source: Bank of Thailand.

Tax privileges of BIBF	*Normal*	*BIBF*
1. Corporate income tax	30%	10%
2. Specific business tax	3.3%	0%
3. Interest income withholding tax	10%	0%
4. Stamp duties	2%	0%

The majority of BIBF funds were channeled to the manufacturing sector (particularly electrical appliances), commerce, banking, and finance. As for loans, most net inflows were targeted at financial institutions, while trade and real estate assumed subsidiary roles. Hong Kong and Singapore were primary sources of funds, and by the mid-1990s loans from Japan and the United States gained growing shares.

Financial liberalization via BIBF considerably enlarged the short-term portion of Thailand's external outstanding debt (table 4.3) because most BIBF credits were on a short-term basis and continually rolled over for long-term uses. Tapping short-term funds in the world market was ordinarily cheaper than long-term borrowing. In order to discourage excessive BIBF inflows, the central authority in October 1995 decided to raise the minimum level of out-in BIBF (representing funds from abroad for domestic use) from U.S.$500,000 to U.S.$2 million. Such measure curtailed the volume of BIBF net inflows afterward.

However, inflows via loans, PI, and NRB rose markedly in 1995–96, while those of BIBF subsided. That was a shift in reverse order to the types of flows that predominated in 1993–94. It clearly demonstrated that most of these short-term non-FDI credits were substitutable. Any controlling measures imposed upon one credit type but not its substitutes are likely to be ineffective because rational economic agents will shift gears or direction toward the plausible and profitable routes.

More disturbing was the fact that private net capital inflows grew incessantly to such an extent that the country's external debt outstanding surged from U.S.$52.1 billion in 1993 to U.S.$90.5 billion in 1996. Worse yet, its short-term component swelled from 36 percent in 1990 to 50 percent in 1995, which made Thailand increasingly vulnerable to changes in market liquidity or foreign investors' confidence. Such a debt buildup was largely attributed to a simultaneous implementation of capital account liberalization and rigid exchange rates.

The period between 1993 and 1996 saw a big jump in PI net inflows from U.S.$386 million per annum in 1990–92 to U.S.$3,178 million per annum. That influx led to a boom in the stock market index, price/earnings (P/E) ratio, and market capitalization. The establishment of the Securities and Exchange Commission in 1992 and widespread initial public offerings since

TABLE 4.3. **External Debt Outstanding (millions of U.S.$)**

	1990	1991	1992	1993	1994	1995	1996	1997	1998
Public sector	11,514	12,810	13,068	14,171	15,714	16,402	16,805	17,166	20,290
Long term	11,257	12,105	12,518	14,171	15,534	16,317	16,751	17,146	20,140
Short term	257	705	550	0	180	85	54	20	150
Private sector	17,793	25,068	30,553	37,936	49,152	66,166	73,731	69,093	54,666
Long term	7,633	10,382	12,189	15,302	20,153	25,155	36,172	34,277	31,293
Short term	10,160	14,686	18,364	22,634	28,999	41,011	37,559	34,816	23,373
Commercial bank	4,233	4,477	6,263	5,279	9,865	14,436	10,682	9,488	7,074
Long term	286	338	731	1,263	3,451	4,443	2,314	3,824	3,753
Short term	3,947	4,139	5,532	4,016	6,414	9,993	8,368	5,664	3,321
BIBF	0	0	0	7,740	18,111	27,503	31,187	30,079	21,892
Long term	0	0	0	1,385	2,969	3,799	10,697	10,317	6,946
Short term	0	0	0	6,355	15,142	23,704	20,490	19,762	14,946
Nonbank	13,560	20,591	24,290	24,917	21,176	24,227	31,862	29,526	25,700
Long term	7,347	10,044	11,458	12,654	13,733	16,913	23,161	20,136	20,594
Short term	6,213	10,547	12,832	12,263	7,443	7,314	8,701	9,390	5,106
Monetary authorities	1	0	0	0	0	0	0	7,157	11,204
Use of IMF credit									3,239
Other									7,965
Total	29,308	37,878	43,621	52,107	64,866	82,568	90,536	93,416	86,160
Long term	18,891	22,487	24,707	29,473	35,687	41,472	52,923	58,580	62,637
Short term	10,417	15,391	18,914	22,634	29,179	41,096	37,613	34,836	23,523

Source: Bank of Thailand.

then attracted strong interest among foreign investors, especially as Thailand's economic growth remained attractive until 1995.

Singapore and Hong Kong were major players in the Thai stock market, especially after 1993. But these countries may not represent original sources, as countries such as the United States and Japan channeled a portion of their investment funds through Singapore and Hong Kong because of double tax agreements and custodianship.

Most PI entered as equity except in the years 1991, 1994, and 1996, during which private local companies issued a large volume of debt securities abroad in formats such as convertible debentures, Floating Rate Certificate of Deposit (FRCD), and subordinate debentures.

Although net inflows through NRB may not represent a major portion of total net inflows in the private sector, inflows and outflows of NRB amounted to more than 90 percent of total inflows and outflows after 1994. The underlying reason is that this NRB functioned as a nostro account serving various transactions such as interest arbitrage, stock transactions, and baht clearing for any foreign-exchange-related transactions. Another outstanding feature of NRB was its volatility due to its multifaceted functions.

In contrast to loans, PI, BIBF, and NRB, net inflows of FDI were much steadier, since investors aimed for returns in the long run. Foreign investors were enticed by means of various special privileges granted by the government's Board of Investment and the continuing rapid pace of macroeconomic expansion. In this category of funds, Japan stood out in 1990–91 as a result of a stronger yen and the consequent relocation of production plants to Thailand. Later, Singapore, Hong Kong, and the United States played more active roles. Sectorwise, industry (especially electrical appliances, machinery, and transportation) absorbed the largest proportion of FDI, whereas trade and real estate commanded smaller but still significant shares (table 4.4).

1.3. 1997–98

The continually rising value of the baht (because of the surging U.S. dollar, to which the baht was tightly pegged) in the midst of several macroeconomic problems (e.g., an ominous current account deficit, mounting short-term external debt, and export stagnation) notably weakened foreign investors' confidence in the Thai economy. This led rating agencies (Moody's and Standard and Poors) to lower Thailand's short-term external debt credibility (from P1 to P2 in September 1996) and to downgrade the country's creditworthiness in both foreign and local currencies (from A to A− and AA to AA−, respectively, in September 1997).

TABLE 4.4. Net Flows of Foreign Direct Investment Classified by Sectors (millions of U.S.$)

	1993	1994	1995	1996	1997	1998	Q1/97	Q2/97	Q3/97	Q4/97	Q1/98	Q2/98	Q3/98	Q4/98
Financial institutions	65	7	26	72	108	497	10	8	52	38	114	132	201	50
Trade	219	341	446	545	1,045	840	201	145	445	254	158	271	166	245
Construction	152	70	36	70	170	145	27	53	−8	98	62	67	−9	25
Mining and quarrying	126	52	57	19	21	63	8	9	−5	9	6	19	4	34
Agriculture	13	−6	9	2	1	0	0	0	0	1	0	0	0	0
Industry	452	512	567	709	1,820	2,035	355	378	629	459	425	587	485	538
Services	19	56	88	125	294	294	39	135	41	80	49	115	85	46
Investment	−16	146	−79	−21	30	309	0	14	3	13	46	39	206	18
Real estate	695	472	854	753	110	489	16	34	32	27	141	141	106	102
Total FDI	1,732	1,323	2,004	2,270	3,645	4,810	654	780	1,211	999	1,019	1,492	1,248	1,052

Source: Bank of Thailand.

Considerable appreciation of the baht against non-U.S. currencies following the third quarter of 1996 gave rise to strong pressures against the baht. Such pressures were largely the result of the withdrawal of funds by foreign investors and (p)repayments of domestic debtors due to slackening confidence in the prevailing exchange rate and were not due to attacks on the baht by speculators or hedge funds. However, from the beginning of 1997 onward these speculators certainly exacerbated the situation when the country's economic status, the stability of its financial system, property market difficulties, and the baht exchange rate stability all became questionable. The attacks by hedge fund speculators were extremely strong in January, February, and May 1997, as evidenced by a gigantic reduction of the Bank of Thailand's international reserves from U.S.$38.7 billion in January 1997 to U.S.$2.5 billion in May 1997. Thailand's NRB accounts were heavily used by foreigners as a means of speculative transactions, engendering outflows of NRB throughout the first half of 1997. The situation was aggravated by the country's lower credit rating to such an extent that a drastic reduction of net capital inflows in the first quarter of 1997 became net outflows in the second quarter, spearheaded by the banking sector.

The Bank of Thailand employed several means to prohibit or constrain baht speculation. For instance, short-term baht interest rates were kept very high, while commercial banks were advised to refrain from accommodating foreign speculators' demand for foreign exchange. In addition, onshore and offshore foreign exchange markets were split, with credit restrictions imposed upon nonresidents. These counteracting measures did not help much in subduing capital outflows, and inevitably the Thai government had to float the baht in July 1997.

After the float, net capital outflows peaked in the third quarter of 1997 and the baht kept on depreciating versus the U.S. dollar until its minimum was reached at 56 baht per U.S. dollar in January 1998. The exchange rate stayed above 40 baht per U.S. dollar throughout the first three quarters of 1998 before it stabilized at around 36 to 38 baht per U.S. dollar from the fourth quarter onward.

The banking sector, including BIBF, received the biggest impact of the financial crisis, with commercial banks recording net outflows in the second quarter of 1997 followed by BIBF in the third quarter. Weakening investor confidence and slackening economic activities discouraged foreign creditors from rolling over BIBF credits. Meanwhile, uncertain exchange rates motivated debtors to (p)repay their obligations, resulting in high net capital outflows throughout the second half of 1997. These BIBF outflows primarily belonged to the manufacturing, commerce, and banking and finance sectors.

Although short-term interest rates in Thailand climbed to as high as 20 percent during the crisis, deteriorating confidence and exchange rate uncertainties led to streams of loan outflows, especially short-term ones, toward the end of 1997 and early 1998. Most of these loan outflows came from the financial and real estate sectors in response to the demands of creditors in Singapore, Hong Kong, and the United States.

The net capital outflows through NRB have one notable characteristic. Whenever NRB scored huge net outflows (e.g., as in the third quarter of 1997 and the second and fourth quarters of 1998), the baht exchange rate registered a drastic movement. An underlying reason for this is that one of the NRB's functions is to clear the settlement of baht-foreign exchange transactions.

Net inflows of PI jumped in the second and third quarters of 1997 as the price/earnings ratio in the stock market dipped below 10 for the first time in the 1990s (table 4.1). However, PI decreased to a large extent in 1998, becoming negative in the second and third quarters, since Thai economic growth in 1998 dropped to −8 percent. The sentiment was particularly poor for financial institutions, as their Non-Performing Loans (NPL) grew to a record high level, necessitating substantial recapitalization and corporate debt restructuring. In the meantime, booms in the U.S. economy and stock market recaptured investment funds from emerging economies, including Thailand. What should be noted here is that, although investors from the United States, China, and Belgium retrieved funds from Thailand, investors from Hong Kong, Singapore, and the United Kingdom injected net inflows. Table 4.1 clearly demonstrates that foreign portfolio investors were not the parties who instigated the 1997 crisis at all. In fact, they did the opposite, that is, they caused net capital inflows for a year and a half, from the beginning of 1997 until the middle of 1998 (table 4.1). Typically, foreign portfolio investors generate very strong momentum and therefore represent highly influential players in local stock markets. This is evident from the fact that the Stock Exchange of Thailand index mostly moved in accordance with the net transactions of foreign portfolio investors (see fig. 4.1).

In contrast, FDI was not at all affected by the crisis and the economic recession. On the contrary, it grew to a remarkable degree in 1997–98 after the baht was floated. This can be attributed to a large number of ongoing projects that are long-term commitments and a number of mergers and acquisitions occasioned by the financial troubles. The increases in FDI helped cushion the private sector's net outflows in other capital categories.

Overall, private capital flows responded very well to policy measures. For instance, before 1993, when BIBF credits were not available, most net inflows came in under the category of nonbank loans. In 1993–94, the BIBF credits, which gave special privileges to borrowers, were opted for by various parties. But such selection declined markedly in 1995–96 when the authorities raised

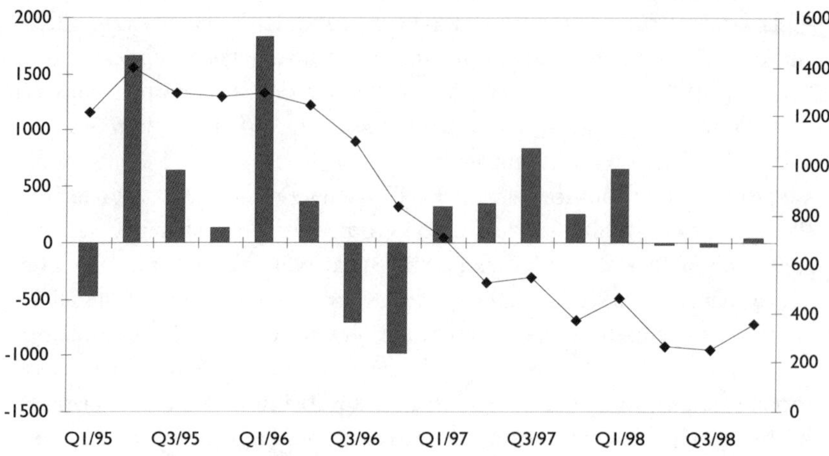

Fig. 4.1. Stock Exchange of Thailand index and net foreign purchases

the minimum level of out-in BIBF in order to reduce the short-term portion of the country's external debt. By 1997–98, the country was experiencing net outflows of both nonbank loans and BIBF because of exchange rate floatation (table 4.1). The other two contrasting types of capital inflows were FDI and PI. Fluctuations in PI were largely attributed to sources in Hong Kong and Singapore. Meanwhile, the stream of FDI was more stable and was largely dominated by Japan, Hong Kong, Singapore, and the United States. Most of these FDI flows were absorbed by the industrial sector (particularly electrical appliances and chemicals), trade, and real estate (table 4.4). Net inflows of FDI and loans as well as BIBF immediately indicate that the following sectors attracted strong attention from foreign investors: real estate, electrical appliances, and trade. These capital inflows generated not only asset price inflation or economic bubbling but dangerous current account deficits or excessive spending.

2. DETERMINANTS

2.1. FOREIGN DIRECT INVESTMENT

Among various types of net capital inflows, FDI was outstanding in its stability. It barely fluctuated with market liquidity or other short-term disturbances because investors' primary concerns were long term. After the baht was floated and the financial crisis erupted in 1997, FDI rose to a notable extent. This was largely attributed to a surge of problem companies seeking takeover partners. In addition, 38 percent depreciation of the baht raised the purchasing power of foreign investors and encouraged acquisitions.

Typically, the following factors motivate FDI or relocation of production bases.

- Exchange rate shifts
- Promising growth in the recipient economy
- Cheap and/or good quality inputs
- Special privileges granted by recipient governments
- Political stability and firm economic policies as well as fundamentals

Thailand possessed all these features (e.g., real GDP growth of 8 percent per year in 1990–95, low wages, Board of Investment privileges, and plentiful economic fundamentals). Unsurprisingly, the high volume of FDI prevailed steadily throughout. Even in 1998, when real GDP fell drastically, FDI remained active.

Flows of FDI into Thailand were dominated by those from Japan. This was largely due to a stronger yen, while the baht was kept intact. Other sources included Hong Kong, the United States, and members of the Association of Southeast Asian Nations (ASEAN) and the European Union (EU). The industries that attracted the strongest interest among investors were electronics, chemicals, metals, and real estate. It is notable that a majority of promoted investment projects were export oriented. One Taiwanese government agency described Thailand as "a key linkage between Asia and Europe, comprising abundant raw materials as well as good quality staff, reasonable land prices and wages, together with accommodative government policies."[1] The Japanese, on the other hand, cited the country's ability to "maintain/expand the sales volume in the local market" as the best reason for relocation of production bases to Thailand.[2] "Exports," "exploring new markets," "secure inexpensive labor," and the "spread of production bases overseas" ranked as secondary reasons for Japanese FDI in Thailand (table 4.5). What is most noticeable is that Japanese investors cared little about "making use of preferential treatments for foreign capital."

Among the three forms of FDI (100 percent ownership, joint ventures, and acquisition/equity participation), 60 percent of Japanese FDI in Asia took the form of joint ventures in 1994–98 (in contrast to the FDI from the United States, Canada, and the EU, most of which was in the form of wholly owned affiliates). The reasons why Japan favored joint ventures are as follows.

1. Host country restrictions on foreign ownership
2. The need to acquire local business know-how
3. The need to secure local sales networks

Thailand was ranked third (behind China and the United States) by Japanese investors. In the automobile industry, Thailand was perceived to command some advantages because it had accommodating markets and served as an export base for other regions.

"Stability of the local currency" was the greatest challenge cited by 69.1 percent of the Japanese firms responding in Thailand. Only 25.2 percent of respondents enjoyed an improvement in price competitiveness as a result of currency devaluation in ASEAN because "we rely on imports for parts and materials."

2.2. NON-FDI FLOWS

Other than foreign direct investment, private capital flows were volatile. They were channeled via several different formats such as loans, portfolio investments, nonresident baht accounts, trade credits, and commercial banking facilities. Nevertheless, they had one common characteristic, being sensitive to opportunity costs or rates of return, confidence-affecting factors, and policy measures. They therefore could easily substitute for one another in response to policy measures aimed at one but not another type of non-FDI private capital flows.

TABLE 4.5. Reasons for Japanese FDI in Thailand (percentages)

	1994	1995	1996	1997	1998	Average
Maintain/expand the sales volume in the local market	46.7	59.0	55.6	58.3	57.4	55.4
Explore new markets	25.0	33.6	35.7	36.9	27.9	31.8
Exports to Japan	31.5	32.8	27.0	31.0	23.5	29.2
Exports to third countries	21.7	33.6	31.7	40.5	33.8	32.3
Spread production bases overseas	25.0	29.5	33.3	29.8	36.8	30.9
Secure inexpensive labor	31.5	39.3	32.5	36.9	29.4	33.9
Supply parts to assembly manufactures	16.3	36.9	34.1	28.6	25.0	28.2
Make use of preferential treatments for foreign capital	2.0	9.0	13.5	14.3	10.3	9.8
Avoid foreign exchange risk	5.4	12.3	9.5	9.5	8.8	9.1
Develop new products designed for the local market needs	3.3	5.7	6.3	8.3	0.0	4.7

Source: Nishiyama, Kushima, and Noda (1999).

In the first half of the 1990s, the weak economic performances of many industrial countries led to accommodative monetary policies, abundant liquidity, and low interest rates. These, in turn, depressed dividend yields as well as ratios of corporate earnings to equity values. Declines in asset yields in industrial countries made emerging countries an increasingly attractive investment opportunity. Moreover, exchange rates in East Asian countries were tightly linked to the U.S. dollar, entailing few exchange risks to investment flows from industrial countries. On the part of recipient countries, efforts to liberalize capital transactions facilitated flows of funds across borders. In addition, international wealth holders were impressed with Asia's strong economic growth, moderate inflation, and higher interest rates (table 4.6). Therefore, East Asia received plentiful capital inflows from industrial countries in 1990–96.

Financial liberalization measures undertaken in Thailand in the first half of the 1990s helped strengthen the confidence of foreign investors in several respects. The first milestone was Thailand's acceptance of obligations under Article VIII of the IMF on May 21, 1990. This was followed by three rounds of exchange control dismantling, the aim of which was to keep the foreign exchange regime in line with globalization and the growing mobility of capital.

The first round, instituted in May 1990, allowed commercial banks to authorize foreign exchange transactions in trade-related activities without prior approval from the Bank of Thailand and increased the limit on foreign exchange purchases to facilitate transfers and travel expenses. Commercial banks were also permitted to remit funds for debt repayment, sales of stocks, or liquidation of businesses within certain limits.

The second round, in April 1991, lifted most controls related to capital account transactions. For the first time, unincorporated Thai entities could open foreign currency accounts provided that the funds originated from abroad. Exporters were allowed to accept baht payments from non-resident

TABLE 4.6. Important Economic Statistics, Periodical Averages

	Economic Growth (%)		Current Account/ GDP (%)		Inflation (%)	
	1987–89	1990–97	1987–89	1990–97	1987–89	1990–97
Thailand	11.7	7.4	−2.3	−6.3	3.9	5.2
Malaysia	7.8	8.7	4.8	−5.8	1.9	3.8
Indonesia	6.1	6.9	−1.9	−2.5	7.9	9.3
Philippines	5.8	3.7	−1.9	−4.3	8.3	10.0

Source: International Financial Statistics, 1998; Bank of Thailand's *Key Economic Indicators*, various issues.

baht accounts without prior approval from the central bank and to use their export proceeds to service external obligations.

The third round of foreign exchange liberalization, in February 1994, raised the limit on outward transfers of direct investment by residents; increased the limit on banknotes taken to countries bordering Thailand, including Vietnam; abolished the limit on travel expenses; and allowed residents to use foreign exchange proceeds that originated abroad to service their external payments. Relaxation of these exchange controls aimed at promoting a more active role for market forces and greater utilization of the baht in regional trade.

The Bangkok International Banking Facilities agency was established in March 1993 as a means of developing international financial services and mobilizing capital to support regional economic growth and development. The BIBF may also have been adopted so as to strengthen competition in domestic financial markets without setting up new commercial banks or finance companies. The BIBF was granted privileges regarding the juristic income tax, the special business tax, and the interest income tax.

On the price front, the authority on June 1, 1989, removed interest rate ceilings on commercial banks' time deposits with maturities longer than one year. Interest rate ceilings on savings deposits (7.25 percent) and short-term time deposits (9.5 percent) were discontinued on January 8, 1992, and ceilings on loan rates (15 percent) were ended five months later. By June 1, 1992, all interest rate ceilings were abolished for commercial banks and finance companies as well as credit fonciers.

Differences in interest rates and the pace of economic growth, together with financial liberalization and the stable exchange rate of the baht, attracted a growing stream of net capital inflows to Thailand, from 2 to 6 percent of GDP in the 1980s to 9 to 12 percent in 1990–96. As the surge in FDI and equity investment was less dramatic, most of the inflows were in the form of loans. These vigorous foreign borrowings resulted in Thailand's swelling external debt outstanding, which more than tripled from U.S.$29 billion in 1990 to U.S.$94 billion in mid-1997. In relative terms, total foreign debt outstanding surged from 34 percent of GDP in 1990 to 59 percent in mid-1997. The majority of these inflows went to the private sector, as the Thai government had enjoyed nine consecutive years of surplus (1988–96) in its cash balance. That was why private external debts accounted for an increasing portion of the country's total debt outstanding, which rose from 61 percent in 1990 to 81 percent in 1996. Such predominance shortened the external debt profile (with short-term debts accounting for 50 percent in 1995 as opposed to 15 percent in 1987) because most credits to which private entities had access were of short-term maturity. The shortening of the country's external debt maturity profile raised the degree of volatility as well as vulnerability.

The volatility is unquestionable in the case of non-FDI capital flows, as demonstrated in table 4.7. During the 1990s, net inflows of FDI stayed within the range of 1.1 to 3.3 percent of GDP. Non-FDI net inflows, in contrast, moved from 12.6 percent of GDP in 1995 to −14.9 percent in 1997. In other words, almost all the volatility of private net capital inflows was for non-FDI reasons.

Capital influx and financial deregulation led to excessive spending or investment, credit extension, and declining asset quality. The economic bubble affected not only real estate but the automotive industry, private hospitals, steel bar manufacturing, and petrochemicals.

On the part of the private sector, the constantly increasing momentum (real economic growth of 12.2 percent per year in 1988–90 and 8.6 percent per year in 1991–95) easily tempted businessmen to invest heavily, especially when they had immediate access to cheap foreign funding under stable exchange rates. However, they tended to mismanage their financial positions by (1) relying too much on debt instead of equity financing; (2) engaging in maturity mismatching, which necessitated frequent debt rollovers, and (3) leaving their net foreign exchange positions unprotected. These financial weaknesses lowered financial institutions' asset quality to an alarming degree.

The situation was aggravated by the shortcomings of domestic banks and finance companies. In contrast to foreign banks, local units were frequently incompetent in evaluating credit applications and cash flow analyses. Instead, they often resorted to collateral or asset-based decision making. Local banks and finance companies hardly tapped long-term deposits while granting too many overdraft facilities for long-term fund uses. Such maturity mismatching entailed liquidity risks for both borrowers and lenders.

Interviews with foreign banks in Thailand, representing either bank branches or representative offices, revealed that credit extension was primarily based on corporate ratings, as indicated by data drawn from annual reports and financial status. Collateral did not receive much attention. Instead, these foreign banks placed their emphasis on exchange risks, especially after the baht was floated. Nonetheless, in credit extension foreign commercial banks had

TABLE 4.7. Thailand's Private Net Capital Inflows (percentage of GDP)

	1990	1991	1992	1993	1994	1995	1996	1997	1998
Total	13.3	9.0	9.7	7.6	9.0	14.0	7.8	11.7	9.8
Private net capital inflows									
FDI	2.6	1.9	1.9	1.2	1.1	1.4	1.2	3.2	3.3
Non-FDI	10.7	7.1	7.8	6.3	7.9	12.6	6.7	14.9	13.1

Source: Bank of Thailand.

neither industry nor currency limits. They were only subject to the country limits specified by their headquarters. Such country limits often varied, hinging upon country ratings and other factors deemed important by those banks.

Overall, the central authority was to bear the blame on three accounts: (1) for liberalizing the country's capital account without freeing up the baht exchange rate, (2) for prematurely liberalizing the practices of domestic financial institutions, and (3) for failing to prudently examine and supervise local financial institutions. Unsurprisingly, the period preceding the financial crisis saw a marked deterioration of both the micro- and macroscenarios.

On the micro side, the number of ailing commercial banks and finance companies troubled by doubtful assets and liquidity shortages grew at a shocking pace. What was more distressing was that the Bank of Thailand had to cope with these predicaments in the absence of a deposit insurance institute. The central bank thus had to rescue numerous unhealthy banks and finance companies, even though such assistance worsened the country's macroeconomic imbalances.

On the macro side, Thailand's current account deficit rose to 8 percent of GDP in 1995–96 as a result of an export downturn and superfluous spending largely funded by foreign capital. The government's efforts to restrain domestic credit extension proved fruitless, since the nonbank private sector resorted to foreign credits instead. In the meantime, the excess of Thai over U.S. inflation, spurred by external borrowing, increased markedly and was not rectified by any exchange rate move. In contrast, the baht was tightly pegged to the U.S. dollar, whose value climbed continually and considerably between mid-1995 and mid-1997. The rising value of the baht, together with growing excess inflation, dampened exports, which were already suffering a slump. Overall, the pegging exchange rate regime hurt the country's current account by encouraging more spending on imports via foreign borrowing and discouraging exports via prices.

It should be noted as well that the policy measures implemented by the Thai government were too little too late. In 1995, the authority tightened regulations on foreign borrowing, for example, by raising the minimum amount for BIBF inflows, and imposing a 7 percent reserve requirement on short-term external debts. By 1996 and the first half of 1997, investor confidence deteriorated to a large degree due to threatening current account deficits, the appreciating value of the dollar and the baht, ailing banks and finance companies, and growing excess inflation (table 4.8). The anticipated baht devaluation triggered a flood of capital outflows to liquidate short-term foreign debts or speculate against the baht. Such huge outflows resulted in a plunge of the central bank's foreign exchange reserves, which made floating the baht unavoidable on July 2, 1997, the onset of the Asian financial crisis.

After the baht's exchange rate was floated, the currency nosedived from 26 baht per U.S. dollar in June 1997 to 47 baht in December 1997 and 56 in January 1998. But it stabilized at 36 to 37 baht toward the end of 1998.

Capital flows thus far had exerted more pressure on exchange rates than did their current account counterparts. The principal reason was that capital flows included not only trade financing but capital and speculative investment.

What made capital flows volatile and therefore formidable was that they hinged upon numerous factors as well as a subjective degree of confidence. For instance, according to one recent survey the following seven factors, which are hardly steady according to several interpretations, strongly affect investor confidence.

- Political stability
- Competence of the economic management team
- External accounts, including the trade balance, current account, and balance of payments
- Efficiency and stability in the financial system
- Foreign exchange reserves
- The asset quality of financial institutions
- Policy inconsistency or rigidity

TABLE 4.8. Thailand's Current Account Balance and Domestic Inflation

	Current Account Balance (% of GDP)	Thai-U.S. Inflation Differential (%)
1982	−3.2	−1.0
1983	−7.8	0.6
1984	−5.1	−3.4
1985	−4.1	−1.2
1986	0.6	0.0
1987	−0.8	−1.2
1988	−2.6	−0.3
1989	−3.5	0.6
1990	−8.5	0.6
1991	−7.7	1.5
1992	−5.7	1.0
1993	−5.1	0.3
1994	−5.6	2.5
1995	−8.1	3.0
1996	−8.0	3.0

Source: Bank of Thailand.

2.3. ECONOMETRIC INVESTIGATION

While there are several forms of capital inflows (e.g., foreign direct investment, portfolio investment, loans, and nonresident baht accounts), various other factors affect these inflows as well (e.g., economic growth potential, stock market returns, interest rate differentials, exchange rate volatility, and macroeconomic stability). These factors influence capital inflows either directly (e.g., via interest rates on loans) or indirectly (e.g., by affecting investor confidence in the recipient economy). Although there are numerous theoretical assertions about how each factor affects each type of capital inflow, little empirical work has been done. This investigation thus has two objectives: (1) to statistically test the influences of each factor on different kinds of capital inflows, and (2) to pinpoint the different degrees of those influences.

The degree of influence is measured by standardized coefficients obtained from ordinary least squares (OLS) estimated equations that link each type of capital inflow to possibly pertinent explanatory variables. The estimation utilizes monthly data from January 1988 to June 1998. The tested explanatory variables are as follows.

- Interest rate differentials
- Returns from the Stock Exchange of Thailand
- Volatility of baht exchange rates versus the U.S. dollar, yen, and the Singapore dollar
- Forward cover or swap premium
- Indicators of macroeconomic stability such as current account deficits, inflation differentials, and the foreign exchange reserves/imports ratio
- Indicators of economic activities such as the private sector's electricity consumption and the manufacturing production index

Some dummies were also included to reflect the crucial impact of economic or political changes, for example, government turnover, shifts in the exchange rate system, and variations in the country's credibility as evaluated by credit rating agencies. Results of this econometric investigation, as shown in tables 4.9 through 4.12, are close to expectations for each type of capital inflow. Meanwhile, the following points deserve some attention.

Foreign Direct Investment

In table 4.9, export performance is the most significant explanatory variable, demonstrating the long-term relationship and the Board of Investment's role. The current account deficit, the second in rank, is probably there because it correlates with foreign investors' confidence. As for the exchange rates, volatility of baht per yen has a stronger impact than those versus other currencies. This could be partly due to the fact that Japan accounted for 38 percent of all foreign direct investment, more than other countries.

Portfolio Investment

In table 4.10, fundamental economic factors (e.g., the manufacturing production index and the stock exchange index) are equally important to technical factors (e.g., baht per U.S. dollar volatility, forward cover, and interest rate differentials). In contrast, the adequacy of foreign exchange reserves (in terms of import expenses) is not very meaningful to foreigners in the stock market as well as not meaningful for direct investment.

Loans

In table 4.11, interest rate differentials and exchange risks are primary determinants of loan inflows. But it is notable that the latter command more weight than the former. In other words, in negotiating cross-border credits lenders and borrowers paid more attention to exchange rate stability than to

TABLE 4.9. Foreign Direct Investment Inflows

Variables (in order of significance)	Standardized Coefficients	*t*-Statistics
Export performance[a]	0.308**	6.094
Current account deficit	−0.158**	−3.968
Growth performance[b]	0.041*	1.895
Baht per yen volatility	−0.035*	−1.551

Note: R^2 adjusted = 0.962; D. W. = 2.23.
[a]Export value is used as a proxy for the export performance.
[b]Due to lack of monthly data, the private sector use of electricity is used as a proxy for growth performance.
*Significant at 10% level; ** significant at 5% level.

TABLE 4.10. Portfolio Investment Inflows

Variables (in order of significance)	Standardized Coefficients	*t*-Statistics
Growth performance[a]	0.267**	4.203
Baht per dollar volatility	−0.245**	−2.750
Stock market performance[b]	0.244**	5.545
Swap rate	−0.236**	−2.399
Interest rate differential	0.224**	2.311

Note: R^2 adjusted = 0.842; D. W. = 2.11.
[a]Due to lack of monthly data, manufacturing index is used as a proxy for growth performance.
[b]Stock Exchange of Thailand index is used as a proxy for the stock market performance.
**Significant at 5% level.

differences in interest rates. This outcome is consistent with the actual situation in 1997–98. During this period, exorbitant interest rates of the baht could not attract much capital inflow because the baht value was under heavy pressure. And when the baht regained its stability, even though Thai interest rates were less than half, there were more capital inflows than during the crisis.

Nonresident Baht Account

In table 4.12, it is not surprising that deposit rate differentials, the forward cover or swap rate, and the stock market index represent important determinants of whether foreign investors will shift their funds to Thailand or not. The following three points are noticeable.

- The foreign exchange reserves to imports ratio, which in a way signifies investor confidence as to how well the debtor country can satisfy its external debt obligations, receives the heaviest weight from foreign investors and more than that of interest rate differentials. This corresponds well with the fact that these nonresident baht deposits (the amounts of which exceeded those of other types of capital inflows) tended to have short maturities and easily fluctuated depending on whether there was any news affecting investor confidence.

TABLE 4.11. Loan Inflows

Variables (in order of significance)	Standardized Coefficients	*t*-Statistics
Swap rate	−0.405**	−4.272
Interest rate differential	0.302**	2.514
Baht per dollar volatility	−0.173**	−1.933
Reserves to imports ratio	0.148*	1.701

Note: R^2 adjusted = 0.764; D. W. = 1.96.
*Significant at 10% level; ** significant at 5% level.

TABLE 4.12. Nonresident Baht Account Inflows

Variables (in order of significance)	Standardized Coefficients	*t*-Statistics
Reserves to imports	0.124**	2.075
Deposit rate differential	0.112**	3.028
Swap rate	−0.084*	−1.777
Stock market performance	0.071*	1.804
Baht to Singapore dollar volatility	−0.061*	−1.623

Notes: R^2 adjusted = 0.922; D. W. = 2.23.
*Significant at 10% level; ** significant at 5% level.

- Interest rate differentials are more important than the stock market index.
- The deposit rate differential that is statistically significant is the one between the baht and the Singapore dollar, not the U.S. dollar or yen. Furthermore, the baht volatility that is statistically important is the baht versus the Singapore dollar, not the U.S. dollar or yen. This corresponds well with the fact that most (roughly 60 percent) of all nonresident baht deposits came from Singapore.

Foreign investors' confidence represents a crucial determinant of capital inflows to Thailand. This is immediately evident from the weight of the current account deficit in the case of foreign direct investment (table 4.9), growth performance in the case of portfolio investment (table 4.10), the reserves to imports ratio in both cases of loans (table 4.11), and the nonresident baht account (table 4.12).

Differences between inflation in Thailand and inflation abroad are not statistically significant. This may be because in the past Thailand had been successful in maintaining price stability most of the time and so this factor hardly affected foreign investors' confidence.

3. IMPACT ON THE ECONOMY

Section 2 examined the influence of the economy on the volume of capital flows. It remains to trace the impact of capital flows on the economy. In doing so, it is convenient to split the discussion into pre- and postcrisis periods, as the economic mechanisms whereby the flows are translated into economic consequences are different.

3.1. PRECRISIS

The volume of capital inflows during the precrisis period had an enormous impact on the macroeconomy. The most obvious consequence was excess aggregate demand. Within the tradable sector, this excess demand found an outlet in an expansion of the current account deficit, which grew continuously until it reached 8 percent of GDP in 1996 on the eve of the crisis. Among the nontradable goods, the excess demand led to a rapid increase in their prices relative to the prices of tradable goods or a decline in the real exchange rate. Figures 4.2 and 4.3 show these impacts.

It has been claimed that in Asia most of the capital inflows went into investment rather than consumption. This is not quite accurate, at least as far

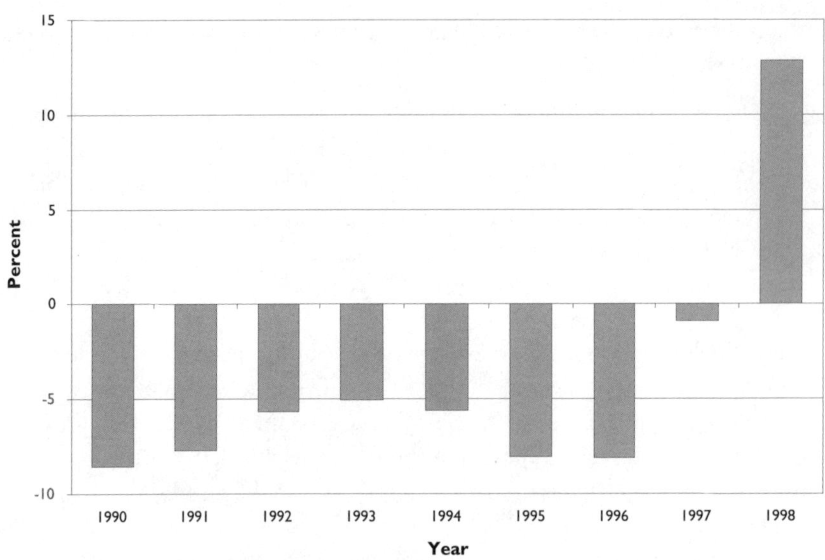

Fig. 4.2. Thailand's current account. (Data from Central Bank of Thailand.)

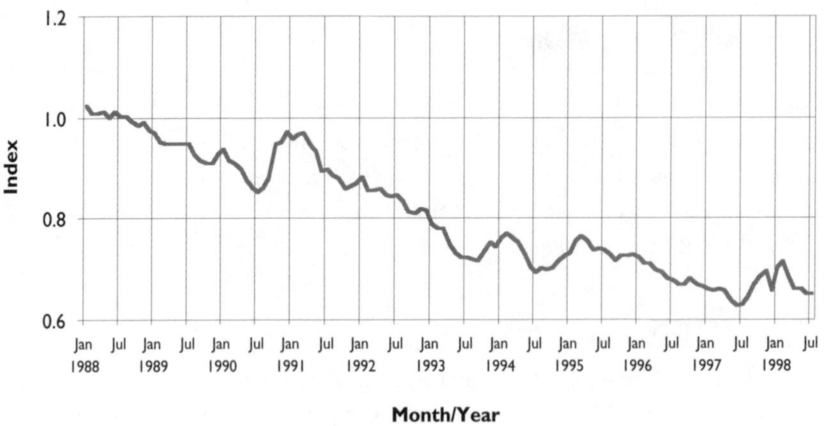

Fig. 4.3. Relative prices of tradable to nontradable goods. (Data from Department of Business Economic.)

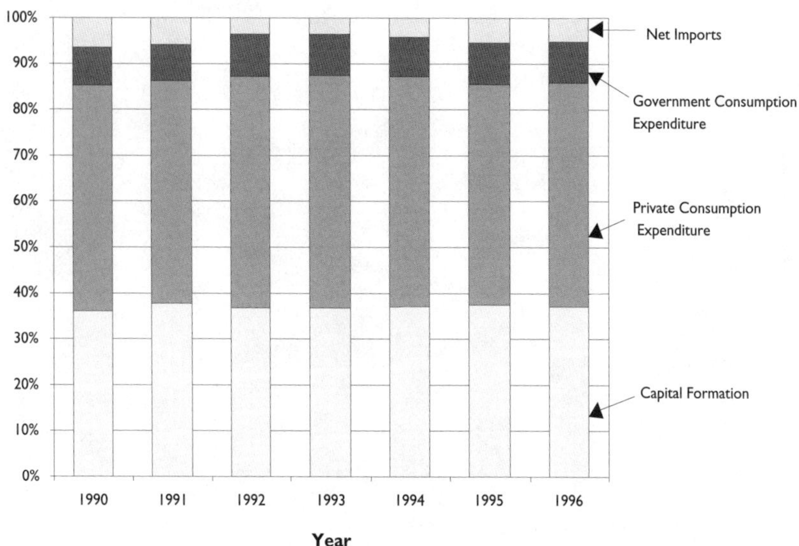

Fig. 4.4. Components of expenditure on GDP, 1990–96. (Data from the National Economic and Social Development Board.)

as Thailand is concerned. While it is true that the share of investment in national expenditure was very high, around 40 percent, this high share preceded the large influx of capital and remained remarkably unaffected by capital inflows (see fig. 4.4).

The high saving rate that accompanied the high investment rate, amid a relatively undeveloped long-term and equity market, implies that banks and finance companies played major intermediary roles. (Finance companies in Thailand are deposit-taking institutions that function almost like banks). After 1993, a rising portion of the capital inflows documented in section 1 of this chapter went to the BIBF; local financial institutions were major players. It is therefore essential to give a brief description of these institutions.

Thai banks and finance companies had long played a very important role in channeling savings to investment. Like financial institutions everywhere, they were subject to stringent regulations, and before 1990 interest rate floors and ceilings were set by the authorities. Their lending portfolios were only lightly controlled by the central bank (compared to controls in countries like Korea or India). The only explicit credit rule stipulated by the Bank of Thailand was that a certain proportion (between 14 and 20 percent) of commercial banks' lending had to be allocated to rural areas. Occasionally, there were instructions from the central bank varying the amounts of these required rural credits. These regulations and controls were gradually lifted in the early 1990s.

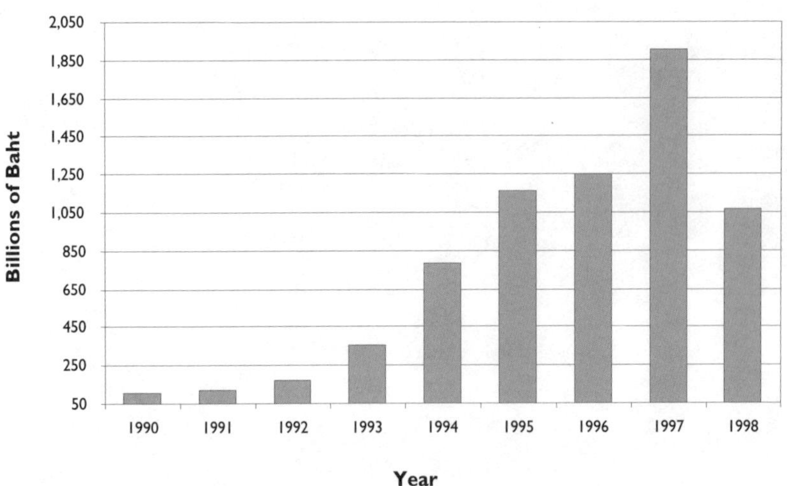

Fig. 4.5. Gross foreign liabilities of the central bank and commercial banks in Thailand. (Data from Bank of Thailand.)

Prior to August 1997, Thailand did not have an explicit deposit insurance system, although on occasion the government had to bail out both banks and finance companies. When these bailouts became necessary, for example, during the early 1980s, depositors received refunds but not immediately and not with interest. In the 1990s, when a bailout became unavoidable again, the government was kind enough to provide interest payments. In August 1997, to head off a bank run, the government enacted an explicit guarantee to all depositors and local as well as foreign creditors.

As exchange controls began to be dismantled along with domestic financial liberalization, commercial banks and finance companies tapped funds from foreign sources for their operations to a greater extent. This reliance on foreign resources can be seen in figure 4.5, which shows the *gross* foreign liabilities of the banks. These inflows made the banking system increasingly vulnerable.

This ratio steadily declined and finally moved into negative territory. The decline was mainly caused by the increase in commercial banks' foreign liabilities. Another index of vulnerability is the short-term portion of external debt outstanding, since the larger ratio means more rollovers will be required. In Thailand, this ratio surged from 22 percent in 1988 to 50 percent in 1995–96 (see fig. 4.6).

The central bank did try to limit the foreign exchange exposure of financial institutions by limiting their *net* foreign exchange open position to 15 to 20 percent of their capital funds. But the financial institutions were not effectively constrained by this regulation, as they could lend to their domestic

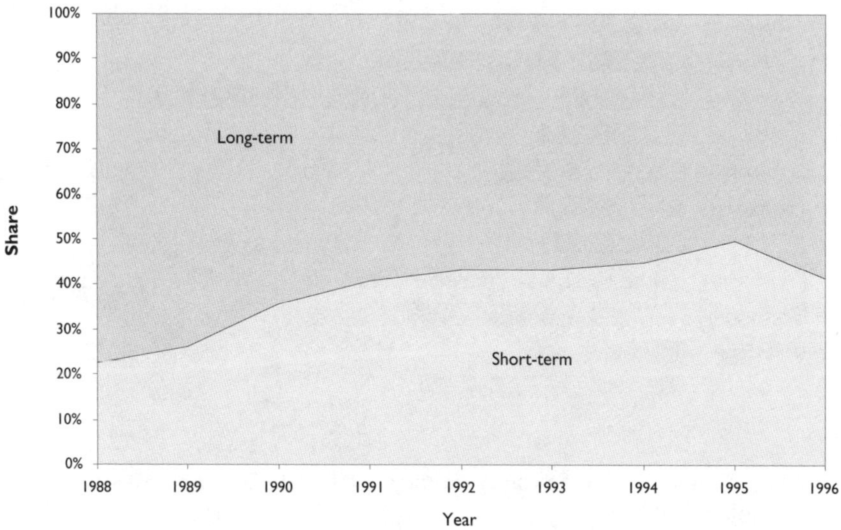

Fig. 4.6. Total external debt outstanding. (Data from Bank of Thailand.)

customers in dollars. While the financial institutions were seemingly insulated from exchange risks, their customers were not (very few final borrowers covered their dollar liabilities). What the regulation did, in effect, was convert exchange risks into credit risks.

This credit risk was quite high since Thai corporations were highly leveraged for five explicit reasons. First, from 1990 onward the Thai central bank liberalized exchange controls to a large extent, especially after 1993 when the BIBF was established as a means of promoting Thailand as a regional financial center. Second, foreign interest rates exceeded local rates on some occasions. Third, the exchange rate was kept at around 25 baht per U.S. dollar with very low volatility. Fourth, debt, instead of equity, financing helped preserve ownership among large Thai families. This particular feature fitted very well with the Asian culture. Finally, according to the revenue code, payments resulting from debt financing (i.e., interest payments) are tax deductible, whereas those that stem from equity financing (i.e., dividend payments) are not. Figures 4.7 and 4.8 demonstrate that Thailand's debt/equity ratio was not only high relative to those in other countries but also rising to some extent.

Problems also occurred on the lender side, as foreign money was mostly committed on a short-term basis while the money involved was used by the banks and end users to finance long-term investments (e.g., in the real estate sector). This maturity mismatching became a major problem both before and after the crisis.

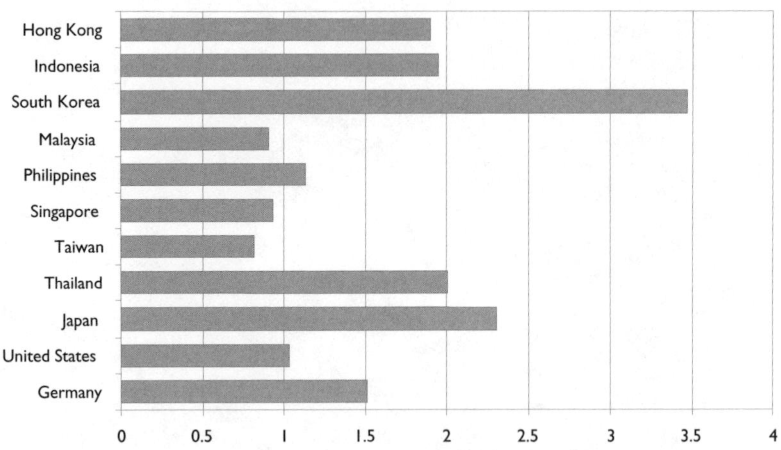

Fig. 4.7. Ratio of debt to equity (average, 1988–96). (Data from Claessens, Djankov, and Lang.)

3.2. THE RUN-UP TO THE CRISIS

Beginning in 1996, signs emerged that the Thai economy was heading toward a crisis. In fact, the real estate sector had been in trouble since 1994. The main turning point came with news release of a dramatically falling export growth rate, which dropped from double-digit levels to zero in one year. By September, overexposure and problem loans in the real estate sector led Moody's to reduce its rating of the country.

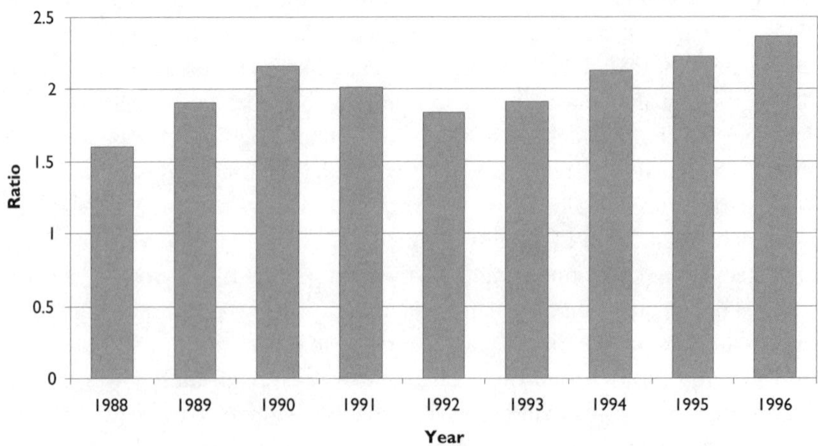

Fig. 4.8. Debt to equity ratio of the listed nonfinancial corporations in Thailand (1988–96). (Data from Claessens, Djankov, and Lang.)

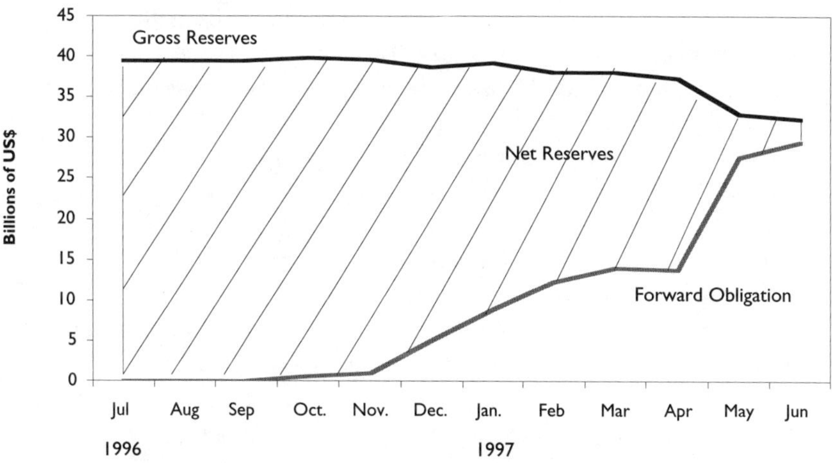

Fig. 4.9. Thailand's net international reserves. (Data from Bank of Thailand.)

Nonetheless, funds were still flowing in throughout 1996 and the first quarter of 1997. The global financial markets chose to respond to predicaments in Thailand by attacking at perhaps the country's most vulnerable point, namely, its exchange rate. Speculative strikes were launched, allegedly by hedge funds, first in November 1996 and then in February 1997. These were followed by a truly massive attack in May 1997.

The central bank chose to counter these attacks by engaging in swapping operations. Instead of selling its dollar reserves on the spot market alone to support the baht, which would over time lead to a rise in interest rates, it simultaneously sold baht for dollars on the spot market and covered this with a reverse trade in the future. The effect of this was basically the same as if it had sterilized the support operations. However, in selling baht on the spot market it handed the currency to foreigners, who could use it to attack the baht again and again. This operation was halted on May 15, 1997, when, after the latest and most severe attack, the Bank of Thailand told Thai banks to cease lending baht funds to foreigners and to try to close down the offshore baht market. This measure effectively stopped the speculators, and indeed imposed severe losses on them, but it was too late because by then the net reserves of the central bank had dwindled to near zero (see fig. 4.9). Six weeks later, on July 2, 1997, the baht was floated.

The reluctance of the central bank to engage in a conventional defense of the baht by selling dollars on the spot market can be partly explained by the weakness of local financial institutions, particularly finance companies. By the beginning of 1997, the real estate sector was truly sick and threatening to pull down many of these institutions. The central bank was forced to provide liquidity to them. In the first quarter of 1997, the central bank began to exert pressure on them to increase capital. When sixteen finance companies were unable to comply, it suspended their operations, thereby triggering a bank run.

The problems with finance companies may appear to be independent of the speculative attacks in the currency markets. But in fact they occurred simultaneously and, as we believe, were closely related. As stated earlier, although there is no guarantee for depositors at the banks and finance companies, political considerations suggest that the government could not stand idly by and let them go bankrupt. The government would then have been liable for a sum that turned out to be very large, negating years of fiscal prudence before 1997. It is this consideration that added fuel to the speculative fire, engulfing the baht.

3.3. THE CRISIS AND ITS AFTERMATH

As noted earlier, capital continued to flow into Thailand until the third quarter of 1997. The speculative attacks on the baht did not appear in any of the numbers we presented in section 1, for they were entirely central bank operations disguised as off-balance-sheet items. The important point is that, although confidence was low, this did not lead to a mass exodus of credit—until July 2.

Once that happened, the outflow was massive, as were the effects on the economy. The situation was aggravated when the contagion spread to other Asian countries, and the effects rebounded back to Thailand. A good measure of the results of the panic is the exchange rate (see fig. 4.10). It was only after May 1998 that the baht stabilized at a level that placed the price of a dollar about 50 percent above the level that prevailed before July 2, 1997. This was the largest currency depreciation Thailand experienced in the last four decades. In addition, the wide fluctuations in exchange rates considerably weakened market confidence and capital continued to flow out of the country, thus debilitating prospects for growth. In its earlier stages, the currency depreciation was accompanied by a very sharp increase in interest rates (see fig. 4.10).

The depreciation of the baht had rather anomalous results. There was, first of all, little increase in exports. While growth in exports to the U.S. and European markets was high, this was offset by declines in exports to Asian markets, which constituted half of Thailand's export markets. Second, the inflation rate was relatively low considering the size of the depreciation. The

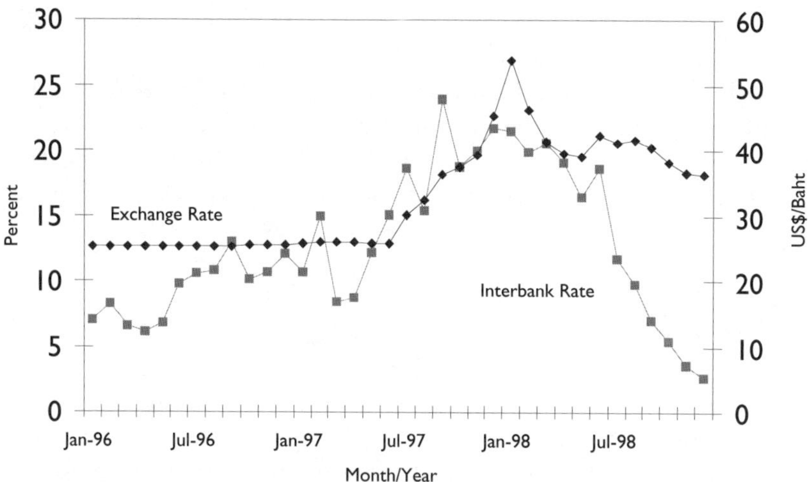

Fig. 4.10. Exchange rate and interest rate movements. (Data from Bank of Thailand.)

consumer price index rose by about 10 percent in the first year after the devaluation and remained flat thereafter.

Sluggish exports together with a sharp drop in investment occasioned by the exodus of capital led to a severe contraction of the economy. Preliminary estimates indicated that in 1998 the gross national product (GNP) fell 8.5 percent below that of 1997. The number of unemployed in February 1998 was 1.1 million more than a year before, and the number of underemployed (those working less than 20 hours a week) was another 0.8 million, out of a total labor force of 30 million. In the beginning, the situation was not helped by the insistence of the International Monetary Fund that the Thai government run a budget surplus of 1 percent. Later, in February 1998, this policy was modified to permit a deficit of 3 percent. In its later explanation, the IMF claimed that the earlier deflationary policy was dictated by its fear of inflation, which could have arisen as a result of an export boom, and that misestimation of export growth was in turn due to its failure to predict the contagion effect.

The combination of a depreciated currency, high interest rates, and declining GNP played havoc with corporate balance sheets. Many companies became insolvent, and more were unable to service their loans. The knock-on effects on the finance sector were enormous. As early as August 1997, an additional 42 finance companies were suspended. With the sixteen suspended in May 1997, this brought the total to 58. Of these, all but two were permanently closed. Later half a dozen more finance companies were taken over by the government, as were four banks.

All these adverse effects on the economy lessened confidence further and induced a greater exodus of capital, the opposite of the boom times, when the strong showing of the economy encouraged inflows. This reinforcing feedback mechanism makes reliance on foreign capital flows a dangerous policy option.

4. LESSONS LEARNED

The story just outlined offers a number of lessons to Thailand and, we believe, for other countries that are entering or are in the same stage of development as Thailand in the 1990s. We divide our account of the lessons learned into two parts. The first is determining which set of policies to adopt during "normal" times in order to prevent a crisis. The second deals with policies to be adopted when, unfortunately, a country cannot avoid a crisis.

First, we would like to repeat what has now become a cliché but nevertheless needs reiteration: a fixed exchange rate regime, an open capital account, and an independent monetary policy are mutually incompatible. The real question is which of these three, or which combination of them, to give up. Clearly, each country has its own political economy, which makes the choice unique. To give up only the independent monetary policy, while retaining the other two, implies that the country must have a currency board, an option that is not viable for most countries. Such a choice would tie the economy unnecessarily to the ups and downs of another country, such as the United States, to which the home currency is tied.

Of the remaining two options, many countries would like to retain a fixed exchange rate regime, as that has many desirable features for agents in the economy. Most businessmen, when asked, will vote overwhelmingly for a fixed exchange rate regime. However, whether that is the best option for the country as a whole is another matter. In the specific case of Thailand, a further point must be borne in mind. As the peg does require adjustment from time to time, it requires the willingness and ability to do so with precise timing. Experience has shown that the Thai authorities were invariably reluctant to adjust the peg, postponing the action until the last minute, as was the case in 1997, when the adjustment costs were very great.

Is an open capital account equally desirable? The one clearly desirable feature for any developing country is to be open to foreign direct investment, as that brings in foreign technology and know-how. Besides, the flows of foreign direct investment are far less volatile than other items in the capital account.

For these other items, events in Thailand and elsewhere in Asia have shown that, on a net basis, there is little to be gained from having an open capital account. The flows were very volatile and were dependent on many considerations other than relative rates of return, such as political stability, manias, and panics in other countries.

In particular, when a country rushes into liberalization of the currency and capital markets without sufficient preparatory steps, then to have an open capital account can be very dangerous. For a country to benefit from the world capital market, it must have in place a balanced and sophisticated capital market of its own. Most Asian countries, and Thailand in particular, were overly dependent on banks and finance companies to intermediate funds between savers and spenders. True, the equity market was being developed, but it never adequately complemented the bank-based system. Indeed, it is arguable that the appearance of an equity market undermined the control that traditional "mainline" banks exerted over companies. The crisis has also shown that the legal structure that underlay these markets was severely underdeveloped. That foreign bankers and investors, who should have known better, discovered these weaknesses along with the rest of us is a telling indictment of the workings of the international capital markets.

The opening of the capital markets also undermined Thailand's banking and financial system. This is because, having liberalized rapidly, the central bank did not sufficiently revise its supervisory roles to match the increasing riskiness that such a system entailed. This was a major policy mistake underlying the Thai crisis.

Note that the arguments against an open capital account still remain even if the exchange rate is allowed to float, for in that case the volatility of the flows would translate itself into the volatility of the exchange rate. It can be argued that the flexibility of the exchange rate will lessen the volatility of the flows (Krugman 1979), but since capital flows depend on so many other extraneous factors as well we do not believe that the reduction of capital flow volatility as a result of exchange rate flexibility will be substantial.

If capital flows ought to be controlled, what instruments should be deployed to achieve the best results? The most market friendly instrument, which even the IMF seems to have found acceptable, is to levy a tax or a tax equivalent on capital inflows. Chile, for example, used to require foreigners bringing in foreign funds to deposit a certain proportion, interest free, with the central bank. This amount can vary to allow the central bank to control the volume of capital inflows.

A second instrument that could be deployed is to prevent foreigners from acquiring large quantities of the home currency. This instrument was used by the Bank of Thailand when the baht was under attack in May 1997 (though it has since been withdrawn, apparently at the urging of the IMF) and also by the Malaysian central bank in September 1998. Indeed, Singapore has employed this measure for a long time.

Discussion of this last instrument and its timing brings us to the instruments that could be deployed once a crisis has occurred. Preventing foreigners from acquiring the home currency has been noted. The Malaysians have actually prevented foreign portfolio investors from repatriating their capital for a year (although that measure was partially rescinded before the year was out). The introduction of this measure was widely criticized in the international capital markets, for it did look very much like a debt moratorium, although it is interesting to note how quickly the Malaysians have been "forgiven" for their trespass in the international markets.

We would like to venture a proposal that developing countries should hold a Malaysia-like set of measures always in reserve and announce that they could use them in the future if there is a pressing circumstance such as a mass exodus (or influx) of capital. This would of course raise the required yield on capital flowing in from outside and would be a taxlike measure that would "add the grain of sand to the machinery of international capital flow."

NOTES

1. Board of Investment 1997, 6.
2. Nishiyama, Kushima, and Noda (1999), 31.

REFERENCES

Bank of Thailand. 1996. "Analysing Thailand's short-term debt," *Bank of Thailand Economic Focus,* July–September: 8.

Board of Investment. 1997. *Foreign direct investment in Thailand* 6. Bangkok.

Krugman, Paul. 1979. "A model of balance-of-payments crises." *Journal of Money, Credit, and Banking* 11, no. 3 (August): 311–25.

Nishiyama, Y. T. Kushima, and M. Noda. 1999. "EXIM Japan 1998 Survey: The Outlook of Japanese Foreign Direct Investment (FDI)—Asian Crisis and Prospects of Foreign Direct Investment by Japanese Manufacturers." *EXIM Review* 19, no. 1.

CHAPTER 5

Capital Flows into and from Malaysia

Jomo K. S.

Together with several other economies in Southeast Asia, led by Thailand, Malaysia experienced a currency crisis in mid-1997, which in turn precipitated a financial crisis and eventually led to a severe recession in 1998, after almost a decade of rapid economic growth and industrialization. There have been many competing explanations for these unprecedented crises. Many popular accounts, especially in the Western-dominated international media, have portrayed the crisis as primarily one of crony capitalism (e.g., Jomo 1999). Others have focused on the vulnerability of the national financial systems in the region that resulted from growing international financial liberalization (e.g., Jomo 1998a, 1998b). Many observers have also highlighted the large current account deficits in Thailand and Malaysia during most of the early and mid-1990s. Such deficits were largely financed by their net capital account surpluses during this period.

It is worthwhile to emphasize at the outset that Malaysia's experience differs from those of other East Asian economies hit by crises in at least four respects. First, although prudential regulation had deteriorated with growing financial liberalization, especially since the mid-1980s, the situation in Malaysia was not as bad as elsewhere in the region. Second, although the Malaysian banking system had contributed to asset price inflation, and was thus severely affected by the crisis, Malaysian banks and corporations had far less access to international borrowing than their counterparts in other crisis-affected economies. Unlike the others, foreign bank loans did not figure as significantly in the story of the Malaysian crisis, whereas capital market flows, especially into and out of the stock market, figured more prominently. Third, as a consequence of its reduced exposure to private bank borrowing from abroad, Malaysia did not have to go cap in hand to the International Monetary Fund (IMF) or others for emergency international credit assistance. Fourth, during most of the second half of 1997, and again beginning in mid-1998, the Malaysian authorities deliberately pursued unconventional measures in response to the deteriorating situation, with rather mixed results.

Hence, while there are important parallels between the Malaysian experience and those of its crisis-affected neighbors, there are also important differences. It is tempting to exaggerate the significance of either similarities or contrasts to support particular preconceived arguments when in fact the nature of their experiences does not allow strong analytical or policy conclusions to be drawn. For example, whereas South Korea, Thailand, and Indonesia experienced positive growth in the first quarter of 1999, the Malaysian economic recovery only began in the second quarter. Critics have been quick to blame Malaysia's unorthodox measures for its later recovery. Conversely, the Malaysian regime has been equally quick to claim success for its approach on the basis of limited evidence of a stronger recovery since then, which critics have just as readily attributed to a technical rebound, the externally induced electronics boom, and "unsustainable" government measures. Hence, it is also important to bear other aspects of the debate on the Malaysian crisis in mind as this chapter focuses on capital flows into and out of the Malaysian economy.

1. FOREIGN CAPITAL INFLOWS

According to orthodox economic theory, foreign capital inflows (FCI) contribute to economic growth by raising investment levels, usually by simultaneously closing the classical two (foreign exchange and savings-investment) gaps. While Rosenstein-Rodan (1961) and Chenery and Strout (1966) have argued that foreign capital inflows contribute to economic growth, Griffin and Enos (1970) and Weisskoff (1972) have dissented. The former regard foreign capital inflows as supplementary to domestic savings, while the latter claim that foreign capital inflows replace domestic savings and thus do not necessarily enhance growth and development since foreign capital inflows may also adversely affect the domestic savings rate. Foreign capital inflows would also increase investment payments abroad—which would detract from their positive contributions.

Empirical assessment of the role of foreign capital inflows in Malaysian economic development between 1966 and 1996 has sought to evaluate their impact on output growth (Wong with Jomo 1999). The analysis considers both the direct and indirect effects of foreign capital inflows discussed in the conventional as well as the critical economic literature, paying particular attention to foreign capital inflows' impact on investments and savings. The composition and magnitude of foreign capital inflows in Malaysia have undergone various shifts over the last three decades. Foreign direct investment (FDI) has been important since the 1960s. The official development assistance of the 1960s grew in the 1970s and early 1980s. Portfolio investments and private borrowings from abroad grew rapidly in the early and mid-1990s.

Much of the early FDI in Malaysia was attracted by the various incentives offered to promote import-substituting industrialization in the late 1950s and export-oriented manufacturing in the late 1960s. A sizable portion of the funds for the large public expenditures of the 1970s through the mid-1980s was obtained through foreign borrowings. Hence, public foreign debt increased from the 1970s until the mid-1980s, ballooning when the ringgit depreciated against the Japanese yen during the mid-1980s (Jomo 1990). While government foreign debt has declined since the late 1980s, private debt has grown, especially in the 1990s, though the central bank has continued to limit corporate borrowing from abroad. The growing share of private—as opposed to public—debt has also resulted in a higher proportion of short-term debt from commercial sources. This trend must have contributed to the rising proportion of short-term inflows—relative to medium- and long-term capital inflows—in the 1990s. Unlike other East Asian economies, which experienced tremendous inflows of short-term bank borrowings, however, the main reason for the more volatile nature of foreign capital inflows in Malaysia in the last decade was the growing share of (easily reversible) foreign portfolio investments.

Analysis by Wong and Jomo (1999) of the impact of long-term foreign capital inflows into Malaysia over three decades from 1966 to 1996 found the following.

- Foreign capital inflows have augmented domestic savings for investment, and have generally served as a supplement to, and not substitute for, domestic savings.
- Foreign capital inflows seem to have adversely affected the domestic savings rate, albeit only indirectly.
- Foreign capital inflows have augmented foreign exchange reserves, for example, by financing additional imports and encouraging current account deficits.
- Foreign capital inflows have adversely affected factor payment outflows, export and import propensities, and the terms of trade and capital flight, worsening the balance of payments.

While there are cumulative long-term effects of foreign capital inflows, in the short term the financial system has also become more vulnerable to volatility. The sudden massive outflow of funds that began in the latter part of 1997 shocked Malaysia's financial system. These outflows formed a vicious cycle with the depreciation of the Malaysian ringgit, as contagion from the Thai baht crisis spread to similarly vulnerable neighboring economies. Stock prices also plummeted with the collapse of investor confidence exacerbated by herd behavior and perceptions of inappropriate government policy responses. The combined effects of currency depreciation, asset price deflation, higher interest rates, economic recession, and loss of investor confidence saddled many Malaysian companies with heavy (mainly domestic) debt and collapsed asset values.

This chapter will attempt to develop a more detailed understanding of the pattern of foreign capital flows and their volatility. Particular attention will be given to the consequences of inflow surges and sudden massive outflows and the changing relationship between such capital flows and the rest of the Malaysian financial system and the real economy. Section 2 presents a brief historical overview of the Malaysian financial system to locate the significance of capital flows. Section 3 assesses the magnitude of foreign capital inflows into Malaysia. Section 4 analyzes the impact of the volatility of foreign capital inflows on the Malaysian economy. This section examines the changing nature and role of capital flows into and out of Malaysia, particularly with a view toward understanding and explaining the recent crisis. A longer view of such flows is taken in order to highlight how such flows have changed in character, magnitude, and significance in the 1990s, as well as to show how the sudden massive reversal of such flows contributed to the crisis after mid-1997. Section 5 looks at Malaysia's unique response to the crisis, that of introducing selective capital controls. Section 6 concludes the study.

2. MALAYSIA'S FINANCIAL SYSTEM

In the colonial era and soon after independence, the financial system in Malaysia had a limited role for the most part. Its main function was to facilitate trade by providing funds for the agency houses, which dominated the exports of the country's primary commodities (tin and rubber) as well as the imports of consumer and capital goods. Effective measures intended to develop the financial system were adopted after the founding of the Central Bank of Malaya, which was renamed Bank Negara Malaysia (BNM) after the formation of Malaysia in September 1963. Since then, the financial system has been restructured, reorganized, and reshaped to meet the increasing and changing investment needs of the growing economy. It has certainly become much deeper, broader, and more diverse, with a host of institutional developments taking place over the decades. The turn of the 1960s also saw aggressive promotion and rapid growth of the capital market. In order to facilitate the mobilization of financial resources for technology development in the manufacturing sector, the government has adopted several measures in recent years to promote the venture capital industry.

2.1. THE BANKING SYSTEM

The government has adopted legislation to regulate the banking system, mainly to prevent banks, domestic or foreign owned, from overinvolvement in corporations. Under the Banking (Control of Acquisition and Holding of Shares) Regulations of 1968, a bank could only invest up to 10 percent of its paid-up capital and reserves (or 10 percent of the net working funds of a foreign bank) in trustee shares. A domestic bank was not permitted to hold shares of companies exceeding 25 percent of the bank's paid-up capital and reserves, while a foreign bank was not permitted to invest in such shares exceeding 25 percent of its net working funds (BNM 1989, 101). Since September 1989, however, the scope of permissible investments by commercial banks has been broadened.[1]

The 1965 establishment of Bank Bumiputra, the first state-owned commercial bank in Malaysia, marked the beginning of active direct government intervention in finance. The government became a major shareholder of Malayan Banking in 1969 after a run on the bank in 1966. By 1976, when the then United Malayan Banking Corporation (UMBC) came under government control, the government dominated the banking system, owning the three largest commercial banks in the country. These state-owned banks were used to facilitate implementation of the New Economic Policy (NEP), which was introduced in 1970, especially to achieve interethnic redistribution and other policy objectives.

The first half of the 1980s saw many abuses in lending operations by the directors and staff of banks and finance companies. Some major Bumiputera-controlled conglomerates emerged at that time,[2] usually under the patronage of powerful politicians, for example, with soft loans from state-owned banks and the award of major projects and lucrative licenses as well as other business opportunities, including privatization (Gomez 1994, 9). The ownership of financial institutions as well as some major corporations by the government and state-owned enterprises, and then the privatization of some of them, served to encourage such developments. Huge loans could be obtained without going through proper procedures and were often given for speculative "get rich quick" schemes rather than productive investments. As such, national developmentalist priorities such as industrial policy have been neglected. While entry and branching restrictions have long been imposed on foreign banks in Malaysia, special incentives have been provided to entice foreign banks to open up in Labuan, where the government set up an international offshore financial center (IOFC) on October 1, 1990. Various measures have been taken to make Labuan comparable to some of the "best" IOFCs around the world, enhancing the attractiveness of Malaysia as an investment center (see Awang 1997). To this end, a relatively liberal regulatory environment has been established on the island. Exchange rate control regulations pertaining to offshore business activities have been made very liberal, with preferential tax treatment for income, profits, dividends, and interest earned from offshore business activities.

In 1989, the Banking and Financial Institutions Act (BAFIA) was passed by Parliament, with vast implications for governance of the financial system. In the mid-1990s, well before the recent crisis, BNM began trying to consolidate Malaysian banks in anticipation of further financial liberalization. A new, two-tier regulatory system was introduced in December 1994. The new system sought to provide incentives for smaller banks to recapitalize and merge. Only larger, "tier-one" banks were allowed to handle the lucrative kinds of transactions denied to other banks, such as opening foreign currency accounts. To qualify for tier-one status, banks must have an equity base of at least RM500 million.

Hence, while "financial restraint" exists in Malaysia,[3] it has primarily sought to achieve interethnic redistribution by ensuring bank profitability, especially with increasing Bumiputera dominance of the Malaysian banking system dating from the 1970s. Banks in Malaysia have also been heavily used by the state to redistribute and accumulate wealth, ostensibly in line with the NEP. As Bumiputeras advanced their interests in the financial sector, rents were created by limiting competition in some areas, especially from foreign banks. However, this was not complemented with other policies to restrict wasteful competition in the banking sector that would erode these rents. For example, generous banking margins have fostered wasteful competition, with too many bank branches competing for limited business in particular areas, resulting in a socially wasteful duplication of services, which also undermines the likelihood of scale economies in the provision of banking services (Chin with Jomo 1996).

Some previous efforts to deregulate the Malaysian financial system encouraged the proliferation of unproductive investments, for example, in the property sector. Following the liberalization of interest rates in October 1978, there was a property boom, reflecting the banking sector's preference for making collateralized loans with high rates of return rather than productive long-term investments. While changes over time in each sector's share of total loans and advances by commercial banks have generally moved in line with changes in capital productivity (i.e., profitability) and share of gross domestic product (GDP) (Zainal et al. 1994, 307), the share of bank credit channeled to the property sector rose from 8.8 percent in 1966–70 to 33.5 percent in 1986–90 before declining slightly to 30.5 percent in 1992–96.

This huge increase in property-related lending contrasts with the relatively modest importance of building and construction in GDP and reflects the greater profitability of real estate investments due to rapid property price appreciation. Loans by the banking system for consumption credit also rose, together with loans for purchases of stocks and shares. Bank lending to the stock market only began in the late 1970s and averaged 3.8 percent during 1992–96. As a result, the share of bank credit to the manufacturing sector rose only modestly, while the proportion of lending to agriculture actually declined during this period, despite a sharp increase in the manufacturing sector's share of GDP and agriculture's continued growth, albeit more modestly.

Only about a quarter of Malaysian commercial bank lending went to manufacturing, agriculture, and other productive activities (see tables 5.1 and 5.2). This modest share for productive investments is likely to be even smaller for foreign borrowings, most of which have been collateralized with assets such as real property and stocks. The lack of incentives for Malaysian bankers to favor long-term lending for productive investments is one reason for the limited development of Malaysian manufacturing capabilities, especially in non-resource-based export-oriented industries, which are dominated by foreign investors instead. Export-oriented manufacturing only accounts for a very small percentage of total outstanding loans extended by commercial banks. With the exception of export credit and some relatively minor financial institutions, there is little evidence of financial policy serving as an important tool in industry promotion in Malaysia (Chin with Jomo 1996, Chin 2000).

Malaysian banks also tend to be conservative, mainly extending loans on the basis of collateral rather than project viability. Banking profitability and other considerations as well as regulations tend to encourage a "cautious and short-term view of investment, profitability and profit allocation and inhibit long-term or high-risk industrial investment" (Hing 1987, 422). Such emphasis on loan security has instead encouraged loans for the real property

TABLE 5.1. Malaysia: Distribution of Bank Credit for Selected Purposes, 1966–96 (percentage shares)

	Manufacturing	Property[a]	Shares	Agriculture
1966–70	2.6	8.8	−9.2	
1971–75	8.5	17.0	—	8.6
1976–80	18.8	22.5	1.8[b]	7.1
1981–85	21.1	32.0	1.8	6.5
1986–90	20.1	33.5	2.4	5.6
1991–96	22.6	30.5	3.8	2.9

Source: Bank Negara Malaysia (BNM) 1994, 506; BNM, *Quarterly Economic Bulletin;* BNM, *Annual Report,* various issues.

[a]Property includes loans for building, construction, real estate, and housing.

[b]1979–80.

TABLE 5.2. Malaysia: Commercial Bank Lending and Advances to Selected Sectors, 1960–96 (percentage shares)

Sector	1960	1965	1970	1975	1980	1985	1990	1991	1992	1993	1994	1995	1996
Manufacturing	10.4	15.3	19.8	19.6	22.3	17.5	23.2	23.8	23.4	22.5	23.0	23.3	21.0
Agriculture	7.2	8.5	10.2	7.5	7.9	6.0	5.2	4.5	4.3	3.4	2.5	2.1	2.0
Commerce	42.2	37.1	32.1	26.6	22.1	17.9	14.4	12.6	11.9	11.4	10.8	10.5	9.8
Property[a]	3.7	7.3	8.8	18.9	25.4	34.7	18.1	28.8	32.0	31.6	29.3	29.3	30.3

Source: 1960–85: Lee 1987, 312–3; 1990–96: Bank Negara Malaysia, *Annual Report,* various years.
[a]Comprises construction, real estate, and housing.

sector, share purchases, and consumption—rather than for production—especially when the property and stock markets have been bullish.[4]

As a consequence of the relative financial disintermediation, which happened in Malaysia due to the rapid growth of the stock market, especially in the early and mid-1990s, banks became less assured of easy and stable sources of income from large loans given to well-established corporations as more and more corporate borrowers resorted to tapping funds directly from the securities market. Due to the shrinking customer base in the lending business following growing competition from the securities market, banks have turned to servicing small and medium enterprises (SMEs) and households, which generally do not have direct access to the capital market. However, Malaysian banks' typical emphasis on loan security (rather than project viability) has discouraged loans, even to viable SMEs, due to lack of collateral.[5] They are more attracted to giving direct loans to consumption, especially with the steady increase in income due to rapid growth and rising household wealth, the result of the appreciation of property and stock market prices that began in the late 1980s.

2.2. STOCK MARKET DEVELOPMENT

The stock market in Malaysia is a more recently developed institution.[6] Although share trading began in the 1970s, involving British companies dealing in international trade, tin, and then rubber, public trading of stocks and shares only began after the Malayan Stock Exchange was established in May 1960. It was renamed the Stock Exchange of Malaysia in 1964, after the formation of Malaysia on September 14, 1963, and renamed again the Stock Exchange of Malaysia and Singapore after the separation of Singapore from Malaysia in 1965. It continued operating as a unified stock exchange with separate trading rooms in Kuala Lumpur and Singapore (Zeti 1989, 92), before splitting into two linked exchanges. The Kuala Lumpur Stock Exchange (KLSE) was formally unlinked from its Siamese twin, the Stock Exchange of Singapore (SES), in 1990, with double listing no longer allowed.[7] Since the independence of the KLSE, which coincided with efforts to promote newly emerging markets, the Malaysian stock market has experienced rapid expansion.

As noted by Singh (1995, 27), contemporary stock market development in many developing countries has not been a spontaneous response to market forces; governments have played a major role in the expansion of these markets. This is particularly true of Malaysia. For instance, government efforts to spur credit financing for pioneer companies, under supervision of the Capital Issues Committee (CIC), induced increased growth in new market issues beginning in 1968 (Zeti 1989, 97).[8] With the promulgation of the NEP in 1970, redistribution, especially along interethnic lines, became the most important government public policy priority. Since 1976, firms issuing shares to the public have had to offer 30 percent of their equity to Bumiputeras. Together with the Capital Issues Committee, the Foreign Investment Committee (FIC) has set the prices of shares issued by local (mainly ethnic-Chinese-owned) and foreign firms to Malay interests, including special government-financed trust agencies and investment funds for Bumiputeras. The prices were usually set below market prices to ensure positive returns for these special investment funds to accelerate capital accumulation and speed up acquisition of corporate assets on behalf of Bumiputeras.[9] Excessive underpricing of new issues has meant good prospects for capital gains from immediate resale on the market after successfully securing allocations of new public offerings. This resulted in considerable oversubscription for new issues, particularly in the case of new KLSE Second Board listings. Since such capital gains have long been tax exempt, there is an even greater incentive to subscribe for new shares (Ng 1989, 44).

The stock market has grown with considerable support from the government and those who have sought to use the stock market and publicly listed firms to capture various types of rents and to secure better access to relatively cheap funds through the securities markets or from financial institutions, which increasingly used stock market listings and performance as loan market signals (Chin with Jomo 2000). The political influence of many key players encouraged such developments. In August 1985, the finance minister allowed and even encouraged banks to give up to 100 percent loan support for share purchases, despite persistent warnings from Bank Negara Malaysia against giving out loans for share speculation (Khor 1987, 101). Thus, increased bank lending to purchase shares increased share trading and stock values. He also directed government-controlled investment institutions, such as the Employees Provident Fund, to invest in share market activities. The privatization of state-owned enterprises further contributed to stock market growth in the country. The substantial amount of funds raised by the capital market since

1990 can be partly attributed to the government's privatization program, which has undoubtedly deepened Malaysia's stock market considerably.

By 1993, however, the Malaysian stock market had gained an international reputation as a kind of casino, with active trading fueled by heady optimism, sudden interest from foreign institutional investors, and frenzies of speculation about corporate takeovers (*Asian Wall Street Journal,* March 26, 1996). The KLSE Composite Index (KLCI) almost doubled to an average of 1,275 points in 1993, before dropping 24 percent to an average of 971 points in the following year. Meanwhile, market capitalization as a proportion of GDP rose more than twofold from the previous year (1992), as the volume of traded shares jumped by more than 450 percent, and rose by more than 650 percent in terms of market value, to reach RM387 billion (see table 5.3).

Successful promotion of the stock market in the 1990s brought about significant financial disintermediation from the banking system to the securities markets, particularly in the bullish years of the early 1990s, though corporate savings continue to account for much of corporate financing. When the stock market was booming, Malaysia's banks lost much of their deposit base to the stock exchange, particularly during the bullish periods in 1993 and 1996. Higher returns on equities, with opportunities for making quick, tax-free capital gains, accounted for portfolio substitution. The Malaysian stock exchange's share of the total deposit base increased significantly from 48.8 percent in 1991 to 53.3 percent in 1992 before reaching almost 70 percent in 1993, while the commercial banks' share dropped from 23.1 percent in 1991 to 13.4 percent in 1993. Such disintermediation was reversed when the stock market turned bearish in 1994.

The Malaysian stock market increased in relative significance as a source of corporate finance, particularly at the expense of domestic and foreign bank loans, and emerged as a more important source of funds than the com-

TABLE 5.3. Kuala Lumpur Stock Exchange: Selected Indicators, 1990–96

	1990	1991	1992	1993	1994	1995	1996
Price indices							
Composite	506	556	644	1,275	971	995	1,238
EMAS	131	141	162	384	284	279	348
Second board	—	127	140	352	261	299	576
Total turnover							
Volume (billions of units)	13.1	12.4	19.3	107.8	60.2	40.0	66.5
Value (RM billions)	29.5	30.1	51.5	387.0	328.1	178.9	463.3
Market capitalization (RM billions)	132	161	246	620	504	566	807
Market liquidity							
Turnover value/market capitalization (%)	22.3	18.7	20.9	62.4	65.1	31.6	57.4

Source: Bank Negara Malaysia, *Annual Report,* various issues.

TABLE 5.4. Malaysia: Commercial Banks' and KLSE's Shares of Funds, 1990–94 (percentage shares)

	1990	1991	1992	1993	1994
Commercial bank deposits[a]	22.8	23.1	20.1	13.4	16.1
KLSE capitalization	48.2	48.8	53.3	69.4	62.1

Source: Adapted from *Banker's Journal Malaysia* 1995, 33.
Note: Allow for +/− 3 percent variation.
[a]Figures do not include negotiable certificates of deposit and repurchase agreements.

mercial banks in the early 1990s. Table 5.4 shows that the early 1990s saw some financial disintermediation, with commercial bank deposits' share of savings declining from 23 percent in 1990 to 16 percent in 1994, and the KLSE's share rising from 48 to 62 percent over the same period. Table 5.5 shows that the stock market became more important as a source of funds, while the share of bank loans as a proportion of total funds raised by the private sector declined correspondingly. Specifically, the share of equity market financing of total funds raised by the private sector rose significantly, from 9 percent during 1980–85 to 19 percent during 1990–96, while the bank loans' share dropped correspondingly from 67 to 51 percent. The additional funds raised through share issues since 1993 are reflected in increased stock market capitalization, especially in terms of share volume. Table 5.6 shows that many of the funds raised from the equity market in 1996 were derived from rights issues, which mobilized 43 percent of the total funds raised during 1993–97, while initial public offerings only accounted for 31 percent.

As table 5.7 shows, the growth of the Malaysian stock market was extraordinary by regional standards, with KLSE capitalization more than double annual gross national product (GNP) by 1996. While total capital inflows into Malaysia were not extraordinarily high, the composition of such inflows was

TABLE 5.5. Malaysia: Funds Raised by the Private Sector (percentage shares)

	1980–85	1990–96
Bank loans	67	51
Private debt securities	1	13
Equity	9	19
EPF[a]	—	3
Foreign borrowing	23	14

Source: Compiled from Bank Negara Malaysia, *Annual Report, 1997,* chart IX.2.

Notes: Excluding loans to individuals and CAGAMAS (National Mortgage Corporation) papers.

[a]Direct equity financing.

TABLE 5.6. **Kuala Lumpur Stock Exchange: New Share Issues, 1992–97 (RM millions, % of shares)**

	1992	%	1993	%	1994	%	1995	%	1996	%	1997	%
Initial public offers	5,415.8	59	912.7	26.6	2,972.9	35	4,175.0	36	4,099.2	26	4,781.0	26
Rights issues[a]	3,437.8	37	1,176.9	34.3	3,436.7	41	5,240.2	46	5,268.5	33	8,524.9	46
Special issues[b]	300.4	3.3	684.2	19.9	1,249.4	15	875.5	7.7	2,002.3	13	1,818.8	10
Private placements	27.5	0.3	658.8	19.2	798.9	9.4	1,146.9	10	4,554.4	29	3,233.6	18
Preference shares	—	—	—	—	—	—	—	—	—	—	—	—
Total	9,181.5	100	3,432.6	100	8,457.9	100	11,437.6	100	15,924.4	100	18,358.3	100

Source: Adapted from Bank Negara Malaysia, *Annual Report, 1997,* 249; *1998,* 290.

Note: Excluding funds raised by the exercise of employee share options schemes, transferable subscription rights, and warrants and irredeemable convertible unsecured loans stocks.

[a]Issues to Bumiputera investors and selected investors.

[b]Including restricted offer for sale.

TABLE 5.7. Southeast Asia: Comparative Precrisis Financial Development Indicators, 1996 (U.S.$bn and as percentage share of GDP)

	Credit[a]		Money[b]		Stocks[c]		Capital Inflows[d]	
	U.S.$bn	%	U.S.$bn	%	U.S.$bn	%	U.S.$bn	%
Indonesia	123.9	55.0	94.9	42.0	43.5	19.0	10.8	4.8
Philippines	40.5	49.0	36.1	43.0	31.3	38.0	7.7	9.3
Malaysia	92.2	93.5	67.1	68.0	223.5	227.0	9.5	9.6
Thailand	185.0	100.0	130.3	70.0	142.0	77.0	19.5	10.5

Source: IMF, *International Financial Statistics* (November 1998), except the Philippines, for which the preliminary figures are from the *Philippine Statistical Yearbook, 1997.* Stock market capitalization figures are obtained from Crosby Research figures as cited in *Euromoney* 1996, 84.

Note: Calculated according to the following exchange rates and GDP values.

	1996 GDP (billions, local currency)	*Exchange rate per U.S.$ (end 1996)*
Indonesia	532,631	2383
Philippines	2,171.9	26.288
Malaysia	249.503	2.529
Thailand	4,689.6	25.343

[a]Claims on private sector held by deposit money banks, end of 1996.
[b]Quasi money.
[c]Stock market capitalization, December 1995.
[d]Net inflows of capital: financial and capital account of the balance of payments, 1996.

quite different, with a much higher proportion going into the stock market rather than coming in as bank borrowings, as in Thailand and Indonesia.

But the Malaysian stock market boom in recent years may not really have mobilized funds for productive investment more effectively since more than half the total funds raised in the equity market through initial public offerings (IPOs) during 1990–96 went to privatized projects (BNM 1997, 149), implying that the stock market booms did not necessarily mobilize funds more effectively for new productive investments. Thus, with privatization "capital resources—which might otherwise have been invested into expanding productive capacity—have instead been diverted into acquiring or transferring existing public sector assets" (Jomo 1995, 51). Adam and Cavendish (1995, 37–39) suggest that such privatization issues may well have crowded out other private investment issues unless total foreign portfolio capital inflows were very high.

3. MAGNITUDE, VOLATILITY, AND THE IMPACT OF FOREIGN CAPITAL FLOWS

The Malaysian government has made efforts to attract foreign capital to supplement domestic savings since Malayan independence in 1957. From the late

1950s until the 1980s, this mainly consisted of foreign direct investment (usually in line with industrialization policy priorities) as well as foreign aid. Foreign investors dominated the new import-substituting industries for over a decade beginning in the late 1950s and non-resource-based export-oriented industries beginning in the 1970s. With rapid development, Malaysia's eligibility for foreign aid declined, but there was a spate of official borrowing—mainly from Japan—in the first half of the 1980s to finance the new heavy industries sponsored by the Mahathir government. Investments from Japan had become significant in the 1970s, and they accelerated, along with other investments from the first-tier East Asian newly industrializing economies, in the second half of the 1980s.

As with many other "newly emerging markets," foreign portfolio flows into Malaysia rapidly grew in significance only in the late 1980s. The separation of the Kuala Lumpur Stock Exchange from the Stock Exchange of Singapore at the turn of the decade gave an added boost to the Malaysian bourse. The Malaysian authorities opened the gates more widely to foreign capital in the 1990s. Like other emerging markets in the region, Malaysia experienced an unprecedented surge of foreign investment inflows, especially from portfolio management funds, attributable to various factors.[10] Liberalization of the financial market provided the impetus for massive portfolio inflows seeking to maximize capital gains in the generally bullish Malaysian stock market. But as tables 5.8 through 5.11 show, net portfolio capital inflows have proved to be very volatile, rising from −1.5 percent of GDP in 1991 to 14.5 percent in 1993 before dropping off to 1.2 percent in 1995. Bank loan flows (presumably mainly to the private sector) have been almost as volatile, while foreign direct investment and official development assistance have been far less volatile.

3.1. FOREIGN PORTFOLIO INVESTMENT

With the lure of fast and lucrative returns and encouragement to diversify internationally, portfolio funds have made inroads into developing countries. Thus, the role and influence of portfolio management funds, including pension, mutual, and hedge funds, expanded dramatically in the 1990s. Stock markets in developing and transitional economies, both of which are packaged as "emerging markets," welcomed the rising tide of portfolio inflows, which seemed to contribute to the general prosperity through asset price inflation.

Table 5.12 compares the withholding tax rates for dividends and long-term capital gains offered by selected emerging markets in Asia to U.S.-based institutional investors as well as restrictions on foreign ownership of listed

TABLE 5.8. Malaysia: Net Capital Inflows by Major Category, 1989–95 (percentage of GDP)

	1989	1990	1991	1992	1993	1994	1995
Net capital inflows	3.5	4.2	11.9	15.2	16.8	1.6	8.5
Official development finance	−2.4	−2.4	−0.5	−1.4	0.6	0.3	2.7
Foreign direct investment	4.4	5.4	8.5	9.0	7.8	6.0	4.7
Commercial bank funds	1.1	2.0	2.8	6.3	6.6	−7.0	0.1
Portfolio equity			−1.5	5.6	14.5	5.7	1.2

Source: Bank Negara Malaysia's Cash BOP Reporting System, as cited by Ong (1998, 222).

TABLE 5.9. Malaysia: Quarterly Foreign Investment Inflows, 1996–98 (RM millions)

	Total Portfolio Investment		External Equity Investment (FDI)		External Investment	
Period	Receipts	Net Inflows	Receipts	Net Inflows	Receipts	Net Inflows
1996Q1	32,131	4,078	1,563	−21	6,508	4,228
1996Q2	32,671	2,257	1,366	−365	6,601	4,177
1996Q3	34,215	−66	2,462	−220	5,871	2,709
1996Q4	45,916	2,497	2,870	1,122	12,101	9,252
1997Q1	47,431	5,647	1,180	−750	7,025	4,404
1997Q2	41,793	−8,584	1,674	−185	11,909	9,373
1997Q3	39,614	−16,000	1,355	−30	9,055	6,252
1997Q4	27,317	−5,492	1,739	−246	7,975	5,476
1998Q1	27,005	5,596	978	−166	6,484	4,663
1998Q2	12,284	−3,275	1,106	−287	6,083	4,237
1998Q3	8,918	−3,669	913	−876	5,333	2,754
1998Q4	5,652	−717	2,946	1,797	9,858	7,691

Source: Bank Negara Malaysia, *Quarterly Economic Bulletin.*

TABLE 5.10. Malaysia: Annual Foreign Investment Inflows, 1991–98 (RM millions)

	Total Portfolio Investment		External Equity Investment (FDI)		External Investment	
Period	Receipts	Net Inflows	Receipts	Net Inflows	Receipts	Net Inflows
1991	19,346	−1,928	4,482	3,944	8,776	7,694
1992	60,935	7,892	3,766	2,991	14,195	12,713
1993	187,782	25,654	3,413	1,355	17,474	13,691
1994	238,454	14,029	7,769	4,477	28,873	22,047
1995	106,414	5,360	5,850	456	26,874	18,938
1996	144,933	8,766	8,261	516	31,081	20,366
1997	156,156	−28,430	5,949	−1,210	35,964	25,506
1998	75,524	−2,065	5,943	467	27,757	19,344

Source: Bank Negara Malaysia, *Quarterly Economic Bulletin.*

TABLE 5.11. Malaysia: Annual Capital Inflows by Type, 1991–98 (U.S.$ millions, % GDP)

	Foreign Portfolio Investment						Foreign Direct Investment						External Loans					
	Inflows		Outflows		Net Inflows		Inflows		Outflows		Net Inflows		Inflows		Outflows		Net Inflows	
Year	% GDP	US$ mil.	% GDP	US$ mil.	% GDP	US$ mil.	% GDP	US$ mil.	% GDP	US$ mil.	% GDP	US$ mil.	% GDP	US$ mil.	% GDP	US$ mil.	% GDP	US$ mil.
1991	16.7	7,035	18.3	7,736	−1.7	−701	3.9	1,630	0.5	196	3.4	1,434	3	1,263	0.4	175	−2.5	−1,088
1992	48.2	23,896	42.0	20,801	6.2	3,095	3.0	1,477	0.6	304	2.4	1,173	7.5	3,611	0.5	248	−7	−3,363
1993	135.2	73,067	116.7	63,085	18.5	9,982	2.5	1,328	1.5	801	1.0	527	2.9	4,784	0.3	571	−2.6	−4,213
1994	157.2	91,013	147.9	85,658	9.2	5,355	5.1	2,965	2.2	1,256	3.0	1,709	13	7,722	2.1	1,263	−10.9	−6,458
1995	63.9	42,396	60.6	40,261	3.2	2,135	3.5	2,331	3.2	2,149	0.3	182	11.6	7,643	1.3	830	−10.4	−6,813
1996	79.1	57,513	74.3	54,035	4.8	3,479	4.5	3,278	4.2	3,073	0.3	205	11.9	8,654	1.3	951	−10.6	−7,703
1997	79.2	55,572	93.6	65,689	−14.4	−10,117	3.0	2,117	3.6	2,548	−0.6	−431	14.8	7,495	1.5	760	−13.3	−6,735
1998	41.4	19,266	42.6	19,793	−1.1	−527	3.3	1,516	3.0	1,397	0.3	119	11.7	5,625	1.6	744	−10.2	−4,881

Source: Bank Negara Malaysia, *Quarterly Economic Bulletin,* various issues.

TABLE 5.12. Selected Asian Stock Markets: Taxes on and Barriers to Portfolio Investments, 1996

	Withholding Taxes on		
Country	Dividends (%)	Long-Term Capital Gains (%)	Foreign Investment Ceiling for Listed Stocks
Malaysia	0.0	0.0	100% in general
Indonesia	20.0	0.1	49% in general; 85% for securities companies
Philippines[a]	15.0	0.5	40% in general; 30% for banks
Thailand	10.0	0.0	10–49% depending on company bylaws
India	20.0	10.0	24% in general
South Korea[b]	16.5	0.0	20% in general; 15% for KEPCO and POSCO
Taiwan	35.0	0.0	25% in general

Source: International Finance Corporation 1997.

[a]Transactions tax in lieu of a capital gains tax.

[b]Rates are for funds in which U.S. investments total more than 25 percent. Tax rates shown include 10 percent resident tax applied to base rates.

stocks in 1996. Malaysia was clearly the most generous and liberalized and thus presumably the most attractive market. The entry of such funds into the Malaysian market was further encouraged by the offer of a zero withholding tax and the absence of entry or exit conditions that might deter massive surges in either direction and thus check severe fluctuations or volatility.

Temporary capital controls introduced after a sudden collapse of the Malaysian stock market in early 1994 were soon withdrawn without the introduction of a more permanent regime of market-based controls that could be flexibly adjusted in response to policy priorities and concerns. The central bank saw the problem as one of excess liquidity due to the massive inflow of short-term funds from abroad due to higher interest rates in Malaysia, the buoyant stock market, and expectations of ringgit appreciation. Several monetary measures introduced in early 1994 were gradually phased out during the course of the year. The following measures sought to manage excess liquidity, to contain speculative inflows, to restore stability in financial markets, and to control inflationary measures (for a fuller account, see BNM's *1994 Annual Report,* especially the foreword, 42–44, boxes A to J).

- The eligible liabilities base for computing statutory reserve and liquidity requirements was redefined to include all fund inflows from abroad, thus raising the cost of foreign compared to domestic funds.
- Limits on non-trade-related external liabilities of banking institutions were introduced; net external liabilities of the banking system declined from a peak of RM35.4 billion in early January 1994 to RM10.3 billion at the end of 1994.

- The sale of short-term monetary instruments was limited to Malaysian residents to prevent foreigners from using such investments as substitutes for placements of deposits (this measure was lifted on August 12, 1994).
- Commercial banks were required to place the ringgit funds of foreign banks in non-interest-bearing vostro accounts.
- Commercial banks were not permitted to undertake non-trade-related swaps (including overnight swaps) and outright forward transactions on the bid side with foreign customers to prevent offshore parties from establishing speculative long forward ringgit positions while the ringgit was perceived to be undervalued (this measure was lifted on August 16, 1994).
- The statutory reserve requirements of all financial institutions were raised three times in 1994—by one percentage point each time—to absorb excess liquidity on a more permanent basis, absorbing an estimated RM4.8 billion from the banking system.

Nevertheless, with the growing ease of moving portfolio funds into and out of Malaysia, both inflows and outflows accelerated intermittently, generating net inflows most of the time. Annual foreign portfolio investment (FPI) inflows rose from RM19.3 (U.S.$7.0) billion in 1991 to RM238.5 (U.S.$91.0) billion in 1994 (table 5.13). Annual inflows fluctuated significantly after 1994, growing more slowly to RM106.4 (U.S.$42.4) billion in 1995 and then soaring once again to RM144.9 (U.S.$57.5) billion in 1996. Annual FPI outflows were also sizable in the 1990s, rising from U.S.$7.7 billion in 1991 to a peak of U.S.$85.7 billion in 1994. Outflows were generally smaller than inflows, resulting in positive net annual inflows from 1992 to 1996. However, focusing

TABLE 5.13. Malaysia: Annual Net Foreign Portfolio Investments by Type, 1991–98 (RM millions)

	Shares and Corporate Securities	Malaysian Government Securities	Foreign Government Securities	Private Debt Securities	Money Market Instruments	Financial Derivatives	Total Portfolio Investments	
							Receipts	Net Inflows
1991	−1,879	17	−66	—	—	—	19,346	−1,928
1992	6,843	890	159	—	—	—	60,935	7,892
1993	24,659	1,944	−949	—	—	—	187,782	25,654
1994	14,432	−894	491	—	—	—	238,454	14,029
1995	5,345	−1,024	1,039	—	—	—	106,414	5,360
1996	6,681	−26	292	−234	2,038	15	144,933	8,766
1997	−22,004	16	−1,243	1,970	−7,247	78	156,156	−28,430
1998	−2,220	−650	81	−497	−2,906	−648	75,524	−6,840

Source: Bank Negara Malaysia, *Monthly Statistical Bulletin,* table VIII.15.

on such annual figures as well as net flows tends to obscure what are often short-term fluctuations. Official figures for quarterly flows, shown in table 5.14, reflect the tremendous fluctuations in net inflows. Net FPI inflows were sometimes paralleled by other movements of funds, including bank loans, foreign direct investment, and other investments, with some cumulative consequences.

Net inflows of portfolio investments were substantial up to the first quarter of 1997. In fact, for all of 1997 inflows totaled RM156.2 (U.S.$55.5) billion, even higher than 1996 inflows in ringgit terms and only slightly lower than

TABLE 5.14. Malaysia: Quarterly Net Portfolio Investment Inflows by Type, 1991–98 (RM millions)

	Shares and Corporate Securities	Malaysian Government Securities	Foreign Government Securities	Private Debt Securities	Money Market Instruments	Financial Derivatives	Total Portfolio Investments	
							Receipts	Net Inflows
1991Q1	229	16	−3	—	—	—	4,316	242
1991Q2	77	−10	76	—	—	—	5,822	143
1991Q3	−1,374	11	−300	—	—	—	5,454	−1,663
1991Q4	−811	0	161	—	—	—	3,754	−650
1992Q1	964	0	290	—	—	—	13,849	1,254
1992Q2	1,982	57	707	—	—	—	12,168	2,746
1992Q3	1,155	457	141	—	—	—	16,201	1,753
1992Q4	2,742	376	−979	—	—	—	18,717	2,139
1993Q1	4,100	392	−15	—	—	—	23,572	4,477
1993Q2	5,827	471	351	—	—	—	41,872	6,649
1993Q3	7,020	866	−1,631	—	—	—	51,777	6,255
1993Q4	7,709	215	346	—	—	—	70,558	8,270
1994Q1	6,973	−189	28	—	—	—	61,255	6,812
1994Q2	−1,805	−842	1,301	—	—	—	46,986	−1,346
1994Q3	7,641	369	−568	—	—	—	69,322	7,442
1994Q4	1,623	−232	−270	—	—	—	60,891	1,121
1995Q1	−2,378	−651	569	—	—	—	32,243	−2,460
1995Q2	6,361	−315	0	—	—	—	28,111	6,046
1995Q3	2,292	−91	60	—	—	—	26,909	2,261
1995Q4	−930	33	410	—	—	—	19,151	−487
1996Q1	3,813	−15	280				32,131	4,078
1996Q2	2,246	−1	12				32,671	2,257
1996Q3	−1,950	−41	0	142	1,779	4	34,215	−66
1996Q4	2,572	31	0	−376	259	11	45,916	2,497
1997Q1	3,625	5	−82	546	1,540	13	47,431	5,647
1997Q2	−7,427	−1	−516	164	−821	17	41,793	−8,584
1997Q3	−11,781	−4	−679	1,121	−4,715	58	39,614	−16,000
1997Q4	−2,422	16	35	139	−3,250	−10	27,317	−5,492
1998Q1	4,224	94	−36	196	1,325	−207	27,005	5,596
1998Q2	−1,693	0	70	−124	−1,290	−238	12,284	−3,275
1998Q3	−2,329	−760	12	−708	309	−193	8,918	−3,669
1998Q4	−2,186	0	−19	1,156	343	−11	5,652	−717

Source: Bank Negara Malaysia, *Monthly Statistical Bulletin,* table VIII.15.

1995's U.S.$57.5 billion in inflows. This swell of FPI was eventually reversed by even more massive outflows, which amounted to RM184.6 (U.S.$65.7) billion in 1997 (table 5.13). Interestingly, although there was net capital flight of RM28.4 billion in 1997, inflows remained reasonably high, possibly reflecting short-selling activity from abroad intended to profit from the falling bear market.

Malaysia experienced net FPI outflows beginning in the second quarter of 1997 (table 5.14). In other words, the reversal began prior to the devaluation of the Thai baht in early July 1997. Clearly, anxiety among investors over the overheating of Southeast Asian economies, especially that of Thailand, was already mounting before the currencies began to fall in July 1997. After the baht was floated on July 2, 1997 and the ringgit fell in mid-July (after an expensive but futile ringgit defense effort), FPI inflows fell drastically and continued to dwindle throughout 1998, falling from U.S.$16.6 billion in the second quarter of 1997 to U.S.$7.2 billion in the fourth quarter of 1997, and to U.S.$1.5 billion in the fourth quarter of 1998.

The massive collapse of the stock market also reflected the leading role that foreign investors had come to play. While remaining a minority (accounting for perhaps a quarter of total stock market capitalization by mid-1997), their behavior had a disproportionate impact on the bourse, owing to their greater activity (compared to domestic institutional investors) and their greater magnitude (compared to "retail players"). Hence, their rapid withdrawal of capital from Malaysia resulted in massive (four-fifths) market decapitalization, from a KLSE Composite Index high close to 1,300 in February 1997 to the low of 262 on September 2, 1998.

The quarterly data on inflows and outflows in table 5.14, reflected in figure 5.1, demonstrate the ebb and flow of foreign funds. For example, net portfolio inflows fell from late 1993 to mid-1994 and again from late 1994 through most of 1995. However, during this period, net inflows fluctuated tremendously, falling to minus RM2 billion from a positive RM8 billion. Inflows began to decline again in early 1997, but net inflows fell the most as the contagion spread in the third quarter of 1997 and the fall of the ringgit precipitated capital flight, mainly from the stock market. This time, outflows overwhelmed inflows. Besides showing the rapid reversal in the wake of the crisis, the figure also reveals the volatile behavior of portfolio capital flows more generally.

Most portfolio investment into Malaysia has been channeled into the stock market. Hence, the trends for aggregate portfolio inflows parallel those for the purchase of shares and corporate securities. In 1991, RM13.6 billion's worth of shares and corporate securities, or 8.5 percent of market capitalization, was purchased by foreign portfolio funds. By 1994, this figure had bal-

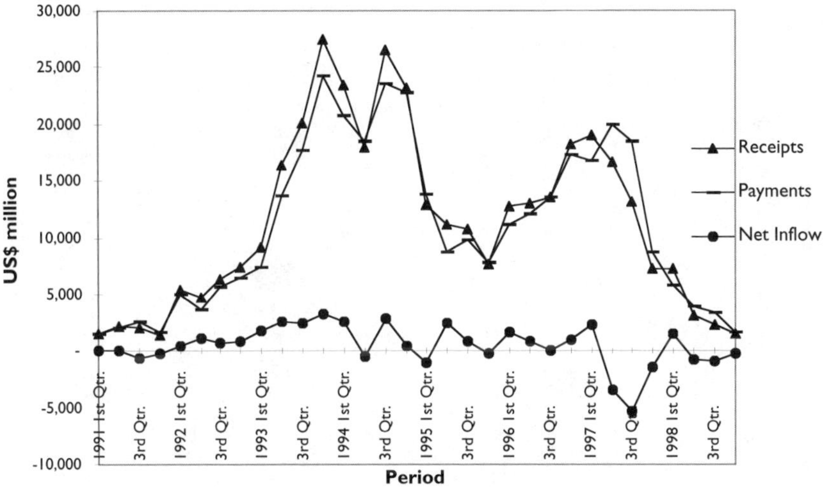

Fig. 5.1. Malaysia: Foreign portfolio investment, by quarter, 1991–98

looned to RM130.0 billion, or 25.5 percent of market capitalization. In contrast, Malaysian government securities have not been very attractive to foreign fund managers. After their introduction in 1996, private debt securities have attracted quite sizable inflows, while advanced money market instruments and financial derivatives have expanded more cautiously. Figure 5.2 underscores the relative volatility of net inflows of portfolio funds, reflecting the ease with which such investments can take flight.

The dominance of the stock market has probably been due to the limited range of investment instruments from which foreign investors can choose. During the period 1991–95, portfolio investment funds accounted for 88 percent of all identified gross capital inflows, while net foreign portfolio investment averaged 5.1 percent of GDP (Ong 1998, 222–23). In 1993 and 1994, portfolio inflows alone surpassed annual GDP in current market prices, reaching U.S.$67 billion and U.S.$87 billion, respectively. Figure 5.2 shows that FPI inflows into private debt securities, money market instruments, and financial derivatives only began in 1995 and have remained modest in comparison with the total funds flowing in and out of Malaysia. Although non-stock-market flows—especially money market instruments, which recorded an inflow of RM15.8 billion and an outflow of RM23.1 billion in 1997—were of increasing importance, such flows remained less significant in the domestic capital market. Some nonetheless served as additional vectors of contagion, while the development of the markets for these instruments has undoubtedly been set back by the financial crisis.

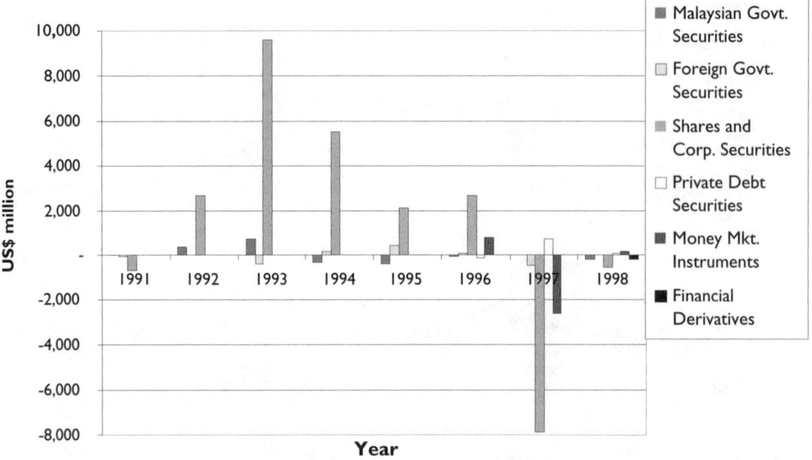

Fig. 5.2. Malaysia: Foreign portfolio investment net inflow, by type, 1991–98

As noted earlier, the increased foreign capital flows into and out of Malaysia, with the growing share of portfolio investment funds involved, allowed foreign institutional investors to exert disproportionately greater influence on the Malaysian stock market. The growing presence of foreign funds also made the Kuala Lumpur bourse much more vulnerable to international vicissitudes of various types. Inevitably, the national economy was increasingly affected by international macroeconomic fluctuations as well as capital flight, rendering the tasks of exchange rate management, controlling inflation, and capital account management much more difficult. The huge short-term capital inflows proved to be especially destabilizing, as they linked two inherently unstable markets, that is, the stock and currency markets. The central bank was reportedly incurring high costs in maintaining a tight monetary policy to sterilize the potentially destabilizing speculative inflows of foreign portfolio funds.[11] After a sudden exodus of such funds in early 1994, temporary controls aimed at limiting portfolio inflows were put in place, but these were removed when speculative pressures on the ringgit declined by the end of the year.

It has been noted that stock market analysts estimate that by mid-1997 about a quarter of the stock listed on the Kuala Lumpur Stock Exchange was in foreign hands, with another quarter held by Malaysian institutions and the remaining half by "retail investors." While most petty Malaysian shareholders only operate within the Malaysian stock market or financial system, foreign institutional investors see the Malaysian stock market as only one of many different investment options in a global financial system that includes many national markets for different types of investment instruments. Unlike the typical Malaysian retail investor, who reputedly chooses between the fixed deposit interest rate on offer and the stock market, foreign investment institutions can shift their funds among various securities markets as well as among other types of financial investment options all over the world. Of course, the specialization among investors that has emerged over the years circumscribes the actual range of investment options available to particular types of investment institutions (e.g., mutual funds, hedge funds, or more specialized investment funds such as fixed income investment funds).

Faced with poor information, which is exacerbated by limited transparency, and the short termism of their investment horizons, many stock market players are prone to herd behavior, especially in response to panic. The nature of foreign fund managers' incentives as well as their much more varied operations and options mean that foreign financial institutions are also more liable to cause such herd behavior to be transformed into the transborder spread of contagion. Although their proportion of share ownership has remained in the minority, the influence of foreign funds grew disproportionately as they became market leaders, with their greater turnover compared to domestic institutions and their far greater clout compared to local "retail players."

3.2. FOREIGN DIRECT INVESTMENT

Foreign direct investment, as it is conventionally understood, is associated with investors with long-term investment commitments.[12] It refers to the establishment or expansion of businesses, including joint ventures, in which the foreign investor has an effective voice in the management of the business. Besides new "green-field" investments, FDI may refer to the reinvestment of profits for business expansion or development as well as to mergers and acquisitions by foreign owners of investments or businesses. Hence, it is generally assumed that FDI is more committed to developing the productive capacity and technological capabilities of the firm. The potential for capturing market share and reducing costs, as well as prospects for product development and production efficiency, among other managerial concerns, are therefore more likely to be investment criteria. Foreign participation in equity investment, or FDI, is often desired for the achievement of long-term development goals, especially in sectors that benefit from foreign expertise and technological hardware that is not sufficiently available domestically.

With the earlier decline of the relative role of overseas development assistance, FDI gained in relative significance. But, with the more recent growth of foreign portfolio investment, foreign direct investment has come to account for a much smaller share of total capital inflows or total foreign investment in Malaysia. Annual inflows of FDI into Malaysia rose from U.S.$1.6 billion in 1991 to peak at U.S.$3.6 billion in 1996 before declining to U.S.$2.1 billion in 1997 and U.S.$1.5 billion in 1998.

Outflows of FDI also increased during the 1990s; with considerable government encouragement, Malaysian direct investment abroad rose from U.S. $196 million in 1991 to U.S.$3.1 billion in 1996. Malaysia remained a net importer of FDI until 1997, when there was an unprecedented net outflow amounting to U.S.$431 million. This can be attributed to the decline of FDI as the crisis set in; uncertainties attributable to the crisis were probably exacerbated by the unorthodox and apparently compromised nature of government policy responses as the crisis unfolded. Direct investment inflows have experienced significant fluctuations, for example, between 1996 and 1997, when inflows dropped from U.S.$3.3 billion to U.S.$2.1 billion, or 36 percent. On balance, then, while net FDI inflows have fluctuated considerably in recent years, these fluctuations have not been of the same magnitude and volatility as FPI. The anomalous increases in FDI can be attributed to major, often "lumpy" investments from one or two source countries, for example, large FDI inflows from Singapore in mid-1994, Germany in late 1996, and the United Kingdom in late 1998.

3.3. EXTERNAL BORROWING

External borrowing has been another source of foreign capital.[13] Malaysian resident individuals and corporations have borrowed increasingly heavily from abroad in the last decade. Inflows of loans amounted to a mere U.S.$1.2 billion in 1991, a small fraction of the U.S.$10.4 billion of debt amassed by 1997.

While Malaysia's net external debt exposure undoubtedly grew quickly during the early and mid-1990s, mainly due to the rapid buildup of private debt as the government accelerated prepayment of public foreign debt, such liabilities were still much smaller than in other crisis-affected economies in East Asia. Also, the relatively negligible amount of loans extended to foreigners contrasts starkly with the amount received.

Many of these foreign loans were borrowed by Malaysian banks that wished to profit from international interest rate differentials. For instance, in January 1997, U.S. and Japanese discount rates (5.0 percent and 0.5 percent, respectively), the U.K. base lending rate (6.0 percent), and the Singapore three-month interbank lending rate (2.6 percent) were all substantially lower than Malaysia's commercial bank base lending rate of 9.2 percent (Bank Negara Malaysia, *Monthly Statistical Bulletin,* table IX.2). Some of these monies were then loaned to domestic borrowers, who were willing to pay relatively higher interest rates, with considerable opportunities for arbitrage. However, strict central bank supervision limited such arbitrage activities compared to those in other crisis-affected economies.

The quasi pegs of the ringgit and most other Southeast Asian currencies to the U.S. dollar facilitated these flows. Most borrowings, regardless of their source (i.e., including those from Japanese or European banks), tended to be U.S. dollar denominated, while the long-standing pegs—despite official claims that the currency's value was based on a basket of currencies of the country's major trading partners—served to enhance export competitiveness as the U.S. dollar declined against the Japanese yen between 1985 and mid-1995. However, the strengthening of the U.S. dollar (especially against the yen) from mid-1995 on effectively appreciated the Southeast Asian currencies, adversely affecting export competitiveness and growth as well as industrial growth and industrial investments more generally.

Figures 5.3 and 5.4 show the growth and distribution of short-, medium-, and long-term foreign debt from 1988 to 1998 (also see tables 5.15 and 5.16). The absolute amount of short-term debt grew at great speed, rising from RM2.4 billion in 1988 to RM43.3 billion in 1997, while the share of short-term debt in the total debt increased from 5.0 to 25.7 percent over the same period. Medium- and long-term debt also increased from RM47.0 billion to RM127.5 billion, although their share of the total debt declined from 95.0 to 74.3 percent. After the massive exodus of capital in early 1994, the Malaysian

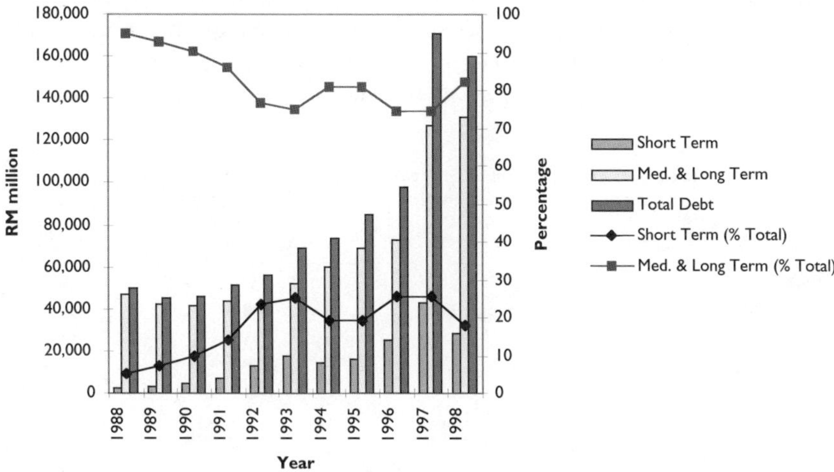

Fig. 5.3. Malaysia: Annual external debt, by maturity

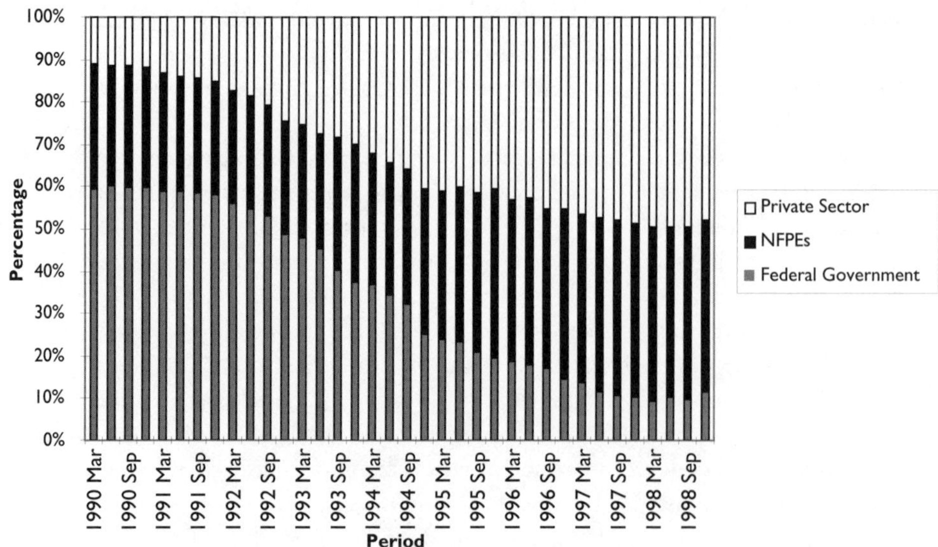

Fig. 5.4. Malaysia: Percentage distribution of external debt

authorities introduced temporary capital control measures, which reduced the inflow of short-term borrowing during 1994–95.

The direction of this external debt by category of debtor is shown in figure 5.4. From 1990 to 1998, the federal government's share of total foreign debt steadily decreased, while the private sector's share increased. Nonfinancial public enterprises (NFPEs) also raised their share of total debt but more slowly than in the private sector. Since greater shares of government and quasi-government NFPE debt were accounted for by medium- and long-term borrowings, the proportion of short-term loans in total private debt

TABLE 5.15. Malaysia: External Debt as Share of GDP, 1991–98 (percentages)

Year	External Loans Received	Short-Term Debt	Medium- and Long-Term Debt	Total Debt
1991	3.0	6.2	37.7	43.9
1992	7.5	10.4	33.9	44.3
1993	2.9	3.9	11.8	15.8
1994	13.0	9.4	39.1	48.5
1995	11.6	9.7	41.3	51.0
1996	11.9	13.7	39.7	53.4
1997	14.8	21.9	64.7	86.6
1998	11.7	15.6	72.0	87.6

Source: Calculated from Bank Negara Malaysia, *Monthly Statistical Bulletin,* tables VIII.10 and VIII.15.

TABLE 5.16. Malaysia: External Debt as Share of Foreign Reserves, 1991–98 (percentages)

Year	External Loans Received	Short-Term Debt	Medium- and Long-Term Debt	Total Debt
1991	11.2	23.5	143.4	166.9
1992	20.0	27.8	90.5	118.3
1993	16.8	22.6	67.8	90.4
1994	28.9	20.9	87.0	107.9
1995	30.4	25.4	107.8	133.1
1996	31.2	35.9	103.7	139.6
1997	51.0	75.6	222.7	298.2
1998	21.5	28.6	131.9	160.5

Source: Calculated from Bank Negara Malaysia, *Monthly Statistical Bulletin,* tables VIII.10 and VIII.15.

must have been much higher. In line with conventional economic wisdom, the buildup of private debt was considered to be less onerous than increases in public debt. It was also generally assumed that private sector agents would make better use of such funds. Due to such beliefs, the rapid accumulation of private debt by the quickly developing East Asian countries was not regarded with much concern, although a much higher proportion of such debt was short term in nature.

The increase in foreign borrowing and other foreign capital inflows financed Malaysia's persistent precrisis current account deficit until 1998 (see tables 5.17 and 5.18): the lowest and highest deficits were RM5.6 billion in 1992 and RM21.3 billion in 1995, respectively. These current account deficits were covered by surpluses in the capital account during the early and mid-1990s, mainly comprised of growing foreign direct and portfolio investments as well as net external borrowings. While the current account comprises transactions in goods and services, the growing significance of foreign portfolio investment flows in the 1990s meant that the capital account was becoming

TABLE 5.17. Malaysia: Current Account and Balance of Payments, 1991–98

	Current Account		Balance of Payments	
Year	U.S.$ millions	% of GDP	U.S.$ millions	% of GDP
1991	−4,234	−10.0	1,246	3.0
1992	−2,205	−4.4	6,566	13.2
1993	−3,084	−5.7	11,377	21.0
1994	−5,606	−9.7	−3,123	−5.4
1995	−8,495	−12.8	−1,625	−2.4
1996	−4,455	−6.1	2,478	3.4
1997	−5,630	−8.0	−3,876	−5.5
1998	9,386	20.2	10,281	22.1

Source: Bank Negara Malaysia, *Monthly Statistical Bulletin.*

much more vulnerable to speculation and volatility. Thus, the Malaysian economy became even more vulnerable to shifting capital market sentiments, including contagion from other economies. To add to this vulnerability, Malaysia's total external debt to foreign exchange reserves ratio was becoming dangerously high before the crisis, reaching 139.6 percent in 1996 before jumping to 298.2 percent in 1997.

As the economic recession deepened in 1998, foreign borrowing decreased to 1996 levels after peaking at RM29.2 billion in 1997. With a lower proportion of short-term loans compared to the other East Asian economies hit by the crisis, fluctuations in foreign bank borrowings in Malaysia have been less severe. It is noteworthy that borrowing from offshore financial centers, namely, the Labuan IOFC and Bermuda, rose in the aftermath of the financial crisis.

The Bank for International Settlements (BIS), banking regulations, and certain banking practices inadvertently encouraged short-term debt—compared to medium- or long-term debt—in the exposure of banks based in Organization for Economic Cooperation and Development (OECD) countries, especially loans to emerging markets or developing countries (e.g., loans for less than a year only required 20 percent capital backing compared to 100 percent backing required for loans for a year or more). Further, the degree of Malaysian exposure to such short-term debt was partly mitigated by more prudent central bank regulations, supervision, and enforcement, as well as limiting foreign borrowing by Malaysian banks and corporations.

Thus, in this regard Malaysia actually fared better than most countries hit by the crisis because it had accumulated relatively less foreign borrowings, with a smaller proportion of debt of short-term maturity. For instance, in June 1997 short-term debt as a share of total reserves for Malaysia was approximately 60 percent, significantly lower than that of South Korea (more

TABLE 5.18. Malaysia: Annual Balance of Payments, 1991–98 (RM millions)

Year	Current Account	Official Long-Term Capital	Corporate Investment	Balance of Long-Term Capital	Basic Balance	Private Capital (net)	Errors and Omissions	Overall Balance
1991	−11,644	−665	10,996	10,331	−1,313	5,135	−395	3,427
1992	−5,622	−2,876	13,204	10,328	4,706	11,957	81	16,744
1993	−7,926	979	12,885	13,864	5,938	13,931	9,370	29,239
1994	−14,689	861	10,798	11,659	−3,030	−8,485	3,333	−8,182
1995	−21,323	6,147	10,464	16,611	−4,712	2,529	−1,896	−4,079
1996	−11,226	748	12,777	13,525	2,299	10,317	−6,371	6,245
1997	−15,820	4,645	14,450	19,095	3,275	−12,913	−1,254	−10,892
1998	36,794	2,137	8,490	10,627	47,421	−20,633	13,513	40,301

Source: Bank Negara Malaysia, *Monthly Statistical Bulletin,* table VIII.1.

than 200 percent), Indonesia (about 170 percent), and Thailand (just under 150 percent) and slightly lower than Brazil (80 percent). Countries with lower ratios included Chile (45 percent) and China (25 percent) (Ishak Shari et al. 1999).

Financial market observers also note that the costs of hedging foreign loans in Malaysia were relatively lower compared to its neighbors (with the exception of Singapore), although there are some anecdotal claims that the central bank actually discouraged Malaysian external borrowers from hedging their debts. In addition, the majority of loan funds disbursed through the Labuan international offshore financial center, which grew rapidly in the 1990s, were secured by residents of Malaysia. For example, before the crisis, of all loans sourced through the Labuan IOFC, approximately 80 percent in 1995 and 70 percent in 1996 were obtained by Malaysians (Awang 1997, 7). There is also anecdotal evidence of Malaysian individuals and companies borrowing offshore, especially in Singapore and Hong Kong, but again systematic evidence is not available.

The Malaysian ringgit vacillated around RM2.5 against the U.S. dollar during the first half of 1997. After the Thai baht was floated on July 2, 1997, like other currencies in the region, the ringgit was under strong pressure, especially because, like Thailand, Malaysia had maintained large current account deficits during the early and mid-1990s. The monetary authorities' efforts to defend the ringgit actually strengthened it against the greenback for a few days before the futile ringgit defense effort was abandoned in mid-July. The aborted ringgit defense effort is widely believed to have cost more than nine billion ringgit. The ringgit—like the currencies of other economies hit by the crisis—fluctuated wildly until mid-1998, weeks before the ringgit was fixed at RM3.8 against the U.S. dollar on September 2, 1999. While much of the downward pressure on the ringgit was externally induced by regional developments as well as adverse perceptions of the regional situation, there is evidence to suggest that inappropriate political rhetoric and policy measures by the political leadership exacerbated the situation. Malaysia's foreign exchange reserves depleted rapidly from July to November 1997, before improving in December, especially after the imposition of capital controls in September 1998.

4. CAPITAL CONTROLS

Malaysian prime minister Mahathir Mohamad's September 1, 1998, announcement of capital controls was important in several regards. Whereas Thailand, South Korea, and Indonesia had gone cap in hand—humiliatingly accepting conditions imposed by the IMF—in order to secure desperately needed credit, the Malaysian initiative reminded the world that there are alternatives to capital account liberalization. The capital control measures were significantly revised in February 1999. As of September 1, 1999, yet another regime came into effect. These modifications recognize the negative impact of the capital controls regime and represent attempts to mitigate it and encourage the return of the often condemned short-term capital.

Unfortunately, there has been a tendency since for both sides in the debate over Malaysia's capital control measures to exaggerate their own cases, with little regard for what has actually happened. Market fundamentalists have loudly prophesied doom for Malaysia ever since, although the evidence does not support their often wild claims. Meanwhile, opponents of capital account liberalization have gone to the other extreme with some wishful exaggeration about what the Malaysian measures actually imply and their consequences (one supporter has extolled its ostensibly virtuous consequences for labor with scant regard for Malaysian realities). Both sides forget that capital controls are often a necessary means to other policy objectives rather than ends in and of themselves. One needs to be clear about these objectives. Will capital controls be used in the interests of workers, consumers, or the nation as a whole? Or are they mainly being used to save the politically well connected?

There are many types of capital control instruments, with different consequences that often vary with circumstances. Before capital account liberalization began in the 1980s, most countries retained some such controls despite significant current account liberalization in the postwar period. Most such measures can only be understood historically, in terms of their original purposes, and there are no ready-made packages available for interested governments.

It is important to establish at the outset what particular controls seek to achieve. With the benefit of hindsight, it is crucial to determine to what extent the measures actually achieve their declared objectives as well as their other consequences, intended or otherwise. For instance, it is important to know whether specific controls are meant to avert a crisis or assist in the recovery from one. In its 1998 *Trade and Development Report,* the United Nations Conference on Trade and Development (UNCTAD) recommended capital controls as a means of avoiding financial crises. Almost as if he were endorsing the Malaysian measures, MIT professor Paul Krugman recommended such measures in his *Fortune* magazine column in early September 1998 to create a window of opportunity for economic recovery—which is another objective, though the considerations involved may not be altogether different.

Did Malaysia's selective capital control measures succeed? The ability of the

Malaysian government's regime of capital controls to deal with the regional currency and financial crisis will continue to be debated for a long time, as the data do not lend themselves to clearly supporting any particular position. Proponents can claim that the economic decline came to a halt soon after and the stock market slide turned around, while opponents can say that such reversals have been more pronounced in the rest of the region. As is now generally recognized, the one-year lock in of foreign funds in the country came too late to avert the crisis or to lock in the bulk of foreign funds, which had already fled the country. Instead, the funds "trapped" were those that had not left in the preceding 14 months. Inadvertently, this "punished" investors who had shown a greater commitment to Malaysia. This is also evidenced by the very low volume of outflow since the end of the lock in on September 1, 1999.

It appears that, at best, its contribution to recovery was ambiguous, while at worst it probably slowed it down and acted to diminish the likely recovery of foreign direct investment—which may yet have an impact on Malaysia's medium-term competitiveness vis-à-vis its neighbors. Further, the regime remains untested in checking currency speculation, as for various reasons such speculation abated shortly after its imposition. In addition, recovery of the Malaysian share market, which had declined much more than other stock markets during the crisis, has lagged behind that of other markets in the region.

Malaysia was most fortunate in the timing of the imposition of capital controls if indeed, as stated by Mahathir in his speech to the symposium on the first anniversary of the controls, it came about almost in desperation. At the time the controls were introduced, the external environment was about to change significantly, while the economy had seen the outflow of the bulk of short-term capital. So in a very real sense the regime was never tested. If the turmoil of the preceding months had continued until the end of 1998, or longer, continued shifts and repegging would have been necessary, with deleterious effects.

Clearly, the ringgit peg brought a welcome respite to businessmen after more than a year of currency volatility. However, exchange rate volatility across the region also effectively abated shortly thereafter due to other factors, and even the later Brazilian crisis did not renew such volatility. Moreover, it is ironic that an ostensibly nationalistic attempt to defend monetary independence against currency traders in effect handed over determination of the ringgit's value to the U.S. Federal Reserve. However, should the U.S. dollar strengthen significantly against other currencies, Malaysia will probably have to repeg to retain export competitiveness.

While interest rates were brought down by government decree in Malaysia, the desired effects were limited. Interest rates have fallen dramatically across the region, in some cases even more than in Malaysia, without the others having to resort to capital controls. For example, while interest rates in Thailand were much higher than in Malaysia for over a year after the crisis began, they declined below Malaysian levels during September 1998. Perhaps more importantly, loan and money supply growth rates actually declined in the first few months after the new measures were introduced, despite central bank threats to sack bank managers who failed to achieve the 8 percent loan growth target rate for 1998. It has become clear that credit expansion will be a consequence of factors other than capital controls. Across the region, countercyclical spending has also grown, again without resort to capital controls.

The Malaysian authorities' mid-February 1999 measures have effectively abandoned the main capital control measure introduced in September 1998, that is, the one-year lock in. While foreign investors were prohibited from withdrawing funds from Malaysia before September 1999, they were allowed to withdraw after mid-February following payment of a scaled exit tax (pay less for staying longer in Malaysia) in the hope that this would reduce the rush for the gates come September 1999. Meanwhile, in an attempt to attract new capital inflows, new investors would only be liable for a less onerous tax on capital gains. The new capital gains tax will hardly deter exit in the event of a panic as investors rush to get out to cut their losses. At best, however, it could serve to discourage some short selling from abroad owing to the much higher capital gains tax rate on withdrawals within less than a year of 30 as opposed to 10 percent. The differential exit capital gains tax rate may have discouraged short selling from abroad, but it did nothing to address other possible sources of vulnerability and will not deter capital flight in the event of a financial panic. In September 1999, the capital gains tax rate was set at a uniform rate of 10 percent, thus eliminating the only feature that might have deterred short selling from abroad. Effectively, Malaysia is once again almost defenseless in the face of a similar sudden exodus of capital in the future, though this may not be the most urgent problem at hand.

By setting the peg at RM3.8 to the U.S. dollar on September 2, 1998, after it had been trading in the range of RM4.0 to 4.2 to the U.S. dollar, the Malaysian authorities were then seeking to raise the value of the ringgit. However, the other currencies in the region strengthened after the U.S. Federal Reserve Bank lowered interest rates in the aftermath of the Russian and Long-Term Capital Management (LTCM) crises in mid-September 1998, strengthening the yen and other regional currencies. Thus, the ringgit became undervalued for about a year instead, which—by chance rather than design—boosted Malaysian foreign exchange reserves from the trade surplus, largely due to import compression as well as some exchange-rate-sensitive exports. Thus, the ringgit undervaluation may have helped the Malaysian economic recovery but certainly not in the way the authorities intended when they pegged the ringgit in September 1998. However, the U.S. Federal Reserve reduced interest rates soon after, with the ringgit considered to be undervalued. While the undervalued ringgit would favor an export-led recovery strategy, this certainly was not the intent. (Meanwhile, however, government efforts continue to be focused on a domestic-led recovery strategy.) The undervalued ringgit may have an unintended "beggar thy neighbor" effect. Due to trade competition, the undervalued ringgit has been discouraging other regional currencies from strengthening. This may even cause China's authorities to devalue the renminbi, which could have the undesirable effect of triggering another round of "competitive devaluations" with concomitant dangers for all.

Industrial output, especially for manufacturing, declined even faster from the time of the introduction of capital controls in Malaysia until November 1998. It continued downward in January 1999 before turning around. Except for a few sectors (most notably electronics), industrial output recovery has not been spectacular since then, except in comparison with the deep recession of the year before. Meanwhile, unemployment has risen, especially affecting those employed in construction and financial services. Domestic investment proposals have almost halved, while green-field FDI seems to have declined by much less, though cynics claim that the figures have been raised by quicker processing of applications.

Thus, contrary to the claims of the Malaysian government, there is no clear evidence that the capital control measures contributed decisively to economic recovery. All the other crisis-affected economies turned around during the first quarter of 1999, while Malaysia was the only one to do so in the second quarter of 1999, when some of the other countries registered even higher growth rates. (Hong Kong, the only place with an even more tightly pegged currency, has been the worst laggard.) On the other hand, Malaysian capital controls have certainly not been the unmitigated disaster that some predicted.

There are now three remaining elements of the controls introduced in September 1998, namely, the ringgit peg; nonconvertibility on the capital account and restricted convertibility on the current account; and the capital gains tax, with the higher rate on capital remaining in effect for less than a year.

With respect to the peg and convertibility, regional currency volatility has largely abated, and there is little risk in the near to medium term of another round of sustained attacks; hence, there is now little need to maintain the peg for this reason. In any case, it is unclear that the Malaysian peg would stand in the event of a sustained attack on neighboring currencies, as evidenced by the need for Taiwan to devalue its currency in 1997. The evidence from Hong Kong, with its rigid peg, is far from encouraging, and its upturn has been the weakest in the region. Ironically, despite the regime's strong anti-Western rhetoric, the status quo leaves Malaysian exchange rate determination in the hands of the U.S. Federal Reserve and, in lesser measure, of the Japanese and European central banks.

The currently undervalued pegged ringgit has negative implications for a broad recovery, which depends upon imported inputs. It appears that the peg has not really given a major boost to exports, as the export figures suggest. The regime has also not had the desired effect with regard to exports, as the export base remains narrow, with the most significant growth coming in electronics, that is, due to fortuitous external demand, while the welcomed increase in the foreign reserves situation has largely resulted from massive import compression. There are costs to maintaining an undervalued ringgit, especially in the context of an economic upturn of what is still a very open economy. An undervalued ringgit may help some exports in the short term, but it also makes imports of capital and intermediate goods more expensive, thus impeding recovery and capacity expansion in the medium term. (Before the crisis, imports were equivalent to more than 90 percent of GDP.) There are already some early indications of a declining trade surplus as the import compression due to the collapsed ringgit declines. This, together with an apparently stubborn negative services balance, will mean a shrinking current account surplus if the economic upturn continues.

While there is a need to continue to press for international financial reform as well as new regional monetary arrangements in the absence of adequate global reform, there is little to be gained by retaining the current regime of controls. Instead, even if it succeeds in attracting short-term portfolio capital, as the various amendments to the regime have sought to do, it would be largely ineffective in the event of another currency and financial panic. The controls should be dismantled while ensuring an adequate and effective regulatory framework to reduce financial vulnerability and to moderate capital flow surges into and out of the country. Malaysia should not be completely defenseless against another round of speculative attacks. While it can afford to return to ringgit convertibility, this should be phased in with effective measures to ensure the noninternationalization of the ringgit to reduce vulnerability to external currency speculation. This can include measures such as not permitting offshore ringgit accounts as well as nonresident borrowing of ringgit.

Contrary to the official claim that the controls have had no adverse impacts, they appear to have had negative effects, among others, on desired long-term foreign direct investments. Even if this has been due to misperceptions, the authorities have had to spend inordinate energy and resources trying to correct this misunderstanding. Confidence in the Malaysian government's policy consistency and credibility has been seriously undermined, as have years of investment promotion efforts. This has not been helped by unnecessarily hostile and ill-informed official rhetoric.

The current regime is now counterproductive and will probably suffer adverse medium-term, indeed long-term, consequences if it is the authorities' intention, as declared by the prime minister, to retain the regime until such time as the international financial system is reformed. Hence, it would be desirable to phase out the existing measures in light of their ambiguous contribution to economic recovery and the adverse consequences of retaining them. While recognizing the utility of portfolio inflows, there is increasing recognition of the need to have protection against rapid massive outflows. Part of that protection has to involve oversight of bank lending to avoid the creation of asset bubbles, which are then used to leverage other activities. Ultimately, however, there are no foolproof guarantees in an increasingly volatile globalized economy.

Since the desired reforms to the international financial architecture are unlikely to materialize in the foreseeable future, the Malaysian government should institute a permanent, but flexible, market-based regime of prudential controls to moderate capital inflows and deter speculative surges, both domestic and foreign, so as to avert future crises. This would include a managed float of the currency with convertibility but no internationalization, meaning, minimally, no offshore ringgit accounts, limits on offshore foreign exchange accounts, and limits on foreign borrowing. There is clearly an urgent need for some degree of monetary cooperation in the region. It is now clear that currency and financial crises have a primarily regional character. Hence, regional cooperation is a necessary first step toward the establishment of an East Asian monetary facility. Only responsible Malaysian relations with its neighbors will contribute to realizing such regional cooperation.

The window of opportunity offered by the capital controls regime has been abused by certain powerfully connected business interests, not only to secure publicly funded bailouts at public expense but even to consolidate and extend their corporate domination, especially in the crucial financial sector. Capital controls have been part of a package focused on saving friends of the political regime, usually at public expense. While ostensibly not involving public funds, the government-sponsored "restructuring" of the ruling-party-linked Renong conglomerate will cost the government, and hence the public, billions of ringgit in foregone toll and tax revenues. In addition, nonperforming loans (NPLs) of the thrice-bankrupted Bank Bumiputra—to be taken over by politically well-connected banking interests—have not been heavily discounted like other banks' NPLs, although the bank has long abandoned its ostensible "social agenda" of helping the politically dominant Bumiputera community.

Other elements in the Malaysian government's economic strategy reinforce the impression that the capital control measures were probably motivated by political considerations as well as the desire to protect politically well-connected businesses. For example, the Malaysian ringgit's exchange rate was pegged against the U.S. dollar on the afternoon of September 2, 1998, just hours before Deputy Prime Minister and Finance Minister Anwar Ibrahim was sacked, probably to preempt currency volatility and speculation after the firing. The Malaysian experiment with capital controls has been compromised by political crises, vested interests, and inappropriate policy instruments. Hence, it would be a serious mistake to reject capital controls on account of the flawed Malaysian experience.

5. VOLATILITY ANALYSES

One major focus of this study has been the volatility of the different types of capital flows into—and out of—Malaysia in the precrisis period as well as after the crisis began in July 1997. The introduction of capital controls in September 1998 adds an additional element of interest to the Malaysian case. In the Malaysian context, the desirability of free international capital flows, involving capital account convertibility, remains a contentious issue. Domestic banking deregulation and official international promotion of Malaysian securities markets, coupled with rapid international financial liberalization, helped create conditions prone to greater market volatility and contagion, thus contributing to the recent financial crisis. In the aftermath of the crisis, there is now greater concern, at least temporarily, for the potential and pitfalls of continuing to allow unrestricted international capital flows. Although the financial crisis in Malaysia was triggered by contagion from abroad and exacerbated by poor policy responses, changes in the economic structure (e.g., increasing influence of the financial system over the real economy, including the manufacturing sector), policy biases (e.g., favoring rent seeking), and the changing institutional context (e.g., the growing influence of the stock market) also increased the vulnerability of the Malaysian financial system in the long term.

An important lesson to be drawn from the East Asian crisis is that Malaysia should have been more prudent in liberalizing its financial sector and capital account. In Southeast Asia, there is considerable evidence that efforts to liberalize domestic financial systems were under way before strong institutions needed for effective prudential regulation, monitoring, and supervision were well established, thus exacerbating the vulnerability of these systems to the potentially disruptive effects of massive trans-border surges of capital. Prudent official regulation is necessary to help maintain a balance between the competitive efficiency of markets and the requirements of a robust and efficient banking system (Park 1994, 21; Chowdhury and Islam 1993, 144). More effective regulation of the capital account to ensure more selective entry would also have served to limit volatility associated with certain types of capital inflows, which would have avoided some of the worst excesses that contributed to the recent financial crises in Southeast Asia in general and Malaysia in particular.

These problems were partly mitigated in Malaysia by its stronger tradition of prudential management of the banking system, its greater restrictions on private foreign borrowings, its relatively less-bank-based financial system compared to the three other most-crisis-affected economies, and its stronger macroeconomic and financial condition before the onset of the crisis. Nevertheless, analysis of prior financial reforms and developments suggests that the Malaysian financial crisis that began in mid-1997 can be traced to financial liberalization and its consequent undermining of effective financial governance or regulation at both the international and national levels. High investments in nontradables, with private external debt and unrestricted portfolio investment inflows arising from financial liberalization, increased the vulnerability of the domestic financial system. The 1997–98 financial crisis points to the importance of prudentially managing risk in the financial system, as failing to do so enhanced its vulnerability. Increasing financial liberalization has exacerbated most of these trends and further reduced the financial sector's support of productive long-term investments.

Furthermore, promotion of securities markets before an effective and mature banking system was well established diminished the franchise value of the banking system. This resulted in increased risk taking and aggravated the fragility of the banking sector. It was also evident in seeming risk management by the excessive (collateralized) bank lending to the property sector observed in the years leading up to the banking crisis in 1985–88 and the recent financial crisis of mid-1997. Such lending for property and share purchases fueled asset price inflation, generating wealth effects and hence raising consumption levels with the help of easier consumer credit. But while such bubbles take months to build up they collapse much more suddenly, usually with devastating consequences. In an increasingly liberalized and integrated international environment, capital flows, especially portfolio investments, seem to have become disproportionately important as the most susceptible to volatility and the most sensitive to trans-border contagion.

Instead of encouraging developing countries to engage in excessively rapid financial market liberalization, Stiglitz (1999) argues that they should focus on finding the right regulatory structure to manage the incentives and constraints that affect financial institutions' exposure to and ability to cope with risk. (He calls this approach to effective financial regulation, from the perspective of risk management, the dynamic portfolio approach.) This, he argues, is due to the fact that financial institutions are both a source of risk to and liable to be affected by risks in the rest of the economy. According to Stiglitz (1999), "the best way to manage risk management in developing countries may differ markedly from that in developed countries, simply because they face larger risks, with poor information and typically have weaker risk management capacities" (3).

While financial restraint can promote banks' commitments to act as long-run agents and enhance their capability to cope with risks, this has not been the case in Malaysia. Insofar as financial restraint has been practiced in Malaysia, it has primarily sought to ensure bank profitability, especially with the increasing ethnic Bumiputera dominance of the Malaysian banking system that began in the 1970s. Banks in Malaysia have been heavily used by the state for the wealth redistribution policies of the NEP. Although it has been utilized to support interethnic economic redistribution and other public policies, financial restraint in Malaysia has not been used very much to favor long-term productive investments, especially in non-resource-based export-oriented manufacturing, which continues to be dominated by foreign direct investment.

Meanwhile, external liberalization in the early 1990s—for example, by encouraging foreign financial institutions to invest in the stock market while continuing to allow free international movement of capital—made the national economy much more vulnerable to both external shocks and capital flight, rendering the tasks of exchange rate management and controlling inflation much more difficult. Unlike the Malaysian banking crisis in the second half of the 1980s, which was triggered by a prolonged world recession that began in the advanced economies in the early 1980s, the recent crisis stemmed from the liberalized financial system itself and was exacerbated by sudden massive withdrawals of funds. Although it was less of a problem in Malaysia than in some other East Asian economies, foreign indebtedness in 1997 was primarily generated by the private rather than the public sector. Also, unlike its neighbors, the main source of volatility and the main transmission mechanism for contagion in Malaysia was through the stock market rather than short-term foreign bank borrowing (and related problems of currency and term mismatches).

Ultimately, how and whether foreign capital contributes to economic development is of the utmost importance. The earlier official enthusiasm for attracting foreign capital inflows, which are generally presumed to be beneficial, has come under more critical scrutiny since the advent of the crisis in mid-1997. Notwithstanding some temporary controls imposed in 1994, which were primarily aimed at limiting portfolio inflows, in their desire to attract more foreign institutional investors the Malaysian authorities did not have enough well-conceived regulatory instruments in place to deal with the surge of destabilizing portfolio investment inflows and the threat of their sudden reversal. With the commanding role of foreign portfolio investors in the Malaysian stock market, declining interest and confidence in the region after early 1997 began a reversal of net portfolio investment flows in the second quarter. The mid-July 1997 collapse of the Malaysian ringgit—after a costly but unsuccessful defense of the currency in the face of regional contagion after the Thai baht float of July 2, 1997—accelerated the unwinding of the asset inflationary buildup, hastening the flight of the very same foreign portfolio capital that had contributed to the share price boom in the first place. The collapse of the bubble was thus speeded by portfolio and other capital outflows and in turn undermined the banking sector, which had become extremely vulnerable to asset price deflation and its concomitant wealth effect. While it is often intended to stem contagion or restore market confidence in the face of increasingly negative investor sentiment, injudicious government policy responses on both sides of an increasingly divided government mainly served to exacerbate the crisis (Jomo 1998b). Thus, what began as a currency and then a financial crisis in Malaysia later became a recession, that is, a crisis in the real economy.

With the benefit of hindsight, it is now clear that the worst was over in the region in the third quarter of 1998. Regional currencies strengthened and stabilized after the greater volatility of the preceding 14 months, as interest rates came down with U.S. rates after the Russian, LTCM, and Wall Street scares of August 1998. Soon renewed foreign investor interest became evident, even if only to take advantage of the "fire sales" occurring in the region. In March 1999, the Malaysian authorities announced that they would consider foreign-led mergers and acquisitions as FDI instead of just green-field investments, which actually add new economic capacity. For the first time since the 1960s, Great Britain became the source country of the most FDI in Malaysia in 1998, with British firms acquiring controlling stakes in previously Malaysian controlled cement plants, electricity generation facilities, and telecommunications firms catering primarily to the domestic market (whereas previously FDI had mainly been encouraged for export-oriented industries).

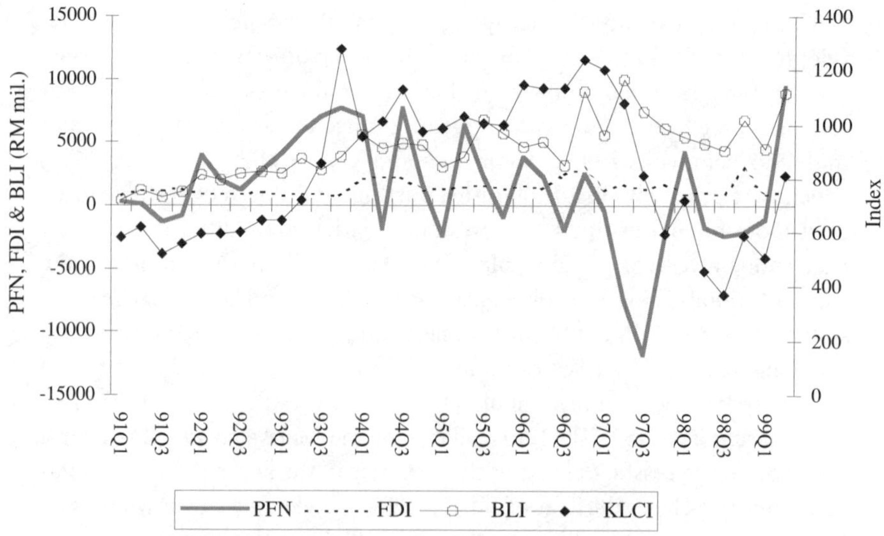

Fig. 5.5. Malaysia: Quarterly net capital inflows and Kuala Lumpur composite index, 1991 to mid-1999

5.1. BROAD TRENDS

Figure 5.5 presents quarterly movements of three types of net capital inflows—namely, portfolio investment inflows (PFN), foreign direct investments, and bank loan inflows (BLI)—compared to the Kuala Lumpur Stock Exchange Composite Index during the period extending from 1991 to mid-1999. The figure suggests broadly parallel movements between FDI and BLI but little else. It also underscores the tremendous volatility of PFN.

Figure 5.6 presents monthly movements of the Malaysian ringgit/U.S. dollar exchange rate compared to the Kuala Lumpur Stock Exchange Composite Index. The figure suggests an indifferent relationship until the onset of the crisis in July 1997, after which one finds broadly parallel movements until the ringgit was pegged to the U.S. dollar in September 1997.

Figure 5.7 plots quarterly changes for these two trends. This time there appears to be some correspondence, perhaps with some lag, with the KLCI seeming to trail forex movements.

5.2. VOLATILITY MEASURES

Interest in the volatility of capital flows has risen in recent years, with growing recognition of the increased volatility of such flows and their implications

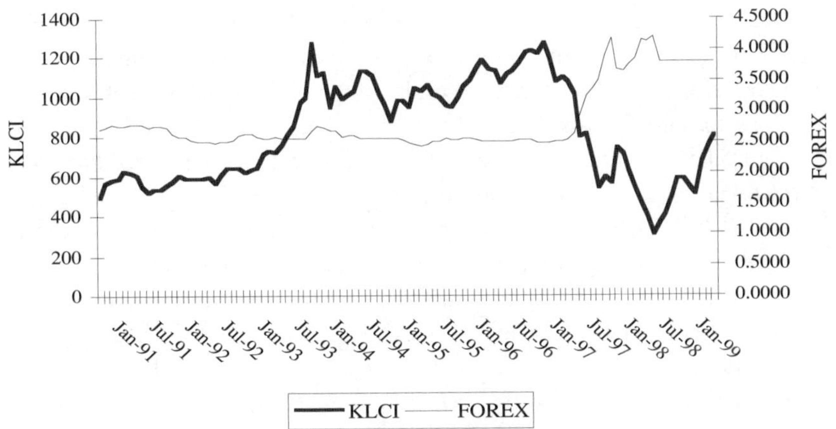

Fig. 5.6. Malaysia: Monthly ringgit/U.S. dollar exchange rate and Kuala Lumpur composite index, 1991 to mid-1999

(Cailloux and Griffith-Jones 1999). There have also been attempts to establish hierarchies of such volatility to help analysts distinguish between relatively "hot" and "cold" flows. Such efforts have remained problematic and controversial. For example, the low frequency of available data reduces the range of econometric tools that can be meaningfully used to gauge the volatility of capital flows. Available data from national and international

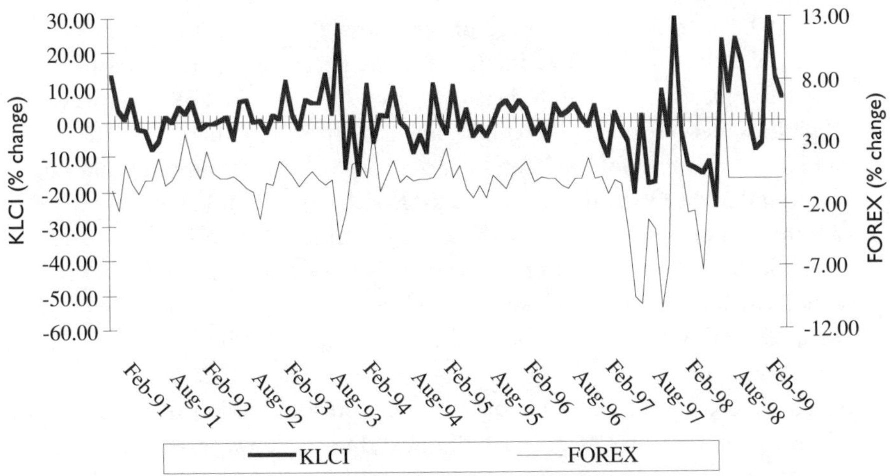

Fig. 5.7. Malaysia: Changes in monthly ringgit/U.S. dollar exchange rate and Kuala Lumpur composite index, 1991 to mid-1999

sources are not always reliable or even consistently defined. Even when they are available, the focus on net flows over particular periods obscures the possibly massive inflows and outflows underlying relatively modest net flows.

Cailloux and Griffith-Jones (1999, 19–21) have correctly criticized the current reliance on the coefficient of variation, that is, the ratio of the standard deviation of flows over their means. Instead they have proposed a new indicator, namely, the standard deviation of the flow of investment at time *m* divided by the moving average of cumulated flows. For them, the moving average—which makes the indicator less sensitive to large shocks occurring just before the new flow is measured—is calculated over the four quarters preceding the inflow. When monthly data have been available, that is, for the precrisis period before July 1997, we have done the same for monthly data. We have considered both portfolio fund inflows and outflows.

My results show that, although the five-quarter moving average adjustment significantly reduces the coefficient of variation, the adjusted measures reiterate the high volatility of other investments, followed by net portfolio investment inflows, with a slightly lower measure for the subset of net inflows of stocks and corporate securities.[14] Foreign direct investments were the least volatile, with bank loans slightly more volatile. According to the quarterly data for the precrisis period (1991 until mid-1997), volatility was also greatest for other investments in this period, followed by net portfolio investment inflows, with the volatility of net inflows for stocks and securities slightly higher. Again, foreign direct investments were the least volatile, followed by bank loans.

Interestingly, when comparing volatility in the precrisis period (1991 to mid-1997) with the entire period under study (1991 to the third quarter of 1999), volatility was greater in the precrisis period for other investments (probably because they only began to grow in the mid-1990s) and even slightly higher for foreign direct investment. Surprisingly, there was little difference in volatility for bank lending, contrary to expectations and the general trend in the rest of the crisis-affected East Asian region. This supports the argument put forward in this chapter that, unlike the case in Malaysia's neighbors, net foreign portfolio investment inflows (and the relatively small other investment inflows) were primarily responsible for the crisis in Malaysia and were the main vector for the spread of the regional contagion to the economy.

Analysis using the monthly data (for the precrisis period only) also included gross data on foreign portfolio investment inflows and outflows. Interestingly, the unadjusted measures of the volatility of inflows and outflows were not significantly different than for foreign direct investment and less volatile than for bank loans and especially net portfolio investment flows.

However, the adjusted measures suggested a hierarchy of volatility, with foreign direct investments the least volatile, followed by bank loans and portfolio investment inflows and outflows, with net flows being the most volatile.

5.3. VECTOR AUTOREGRESSION ANALYSIS

The goal of vector autoregression (VAR) analysis is to determine the interrelationships among the variables (not the parameter estimates). To assess the impact of a shock on the different flows, we create an impulse response function using VAR analysis. An impulse response function traces the response of the endogenous variables in the system to shocks in the errors. By analyzing the response pattern, we may be able to see the direction of interrelationships among variables and to determine whether or not a particular variable is volatile over time. The equation, consisting of four variables (KLCI, PFN, BLI, and FDI), is stated as follows.

$$Y_t = A_0 + A_1Y_{t-1} + A_2Y_{t-2} + A_3Y_{t-3} + e_t,$$

where Y_t is a (4×1) vector containing KLCI, PFN, BLI, and FDI, respectively, at time t; A_0 is a (4×1) vector of intercept terms; A_i is a (4×1) matrix of coefficients; and e_t is a (4×1) vector of error terms.

To determine the specification of the lags in the VAR equation, we use the Akaike information criterion (AIC) and the Schwarz criterion (SC) (see Pindyck and Rubinfeld 1997, 238–39). In our tests, the best results were obtained from VAR equations with one- to three-month lags, and only these are presented here. Our monthly observations are from January 1991 to June 1997, that is, after capital inflows increased but before the crisis began in July 1997, as BNM ceased to publish monthly data after July 1997.[15]

From the t-statistics obtained, KLCI appears to be highly correlated with its own past values, especially in the previous month, and to a lesser extent with net portfolio inflows three months before. PFN appears to be highly correlated with KLCI values in the previous two months but with little else. BLI also seems to be highly correlated with KLCI two months earlier but little else. FDI seems little correlated with its own and other past values. The set of graphs in figure 5.8 plots the impact of a of one-standard-deviation shock involving each of the different variables on the other variables, illustrating the same trends more graphically.

- From the graphs in the figure, it can be seen that the impact of a one standard deviation KLCI shock caused the KLCI to respond positively and PFN to respond positively before turning negative and fluctuating around zero. The response of BLI is generally modest but positive. The impact on FDI is not very significant, converging towards zero over time.

- The strong initial response of PFN to a one standard deviation PFN shock quickly petered out, whereas the KLCI responded negatively after some time to the same. Both BLI and FDI do not respond strongly to such a shock.
- After a strong initial response of BLI to a one standard deviation BLI shock, the response becomes modestly positive. However, the KLCI responds positively after some time. PFN responds positively after a short lag before petering out, whereas FDI responds both positively and then negatively before quickly petering out.
- FDI seems to initially respond positively to a one standard deviation FDI shock before petering out. After a slow initial response of KLCI to such a shock, the response seems to be consistently negative! Both PFN and BLI responded modestly but negatively to such FDI shocks before petering out.

Given the nature of VAR analysis, one would expect the strong positive response of each variable to a one standard deviation shock on itself. However, only the KLCI seemed to respond positively over time, suggesting likely reinforcement of the self-perpetuating nature of virtuous as well as vicious cycles involved in share price inflation and deflation. Such a finding would not contradict the possibility of herd behavior as well as speculative bubbles and their bursting.

Ironically, both PFN and FDI seem to have negative impacts on KLCI after an initially modest response. The negative impact of PFN on KLCI may suggest the likelihood of boom and bust cycles associated with foreign portfolio capital inflows and PFN as a vector for contagion from abroad. Conversely, KLCI seems to respond positively to BLI, suggesting that foreign borrowing probably contributes to share price inflation.

Other inflows, including KLCI, do not seem to affect FDI very much. This suggests that unexpected drops in KLCI do not necessarily lead to sudden pullouts of FDI. On the other hand, the strong initial responses of PFN to PFN, KLCI, and BLI seem quite significant. Given this analysis, PFN appears to be much more volatile than FDI and even BLI.

5.4. FOREIGN PORTFOLIO INVESTOR PERSPECTIVES

To understand the perceptions and behavior of foreign portfolio investors operating in the Malaysian capital market, several foreign managers and an-

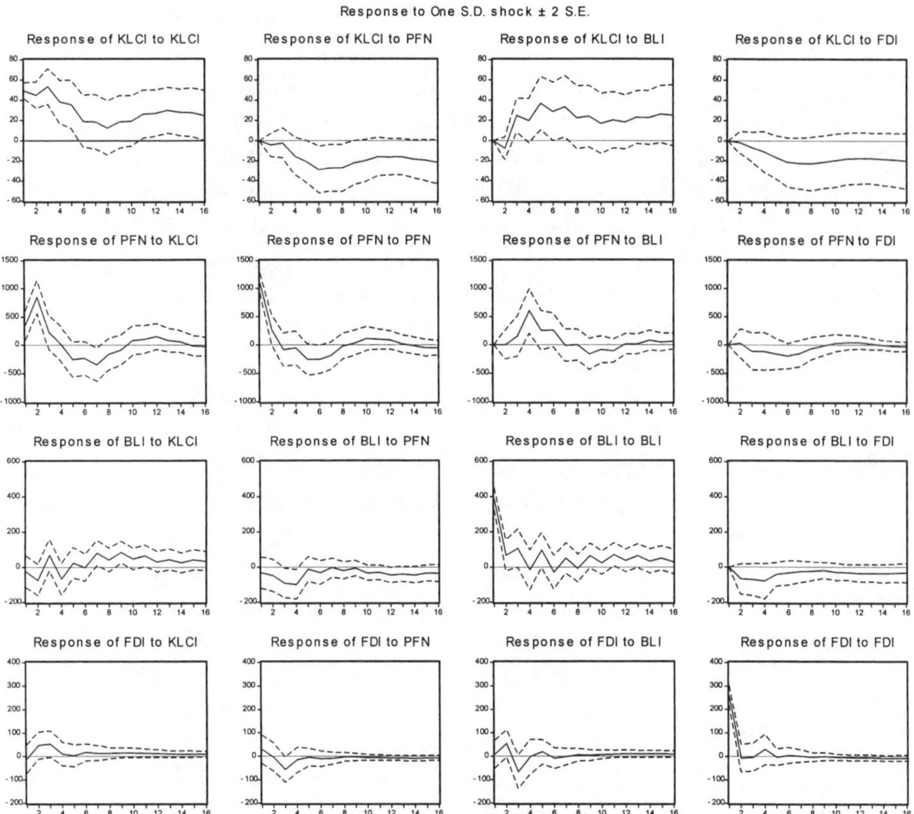

Fig. 5.8. VAR analysis: Responses to one-standard-deviation shock

alysts were interviewed.[16] These interviews were conducted to get a sense of what they perceived to be significant in making investment as well as divestment decisions. An open-ended questionnaire format was used to determine their personal and company investment frameworks and guidelines. Such information proved useful and complementary to the statistical and other analyses employed to understand foreign capital inflows into and out of Malaysia.

Before the crisis, most respondents had most of their holdings in corporate securities (most commonly around 80 percent, if not more), with the remainder usually in money market instruments or cash. Everyone agreed that the market for financial derivatives was very small before the crisis, and this was even more true by the time of the interviews in September 1999. Because money market rates were so low then, most foreign fund managers seemed to be holding cash if they were holding anything. Malaysian government securities and private debt securities were not being held by anyone interviewed. They were considered illiquid before the crisis and were only held by local funds and insurance companies. Everyone was almost exclusively focusing on corporate securities, and the overall percentage allocated to them—as opposed to fixed income securities—did not change postcrisis, remaining at around 20 percent. Over the previous 18 months, there had been a significant shift from assets to cash (and then back to assets) because the capital controls tax was imposed on the repatriation date, not on the date of sale.

All comments addressed only corporate securities, virtually "the only game in town." There was broad variation in average holding time. Of the five fund managers, three viewed six to 12 months as long term, with the other two investing on a two-year time horizon before, during, and after the crisis, in line with standard fund practice, though they agreed that this was rare. The three fund managers in Singapore all said that they were managing long-term money, six to 12 months in one case, two years in another, and three to four years in the third. All stated that holding time was basically unchanged postcrisis.

Everyone interviewed saw hedge funds as having the shortest average holding period, ranging from weeks to three months. They reasoned that this is because hedge fund managers do not have to worry about trustees and because they are trading on volatility, not on fundamentals. Mutual funds are seen as medium to short term, averaging from six to 12 months. Pension and insurance funds (especially from Japan) tend to be more long term, ranging from one to three years. These responses corroborated Maxfield's findings (1997, 72).

Basically, everyone interviewed was in search of higher returns, but if they were covering the spread according to Morgan Stanley Capital International (MSCI) then that also entailed diversification. According to a 1990s' Credit Lyonnais survey of fund managers, 80 percent of them were operating with the MSCI benchmark. In effect, what most people were saying in September 1999 was that the main reason for investing in Malaysia was to cover the benchmark in anticipation of Malaysia being restored to the MSCI benchmark in February 2000 (since postponed to May 2000).

The only push factors mentioned for precrisis investment in Malaysia and the rest of the region were the European recession in 1992 and low interest rates in Euro-American markets in the 1990s. This response could have been affected by the interview sample, which consisted of local agency brokers, local brokers, local analysts, and Singapore-based fund managers. The basic division of labor within global funds between "strategists" (who focus on liquidity and push factors) and "economists" (who focus on countries and hence more on pull factors) means that the sample did not include those who carefully compare emerging markets in relation to more developed markets.

Everyone claimed that they or their clients were investing in East Asia because they considered it to be the best of the emerging markets.

Specific pull factors cited for Malaysia, as opposed to other countries in the region, were good infrastructure, political stability, the size of the market (implying a bigger industrial spread), good economic fundamentals, and good corporate governance. Part of the reason for the strong flows to Malaysia before the crisis (e.g., in 1995–96) was the fact that it was listed on both the Developed Markets' and the Emerging Markets' MSCI indices; this apparent anomaly was due to the pre-1990s' Siamese twin relationship between the Kuala Lumpur Stock Exchange and the Stock Exchange of Singapore. The absence of barriers to portfolio investment was not seen as a crucial positive factor.

Geographical Differences

American fund managers are perceived by Malaysian analysts and brokers as overemphasizing political risks and uncertainties. They also tend to cover all emerging markets, not just those in Asia, and so tend to pay less attention to local information. However, others saw Hong Kong fund managers as also worried about the political risk factor. Singapore fund managers seemed to be much better informed about the political situation in Malaysia and were less likely to make inappropriate comparisons with Indonesia. But in general in September 1999 everyone interviewed was focused on the (November 29, 1999) elections (which were later suspended) and the government-announced forced bank mergers as key indicators.

Attractive Stocks

Nothing on the KLSE second board was recommended by those interviewed. Gaming, utilities, and consumer-oriented stocks were seen to have great upside potential. Banking was seen as a mixed bag, but everyone seemed positive about Maybank, the largest bank controlled by the government. Investors were mainly looking for secure returns, low risks, and liquidity. In 1996, before the crisis, they were mainly looking at privatization, "national service" (implying good political connections and implicit government guarantees) projects, and small companies, including the second board. After the crisis, in September 1999, they were looking more at banking, manufacturing, electronics, utilities, and export-oriented companies.

Hedge Funds

Tracking hedge fund activity and flows proved to be especially difficult. Anecdotally, they seemed unaffected by the controls because lots of funds were contracting with stock lenders offshore and then short-selling the stocks to domestic buyers. When the controls came in, they simply worked out cancellation agreements with the stock lenders. Also anecdotally, most of the "new" money in recent flows to the KLSE is, ironically, hedge fund money.

Capital Controls

Most of those interviewed saw the institution of capital controls as generally contributing to the economic recovery, but they questioned the timing and manner of their implementation. Most people thought the controls would have helped more if they had been instituted in February or even June 1998. Many argued that for local business and manufacturing they were crucial. A few people were uncertain whether the controls had a positive or negative effect and insisted on waiting to see what the medium- to long-term impacts on FDI and portfolio flows would be. Two people rejected the majority's positive assessment of capital controls, arguing that they had come too late and, as instituted, had simply caused a suspension of international flows. All agreed that a clear schedule for their implementation and removal would be beneficial and, as they stood then, the exit tax and capital gains levy were serving to deter inflows because foreign fund managers cannot or do not want to cope with the messy accounting required to track old and new money and so are staying out entirely. In Singapore, the fund managers saw Malaysia's recovery as paralleling those of other Southeast Asian economies, and argued that the recovery was not necessarily linked to the controls. One fund manager stated that they were mainly politically—not economically—motivated. None of the Singapore fund managers interviewed was affected by the Central Limit Order Book (CLOB) issue.

Everyone interviewed in Malaysia was either slightly or very positive about the prospects for the next five months (October 1999 to February 2000). Most were recommending increased exposure, with all fund managers planning small increases. However, no one expected a major increase in inflows until the beginning of 2000. In Singapore, everyone was much closer to neutral, looking especially at political uncertainty. All three were going to remain at current levels—8, 6, and 4 percent of total allocations—at least until the then expected February 2000 reinstatement on the MSCI. One fund manager was looking for major political change, either in paradigm or leadership, before increasing his exposure.

6. CONCLUSION

Foreign capital inflows into Malaysia augmented the high domestic savings rate to raise the domestic investment rate as well as Malaysian investments abroad in the 1990s. Thus, although there is some evidence that foreign capital inflows may have adversely affected the domestic savings rate indirectly, foreign capital inflows generally supplemented rather than substituted for domestic savings. It is difficult to be conclusive on this point, as the nature of foreign capital inflows has changed significantly over time. For example, even if earlier foreign capital inflows had adversely affected domestic savings, it is quite possible that the changed composition of recent foreign capital inflows may no longer adversely affect foreign capital inflows.

Increased foreign capital inflows have also reduced foreign exchange constraints, allowing the financing of additional imports but also inadvertently encouraging current account deficits. Finally, foreign capital inflows into Malaysia appear to have adversely affected factor payment outflows, export and import propensities, the terms of trade and capital flight, and thus the balance of payments. These results suggest caution in determining the extent to which foreign capital inflows should be encouraged. Also, Malaysia's heavy dependence on foreign direct investment in gross domestic capital formation, especially manufacturing investments, has probably also limited the development of domestic entrepreneurship as well as many other indigenous economic capabilities by requiring greater reliance on foreign capabilities, which are often associated with some types of FDI.

After mid-1995, the Southeast Asian currency pegs to the U.S. dollar—which had enhanced the region's competitiveness as the dollar declined for a decade after the 1985 Plaza Accord—became a growing liability as the yen began to depreciate once again. The overvalued currencies became attractive targets for speculative attacks, resulting in the futile but costly defenses of the Thai baht and Malaysian ringgit and the rapid regional spread of the herd panic called contagion. The resulting precipitous asset price collapses—as the share and property market bubbles burst—undermined Malaysia's heavily exposed banking system for the second time in little over a decade, threatening financial system liquidity and hence economic recession.

Undoubtedly, international financial liberalization succeeded in generating net capital inflows into East Asia, including Malaysia, unlike the case in other developing and transitional economies, many of which experienced net outflows. But it also exacerbated systemic instability and reduced the scope for the developmental government interventions that were responsible for the region's economic miracle. In Southeast Asia, especially Malaysia, FDI domination (well above the average for developing countries) of internationally competitive manufacturing had weakened domestic industrialists, inadvertently enhancing the dominance of finance capital and its influence over economic policy making.

Prior to the crisis, there had been a steady trend toward financial liberalization in Malaysia dating back to the mid-1980s. This had included considerable promotion of the Kuala Lumpur's "newly emerging" stock market, growing central bank speculative activity abroad (until it lost at least 20 billion ringgit, about U.S.$8 billion, after the sterling collapse of September 1992), and greater capital account convertibility. As in the rest of fast-growing East Asia, Malaysia succeeded in attracting a great many capital inflows. However, unlike the other crisis-affected economies, which succeeded in attracting considerable, mainly short-term, U.S. dollar bank loans to their more bank-based financed systems, Malaysia's vulnerability was mainly to the volatility of international portfolio capital flows, primarily into its stock market.

As a consequence, the nature of Malaysia's external liabilities at the beginning of the crisis was quite different from that of the other crisis-stricken East Asian economies. A greater proportion consisted of equity rather than debt. Much more of this liability, including the debt, was private—rather than public—compared to Malaysia's exposure in the mid-1980s. Compared to the others, much more Malaysian debt in the late 1990s was long term—rather than short term—in nature. Monetary policy as well as banking supervision in Malaysia had generally been much more prudent compared to the other crisis victims. Banks in Malaysia had not been allowed to borrow heavily from abroad to lend in the domestic market, as in the other economies. Such practices involved currency and term mismatches, which increased financial system vulnerability to foreign bankers' confidence as well as pressure on the exchange rate pegs.

These differences have lent support to the claim that Malaysia was an "innocent bystander" that fell victim to the regional contagion because it was in the wrong part of the world at the wrong time. Such a view takes a benign perspective on portfolio investment inflows, and does not recognize that such inflows are even more easily reversible and volatile than bank loan inflows. The magnitude of the gross inflows and outflows reflect the much greater volatility of these flows, which was often obscured by focusing on net flows. But even the net flow data indicate the relative size of these flows. A net sum of more than RM30 billion of portfolio investments flowed out in the last three quarters of 1997, much more than the total net inflows from 1995 and equivalent to almost a fifth of annual GNP. This exodus included RM21.6 billion of shares and corporate securities and RM8.8 billion of money market instruments. In just one quarter, from July to September 1997, a net RM16 billion of portfolio investments left the country.

Contrary to the innocent bystander hypothesis, Malaysia's experience may actually suggest the greater vulnerability of its heavy reliance on the capital market. As a consequence, the Malaysian economy became hostage to international portfolio investor confidence. Hence, when the government leadership engaged in rhetoric and policy initiatives that upset such investment confidence Malaysia paid a heavy price as portfolio divestment accelerated. Prescriptions of the IMF and conventional policy-making wisdom urged government spending cuts in the wake of the crisis. Such contractionary measures transformed what had begun as a currency crisis into a full-blown financial crisis, a crisis of the real economy. Thus, all the region's economies that had previously enjoyed massive capital inflows—whether in the form of short-term bank loans or portfolio investments—went into recession during 1998, following Thailand. From 7.7 percent growth in 1997, including 6.0 percent in the last quarter, the Malaysian economy shrank by −6.7 percent in 1998, or by −2.8, −6.8, −9.0, and −8.1 percent in the four quarters. The stock market dropped more dramatically, from almost 1,300 in February 1997 to a low of 262 in early September 1998, just 18 months later.

NOTES

I am grateful to Chin Kok Fay, Laura Kaehler, Liew San Yee, Lee Hwok Aun, and Wong Hwa Kiong for their research support, cooperation, and assistance. I am also appreciative of the comments and suggestions made by Jacques Cailloux and Stephany Griffith-Jones as well as Andy Haldane and other participants in the workshop convened at the Institute of Development Studies in Sussex in September 1999. The usual disclaimer applies.

1. The extension of limits allows banks to invest in Malaysia Airline System Berhad (MAS), the Malaysian International Shipping Corporation (MISC), and other approved "blue chip" shares as well as the shares of manufacturing companies and property trusts, subject to prescribed limits (for details, see BNM 1989, 101; and Lee 1992, 281). As for investments in the shares of manufacturing companies, the shares held by a commercial bank should not exceed 10 percent of its paid-up capital and reserves or 5 percent of a foreign bank's net working funds, whichever is lower. The sum of these shares should not exceed 25 percent of a domestic bank's paid-up capital and reserves, or 25 percent of a foreign bank's net working funds.

2. *Bumiputera* refers to the "indigenous" population of Malaysia, which is mainly composed of the Malays of Peninsular Malaysia.

3. Advocated by Hellmann, Murdock, and Stiglitz (1995), financial restraint attempts to create and channel rents in the financial and productive sectors in order to induce agents in the financial sector to engage in desirable or beneficial activities to economic agents. Unlike financial repression, wherein the government extracts rents from the private sector, financial restraint involves the government creating rent opportunities for the private sector. Financial restraint permits the government to create rent opportunities, but it also allows profit-maximizing firms to pursue and capture these rents, thus enabling private information to be utilized in making allocation decisions.

4. A BNM Survey of Private Investment in Malaysia found that this reduction in the share of bank credit to the manufacturing sector caused firms to increasingly rely on internally generated funds. On average, the surveyed firms financed 52 to 66 percent of

their capital expenditures from internally generated funds in the period 1986–90. Bank financing only accounted for between 10 to 14 percent of total financing. Although banks still provided a larger share of external finance than the capital market (ranging from 1 to 8 percent), this probably reflected the less developed state of the capital market vis-à-vis the banking system then. Company size was also found to be an important determinant of access to credit, while larger companies enjoyed lower credit costs on average. This could be due to the less stringent requirements imposed by financial institutions on large companies with better track records and reputations (see Zainal et al., 1994, 313). Such "discrimination" was more pronounced during the recession of 1985–86, when the average cost of credit for large companies was almost 11 percent lower than for small and medium-sized enterprises.

5. In a televised interview with a local station, Looi Teong Chye, the president of the Small and Medium Industries Association of Malaysia, mentioned that some bankers requested collateral of double the value of loans applied for by small-scale entrepreneurs.

6. Part of this section draws from Chin 1999.

7. However, there continued to be active trading of Malaysian counters in Singapore through the over the counter Central Limited Order Book (CLOB) market, before this was declared illegal on September 1, 1998.

8. In the 1960s, the stock market had mixed fortunes, with a boom from September 1961 to June 1964, followed by a bearish phase (Drake 1975), which the government addressed partly through this policy of requiring companies granted pioneer status to go public.

9. Ariff and Lee (1993) argue that excessive underpricing of Malaysia's initial public offerings (IPOs) was mainly due to government intervention in price setting and not merely the consequence of asymmetric information, winner's curse, or ex ante uncertainty. One may disagree by arguing that shares that are issued at their intrinsic values can be bid up by an overly optimistic market, leading us to wrongly interpret demand pressures as underpricing. However, demand pressure at or after listing may push prices above their intrinsic values in the short run, as prices of new issues decline in the longer run after demand pressure subsides.

10. See Akyuz 1995 and Griffith-Jones 1997.

11. For further details, see Bank Negara Malaysia 1993. For instance, the BNM had to absorb large interest payments for issuing bonds to mop up extra liquidity in the financial system.

12. Foreign Direct Investment is used here to refer to what Bank Negara Malaysia refers to as external equity investment, which refers specifically to the establishment or expansion of businesses, including joint ventures, in which the foreign investor has effective control of the business.

Official BNM data understate actual FDI by omitting reinvested earnings as well as equity in the form of imported plant and equipment, as the following letter concerning Bank Negara Malaysia data on capital flows from a BNM official to Jacques Cailloux, dated July 27, 1999, makes clear (my italics): "For your information, the data on FDI, portfolio flows and loans that you retrieved from the Bank Negara Malaysia website are sourced from the Cash BOP Reporting System of Bank Negara Malaysia and should be used as an indicator only. At present, the Malaysian Department of Statistics, the official compiler of balance of payments statistics, *does not publish data on FDI in Malaysia.* The FDI is currently reflected in the net private long term capital account, which also includes Malaysian investment overseas and foreign borrowing by Malaysian-owned companies. The Department is, however, in the process of conducting a new survey to capture the gross flows of private capitals into and out of Malaysia. . . . 2. The Cash BOP Reporting System was implemented by Bank Negara to capture transactions, on a cash basis, between residents and non-residents effected through the domestic banking system, as well as inter-company and overseas accounts. Since the System captures data on a cash basis, it *does not capture data on reinvested earnings as well as direct equity that came into Malaysia in the form of machinery.*"

13. Stiglitz (1999) calls this approach to effective financial regulation from the perspective of risk management the dynamic portfolio approach. Bank of International Settlements data understate Malaysian external debt, as the following clarification from a BNM official dated July 27, 1999, makes clear (my italics): "3. As for the data on loans, the data that you retrieved refer to gross borrowings by the Federal Government as well as the non-bank private sector that are sourced from the Cash BOP Reporting System. This data gives an indication on the countries that extended or received loans to/from Malaysia. The official data on External Debt, which is published in Table VIII.10, is sourced from various sources, such as the Accountant General's Office, quarterly report [*sic*] from the non-bank private sector as well as from the banking institutions. Table VIII.10 refers to the *outstanding balance of external loans* (by type of borrower), which *comprise inter-company loans, bonds raised in the international capital markets as well as bank lending.* On the other hand, the *BIS data refers only to bank lending.* As such, the data reported by BIS is *much lower compared with BNM data* (as at end-1998, BNM: RM161.9 billion. US$42.6 billion); BIS: US$20.8 billion."

14. The results can be found in a more complete version of this chapter; see Jomo 1999.

15. The results of the analysis can be found in ibid.

16. For further details on the methodological approach used for the interviews, see ibid.

REFERENCES

Adam, C., and W. Cavendish. 1995. "Early prioritization." In *Privatizing Malaysia: Rents, rhetoric, realities,* ed. Jomo K. S., 219–35. Boulder, Colo.: Westview Press.

Akyuz, Y. 1995. "Taming international finance." In *Managing the Global Economy,* edited by J. Michie and J. G. Smith. New York: Oxford University Press.

Ariff, M., and D. Lee. 1993. "Share-price-changes-volume relation on the Singapore equity market." *Applied Financial Economics* 3, no. 4:339.

Awang Adek Hussin. 1997. "Offshore Financial Centre: The Labuan experiment." Paper presented at the MIER National Outlook Conference, Kuala Lumpur, December 2–3.

Bank Negara Malaysia. 1987. *Quarterly Economic Bulletin,* 2, no. 3.

———. 1989. *Annual Report, 1988.* Kuala Lumpur: BNM.

———. 1994. *Annual Report, 1993.* Kuala Lumpur: BNM.

———. 1994. *Money and Banking in Malaysia, 1959–1994,* 35th anniversary ed. Kuala Lumpur: BNM.

———. 1995. *Annual Report, 1994.* Kuala Lumpur: BNM.

———. 1997. *Annual Report, 1996.* Kuala Lumpur: BNM.

———. *Monthly Statistical Bulletin.* Various issues.

Banker's Journal Malaysi. 1995. October/November.

Cailloux, Jacques, and Stephany Griffith-Jones. 1999. *International capital flows, what do we know about their volatility? Evidence from Latin American countries.* Brighton: Institute of Development Studies, University of Sussex.

Chenery, H. B., and A. Strout. 1966. "Foreign assistance and economic development." *American Economic Review* 56, no. 4 (September): 679–733.

Chin Kok Fay. 1999. "The stock market and economic development in Malaysia." IKMAS Working Paper 16." Universiti Kebangsaan Malaysia, Bangi, March.

———. 2000. "Financing manufacturing in Malaysia: Experience, issues, and challenges." In *Southeast Asia's Ersatz industrialisation,* ed. Jomo K. S. Hammondsworth: Macmillan.

Chin Kok Fay, and Jomo K. S. 1999. "Financial reform and crisis in Malaysia." Paper presented at the workshop Big Bang in East Asia. Hosei University, March.

Chin Kok Fay, with Jomo K. S. 1996. "Financial liberalization and economic development in Malaysia." Paper presented at the conference Globalisation and Development. Faculty of Economics and Administration, University of Malaya, August.

———. 2000. "Financial intermediation and restraint." In *Globalisation versus development: Heterodox perspectives,* ed. Jomo K. S. and Shyamala Nagaraj. Hammondsworth: Macmillan.

Chowdhury, A., and I. Islam. 1993. *The newly industrializing economies of East Asia.* London: Routledge.

Drake, P. J. 1975. "The New-Issue Boom in Malaysia and Singapore 1961–1964." Reprinted in *Readings on Malaysian economic development.* Ed. D. Lim. Kuala Lumpur: Oxford University Press.

Gomez, E. T. 1994. *Political business: Corporate involvement of Malaysian political parties.* Townsville, Queensland: James Cook University of North Townsville.

Griffin, K., and J. Enos. 1970. "Foreign assistance: Objectives and consequences." *Economic Development and Cultural Change* 18, no. 3 (April): 313–27.

Griffith-Jones, S. 1997. "Regulatory challenges for source countries of surges in capital flows." Paper prepared for the FONDAD conference, November 18–19. Available at <http://www.ids.ac.uk/ids/research/easia.html>.

Hellmann, T., K. Murdock, and J. Stiglitz. 1995. "Financial restraint: Towards a new paradigm." Mimeo, Stanford University.

Hing Ai Yun. 1987. "The financial system and industrial investment in West Malaysia." *Journal of Contemporary Asia* 17, no. 4:409–35.

International Finance Corporation. 1997. *Emerging stock market factbook, 1997.* Washington, DC: International Finance Corporation.

International Monetary Fund. (1998). *International Financial Statistics.* November 1998.

Ishak, Shari, et al. 1999. "Social impact of financial crisis: Malaysia." Report submitted to the United Nations Development Program. Kuala Lumpur.

Jomo K. S. 1990. *Growth and structural change in the Malaysian economy.* London: Macmillan.

———. 1995. *Privatizing Malaysia: Rents, rhetoric, realities.* Boulder: Westview.

———, ed. 1998a. *Tigers in trouble: Financial governance, liberalisation, and crises in East Asia.* London: Zed.

———. 1998b. "Malaysia's debacle: Whose fault?" *Cambridge Journal of Economics* 22, no. 6:707–22.

———. 1999a. "Beyond crony capitalism: Rent-seeking, financial restraint, and economic development." Report prepared for Centre for Development and Entrepreneurship, Johannesburg. Project on Entrepreneurship and Expanding the Business section in South Africa.

———. 1999b. "Capital flows into and out Malaysia." Paper presented at the workshop Global Capital Flows, IDS, Sussex, September.

Khor Kok Peng. 1987. *Malaysia's economy in decline.* Penang: Consumers' Association of Penang.

Kuala Lumpur Stock Exchange. 1996. *KLSE Statistics, 1996.* Kuala Lumpur: KLSE.

Lee Hock Lock. 1987. *Central banking in Malaysia: A study of the development of the financial system and monetary management.* Singapore: Butterworths.

———. 1992. *Regulation of banks and other depository institutions in Malaysia: A study in monetary, prudential, and other controls.* Singapore: Butterworths.

Maxfield, Sylvia. 1997. *Gatekeepers of Growth: Central Banking in Developing Countries.* Princeton: Princeton University Press.

Ng Beoy Kui, ed. 1989. *The development of capital markets in the SEACEN countries.* Kuala Lumpur: South East Asian Central Banks Research and Training Centre.

Ong Hong Cheong. 1998. "Coping with capital flows and the role of monetary policy: The Malaysian experience, 1990–95." In *Coping with capital flows in East Asia,* ed. C. H. Kwan, Donna Vandenbrink, and Chia Siow Yue. Singapore: Institute of Southeast Asian Studies; Tokyo: Nomura Research Institute.

Park, Y. C. 1994. "Concepts and issues." In *The Financial Development of Japan, Korea and Taiwan: Growth, Repression and Liberalization,* ed. H. T. Patrick and Y. C. Park. New York: Oxford University Press.

Philippine Statistical Yearbook (1997). Manila. National Statistical Coordination Board.

Pindyck, Robert S., and Daniel L. Rubinfeld. 1997. *Econometric models and economic forecasts.* 4th ed. Singapore: McGraw-Hill.

Rosenstein-Rodan, P. N. 1961. "International Aid for Underdeveloped Countries," *Review of Economics and Statistics* 43: 103–38.

Singh, A. 1995. *Corporate financial patterns in industrializing economies: A comparative international study.* Technical Paper 2. Washington, DC: IFC.

Stiglitz, J. 1999. "What have we learned from the recent crises? Implications for banking regulation." Remarks delivered at the conference Global Financial Crises: Implications for Banking and Regulation, Federal Reserve Bank of Chicago, Chicago, May 6.

United Nations Conference on Trade and Development (UNCTAD). 1998. Trade and Development Report. Geneva: UNCTAD.

Weisskoff, T. E. 1972. "An econometric test of alternative constants on the growth of underdeveloped countries." *Review of Economics and Statistics* 54(1), Part II: 67–78.

Wong Hwa Kiong, with Jomo K. S. 1999. "The impact of foreign capital inflows on the Malaysian economy, 1966–1996." Mimeo.

Zainal, Aznam Yusof, et al. 1994. "Financial reform in Malaysia." In *Financial reform: Theory and experience,* ed. Gerard Caprio Jr., et al. New York: Cambridge University Press.

Zeti, Akhtar Aziz. 1989. "Development of capital markets in Malaysia." In *The development of capital markets in the SEACEN countries,* ed. Ng Beoy Kui. Kuala Lumpur: Research and Training Centre, South East Asian Central Banks.

CHAPTER 6

The Recent Economic Crisis in Indonesia: Causes, Impacts, and Responses

Anwar Nasution

The crisis that hit Indonesia in the late 1990s was a combination of political and economic crises. The economic crisis itself was to an important extent a financial crisis in that it was a mix of banking and external debt crises that was mainly centered around private sector debt. This chapter argues that this financial crisis was caused by a number of factors. The first major factor was excessive corporate sector short-term external borrowings. A large share of these were not invested productively, particularly because the distorted products and financial markets structures prevented them from being used efficiently. As a result, the external loans were not invested in ways that would significantly increase productivity and generate the stream of profits and export earnings necessary for repayment. Second, the financial sector reform of 1988 (discussed subsequently) was not accompanied by strict implementation of the rules and regulations governing the financial system. Moreover, the liberal "entry policy" in the financial sector was not accompanied by a clear-cut "exit policy."

In addition, there had been a pervasive lack of confidence in the government. This was partly caused by the closure of 16 financially distressed banks in November 1997 and confusing government policies. The lack of confidence precipitated a bank run, panic buying, and capital flight, which led to both an internal and an external liquidity crunch and a sharp increase in the velocity of money. Imports had to be restrained, as foreign banks became reluctant to roll over short-term debt and accept letters of credit from Indonesia. The fear of further currency depreciation put the exchange rate and interest rates under more pressure. Government decisions to limit access to foreign borrowings and to shift public sector deposits from (mainly state-owned) commercial banks to the central bank squeezed liquidity. With banks suddenly illiquid, bankruptcies and the risks of default by corporate borrowers also increased. The fact that Bank Indonesia moved, in mid-August 1997, to a floating exchange rate system suggests that it had limited external reserves with which to defend the exchange rate.

The financial crisis occurred in Indonesia at an unfortunate time. On the domestic front, the weather problem associated with a long drought and forest fire in 1997 and 1998 had had seriously damaging effects on production in the forestry and agriculture sectors. Because of the drought, crop production fell by 1.8 percent and the growth of agricultural production dropped to 0.6 percent in 1997. On the external front, there was a combination of negative terms of trade and reduced capital inflows. The fall in oil prices and low demand for Indonesian exports (such as wood-based products) reduced foreign exchange revenues. Meanwhile, slow growth in Japan and Korea drained capital flows from those countries.

The economic problem was magnified by political uncertainty and a flip-flop government policy in effect since the general elections in 1997. Angered by rising prices and unemployment, violent riots erupted in a number of towns, which led to the resignation of President Suharto, who had been re-elected for a seventh term in March 1998. Even with his departure, political uncertainty remains. President Burhanuddin Jusuf Habibie, in power from May 1998 to October 1999, who was known as a protégé of Mr. Suharto, had a reputation as a big spender and possessed no strong political base. The relatively peaceful general election in June 1999 was not a guarantee of a smooth presidential election in the general sessions of Indonesian People's Assembly (MPR)—the People's Assembly Sessions held in October–November 1999.

The International Monetary Fund (IMF) was partly responsible for aggravating the crisis. First, it recommended closing the banks in November 1997 without adequate preparation. The combination of the sharp devaluation of the rupiah, high nominal interest rates, and tight liquidity pushed the already fragile banks and their customers into bankruptcy. The capital flight caused a massive migration of assets denominated in domestic currency to foreign currencies and from the domestic financial market to international financial centers. The tight monetary and austere fiscal policies led to an economic contraction that had high social costs in terms of eroding real wages and high unemployment rates. Second, not until April 1998 did the IMF make a monumental shift toward recommending fiscal stimulus, the creation of social safety nets, and the resolution of the external debt overhang. As a result, the severe cut in government expenditures undertaken up to that time magnified the domestic economic recession.

This chapter reviews the economic crisis in Indonesia, its causes and impacts, and the government responses to it. It is divided into four sections. Section 1 examines recent macroeconomic developments prior to the crises. Section 2 discusses the banking crisis. Section 3 analyzes policy responses undertaken to cope with the capital inflows since the early 1990s and an analysis of stabilization and adjustment under the IMF program. Conclusions are presented in section 4.

1. WEAK MACROECONOMIC FUNDAMENTALS

Indonesia was indeed in need of adjustment, particularly because of the weaknesses of its economic fundamentals and changes in the international environment that began in 1995. On the domestic front, the massive capital inflows and the change in its composition toward short-term private capital between the early 1990s and 1997 caused bouts of domestic economic overheating. The rapid economic growth had been accompanied by rising domestic inflation and interest rates and a widening current account deficit (table 6.1). The low rate of inflation, high growth of GDP, and high rate of growth of nonoil exports, which were often quoted as indicators of sound economic fundamentals, were largely artificial. The government had to pay expensive subsidies to control prices of state-vended products to keep the inflation rate low, below 10 percent per annum between 1990 and 1996.

The high rate of growth in the gross domestic product (GDP) during the 1990s was mostly associated with the "bubble" industries, including construction, public utilities, and services in the nontraded sector of the economy (table 6.2). Moreover, most of the growth rates of nonoil exports during the 1990s consisted of those sectors that, like electronics, sport shoes, and textiles and garments, relied the least on domestic inputs and were associated with firms from East Asia (mainly Japan, South Korea, and Taiwan) with strong currencies. In contrast, those domestically owned sectors that relied heavily on domestic inputs fared poorly. Part of the problem was due to the fact that exports of palm oil and wood-based products were subject to quotas (table 6.3). Revenue from oil exports also declined because of the drop in oil prices.

The 1997–98 crisis seriously affected the economy and damaged the banking and corporate sectors. The move to a flexible exchange rate system sharply raised the nominal exchange rate from Rp2,599 to one U.S. dollar in July 1997 to Rp10,400 in January 1998 and Rp14,900 in June 1998 (figs. 6.1 and 6.2). The combination of sharp depreciation of the rupiah and the meltdown of the banking system forced an increase (weighted average) in annual lending interest rates from 15.45 percent in July 1997 to 70 percent in April 1998 and nearly 82 percent in August 1998. Despite large budget subsidies intended to control the prices of state-vended products, the inflation rate rose to 77.63 percent in 1998, compared to 11 percent in 1997 and 6.47 percent in

1996. Because of the fiscal distress, the budget deficit rose to 2 percent of GDP in the fiscal year 1998–99 (ending in March). The economy (measured as GDP) contracted by −13.6 percent in 1998, compared to positive growth of more than 6 percent per annum on average during the previous 25 years.

The rise in unemployment and inflation rates increased the number of people living below the poverty line from 22.5 million (11.3 percent of the total population) in 1996 to 34.2 million (16.7 percent of total population) in 1998. The poverty issue was more pronounced in the nontraded sector of the economy, in the agriculture sector, and on the island of Java, as it relies heavily on rice farming, which requires plenty of water. It was estimated that over 45 percent of the rural population, or 56.8 million people, were living below the poverty line. Java absorbs more than two-thirds of over 200 million of the total population of Indonesia.

On the external front, the current account balance improved following the crisis, mainly as a result of the impact of the sharp depreciation of the rupiah on imports rather than exports. A combination of yen depreciation vis-à-vis the U.S. dollar since 1995 and the continuing weak banking system in Japan slowed the inflow of Japanese foreign direct investment to Indonesia. Capital flows from Newly Industrialized Economies (NIEs) also dried up due to slow growth of their exports and strains in their financial systems and companies (in the case of Korea). The rise in interest rates and investment returns in the United States further reduced capital inflows, as they made investment in emerging countries, including Indonesia, less attractive. The combination of these internal and external factors ignited an interruption and reversal of foreign capital inflows.

1.1. EXCHANGE RATE MOVEMENTS

The exchange rate is the single most important relative price in the economy. In a more open economy, monetary transmission operates through exchange rate effects on net exports and interest rate effects on financial portfolios. The exchange rate policy in Indonesia, jointly with other policies, had traditionally been used mainly to remove distortions in the domestic economy and to help safeguard international competitiveness.[1]

Bank Indonesia, the central bank, used to intervene in the foreign exchange market by buying and selling the rupiah in an "intervention band" around the central rate. Prior to the crisis, the authorities had targeted nominal depreciation of the rupiah against the dollar between 3 to 5 percent per annum. Before shifting to the present flexible exchange rate regime, Bank Indonesia had tried to defend the moving band system from speculative attacks by widening the intervention band to 12 percent effective in July 1997 (fig. 6.2). In the end,

TABLE 6.1. Indonesia: Selected Key Indicators, 1990–99 (percentages of GDP, unless otherwise indicated)

	Annual Average											
	1980s	1990s	1990	1991	1992	1993	1994	1995	1996	1997	1998	1999[a]
Internal stability												
Gross domestic product real GDP												
(% of growth rate)	6.6	5.2	9.0	8.9	7.2	7.3	7.5	8.1	8.0	4.6	−13.6	−1.7[b]
Consumption	73.4	67.8	63.7	63.9	62.0	67.5	65.1	69.1	70.3	70.4	78.3	79.6
Private	63.0	59.2	53.9	54.0	52.2	58.5	56.5	61.0	62.7	63.1	70.9	
Government	10.4	8.6	9.8	9.8	9.8	9.0	8.6	8.0	7.6	7.3	7.4	
National Saving		27.7	27.5	26.9	26.9	27.0	28.4	28.0	29.3	28.0		
Private		20.5	19.1	19.8	20.5	20.4	22.0	22.4	23.0	17.2		
Public		7.3	8.4	7.1	6.4	6.6	6.4	5.6	6.3	10.8	8.0	
Investment	23.8	29.3	30.1	29.9	29.0	28.3	30.3	31.3	32.7	31.0	20.9	18.9
Private	13.5	22.6	23.5	21.7	20.9	20.9	24.0	25.8	27.4	25.0	14.0	
Public	10.3	6.6	6.6	7.7	7.8	7.4	6.3	5.5	5.3	6.0	6.9	
Inflation (Consumer Price Index [CPI])	8.5	16.4	9.5	9.5	4.9	9.8	9.2	8.6	6.5	11.6	77.6	10.6
Fiscal balance		0.1	0.4	0.4	−0.4	−0.6	0.1	0.8	0.2	−0.2		
External stability												
Current account balance	−1.2	−2.4	−2.8	−3.7	−2.2	−1.6	−1.7	−3.6	−3.7	−2.7	0.1	10.9
Real effective exchange rate (1997 =100)	44.1	113.5	95.1	93.2	90.8	85.6	82.5	80.1	78.0	100.0	315.8	101.4

Nominal exchange rate/CPI (1997 = 100)	65.1	114.0	111.3	107.7	104.2	97.7	93.2	88.6	85.5	100.0	238.1	431.6
Net capital inflows	1.9	−2.3	4.9	5.0	3.8	1.7	2.0	4.0	5.4	−1.1	0.1	−20.6
Of which:												
Net direct investment	2.1	1.2	1.0	1.3	1.4	1.0	0.8	1.9	2.5	2.1	−0.7	−4.1
Net portfolio investment	0.3	−0.9	−0.1	0.0	−0.1	1.1	2.2	2.0	2.2	−1.2	−14.4	−4.3
Other capital		−1.6	3.3	3.6	3.5	1.4	−0.9	1.2	0.1	−0.2	−26.1	−12.2
Net error and omissions	−0.5	−1.0	0.7	0.1	−1.0	−1.9	−0.1	−1.1	0.6	−1.8	−4.6	0.1
Net resource transfer/GDP (1997 = 100)	−60.8	−99.5	−100.1	−86.1	−535.6	−749.0	−309.7	396.3	198.5	100.0	190.3	−329.3
Reserves (in months of imports)	5.1	5.1	4.7	4.8	5.0	5.2	5.0	4.4	5.1	4.4	7.3	10.6
Ratio M2 to reserves (%)	345.7	556.4	514.0	539.0	552.6	602.3	643.4	690.3	638.6	419.9	407.5	289.4
Total external debt		72.0	65.9	68.4	69.0	56.7	55.5	54.8	49.3	101.4	127.1	
Total external debt (percentage of exports of goods and services)		218.1	222.0	236.9	221.8	211.9	197.4	197.4	188.7	255.0	232.2	
Short-term debt (percentage of total external debt)		22.1	15.9	17.9	20.5	21.0	19.6	22.2	27.1	27.2	27.2	
Short-term debt (in U.S.$ billions)		24.9	11.1	14.3	18.1	18.8	21.1	27.6	35.0	37.0	41.0	55.5
Debt-service ratio (percentage of exports of goods and services)	15.3	36.4	30.9	32.0	33.0	33.6	32.6	30.3	35.9	40.5	58.6	51.6
Exports of goods and services (percentage of GDP)	14.9	25.6	25.1	28.1	30.2	26.8	26.9	27.2	27.1	27.5	11.5	
Exports of goods (% of growth rate)	5.9	12.1	15.9	13.5	16.6	8.4	8.8	13.4	9.7	7.5	15.4	−8.7[b]

Sources: IMF, *International Financial Statistics,* various issues; World Bank, World Debt Tables: External Finance for Developing Countries, 1996; World Bank 1998; Bank Indonesia, *Indonesian Financial Statistics,* various issues. BPS, Statistics of Balances of Central Government, 1999.

[a]Up to the third quarter of 1999.

[b]Compared to that of the third quarter of 1998.

TABLE 6.2. Indonesia: Share and Rate of Growth of Real Gross Domestic Product by Industrial Origin (at 1983 constant market prices for 1985–93 and 1993 constant market prices for 1994–99)

	Share		Rate of Growth									
	1985	1995	1990	1991	1992	1993	1994	1995	1996	1997	1998	1999[a]
Gross domestic product	100.0	100.0	7.2	7.0	6.5	6.5	7.6	8.1	8.0	4.6	−13.2	−4.1
Gross domestic product nonpetroleum	78.7	91.3	7.6	6.5	8.4	7.8	8.1	9.1	8.3	5.3	−14.3	−4.4
Agriculture. livestock. forestry, and fishery	22.6	16.1	2.0	1.6	6.7	1.4	0.9	3.8	3.2	0.7	0.8	5.1
Farm food crops	14.0	8.6	0.5	−0.5	7.7	−1.2	−2.1	4.6	2.4	−2.7	1.9	8.1
Nonfood crops	3.6	2.6	4.9	5.4	4.8	5.8	5.1	4.7	4.2	1.2	2.8	6.9
Livestock and products	2.4	1.8	3.7	6.0	7.9	5.6	4.0	4.2	6.1	4.9	−7.1	−0.4
Forestry	1.0	1.6	3.0	0.0	−2.2	1.7	0.5	0.0	1.3	8.0	−1.8	−4.5
Fishery	1.6	1.6	5.0	5.2	5.8	5.7	8.8	1.9	4.6	5.8	4.1	2.0
Mining and quarrying	18.2	9.3	5.2	10.2	−1.9	2.2	5.6	6.7	5.8	1.7	−3.1	0.1
Crude petroleum and natural gas	17.1	6.2	4.2	9.3	−4.5	−0.3	2.6	0.0	1.4	−0.6	−2.1	−4.5
Other mining and quarrying	1.1	3.1	18.0	20.1	24.0	20.8	13.9	23.5	14.6	5.2	−4.7	8.5
Manufacturing industries	15.8	23.9	12.5	10.1	9.7	9.3	12.5	10.7	11.7	6.4	−11.9	−2.3
Nonoil and gas manufacturing	11.5	21.3	13.0	10.9	11.0	11.6	13.5	13.0	11.7	7.4	−13.4	8.2
Oil/gas industry	4.3	2.5	11.0	7.4	5.3	1.3	5.6	−5.4	11.1	−2.0	1.6	−3.7
Electricity. gas, and water supply	0.4	1.1	17.9	16.1	10.1	10.1	12.5	15.5	13.2	12.3	1.9	0.2
Construction	5.3	7.6	13.5	11.3	10.8	12.1	14.9	12.9	12.8	6.4	−40.5	−7.2

Trade, hotel, and restaurant	14.6	16.7	7.1	5.4	7.3	8.8	7.6	7.7	8.2	5.8	−18.0	−13.3
Wholesale and retail trade	12.2	13.4	6.8	5.1	7.4	9.0	6.8	7.7	8.2	5.9	−18.5	−15.2
Hotels and restaurants	2.3	3.3	8.7	7.0	7.2	7.7	11.1	7.9	8.2	3.8	−16.3	−5.8
Transportation and communication	5.3	7.2	9.6	7.9	10.0	9.9	8.3	9.4	7.8	8.3	−15.1	−10.3
Transportation	4.7	6.0	8.6	7.3	10.0	8.9	6.5	7.3	6.4	6.4	−19.9	−15.4
Communication	0.5	1.2	16.9	12.3	10.0	16.4	20.4	21.1	14.5	17.4	4.8	7.5
Financial. ownership, and business	6.4	9.0	10.1	9.7	9.8	10.3	10.2	11.2	8.8	6.5	−26.6	−16.5
Banking and other financial intermediaries	3.5	4.7	14.1	13.1	13.0	13.0	13.8	13.9	9.6	5.3	−34.0	−22.2
Building rental	2.9	2.8	4.2	4.0	4.2	5.0	4.0	5.5	5.8	5.0	−19.9	−11.9
Business services		1.4					12.0	14.2	12.1	8.5	−16.7	−10.8
Services	11.3	9.2	4.7	3.7	4.3	4.3	2.8	3.3	3.4	2.8	−3.2	3.1
Public administration and defense	7.6	6.0	4.6	3.1	3.0	2.0	1.3	1.3	1.3	1.2	−7.3	1.9
Private services	3.7	3.2	5.0	5.2	7.3	8.9	5.8	7.2	7.4	5.7	3.7	4.9
Traded sector[b]	40.2	38.9	8.5	9.3	4.5	6.2	9.5	8.5	9.1	5.2	−8.4	−1.2
Nontraded sector[c]	59.8	61.1	6.4	5.3	7.8	6.7	6.5	7.9	7.3	4.5	−16.6	−6.0

Source: Central Bureau of Statistics. *Economic Indicators,* various issues.

[a]Preliminary data. Growth as of the second quarter of 1999 compared to that of 1998.

[b]Comprised of nonfood crops, forestry, fishery. Mining and quarrying and manufacturing industries.

[c]Comprised of farm food crops, livestock and products, electricity, gas, water supply, construction, trade, hotels, and restaurants. Transportation & Communication. Financial. Ownership and Business and Services.

TABLE 6.3. Indonesia: Export Value by Commodity Group

Total Exports	1990	1991	1992	1993	1994	1995	1996	1997	1998	1999[b]
In billions of U.S.$	25.68	29.14	33.97	36.82	40.05	45.42	49.81	53.44	48.85	10.17
Agriculture	2.08	2.28	2.21	2.64	2.82	2.89	2.91	3.13	3.65	0.66
Industrial product	11.88	15.07	19.61	22.94	25.70	29.33	32.12	34.99	34.59	6.95
Forestry-based products[a]	3.48	3.87	4.53	6.01	5.86	6.00	6.09	6.24	5.85	1.25
Garments and textiles	2.93	4.08	6.06	6.18	5.80	6.20	6.55	5.27	6.53	1.37
Electronics	0.29	0.67	1.10	1.64	0.72	0.92	1.41	1.37	1.49	0.33
Mining and minerals	0.64	0.89	1.45	1.46	1.80	2.69	3.02	3.11	2.70	0.67
Other sectors	0.01	0.01	0.02	0.03	0.04	0.05	0.04	0.60	0.02	0.05
Total nonoil exports	14.60	18.25	23.30	27.08	30.36	34.95	38.09	41.82	40.96	8.33
Oil and gas exports	11.07	10.89	10.67	9.75	9.69	10.46	11.72	11.62	7.87	1.87
As a percentage of total exports	100.0	100.0	100.0	100.0	100.0	100.0	100.0	100.0	100.0	100.0
Agriculture	8.1	7.8	6.5	7.2	7.0	6.4	5.8	5.9	7.5	6.5
Industrial products	46.3	51.7	57.7	62.3	64.2	64.6	64.5	65.5	70.8	68.3
Forestry-based products[a]	13.6	13.3	13.3	16.3	14.6	13.2	12.2	11.7	12.0	12.3
Garments and textiles	11.4	14.0	17.8	16.8	14.5	13.7	13.2	9.9	13.4	13.5
Electronics	1.1	2.3	3.2	4.4	1.8	2.0	2.8	2.6	3.1	3.3
Mining and minerals	2.5	3.1	4.3	4.0	4.5	5.9	6.1	5.8	5.5	6.6
Others sectors	0.0	0.0	0.1	0.1	0.1	0.1	0.1	1.1	0.0	0.5
Total nonoil exports	56.9	62.6	68.6	73.5	75.8	77.0	76.5	78.3	83.8	81.9
Oil and gas exports	43.1	37.4	31.4	26.5	24.2	23.0	23.5	21.7	16.1	18.4
As a percentage of annual growth[c]	15.9	13.5	16.6	8.4	8.8	13.4	9.7	7.3	−8.6	−18.8
Agriculture	7.2	9.5	−3.1	19.5	6.6	2.5	0.8	7.5	16.6	−17.8
Industrial products	7.7	26.8	30.2	17.0	12.0	14.1	9.5	8.9	−1.1	−21.1
Forestry based products[a]	7.9	11.1	17.0	32.7	−2.4	2.4	1.4	2.5	−6.3	0.5
Garments and textiles	46.3	39.1	48.7	2.0	−6.2	7.0	5.6	−19.6	24.0	−12.6
Electronics	50.5	133.9	64.0	49.2	−56.2	28.5	53.0	−2.9	8.8	0.8
Mining and minerals	26.4	39.8	63.4	0.8	23.0	49.5	12.2	2.9	−13.2	9.4
Other sectors	10.3	35.9	108.0	38.1	54.4	19.2	−22.6	1,574.4	−96.7	−32.4
Total nonoil exports	8.3	24.9	27.7	16.2	12.1	15.1	9.0	9.8	−2.1	−19.0
Oil and gas exports	27.5	−1.6	−2.1	−8.7	−0.5	8.0	12.0	−0.8	−32.3	−17.8

Source: Central Bureau of Statistics. *Economic Indicators,* various issues.

[a]Comprised of processed wood, paper, and paper goods.

[b]As of the first quarter of 1999.

[c]For 1999 compared to the first quarter of 1998.

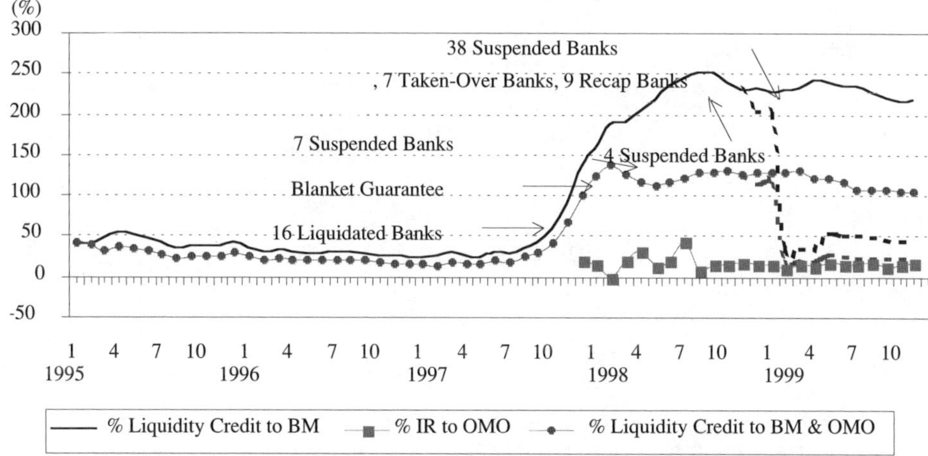

Fig. 6.1. Indonesia: Share of liquidity credit to base money (BM), share of intervention (IR) to open market operation (OMO), and share of liquidity credit to BM and OMO, 1995–99. (Data from Bank Indonesia.)

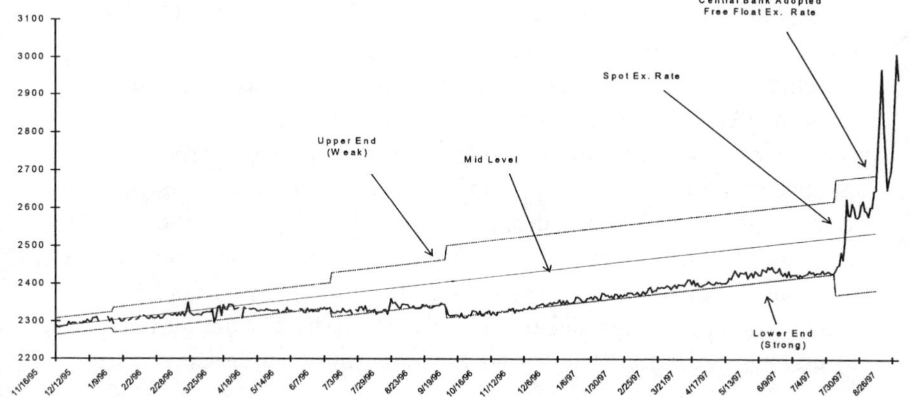

Fig. 6.2. Indonesia: Rupiah exchange rate and its intervention bands, November 1995 to August 1997. (Data from Bank Indonesia, Indonesian Financial Statistics, various issues; and University of British Columbia data base.)

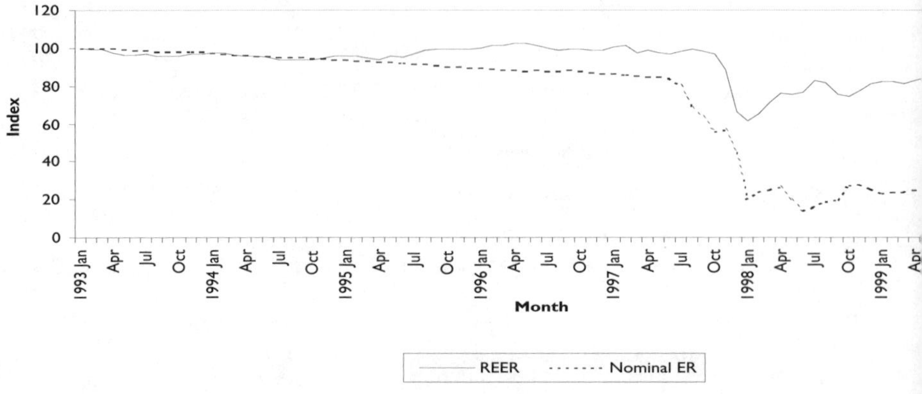

Fig. 6.3. Indonesia: Nominal and real effective exchange rate, 1993–99 (U.S.$/Rp, 1993 = 100). The declining of the index means that the rupiah has depreciated. (Data from J. P. Morgan Web site, Real Broad Effective Exchange Rate; and Bank Indonesia, Indonesian Financial Statistics, various issues.)

Bank Indonesia had to abandon the moving band system, adopted in 1992, in order to defend its foreign exchange reserve position.

Figure 6.3 shows a steady appreciation of the effective exchange rate of the rupiah between 1990 and 1996, which indicates a slight change in government policy with respect to the exchange rate. The rupiah appreciation was also due to the rising value of its main external anchor, the U.S. dollar, vis-à-vis the Japanese yen. The rupiah appreciation helped reduce inflation and interest rates in 1996. However, it also eroded the external competitiveness of the economy, distorted saving and investment decisions, and squandered scarce savings upon unproductive investment projects. The decline in the inflation rate, on the other hand, helped stabilize rupiah appreciation.

1.2. THE WIDENING CURRENT ACCOUNT DEFICIT

Having been maintained at below 2 percent of annual GDP in 1993 and 1994, the current account deficit rose to 3.6 percent in 1995 and 3.7 percent in 1996. Table 6.1 shows that the widening current account deficit between 1990 and 1996 was the result of, first, an increase in overall investment—from 30.1 to 32.7 percent of GDP. One of the links was the banking system, which converted part of the increased liquidity into loans to finance investment, including those in land-based industries (hotel and tourist resorts, amusement and industrial parks, real estate, commercial buildings, and shopping malls), excessive infrastructure, and other nontradables. Most of the private debt was, however, directly borrowed from foreign lenders, and only a small fraction of it was intermediated through the banking system.

Second, the widening current account deficit reflected high consumption levels, as part of the capital inflows was probably used to finance consumption. This is partly shown by a slight decline in the savings rate in the national account data. In addition, there was a rapid increase in the number of credit cards issued and the number of transactions using them. In the fiscal year 1996–97, ending in March, the number of credit cards in circulation was 1.6 million (an increase of nearly 30 percent compared to 28 percent in the preceding year). In the same year, the value of transactions using credit cards amounted to Rp4.7 trillion (an increase of 35 percent compared to 22 percent in the previous year). As of the time of writing, there were 17 banks and 84 finance companies (operating with 40,000 merchant outlets throughout the country) licensed in the credit card business.

The widening external deficit was not due to irresponsible fiscal behavior. A combination of a greater tax effort, tightening fiscal policy, and improvement in the operations of state-owned enterprises had reduced the government budget deficit and increased public sector savings. While formally maintaining the "balanced budget principle," in reality the government had run an annual budget surplus between 0.2 and 0.8 percent of GDP since fiscal year of 1993–94. This small budget surplus, however, was not powerful enough to offset the rapid expansion of private sector investment, which was partly supported by external borrowings. Moreover, the budget surplus figure did not necessarily reflect the true picture, as a significant part of the bank and corporate sectors' external debt was either explicitly or implicitly guaranteed by the government.

1.3. THE STOCK OF EXTERNAL DEBT

Mainly because of the surge in private sector direct borrowing from abroad, the stock of external debt of Indonesia rapidly increased from $66.9 billion in 1990 to $151 billion in December 1998 (table 6.4). This level of external debt was alarming by world standards. The World Bank considers a debt to GNP ratio of more than 80 percent as high risk. In terms of total debt service to exports, the World Bank considers 18 percent the "warning" threshold. The stock of external debt of Indonesia in December 1998 amounted to around 308 percent of export value and about 321 percent of annual GDP. The debt service ratio was ranging between 30 to 34 percent, and interest payments

TABLE 6.4. Indonesia: External Debt Outstanding, 1989–99

	1989	1990	1991	1992	1993	1994	1995	1996	1997	1998	1999[a]
In millions of U.S.$											
External debt outstanding	51,974.7	62,820.6	65,697.2	73,358.9	80,591.8	96,500.1	107,831.9	110,170.8	134,794.3	150,886.1	142,415.2
Public sector	39,576.9	45,100.2	45,724.7	48,768.7	52,461.4	58,615.6	59,588.2	55,302.6	53,865.0	67,328.2	70,786.0
Private sector	12,397.8	17,720.4	19,972.5	24,590.2	28,130.4	37,884.5	48,243.7	54,868.2	80,929.3	83,557.9	71,629.2
The structure of private sector external debt (%), by debtors											
Banks	6.4	14.8	17.1	23.4	27.6	21.7	20.9	16.5	17.7	12.9	13.4
State-owned banks	3.4	6.4	7.0	10.3	11.1	7.3	8.0	5.4	7.3	5.7	6.0
Private banks	3.0	8.4	10.2	13.1	16.5	14.4	12.9	11.1	10.4	7.2	7.4
Nonbank	93.6	85.2	82.9	76.6	72.4	78.3	79.1	83.5	71.2	80.8	82.1
State-owned enterprise	26.0	17.6	16.8	18.4	18.0	13.4	10.0	6.8	4.9	5.0	5.8
Foreign investment enterprise	26.4	26.4	25.8	22.7	21.2	25.3	27.0	29.9	29.0	38.8	41.8
Domestic investment enterprise	23.0	23.0	22.5	19.8	18.5	22.1	23.5	26.1	20.4	24.1	21.3
Financing institution	3.9	3.9	3.8	3.3	3.1	3.7	3.9	4.4	4.2	2.5	2.2
Others	14.4	14.4	14.1	12.4	11.6	13.8	14.7	16.3	12.6	10.4	10.9
By Maturity											
Short term	6.9	6.9	6.9	6.9	6.9	6.9	6.9	6.9	6.1	6.5	6.6
Long term	93.1	93.1	93.1	93.1	93.1	93.1	93.1	93.1	82.8	87.2	88.9
Memo items											
Share of government debt to total debt (%)	76.1	71.8	69.6	66.5	65.1	60.7	55.3	50.2	40.0	44.6	49.7
Share of private debt to total debt (%)	23.9	28.2	30.4	33.5	34.9	39.3	44.7	49.8	60.0	55.4	50.3
Share of total debt to real GDP (%)	36.7	43.2	44.6	48.4	51.2	59.1	63.6	62.5	99.4	396.2	
Share of total debt to exports (%)	234.5	244.7	225.4	216.0	218.9	240.9	237.4	221.2	252.2	308.9	

Source: Bank Indonesia, *Recent Economic Indicators*, various issues.
[a]As of August 1999.

alone amounted to 12 percent of total exports between 1990 and 1996. The sharp depreciation of the external value of the rupiah added significantly to Indonesia's debt burden.

Over 55 percent of the external debt in December 1998 ($83.6 billion) was owed by the private sector, and over 80 percent of it was borrowed by nonbank corporate entities. The average maturity of this external debt was approximately 1.5 years (J. P. Morgan 1998, 70). As noted, some of the private sector's external debt was explicitly or implicitly guaranteed by the government. Sovereign guarantees covered not only the external debt of the state-owned banks and nonbank companies but the foreign liabilities of the private sector, particularly the politically well connected private infrastructure providers.

2. THE BANKING CRISIS

The indicators of banking system fragility are presented in table 6.5. In terms of total assets and number of offices, the system is the core of the financial sector in Indonesia (Nasution 1996). The banking industry plays an important role in the economy, as it has been the main source of external financing for the corporate sector in Indonesia, which traditionally adopts financing strategies with high debt-equity ratios. As a result, the rise in interest rates and the credit crunch resulting from the banking troubles precipitated a collapse in trade and production and aggravated an already deep recession, as traders and producers could not get credit lines to purchase the goods and inputs required in the production process.

On the other hand, faltering economic activity, the sudden depreciation of the rupiah, high interest rates, and the bank run dealt a devastating blow to the financial system. Banks became short of liquidity because of client withdrawals of deposits. Indonesian banks prior to the crisis had received, borrowed, deposited, and made loans denominated in foreign currency (primarily U.S. dollars). The sharp devaluation of the rupiah shifted many of these loans into "the nonperforming category," but they did nothing to relieve banks of their foreign currency obligations to their lenders and depositors.

2.1. THE OVEREXTENDED BANKING SYSTEM

The banking system was over stretched at the onset of the financial crisis in 1997, as shown by the rising loan to deposit ratio (LDR) and excessive credit expansion. The banking system's LDR rapidly rose from 106 percent in 1988 to 129 percent in 1992 and peaked at 240 percent in 1994, 1995, and 1996 (table

6.5). These levels were much higher than the maximum allowable LDR ratio of 110 percent. On average, the credit outstanding of commercial banks increased by over 24 percent per annum between 1992 and 1997. This was over three times the average annual rate of growth of the economy during the same period. The average annual growth rate of bank loans was also much higher than that of the manufacturing industry, the most dynamic sector of the economy.

The rapid growth of credit expansion in the banking system between 1990 and 1997 was induced by a combination of lifting restrictions on bank lending and regulations on asset portfolios, lowering reserve requirements, market opening, privatization, and greater access to offshore markets. The presence of new entrants in a more competitive market environment may well increase the pressures on banks to engage in riskier activities. Yet bank credit officers reared in an earlier controlled environment may not have the expertise needed to evaluate new sources of credit and market risk. When the economy is booming, it is difficult to distinguish between good and bad credit risks because most borrowers look profitable and liquid. Lifting restrictions on bank lending immediately expanded credit to land-based industries and excessive infrastructure projects. Part of this credit expansion was financed by means of foreign borrowing. In addition, the surge in private capital inflows relative to the size of the equity market drove up equity prices following financial market deregulation in 1988.

The financial sector reform of 1988 relaxed the requirements domestic banks had to meet in order to engage in foreign exchange transactions and to open branch offices overseas. It also allowed greater penetration of foreign banks in the domestic economy and greater ownership by foreign investors of domestic assets. Moreover, the new rules and regulations replaced the administrative ceilings on offshore borrowing by commercial banks with a more rational system of net open positions. Along with privatization, in 1997 the authorities abolished the limits on inflows of FDI and foreign ownership of equities issued in domestic stock markets. Prior to the more recent reform, Indonesia, in 1971, had adopted a relatively open capital account and a managed unitary exchange rate. Under this system, there is no surrender requirement for export proceeds or taxes or subsidies on the purchase or sale of foreign exchange. Indonesian citizens and foreign residents are free to open accounts in the rupiah (the national currency) or foreign currencies at the authorized banks (*bank devisas*). These banks are authorized to extend credit in foreign exchange in the domestic market.

To encourage inflows of foreign investment, between January 1979 and December 1991 a special effective exchange rate was made available to domestic borrowers by providing an explicit subsidy on the exchange rate. The subsidy was extended through the exchange rate swap facility. Under this

TABLE 6.5. Indonesia: Banking Sector Indicators, 1985–97

	1985	1986	1987	1988	1989	1990	1991	1992	1993	1994	1995	1996	1997
Number of banks	114	110	109	108	145	171	192	208	234	240	240	239	222
Private banks	69	65	64	63	88	109	129	144	161	166	165	164	144
State-owned banks[a]	5	5	5	5	5	7	7	7	7	7	7	7	7
Foreign banks and joint venture banks	11	11	11	11	23	28	29	30	39	40	41	41	44
Regional development banks	27	27	27	27	27	27	27	27	27	27	27	27	27
Loan to deposit ratio (%)	102.9	96.3	101.9	105.7	112.6	118.2	130.7	129.3	132.4	134.9	137.7	131.0	123.7
LGR minus GDPGR (%)	14.7	19.8	8.8	23.1	31.2	48.1	−9.9	7.7	6.9	5.7	4.0	4.7	12.1
LGR minus IPGR (%)	29.0	20.8	35.9	34.4	44.2	61.4	9.0	25.9	22.4	16.0	23.1	22.5	16.2
NFL to TBL (%)	−20.0	−23.6	−18.2	−14.1	−10.6	0.9	0.7	2.2	4.9	5.8	3.8	2.8	5.2
M2 multiplier[b]	3.4	3.4	3.8	5.0	5.4	6.7	7.7	7.0	7.8	7.4	8.0	7.5	7.6
M2/FOREX reserves (%)	414.2	415.4	367.5	481.5	597.2	596.8	539.0	552.6	602.3	643.4	690.3	638.6	419.9
M2/GDP (%)						43.0	43.6	46.4	44.0	45.7	49.0	54.2	56.9
Nonperforming loans[c] (%)							9.2		14.2	12.1	10.4	8.8	14.0
Bad debt (%)							1.7		3.3	4.0	3.3	2.9	2.3
Cash assets to deposit ratio (%)	15.9	13.3	12.4	14.5	11.1	6.5	13.7	3.2	2.6	2.5	2.6	4.7	5.8
Loans to assets ratio (%)		53.3	58.2	61.5	65.4	73.4	76.2	73.7	75.4	80.3	79.2	77.0	71.9
Credit in U.S.$ to total credit (%)						12.2	15.6	17.9	19.4	19.1	19.5	19.9	30.8
Dollar deposits to M2 ratio (%)						20.6	21.2	20.8	21.7	21.7	19.8	19.5	31.1
EL to TL in U.S.$ (%)						9.1	7.4	12.0	12.8	8.3	5.7	4.0	6.1

Source: IMF, *International Financial Statistics,* various issues; Bank Indonesia, *Annual Report,* various issues. Data as of June 1999.

Note: LGR: loan growth rate; GDPGR: GDP growth rate; IPGR: industrial production growth rate; NFL: net foreign liabilities; TBL: total bank liabilities; EL: excess liquidity; TL: total liquidity.

[a]Including 12 banks taken over by the IBRA-Indonesian Banks Restructuring Agency as of June 1999.

[b]Ratio of M2 to reserve money.

[c]As a percentage of total loans outstanding of commercial banks. Nonperforming loan data tend to be underestimated. The decline of nonperforming loans to 8.8 percent of total credit in 1996 was mainly due to writeoffs of the bad loans at state-owned commercial banks and private "non-foreign-exchange" banks. As of the end of March 1998, bank nonperforming loans reached over 70 percent of total loans for several banks.

facility, Bank Indonesia provided forward cover to foreign exchange borrowing contract swaps to banks and nonbank financial institutions (NBFIs) and to customers with a foreign currency liability. The subsidy came about because of the time lag in an upward adjustment of the swap premium, a nominal depreciation of the rupiah, or a combination of both.

Herd behavior of foreign investors also had a role to play in increasing capital inflows and outflows to and from Indonesia. They did buy stock, commercial papers, and even real estate, and they invested in infrastructure projects extensively. The reform, which covered nearly all aspects of the economy, combined with the perception of Indonesia as a stable country and one of Asia's success stories, generated a massive capital inflow beginning in the early 1990s. No guarantee was needed, as the government supported the exchange rate and had the reputation to take over the private sector's external debt if things went wrong. Demand for securities issued by Indonesian (state- and privately owned) companies increased, as foreigners are allowed to own up to 49 percent of the listed shares issued by national companies (except banks). The national companies are also allowed to raise funds by selling securities in domestic and international stock and bond markets.

Capital inflows were encouraged further as domestic interest rates (adjusted for relatively limited actual exchange rate movements) rose and were sustained through the 1990s. Peregrine, an investment bank based in Hong Kong, collapsed in early January 1998 due to a single massive bad loan ($265 million) to PT Steady Safe, a local taxi and city bus company in Jakarta. Steady Safe used $145 million to buy 14 percent of a toll road building company owned by Ms. Siti Hardiyati Rukmana (Tutut), the eldest daughter of President Suharto. She was then named to Steady Safe's board (*Time* 1998, 14–16). At that time, a close link to the family of President Suharto was solid insurance.

2.2. INCREASING BANK LIABILITIES WITH LARGE MATURITY/CURRENCY MISMATCHES

The combination of a liberal capital account, financial sector reform, and advances in technology and information processing has made it easier for Indonesians to alter the currency composition of their deposits. A number of indicators pointed to a rising percentage of debt instruments denominated in foreign currency, particularly the U.S. dollar. These include higher ratios of broad money (M2) to GDP, dollar deposits as percentage of M2, credit in dollars as a percentage of total credit, and excess liquidity of commercial banks held in U.S. dollars (table 6.5). As emphasized by Calvo (1994) and Mishkin (1997), this makes it more difficult to manage both the banks' portfolios and the macroeconomy.

When domestic interest rates are high, there is a strong temptation for them to denominate debt in foreign currency. *Bank devisas* (which are licensed to deal in foreign exchange transactions) turned to short-term, foreign-currency-denominated borrowing in the interbank market to fund long-term bank loans. The ratio of external liabilities of the commercial banks to their assets rose from 9.5 percent in 1993 to over 18 percent in March 1998. The ratio of net external liabilities to total liabilities rapidly rose from −14.1 percent in 1988 to 0.7 percent in 1991, 5.8 percent in 1994, and 5.2 percent in 1997. External borrowing by the financial sector in Indonesia rose from $6 billion in 1993 to $12.1 billion in 1995; it then fell to $11 billion in 1996 and 10.1 billion in mid-1997.[2] All of these figures indicate higher exposure of the banking system to foreign exchange risk.

Due to a combination of factors, a large portion of the external debt was not hedged. These factors included the historically predictable low rate of the rupiah depreciation, the availability of exchange rate swaps at subsidized rates, and the reputation of the government to stand by public companies and companies owned by the politically well connected. The large amount of unhedged external debt made banks and their customers more vulnerable, but it also made it harder to deal with the banking crisis, the rise in interest rates, and the sharp devaluation of the rupiah. Depreciation of the rupiah deteriorated banks' and firms' balance sheets because much of their debt was denominated in foreign currencies. The substantial drops in the external value of the rupiah to the dollar rapidly raised the cost of renewing or rolling over the short-term floating rate dollar or yen loans in real terms. The indebtedness level of Indonesian banks and firms went up, and their net worth fell. The vulnerability of banks increased in line with the decline in their capacity to absorb negative shocks because of currency and maturity mismatches. The rise in interest rates caused interest payments to rise, resulting in deterioration in the balance sheets of the banks and their customers.

The risks of maturity mismatches were higher for the unlisted banks, which have no access to long-term sources of funding (by selling bonds, shares, and other types of securities) in stock markets. Selling equity in stock markets can also spread or share risks. The risks were high, as most companies in Indonesia rely exclusively on bank loans for financing, with land being the main collateral used to obtain credit. Only a handful of them supplement bank finance with equity offerings. The high loan to value ratio of bank loans to companies, such as property developers, exposed the Indonesian banks to a sharp decline in real estate prices. This and the plunge in equity prices depressed the market value of the collateral and assets of the banks. The liquidity problem became more difficult because there was no securitization of mortgages and no market for government bonds.

2.3. THE WEAK FINANCIAL POSITIONS OF BANKS AND HIGHLY CONCENTRATED PROBLEM LOANS

Liberalization of the banking industry will surely produce long-term benefits for Indonesia. In the short run, however, deregulation inevitably presents banks with new risks, which, without proper cautions, can lead to a banking crisis, as was the case in Indonesia. A combination of economic crisis and improvements in accounting systems sharply increased the ratio of nonperforming loans (NPLs) from below 10 percent in 1997 to over 50 percent in the first quarter of 1999 (fig. 6.4). The rising numbers of NPLs drove up the operating costs of the banks. To cover the immediate losses from NPLs, banks are required to accumulate provisions until they can recover part of the credit or write it off their balance sheets. The high NPL rate has also caused a negative spread between lending and deposit interest rates.

The NPL problems are more severe at state-owned and "non-foreign-exchange" banks. Traditionally, the state-owned banks were undercapitalized. The state-bank group was the main provider of credit programs, with subsidized interest rates and nearly zero credit risks, during the long era of financial repression. This group of banks has also been the main victim of such erratic government policies as shifting public deposits from these banks to the central bank. The four banks (PT Bapindo, PT Bank Bumi Daya, PT Bank Dagang Negara, and PT Bank Eksim), which have now been merged into one PT Bank Mandiri, were technically insolvent, as the amount of their bad loans was much greater than that of their capital.

The financial position of private sector banks was not much better. Many of them did not meet the capital adequacy ratio and the legal lending limits regulations. The latter restrict the aggregate amount of loans and advances to insiders, a single borrower (person or firm), or a group of borrowers.[3] It was reported that on average over half of all loans provided by private banks was given to companies in the same groups. Over 90 percent of the loans of PT Bank Dagang Nasional Indonesia (BDNI) and PT Danamon, two of the large private banks, was channeled to their own groups. Such large group lending has reduced the franchise value of the private banks.

2.4. HEAVY GOVERNMENT INVOLVEMENT IN THE SELECTION OF CREDIT CUSTOMERS

Despite privatization, the six state-owned banks (Bank Bumi Daya, Bank BNI, Bank Exim, Bank Rakyat Indonesia, Bapindo, and Bank Tabungan Negara) still retained over 30 percent of all bank assets in Indonesia prior to the 1997 crisis. This figure would be even higher if it were computed under a

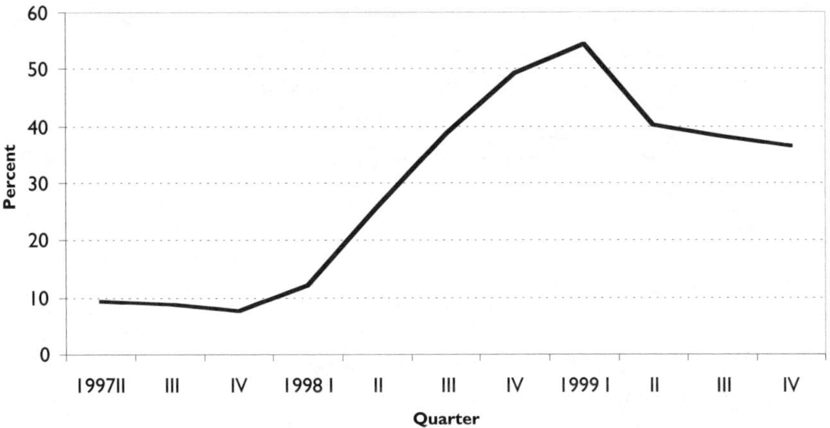

Fig. 6.4: Indonesia: The development of nonperforming loans, 1997–99. (Data from Bank Indonesia.)

broad definition of *indirect ownership,* as Bank Indonesia, state-owned banks, line ministries, and various branches of the armed forces also own banks. In addition, each of the 27 provinces has a regional development bank (RDB).

For decades, the loan decisions of state-owned banks and RDBs had been subject to explicit or implicit government direction. All too often, the creditworthiness of the borrowers did not receive sufficient weight in credit decisions, with the result that loans of state banks were vehicles for extending government assistance to particular industries and a handful of politically well connected business groups. These groups of large companies—the conglomerates—control a large proportion of GDP and a vast range of mainly rent seeking activities. Until the crisis, deregulation had not ended government intervention in the lending decisions of state-owned banks and finance companies.

2.5. LENDER OF LAST RESORT

At present, there is no deposit insurance scheme in Indonesia. However, even long before the crisis Bank Indonesia had been acting as the lender of last resort on an ad hoc and nontransparent basis, particularly to state-owned banks and politically well connected institutions. Resources from state-owned pension funds and insurance companies had also been used to rescue banks owned by the politically well connected conglomerates. The bailout program introduced in November 1997 has enabled Bank Indonesia to indiscriminately provide financial support to financially distressed banks. This financial support includes liquidity credit, emergency financial assistance, and long-term subordinated loans that carry negative real interest rates and nearly zero risk. The rapid growth of Bank Indonesia's support to the financially distressed banks was reflected by the rapid growth of the claims of the monetary system on the private sector, which includes claims of the central bank on commercial banks.

3. POLICY RESPONSES

Indonesia signed a letter of intent with the IMF in October 1997. The standard IMF program consisted of the following measures: (1) a short-term stabilization policy to reduce domestic absorption; (2) medium-term, economywide reforms to remove economic distortions and improve productivity and efficiency, and (3) measures intended to strengthen the market infrastructure (accounting and legal systems), improve symmetry of information, and reduce transaction costs.

A combination of fiscal distress, fragility of the banking system, and other internal and external factors has, however, constrained Indonesia from adopting full-fledged economic stabilization and recovery programs. The factors include slow disbursement of external assistance due to its conditionality, instability of domestic political and social systems, and lack of commitment to implement the stabilization and economic recovery programs. Moreover, the quality of the government policy response was affected by the erosion of the quality of technical competence and the integrity of President Suharto's cabinet ministers, as he relied mostly on his family members and cronies for advice.

Prior to President Suharto's fall from power in May 1998, his regime had wasted six months in considering a number of alternative solutions to the economic crisis. Unhappy with the severe cuts in their pet projects and the slow results of the IMF program, in February 1998 President Suharto considered as policy alternatives to the IMF program the currency board system as well as capital controls. None of these alternatives was feasible, however.

The country is large, with more than 17,000 big and small islands. In the middle of the archipelago, there is Singapore, the leading financial center in the region. The large size of the country, the significant role of the nontraded sector in the economy, inadequate external reserves, a distressed banking system, lax discipline, and weak market infrastructure (particularly the legal and accounting systems)did not permit Indonesia to adopt the currency board system.

With regard to the exchange control option, Indonesia simply does not have the administrative capability to implement exchange controls. This was one reason for adopting the open capital account system in 1971.

3.1. THE SIZE AND TERMS OF EXTERNAL ASSISTANCE

The IMF program secured $36.4 billion in financial assistance from the international community, which amounted to around 17 percent of Indonesia's annual GDP. Of this, $10.1 billion was provided by the IMF and $8 billion was pledged by the World Bank and the Asian Development Bank. The funds pledged by multilateral institutions are to be disbursed in steps according to the progress of the stabilization and deregulation packages as they are subjected to conditionality and programs in specific economic sectors. Another $18 billion of external financial assistance pledged by a group of bilateral creditors in the form of a "second line of defense" had terms and conditions that were not clearly specified.[4] To date, none of this "second line of defense" financing has been disbursed. This and political uncertainties have failed to restore confidence in the private sector.

In October 1998, the Japanese government introduced the Miyazawa Initiatives (named after Minister of Finance Miyazawa) by pledging $30 billion to support short-term economic adjustment and medium- and long-term economic restructuring and institutional building in the crisis countries of Asia. Indonesia received $2.9 billion of Miyazawa program funds. Some of this was used to cofinance reform packages with the IMF, the World Bank, and the Asian Development Bank.

3.2. MONETARY POLICY

There are three conflicting elements of monetary policy in the IMF program. The first is to replace the relatively rigidly fixed exchange rate system with a float system. The second is to use the target of rate of growth of the monetary base as the performance criteria of the monetary policy. Later this criteria was replaced with inflation targeting as the nominal anchor of the monetary policy. The third element is to speed up a bank restructuring program, which is the core of Indonesia's financial system. Gradually, the structure of the financial system is to be changed from the present bank-based system to one that is capital market based. The first two elements of the monetary policy require a tight monetary policy, which is needed to help control the inflation rate and stabilize the exchange rate without sacrificing many external reserves. On the other hand, the tight monetary policy would have limited the ability of the central bank to act as a lender of last resort to rescue the financially ailing banks.

In practice, monetary policy in Indonesia has been swinging back and forth between defending the exchange rate position of the central bank and lowering interest rates. The present system of a flexible exchange rate, adopted on August 14, 1997, was not a pure float. The central bank keeps intervening in the foreign exchange market. Traditionally, the pressures of a rising inflation rate resulting from rapid monetary expansion and the depreciation of the rupiah have been partly suppressed by the government's policy of subsidizing the prices of state-vended products[5] and adopting a more vigorous trade liberalization program. Trade policy reform and productivity gains generated by the economywide reforms help relax the supply constraint and check inflationary pressures.

The move toward a floating exchange rate system allows interest rates to rise precipitously. A combination of a rise in interest rates and depreciation of exchange rates has further weakened the financial position of both the banks and the corporate sector, particularly those with high debt-equity ratios and large unhedged foreign liabilities. To lower interest rates and stabilize the external value of the rupiah, Bank Indonesia indiscriminately injected massive liquidity credit into the banking system and used its external reserves to intervene in the foreign exchange market. The liquidity injection was also intended to address the liquidity and solvency problems of the financially distressed banks. Because of the injection of the liquidity credit scheme, net domestic assets of the central bank rose by over twice the stock of the monetary base between November 1997 and March 1998.

The massive expansion of liquidity was partly sterilized by the issuance of Bank Indonesia Certificates (SBI)—Bank Indonesia's certificates of deposit (fig. 6.5). Other measures intended to absorb liquidity included the depletion of scarce external reserves and shifting the public sector's deposits from commercial banks to the central bank. The shift in public sector deposits (including that of state-owned companies) seriously damaged state-owned banks, as stipulated by government regulations, they had an exclusive monopoly over deposits of public sector funds.

As the injection of liquidity credit was not enough to save the financially weak banks, the authorities in November 1997 provided a guarantee for deposits of all commercial banks operating in Indonesia up to the equivalent of around $5,000. This encouraged large depositors to shift their funds from domestic banks to foreign institutions (including overseas institutions) and convert them into foreign denominated assets. To help stop the destabilized portfolio adjustments, on January 26, 1998, the authorities introduced a blanket guarantee to all depositors (both domestic and foreign) and creditors of all banks incorporated in Indonesia. The guarantee scheme would be effective for at least two years. Its discontinuation would be an-

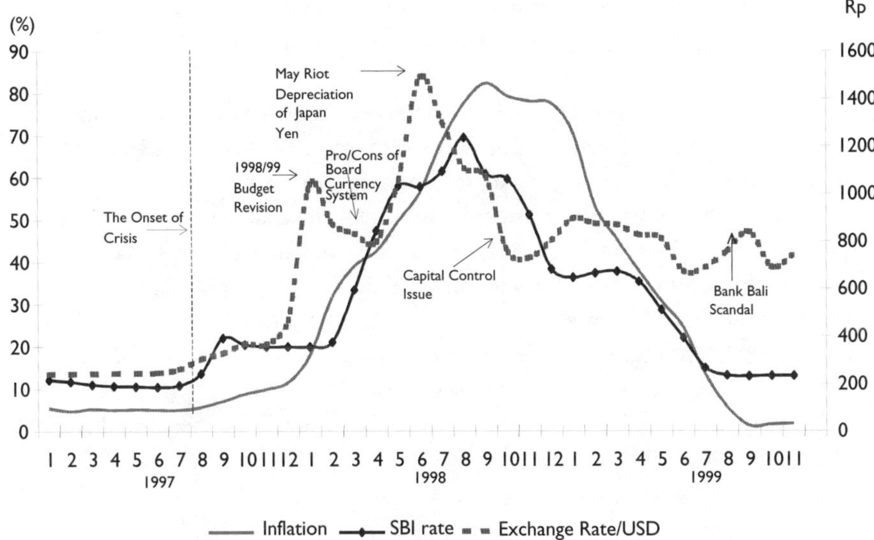

Fig. 6.5. Indonesia: Inflation, one-month SBI Rate, and exchange rate, 1997–99

nounced six months in advance and would be replaced with a deposit insurance scheme.

The mix of injection of liquidity credit, provision of government bonds, and relaxation of the prudential rules and regulations governing the banking industry has not significantly improved the ability of the banking system to extend new credit. As a result, the corporate sector has relied on internally generating funds for working capital. This includes depreciation funds and deferred payments of taxes and loans. Only a handful of reputable companies can raise funds through the capital market or borrow overseas.

3.3. FISCAL POLICY

The economic crisis has caused fiscal distress (table 6.6), as government revenues are insufficient to meet rising expenditures. Government expenditures for, among other purposes, financing soaring costs of servicing both domestic and external debts, overhauling the financial system, and extending the social safety net and fiscal stimuli have been rising fast. As mentioned earlier, a mix of slow disbursement of external assistance, rigidity due to conditionality, and delays in allocating spending authority has limited the use of fiscal policy as an "automatic stabilizer" or countercyclical measure to avoid a major domestic recession. The realized budget deficit in fiscal year (FY) 1998–99 was only 2 percent of GDP, much lower than the budget target 7.8 percent.

The present economic crisis forced the authorities to redefine the scope of government and to change its policy on the role of the public budget. Prior to the crisis, the public budget had been mainly used as a tool of resource allocation. At present, it is a principal instrument of macroeconomic policy. The rise in both the domestic and external debt burdens requires a deep cut in nondebt expenditures. As noted, this public debt burden is very sensitive to developments in interest, inflation, and exchange rates. Following the crisis, the domestic interest burden rose rapidly from 0.02 percent of GDP in FY1998–99 and 1999–2000 (April–March) to around 4 percent in FY2000 (March–December). The burden of domestic debt will increase further in 2003 when the government is scheduled to begin retiring bank recapitalization bonds. As noted, some of the government domestic bonds either carry variable interest rates or are indexed with inflation rates. The sharp depreciation of the rupiah has added to external debt burden significantly.

As the inflexible tax system cannot be expected to pursue an equity objective, the expenditure side of the government budget is also expected to carry multiple tasks, including pursuing this equity objective. This goal can be pursued by increasing the portion of nondebt budget expenditures toward the nontradable sector of the economy. Such expenditures include public schools, extension and outreach services, public health care programs, and labor-intensive public works programs in rural areas. The rise in oil and nonoil exports helped expand these employment creation programs in FY2000.

Privatization of state-owned enterprises (SOEs) is part of the process of scaling back the role of government in providing private goods and services. Privatization also serves as an instrument for improving the efficiency and productivity of SOEs. The proceeds of privatization are needed for financing the growing budget deficit. The other source of government revenue is the sale of banking assets now controlled by the Indonesia Bank Restructuring Agency (IBRA). The authorities have also introduced various measures to raise revenues by means of taxation. These tax efforts, however, have had limited success due to the inflexibility and inefficiency of the regressive tax system (UN-ESCAP 1995).

To help reduce budget expenditures, the authorities have reduced subsidies to state-vended products. The removal of subsidies also promotes the efficient use of resources. Another major change in the government budget is improving fiscal transparency and practices by integrating off-budget transactions into the formal budget. These include explicit and implicit guarantees to third-party liabilities of the banking system, to private infrastructure projects,

TABLE 6.6. Indonesia: Central Government Budget Summary, 1994–95 through 2000–2001 (in billions of rupiah unless otherwise stated)

	1994–95	1995–96	1996–97	1997–98	1998–99	1999–2000	2000–2001
Revenue and expenditure							
Domestic revenues	66,418	73,014	84,792	108,814	159,135	149,303	140,804
Routine expenditures[a]	44,069	50,435	61,568	84,606	140,535	171,205	134,556
Development expenditures	30,692	28,781	33,454	46,398	65,750	92,683	83,648
Budget deficit (= 2 + 3 − 1)	8,343	6,202	10,230	22,190	47,150	114,585	77,400
Government saving (= 1 − 2)	22,349	22,579	23,224	24,208	18,600	−21,902	6,248
Borrowing fund							
Program aid	0	0	0	0	24,926	74,045	47,400
Project aid	9,838	9,009	11,048	23,817	25,313	40,541	30,000
Total borrowing (= 6 + 7)	9,838	9,009	11,048	23,817	50,239	114,586	77,400
Change in balances (= 8 − 4)[b]	1,495	2,807	818	1,627	3,089	1	0
Memorandum item							
Share of deficit to total expenditure (%)	11.2	7.8	10.8	16.9	22.9	43.4	35.5
Share of government saving to domestic revenues (%)	33.6	30.9	27.4	22.2	11.7	−14.7	4.4
Share of program aid to total borrowing (%)	0.0	0.0	0.0	0.0	49.6	64.6	61.2
Share of project aid to total borrowing (%)	100.0	100.0	100.0	100.0	50.4	35.4	38.8
Share of balances to domestic revenues (%)	2.3	3.8	1.0	1.5	1.9	0.0	0.0
Share of balances to total expenditures (%)	2.0	3.5	0.9	1.2	1.5	0.0	0.0
Share of balances to total borrowing (%)	15.2	31.2	7.4	6.8	6.1	0.0	0.0

Sources: Ministry of Finance; World Bank 1999.

[a]Including debt service payments.

[b]Positive means increasing.

to the pension funds of civil servants, and to the contingent liabilities of state-owned enterprises.

3.4. DEALING WITH THE EXTERNAL DEBT OVERHANG

Soaring external debt repayments in the middle of economic crisis required the transfer of larger portions of Indonesia's export earnings and GDP to foreigners. To ease the pressure, Indonesia needs temporary debt relief.

Public Sector External Debt

It is true that the bulk of public sector external debt is long term in nature. However, the associated principal and interest servicing cost still runs high, some $9 billion a year. To be able to repay its external debt, the public sector has to accumulate a budget surplus as well as a surplus in the balance of payments. To ease the pressures on the public budget and the balance of payments, on September 23, 1998, the Paris Club creditor nations agreed to reschedule $4.2 billion in principal repayments of Indonesia's public external debt.

Private Sector External Debt

Three institutions have been established to work out the private sector external debt, namely, the Frankfurt Agreement, Indonesian Debt Restructuring Agency (INDRA), and the Jakarta Initiative. The private sector external debt is relatively more difficult to settle, however, as there is a large number of both foreign lenders and domestic borrowers. Each individual debtor has a distinct willingness and ability to pay. Foreign lenders include foreign private banks, institutional investors, and other nonbank entities. The progress of the external debt workout, however, is very slow, partly because of weak bankruptcy law.

The private sector external debt is to be solved on a voluntary basis based on a combination of Mexico's Ficorca program and the Korean scheme. The Korean idea is to take the short-term and nontrade debts of Indonesian banks and restructure them into loans with one- to four-year maturities. Interest rates on the new loans will be paid based on Libor plus margin, ranging between 2.75 and 3.50 percent.

In June 1998, the Frankfurt Agreement was signed by the government with international private bankers to restructure and maintain trade credit at the April 1998 level for one year. The trade credit was fully guaranteed by the government (administered by Bank Indonesia) and was extended for another year to April 2001. The nonbank corporate debt has been rescheduled and restructured along the lines of the Mexican program. A trust institution, called INDRA, is already established under the central bank. This institution provides exchange rate risk protection and assurances of the availability of foreign exchange to private debtors that agree with their foreign creditors to restructure their external debts for a period of eight years with three years of grace during which no principal will be payable. By the end of 1998, the program only attracted one debtor with a total debt value of $2.9 billion. As a result, the authorities have decided to close INDRA.

The Jakarta Initiative is the third institution to deal with private sector external debt. It is a private sector agency that receives financial support from the government. Modeled after the London Initiative, the Jakarta Initiative facilitates resolutions of debts among international creditors and domestic debtors outside the court system. Despite a large degree of participation, the amount of debt worked out through the Jakarta Initiative has been limited.

3.5. THE BANK RESTRUCTURING PROGRAM

To restructure the banking industry, the authorities adopted three broad policies. The first element of the bank restructuring program is to strengthen the capital base of the banks. The risk base capital adequacy ratio (CAR) of the banks was temporarily lowered in November 1998 to 4 percent to be raised to a minimum of 8 percent by 2003. The second component of the program is to improve governance of the banking system. For this objective, Indonesia now adopts stricter prudential rules and regulations and accounting standards—on a par with international standards—and improves their enforcement and implementation. Resolution of financially ailing banks and exit procedures are now clearer than before. Meanwhile, the quality of controlling shareholders and the management of the banks have been improved, as they are now required to take fit and proper tests to carry out bank business and each major bank is required to have a compliance director.

The banking system has been practically nationalized, as major private banks are now controlled by the IBRA–Indonesia Bank Restructuring Agency. Established in early 1998, IBRA takes over nonperforming loans of the financially distressed banks. The NPL has been reduced from its peak, over 50 percent, in early 1998 to around 28 percent since June 2000. Together with the banks' shareholders, IBRA prepares and implements immediate rehabilitation plans by means of restructuring or mergers with other banks.

The Asset Management Unit (AMU) has been established under IBRA with the role of purchasing nonperforming loans from banks and administering the pledged assets from shareholder settlements. This allows banks to focus on their traditional activities, namely, deposit taking and lending. The purchase of NPLs will significantly add to resources available to banks for lending purposes. To some extent, IBRA adopts the Swedish model by trying to save both the banks and the borrowers by injecting better management methods and fresh capital into the companies. By the end of January 2000, IBRA controlled about $60 billion of bank assets.

The bank recapitalization program was announced on December 9, 1998. The objective of the program is to increase the banks' capital adequacy ratio to 4 percent, or a half of the 8 percent minimum standard set by the Bank for International Settlements (BIS). The program is only available to national commercial banks that have a CAR between −25 percent and 4 percent. The 40 banks with a CAR below 25 percent are required to inject fresh capital within 30 days or risk being closed down. The 10 foreign banks and 32 joint venture banks are excluded from the program.

The government has recapitalized Bank Indonesia (the central bank) and 126 national commercial banks at a cost of Rp610 trillion (U.S.$87 billion at an exchange rate of Rp7,000 per U.S. dollar) or nearly 60 percent of Indonesia's GDP.

The recapitalized banks include seven state banks, 49 private banks (including 13 taken over by the government), and 15 provincial development banks. Four of the seven state-owned banks (PT Bapindo, PT Bank Dagang Negara, PT Bank Ekspor Impor Indonesia, and PT Bank Bumi Daya) have been merged with the newly established PT Bank Mandiri. As shown in table 6.5, the number of banks was reduced from 208 in December 1998 to 167 in June 1999. The number of banks under the control of local and central governments expanded from 34 in June 1997 to 48 at present, with a combined market share of about 73 percent.

The mix of temporarily lowering prudential standards and injecting government bonds into the ailing banks has made them solvent. These banks have not solved their liquidity problems, however, as the long-term government bonds have no secondary market and can be sold in only small amounts at deep discounts. As a result, the illiquid banks still rely on a relatively narrow and shallow interbank money market for cash. This has limited their ability to lower interest rates and expand credit. The slow progress of corporate restructuring that makes banks more careful in selecting loan customers is another reason for the credit crunch. On the demand side, the high interest rates reduce demand for credit.

To ease the fiscal costs of the bank restructuring program and to help relax the credit crunch, the authorities have encouraged the participation of foreign investors in the banking system in Indonesia. This has been done, for example, by allowing foreign banks to rapidly expand their branch networks and permitting foreign investors to own 100 percent of domestic banks. Nevertheless, the massive migration of deposits from ailing domestic banks to branches of foreign banks since 1998 has caused another kind of financial instability.

3.6. POLICY MEASURES INTENDED TO STRENGTHEN MARKET INFRASTRUCTURE

The economic crisis in Indonesia was partly attributed to deficiencies that undermined bank and corporate governance and healthy market competition. Underregulated banks lead to excessive investment by the economy as a whole (McKinnon and Pill 1996). Moreover, private banks belong to business conglomerates and are not tough on affiliated companies, particularly as they can expect assistance from the central bank. Attaching collateral is a costly and time-consuming process that reduces the effectiveness of collateral in solving problems of adverse selection (Mishkin 1997).

A number of policy measures have been implemented to improve governance and promote competition so as to reduce transaction costs. The first is to review and dismantle government contracts that were offered through corruption, collusion, and nepotism. The second is to improve domestic competitive policy by eliminating various types of explicit and implicit marketing arrangements. This includes discontinuing the exclusive access of state-owned banks to public sector deposits. In addition, governance of state-owned enterprises was improved during the preparation for their privatization. Seeking management contracts and twinning programs with reputable international institutions is one of the requirements for the recapitalization of state-owned banks. The third component is to restructure, corporatize, and privatize state-owned enterprises. The fourth is to speed up trade and policy reforms. The fifth is to improve disclosure requirements, to strengthen accounting and legal systems, and to improve both market transparency and contract enforcement. Indonesia is committed to adopting the Basle principles on the prudential rules and regulations that govern the banking system. The sixth component is to improve "exit policy" by modernizing the antiquated bankruptcy code (Lindsey 2000).

4. SUMMARY AND CONCLUSIONS

Deregulation of the banking industry and opening up the capital account of the balance of payments in Indonesia since late 1980s has not been accompanied by significant improvements in market competition, nor by prudential rules and regulations that can govern the banking and corporate sectors. Prior to the crisis, bad policies such as maintaining the relatively rigid exchange rate system, the provision of subsidies on an exchange rate swap facility, and explicit and implicit sovereign guarantees for private sector external debt had provided incentives for the poorly regulated banks and companies to borrow heavily on international markets. The availability of risk covers allowed them to incur unhedged short-term debt.

Microeconomic weaknesses of banks and companies, such as high debt to equity ratios and their overdependence on unhedged short-term external borrowings undermined macroeconomic strengths of Indonesia. The financial structure was vulnerable to interest and exchange rate vagaries. The problems became more difficult as the borrowers invested the borrowed external funds in the progressively less productive sectors of the economy that produce low profits and generate no foreign exchange, which are needed to service the external debt. The fiscal policy could not be implemented as an automatic stabilizer, as the small surplus in the public budget was not large enough to offset the private sector investment boom, which was partly financed by the short-term capital inflows. As a result, the massive short-term capital inflows appreciated the real effective exchange rate (REER). The appreciation of REER eroded the competitiveness of the economy in international markets and shifted the allocation of resources in the domestic economy away from the trading sector.

Since the crisis, monetary policy in Indonesia has been swinging back and forth to achieve two objectives, namely, defending the central bank's external reserve position and lowering interest rates. To keep the financially distressed banks operating, Bank Indonesia pumped massive liquidity credit into these institutions between November 1997 and April 1998, which doubled the monetary base. Part of the rapid growth of money was offset by selling Bank Indonesia's certificates of deposit and shifting public deposits from state-owned commercial banks into the central bank. The shift in policy to defend the external reserve position was initiated in April 1998 by allowing interest rates to adjust freely.

The crisis forced the government to redefine the scope of government and change the role of the public budget from what was previously a main tool of resource allocation to what is now a principal instrument of macroeconomic policy. The rise in both the domestic and external debt burden requires the government to cut nonbudget expenditures. The slow disbursement and rigidities of external assistance have limited the use of fiscal policy as an "automatic stabilizer."

The economic crisis in Indonesia was aggravated by political uncertainty and inconsistent government policy. Prior to his departure from office, President Suharto wasted six months in considering a number of alternative solutions to the economic crisis, including capital controls and the currency board system. The transition to a democratic political system and local autonomy is still a very difficult process.

NOTES

1. The exchange rate policy includes devaluation, speeding up depreciation of the rupiah, widening the intervention band, and raising transaction costs in the foreign exchange markets.

2. J. P. Morgan 1997, 70.

3. Through networks of ownership and business and management interlocking all of the domestic private banks are closely connected to large business conglomerates. The collapse of a number of large conglomerates since 1990 indicates that certain sectors within the conglomerates could become burdensome, in part because of their strategy of being highly leveraged, which may have been suitable in the past era of subsidized interest rates and highly protected domestic markets (Nasution 1995, 185–86).

4. Indonesia committed $5 billion of its own external reserves to the second line of defense.

5. These include staple foods (such as rice, sugar, and wheat flour), building materials (such as Portland cement), energy (such as electricity and petroleum products), and services (such as transportation fares and school tuition).

REFERENCES:

Calvo, G. A. 1994. "Comment on Dornbusch and Werner." In *Brookings Papers on Economic Activity,* no. 1.

Calvo, G. A., L. Leiderman, and C. M. Reinhart. 1993. "Capital inflows and real exchange appreciation in Latin America: The roles of external factors." *IMF Staff Papers* 40, no. 1:108–51.

Claessens, Stijn, M. P. Dooley, and Andrew Warner. 1995. "Portfolio capital flows: Hot or cold?" *World Bank Economic Review* 9, no. 1:153–74.

Cole, David C., and Betty Slade. 1998. "Why has Indonesia's financial crisis been so bad?" *Bulletin of Indonesian Economic Studies* 34, no. 2 (August): 61–66.

Corden, Max. 1999. *The Asian crisis. Is there a way out?* Singapore: Institute for Southeast Asian Studies.

Dornbusch, Rudiger, I. Goldfajn, and R. O. Valdes. 1995. "Currency crises and collapse." *Brookings Papers on Economic Activity,* 2:995, 219–70.

Frankel, J. A. 1994. "Sterilization of money inflows: Difficult (Calvo) or easy (Reisen)?" Working Paper 159, International Monetary Fund.

IMF (International Monetary Fund). 1997. "IMF approves stand-by credit for Indonesia." Press release no. 97/50, November 5.

J. P. Morgan. 1997. *Emerging markets data watch.* July.

———. 1998. *Global data watch.* January 16. Periodical Publication by J. P. Morgan.

"Joint statement of the Indonesian Bank Steering Committee and representatives from the Republic of Indonesia." 1998. Press release, June 4.

Kaminsky, Graciela, Saul Lizondo, and Carmen M. Reinhart. 1997. *Leading indicators of currency crises.* Working Paper 36. College Park: Center for International Economics, Department of Economics, University of Maryland, College Park.

Krugman, Paul. 1998. "Saving Asia: It's time to get radical." *Fortune,* September 7, 32–37.

Lane, Timothy, Atish R. Gosh, Javier Hamann, Steven Philips, Marianne Schulze-Ghattas, and Tsidi Tsikata. 1999. *IMF-supported programs in Indonesia, Korea, and Thailand: A preliminary assessment.* Washington, DC: International Monetary Fund. Preliminary copy, January.

Lindgren, C-J., G. Garcia, and M. I. Saal. 1996. *Bank soundness and macroeconomic policy.* Washington, DC: International Monetary Fund.

Lindsey, Timothy, ed. 2000. *Indonesia: Bankruptcy, law reform, and the commercial court—comparative perspectives on insolvency law and policy.* Sydney: Desert Pea Press.

McKinnon, R. I., and H. Pill. 1996. "Credible liberalization and international capital flows: The overborrowing syndrome." In *Financial deregulation and integration in East Asia,* ed. T. Ito and A. O. Krueger. Chicago: University of Chicago Press.

Mishkin, Frederic S. 1997. "Understanding financial crises: A developing country perspective." In *Annual World Bank Conference on Development Economics, 1996.* Washington, DC: World Bank.

Miyazawa, Kiichi. 1998. "Towards a new international financial architecture." Speech delivered at the Foreign Correspondents Club of Japan, December 15.

Nasution, Anwar. 1995. The opening-up of the Indonesian economy, 1980–1993. In *Indonesian economy in the changing world,* ed. D. Kuntjoro-Jakti and K. Omura. Tokyo: Institute of Developing Economies.

———. *The banking system and monetary aggregates following financial sector reform: Lessons from Indonesia.* Research for Action, no. 27. Helsinki: United Nations University (UNU) and the World Institute for Development Economics Research.

———. 2000. "The meltdown of the Indonesian economy. Causes, responses and lessons." *ASEAN Economic Bulletin* 17, no. 2 (August): 148–62.

Radelet, Steven. 1995. Indonesian foreign debt: Headed for a crisis or financing sustainable growth? *Bulletin of Indonesian Economic Studies* 31, no. 3:39–72.

Reisen, Helmut. 1996. "Managing volatile capital inflows: The experience of the 1990s." *Asian Development Review* 14, no. 1:72–96.

Sachs, Jeffrey, and Steven Radelet. 1998. "The onset of the East Asian financial crisis." Manuscript, March. Downloaded from <http://www.hiid.harvard.edu/pub/other/asiacrisis.html>.

Sachs, Jeffrey, A. Tornell, and A. Velasco. 1996. "Financial crises in emerging markets: The lessons from 1995." *Brookings Papers on Economic Activity* 1:147–96.

Time. 1998. "The hunt is over." January 26, 14–16.

United Nations, ESCAP. 1995. *Issues and experiences in tax system reforms in selected countries of the ESCAP region.* Pt. 2: *The case study on Indonesia.* New York: United Nations.

World Bank. 1998. *Indonesia in crisis: A macroeconomic update.* Washington, DC: World Bank.

———. 1999. *Indonesia: From crisis to opportunity.* Washington DC: World Bank.

———. 2000a. *Indonesia: Public spending in a time of change.* Poverty Reduction and Economic Management Sector Unit, East Asia and the Pacific Region of the World Bank. Washington, DC: World Bank.

———. 2000b. *East Asia. Recovery and beyond.* Washington, DC: World Bank.

CHAPTER 7

Who Destabilized the Korean Stock Market?

Yung Chul Park and Innwon Park

A number of recent empirical studies provide some evidence that foreign portfolio investors in emerging financial markets have been engaged in positive feedback trading: buying when the market is booming and selling when it is slumping. These same studies suggest that foreign investors exhibit herd behavior. This behavior set, regardless of its rationality, could have deepened the crisis in East Asia and might have provided some justification for controlling capital inflows in emerging market economies.

The available evidence, however, is not conclusive. Positive feedback trading itself does not necessarily mean that foreign portfolio investors were destabilizing or increasing the volatility of the market.[1] Furthermore, none of these studies provides credible reasons as to why foreign portfolio investors engage in such trading activities. It is sometimes argued that foreign investors do not have as much information as domestic investors do on economic fundamentals and market development, but this "information asymmetry" explanation is not satisfactory. Foreign portfolio investors, in particular institutional ones, employ local agents or brokerage houses to gather and analyze market-related information. In recent years, they have had access to all sorts of information on the market and the economy supplied by financial and research institutions. A lack of information has not been a serious problem for foreign portfolio investors in most emerging markets. In fact, many domestic investors believe that foreign investors in general have a better ability to analyze the available information and have predicted market movements better. Given this perception, it would not be surprising to find that domestic investors closely mimic the portfolio decisions of foreign investors at least in some emerging markets.

De Long, Shleifer, Summers, and Waldman (1990) develop a theoretical model in which rational investors are shown to follow positive feedback trading and their rational speculation destabilizes prices. Tesar and Werner (1993, 1995), Bohn and Tesar (1996), and Brennan and Cao (1997) provide evidence for a positive correlation between international portfolio investment inflows and the dollar rate of returns on stocks. Froot, O'Connell, and Seasholes (1998) also examine the relationship between international portfolio flows and the stock returns of emerging stock markets. They find both that international inflows have some ability to forecast returns in emerging markets and that stock prices may rise subsequent to the inflows for a long period of time.

There are a number of studies examining foreign investors' trading behavior in emerging stock markets. Among them, Bekaert and Harvey analyze stock market volatility in emerging capital markets, including that of Korea. However, this chapter covers the period before the crisis, when the Korean market was not fully open to foreign investors. Moreover, Bekaert and Harvey's work is directed toward finding common world factors, which may explain volatility by means of a cross-country comparison rather than focusing on the behavior of foreign investors in individual country markets.

Choe, Kho, and Stulz 1998 and Kim and Wei 1999 are the first serious attempts to examine whether the trading patterns of foreign portfolio investors destabilized the Korean stock market in the late 1990s by engaging in positive feedback trading and herding. These studies attempt to gauge the impact of foreign investors' trading on Korean stock returns using trading data on the Korea Stock Exchange (KSE). Using foreign investors' trading data on the KSE, they estimate several ratios to determine whether foreign investors follow positive feedback strategies and whether they herd. Choe, Kho, and Stulz (1998) find evidence of positive feedback trading and herding by foreign investors but no evidence of a destabilizing effect during the period before the crisis and the last three months of 1997. However, their study fails to explain foreign investors' behavior after the crisis and does not answer the question of who destabilized the market if foreign investors were not responsible. Kim and Wei (1999) improve and update information on trade data on the KSE. They find strong evidence of positive feedback trading and herding by foreign investors before, during, and after the crisis but fail to explain whether foreign investors were largely accountable for destabilizing the market.

Most of the earlier studies are incomplete in that they do not compare the behavior of foreign investors to that of domestic investors. The trading share of foreign investors in the Korean stock market before the crisis was only 6 percent. Could such a small segment of the market participants alone destabilize the market and bring about the crash? If foreign investors as a whole followed positive feedback trading, it follows that domestic investors as a whole were engaged in negative feedback trading. Therefore, if the positive feedback trading by foreign investors destabilized the market, then the negative feedback trading by domestic investors should have tended to stabilize the market. On the other hand, if their positive feedback trading was a rational response to the market signal, the negative feedback trading by domestic investors was an irrational response to the signal and would increase market inefficiency and instability. In order to understand the role of foreign investors in the Korean stock market, one must consider the behavior of domestic investors as well. Otherwise, the ex post facto data analysis may not convey any significant information on the extent to which foreign portfolio investors contributed to market instability.

In this chapter, we use updated data sets, including that of the period after the crisis, in order to examine the trading patterns of all investors in the Korean stock market and to determine which investor group should be held responsible for the increase in market instability. First, we analyze the monthly data set using a methodology similar to the one chosen by Kim and Wei (1999) and Lakonishok, Shleifer, and Vishny (1992) to determine whether foreign investors follow positive feedback trading in the Korean stock market. Second, we run a vector autoregressive regression (VAR) estimation to analyze the relationship between investors' behavior and the market return. This estimation is compared with a Granger causality test using the daily record of stock trading in the KSE. Finally, we construct a generalized autoregressive conditional heteroskedasticity (GARCH) model to find out whose trading activities contributed to the increase in volatility in the Korean stock prices.

This chapter is organized as follows. We briefly explain the data sets we use in section 1. In section 2, we introduce the methodologies adopted to examine investors' trading patterns in and their impact on the Korean stock market. Section 3 discusses the results of the Granger causality test and the VAR estimation for a possible linkage between investors' portfolio decisions and the market return. The GARCH model is also estimated to evaluate the likely effects of investors' portfolio decisions on the volatility of the stock rate of return in the KSE. Section 4 briefly explains the important role of indirect foreign capital flows through domestic financial institutions during the late 1997 period as a main cause of the Korean currency crisis. Section 5 summarizes our findings.

1. DATA

This study uses two data sets. The first is the monthly data set, which is used for an analysis of feedback trading of investors by country of origin and type (individual or institutional investor). The second is the daily data set for an analysis of changes in the volatility of Korean stock market returns and the sources of that volatility.

1.1. MONTHLY DATA SET FOR FEEDBACK TRADING

This data set includes two subsets, one for stocks traded and another for foreign investors' trading records in the Korean stock market.[2] The monthly data set extends from December 1996 to April 1999. The stock data set contains information on code number, industrial specification, month-end price, month-end number of shares outstanding, monthly transaction volume, and whether or not the investment ceiling was binding in that month.

The data set for foreign investors contains information on month-end shareholding for each stock listed on the KSE and on whether or not the investment ceiling was binding for that investor during that month. Investors are identified by four-digit identification (ID) codes—the first digit for nationality, the second digit for residential classification, the third digit for the individual-institutional breakdown, and the last digit for the classification of investors by their trading volumes. For the last digit, we divide independent investors from the same country into 10 different groups according to the size of outstanding shares in June 1997. Because of this grouping, the data set for investors used for this study contains the trading behavior of 10 groups from each country rather than those of independent investors from each country. This is a weakness of the data set, but we were not able to collect better data because of strict regulations on the reporting of stock-trading information under the "Real Name Financial System." The Korea Financial Supervisory Committee (KFSC) does not permit publishing the history of an individual investor's trading activity, even with a randomly assigned ID code.[3]

In general, this data set is similar to that used by Kim and Wei (1999), but it is longer, extending until June 1998, when the stock market had not yet recovered from the crisis. By updating the sample period, we can examine trading patterns of foreign investors in the market after the Korean financial crisis. Moreover, by identifying foreign investors by country of origin, we may discover differences in trading patterns by nationality.

Certain categories of observations on investors and stock-months are excluded to avoid biased information and the outlier problem. They are: (1) stocks that were not listed in December 1996, (2) investors who were not registered for the whole period, (3) stocks that have reached foreign ownership limits, (4) stocks that are not initially owned by any foreign investor, and (5) stock-months with dollar rates of return that are too high or too low. For the month-end exchange rate of the Korean won against the U.S. dollar, we use International Monetary Fund (IMF) data.

1.2. DAILY DATA SET FOR CAUSALITY BETWEEN INVESTORS AND MARKET RETURN

The daily data set includes the Korea Composite Stock Price Index (KOSPI) and information on the daily transaction volumes and values of listed stocks bought and sold by domestic and foreign investors.[4] The domestic investors are divided into eight subgroups such as (1) stock companies, (2) insurance companies, (3) investment trust companies, (4) banks, (5) merchant bank and savings and finance companies, (6) mutual aid funds, (7) government funded institutions, and (8) individuals. The data set runs from November 30, 1996, to April 30, 1999.

2. METHODOLOGY

2.1. FEEDBACK TRADING

As the first attempt to find out whether foreign investors could be identified as the group destabilizing the Korean stock market, we analyze, following the methodology used by Kim and Wei (1999) and Lakonishok, Shlleifer, and Vishny (1992), the relationship between portfolio decisions by foreign investors and the dollar rate of return on the listed stocks in the KSE.

For a given period, we divide all the observations on stock-months into five groups of approximately the same size, from the best-performing portfolio (highest 20 percent) to the worst-performing portfolio (lowest 20 percent), by the previous month's dollar rate of return on the stocks. The dollar rate of return on stock i from month $t-1$ to t is defined as:

$$[\ln P_{i,t} - \ln P_{i,t-1}] - [\ln \mathrm{KOSPI}_t - \ln \mathrm{KOSPI}_{t-1}] - [\ln e_t - \ln e_{t-1}], \quad (1)$$

where $P_{i,t}$, KOSPI_t, and e_t are the price of stock i, the KOSPI index, and the exchange rate of the Korean won against the U.S. dollar.

For the analysis of foreign investors' trading patterns, we use three measures of investors' portfolio decisions in a given period: the S-ratio, D-ratio, and N-ratio. The S-ratio measures scale-adjusted net buys of shares in number, the D-ratio measures scale-adjusted net buys of shares in the dollar value, and the N-ratio measures the buyers' ratio. These ratios are defined as follows:

$$S\text{-ratio} = \frac{\text{Number of Shares Bought} - \text{Number of Shares Sold}}{\text{Number of Shares Bought} + \text{Number of Shares Sold}}, \quad (2)$$

$$D\text{-ratio} = \frac{\text{Dollar Value of Shares Bought} - \text{Dollar Value of Shares Sold}}{\text{Dollar Value of Shares Bought} + \text{Dollar Value of Shares Sold}}, \quad (3)$$

$$N\text{-ratio} = \frac{\text{Number of Buyers}}{\text{Number of Buyers} + \text{Number of Sellers}}. \quad (4)$$

For each and every category of stock-months, we estimate the average performance of foreign investors. If the differences between the mean of the best-performing portfolio and that of the worst-performing portfolio based on the *S*-, *D*-, and *N*-ratios are positive (negative) and statistically significant, we may conclude that foreign investors are positive (negative, respectively) feedback traders.

2.2. CAUSALITY TEST

A set of Granger causality tests is run to examine whether the behavior of a particular investor group leads to changes in Korean stock prices or is passive in that the group responds to price changes with lags. In doing so, we may learn whether investors respond to market changes in a rational manner or whether they destabilize the market.

2.3. VAR ANALYSIS

The ratio analysis in the previous section may reveal investors' responses to changes in the market return, but does not explain the causality between them. The Granger test helps determine causality but not the pattern of response. In order to find the pattern of investors' responses to the market signal and the effect of investors' portfolio decisions on the market return, we conduct a VAR estimation using the daily data set. By analyzing the response pattern, we may able to determine whether a particular investor group is a positive or negative feedback trader. In addition, we may also be able to evaluate whose portfolio decisions most affect the market return.

Suppose that the net buys of Korean stocks by an investor group and the rate of return that is calculated from change in KOSPI are jointly determined by a two-variable VAR with a constant as follows.[5]

$$X_t = C + A(L)\,X_t + \varepsilon_t, \qquad t = 1, 2, 3, \ldots n, \tag{5}$$

$$A(L) = \sum_{i}^{p} A_i L^{i-1}, \tag{6}$$

where X_t is a vector of the two endogenous variables mentioned earlier, L is a lag operator, and C is a constant.

By estimating the model and analyzing impulse responses, the causal relationship between the portfolio decision by a particular investor group and the rate of return on stocks will be evaluated. Prior to estimating the VAR model, we will perform a unit root test to check whether the two variables are stationary.

2.4. GARCH MODEL FOR VOLATILITY TEST

We first go through raw data to determine the periods in which sudden changes in volatility of the Korean stock market returns (R_t) occur and then estimate a GARCH model with periodic dummies to measure the variance of those sudden changes. Similar to Aggarwal, Inclan, and Leal 1999, which examines volatility in emerging stock markets by using GARCH(1,1) with dummies, we construct the following GARCH model with dummies. In addition to dummy variables, we include one more exogenous variable to gauge the effect of net buys by different groups of investors on changes in volatility.

$$R_t = a_0 + b_i \sum_i R_{t-i} + c_i Y_t + d_t D + \varepsilon_t, \tag{7}$$

$$h_t = \omega_0 + \omega_1 Y_i^2 + \omega_2 D + \sum_i \alpha_i \varepsilon_{t-i}^2 + \sum_i \beta_i h_{t-i}, \tag{8}$$

where R_t is the rate of return on the listed stocks in the KSE, Y_t is the value of net buys by a particular investor group, D's are dummy variables for periodic specification, and h is the conditional variance.

The first equation is the mean equation, which is a function of own lagged variables (R_{t-i}), an exogenous variable (Y_t), dummies (D), and an error term (ε_t). The second equation is a function of five terms: (1) the mean ω, (2) the square of net buys Y^2, (3) dummies D, (4) news about volatility from the past periods measured by the lagged squared residual from the mean equation ε^2 (the ARCH term), and (5) past periods' forecast variance h (the GARCH term).[7] The first equation may tell us whether the net buys by a particular investor group and dummies explain the average change in the return. The result from the second equation may indicate whether variations of net buys by a particular investor group explain the volatility of the market return.

3. EMPIRICAL RESULTS

We divide the whole period into three subperiods: before, during, and after the crisis. The period before the crisis extends from November 30, 1996, to October 23, 1997 (December 1996 to October 1997), when the Hong Kong stock market crashed. The crisis period runs from October 24, 1997, to September 3, 1998 (November 1997 to September 1998), when the Korean government announced the restructuring of the big five industrial groups (*chaebols*). The period after the crisis extends from September 4, 1998, to April 30, 1999 (October 1998 to April 1999 for the monthly data set, respectively).

3.1. DESCRIPTIVE STATISTICS

Table 7.1 summarizes the descriptive statistics of key variables in the Korean stock market. These statistics are reported for the daily stock index, the exchange rate and its changes, and the dollar and local rates of return over time. The KOSPI plunged to an all-time low and the exchange rate depreciated by almost 100 percent when the crisis broke out, but since then they have returned to a normal level, as illustrated in figure 7.1. These changes contributed to the negative dollar rate of return on the listed Korean stocks during the crisis period.

In table 7.2 and figure 7.2, which depict investors' portfolio decisions over time, we observe that foreign investors, domestic investment trust companies, and domestic individual investors were in general net buyers and others were net sellers for the whole period. In particular, foreign investors were net sellers during the early stage of the crisis but then returned to the market and actively increased their shares, as illustrated in figure 7.2(a). In contrast, domestic individual investors initially increased their shares, reduced

TABLE 7.1. Key Variables of the Korean Stock Market: Daily Values

	Period	Mean	Standard Deviation	Max.	Min.	Skewness
Stock index	All	545.35	153.50	793.98	280.00	−0.17
(KOSPI)	Before crisis	699.17	46.52	792.29	565.64	−0.29
	In crisis	417.74	87.82	574.35	280.00	0.12
	After crisis	500.38	132.23	793.98	291.93	0.15
Exchange rate	All	1,166.02	262.39	1,964.80	828.70	0.35
(won/U.S.$)	Before crisis	883.60	22.53	922.70	828.70	−0.72
	In crisis	1,394.51	205.69	1,964.80	927.90	−0.19
	After crisis	1,257.16	72.06	1,403.90	1,149.00	0.52
Rate of return (%)	All	0.04	2.53	8.50	−8.10	0.21
	Before crisis	−0.06	1.39	6.08	−4.22	0.42
	In crisis	−0.20	3.22	8.50	−8.10	0.16
	After crisis	0.54	2.66	7.80	−5.84	0.27
Dollar rate of return (%)	All	−0.03	3.57	25.50	−24.08	0.47
	Before crisis	−0.10	1.44	6.25	−4.26	0.38
	In crisis	−0.40	5.11	25.50	−24.08	0.51
	After crisis	0.61	2.93	9.58	−5.91	0.37
Exchange rate depreciation	All	0.07	1.86	16.58	−18.28	−0.65
against the U.S. dollar (%)	Before crisis	0.04	0.22	0.90	−2.21	−3.86
	In crisis	0.19	2.99	16.58	−18.28	−0.53
	After crisis	−0.06	0.66	2.52	−2.26	−0.11

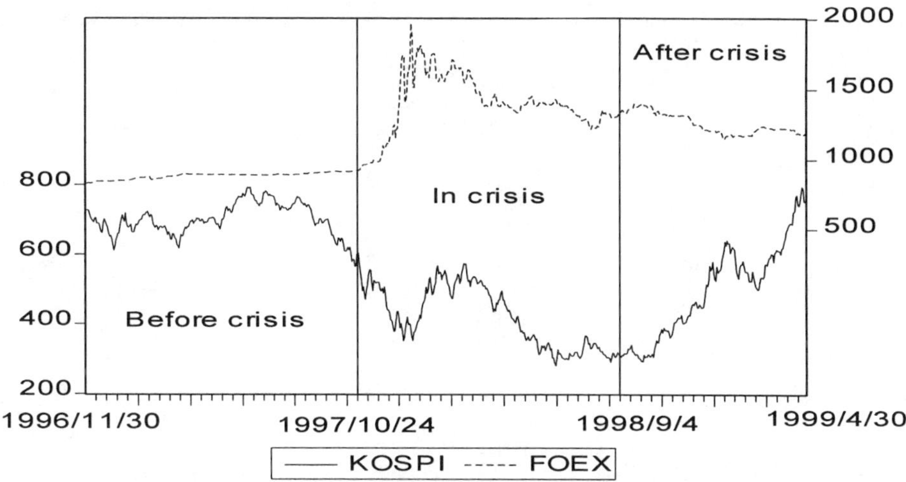

Fig. 7.1. Korea stock price index (KOSPI) and the exchange rate of the Korean won against the U.S. dollar (FOEX)

their holdings shortly after the crisis, and then returned to the market. Most domestic institutional investors reduced their shares for the whole period. The quick recovery of the market after the crisis was achieved through a sharp increase in the demand by foreign investors and domestic investment trust companies.

Did the net sells by foreign investors from late October through early November in 1997 trigger the crisis by leading to net sells by domestic investors? In order to check whether domestic investors deepened the crisis by following foreign investors' trading pattern at that time, we zoom in on the trading patterns during the early stage of the crisis in figure 7.2(b), which illustrates that foreign investors, domestic investment trust companies, and domestic merchant and savings and finance companies all show a similar trading pattern. However, we could not find a causal relationship among those three investor groups during the early stage of the crisis.

As illustrated in figure 7.3, the total transaction share of foreign investors in the Korean stock market during the crisis period was higher than their overall average. This was the result of the abnormally high share of net buys by foreign investors during the crisis period (see figure 7.2) due in part to the rapid upward adjustment of foreign ownership limits (see table 7.3) and the recovery of international confidence in the Korean economy. The buy and sell shares of investor groups are summarized in table 7.4.

TABLE 7.2. **Descriptive Statistics for Net Buys by Type of Investor: Daily Values (100 million won)**

	Period	Mean	Standard Deviation	Max.	Min.	Skewness
Net buys by foreign investors	All	131.49	521.22	6,114.06	−1,348.96	4.06
	Before crisis	38.64	444.57	6,114.06	−881.44	9.86
	In crisis	141.45	548.32	3,251.42	−1,348.96	2.06
	After crisis	257.67	561.41	3,835.82	−787.24	2.48
Net buys by domestic stock companies	All	−45.30	244.37	1,708.77	−1,856.57	−0.62
	Before crisis	−37.52	145.92	411.47	−1,288.46	−3.07
	In crisis	−44.94	142.97	376.20	−543.11	−0.20
	After crisis	−57.62	420.35	1,708.77	−1,856.57	−0.21
Net buys by domestic insurance companies	All	−27.60	132.40	479.10	−1,384.97	28.93
	Before crisis	4.84	51.78	423.49	−154.13	21.51
	In crisis	−18.53	70.29	102.45	−420.26	13.81
	After crisis	−90.23	230.79	479.10	−1,384.97	−1.89
Net buys by domestic investment trust companies	All	15.70	345.02	2,636.74	−2,704.94	1.80
	Before crisis	−17.09	224.44	786.69	−2,704.94	−6.53
	In crisis	−70.04	233.05	737.42	−1,611.35	−1.49
	After crisis	192.09	526.06	2,636.74	−773.79	2.16
Net buys by domestic banks	All	−68.83	125.69	328.02	−755.88	−2.36
	Before crisis	−23.71	56.25	264.99	−402.55	−1.42
	In crisis	−77.87	136.52	106.45	−753.84	−2.37
	After crisis	−123.96	157.19	328.02	−755.88	−1.36
Net buys by domestic merchant banks and savings and finance companies	All	−4.00	66.25	571.07	−321.43	0.65
	Before crisis	9.47	27.51	147.35	−95.54	0.77
	In crisis	−9.71	71.39	571.07	−270.80	2.23
	After crisis	−16.01	91.92	402.75	−321.43	−0.11
Net buys by domestic mutual aid funds	All	−5.24	200.96	304.06	−5,163.81	−24.66
	Before crisis	−2.59	12.47	76.06	−50.07	1.39
	In crisis	0.58	26.11	145.31	−129.44	0.47
	After crisis	−17.84	400.68	304.05	−5,136.81	−12.41
Net buys by domestic government-funded institutions	All	−9.98	158.27	830.09	−1,111.82	−2.43
	Before crisis	4.03	61.26	290.63	−329.53	−1.06
	In crisis	4.99	94.39	502.92	−616.67	−1.76
	After crisis	−52.86	281.16	830.09	−1,111.82	−1.20
Net buys by domestic individuals	All	13.74	557.91	3,620.31	−2,339.26	0.26
	Before crisis	23.88	254.06	1,122.74	−1,350.31	−0.59
	In crisis	74.40	481.30	1,601.50	−1,870.38	−0.52
	After crisis	−91.24	889.46	3,620.31	−2,339.26	0.66

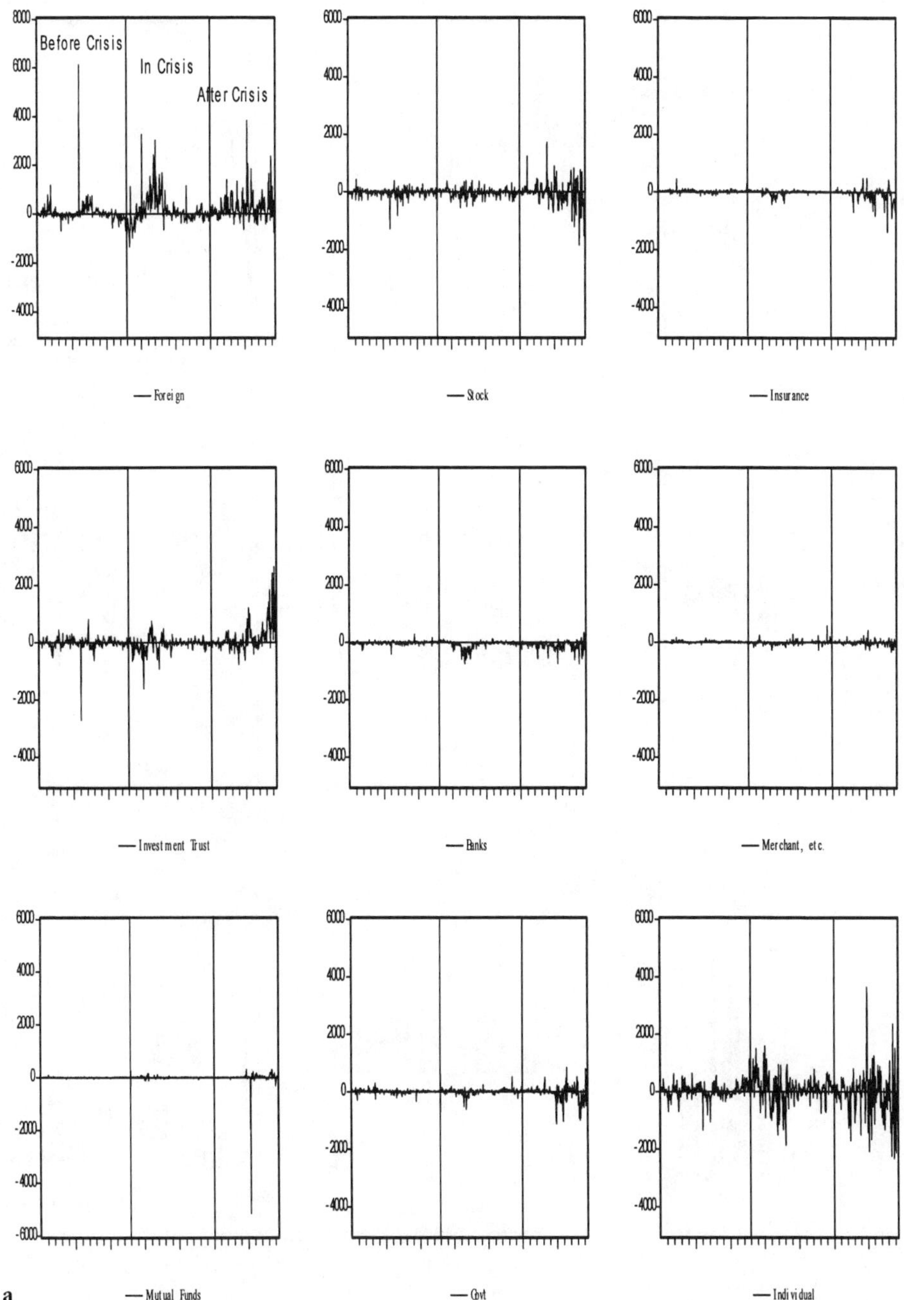

a

Fig. 7.2. Net buys: *a,* by type of investor; *b,* by type of investor during the early stages of the crisis

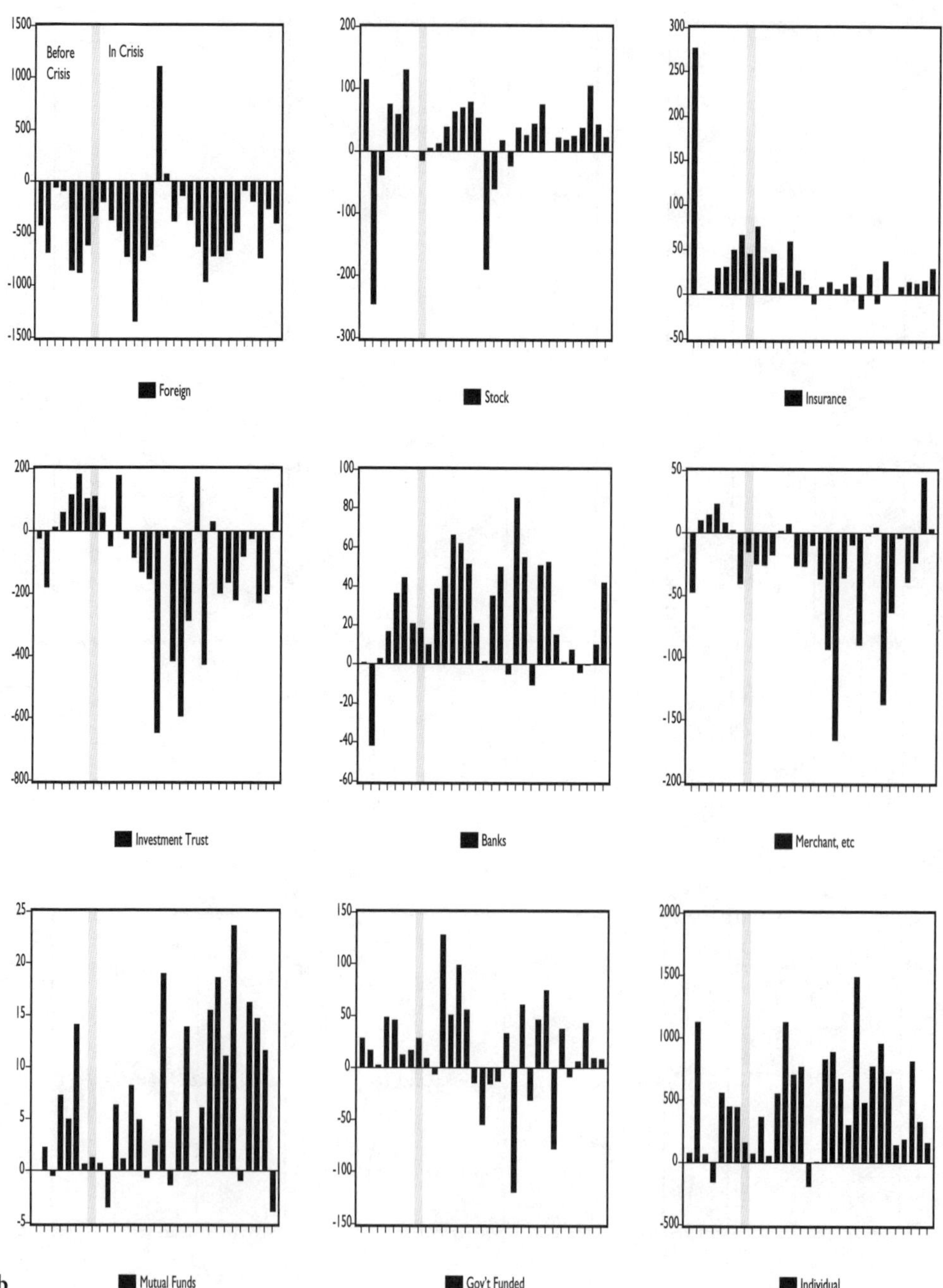

Fig. 7.2. Continued

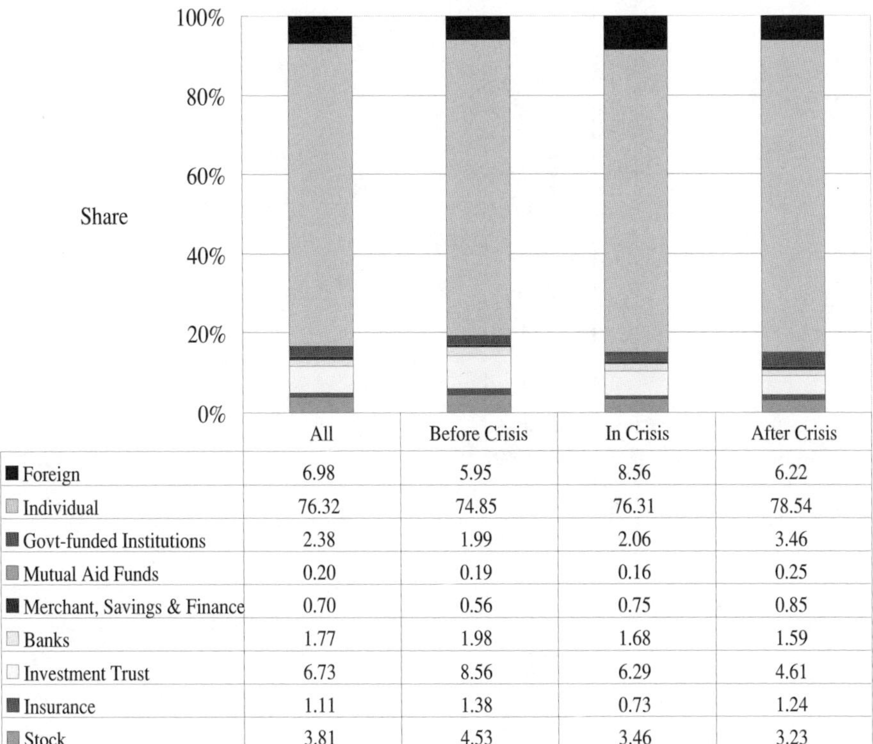

	All	Before Crisis	In Crisis	After Crisis
Foreign	6.98	5.95	8.56	6.22
Individual	76.32	74.85	76.31	78.54
Govt-funded Institutions	2.38	1.99	2.06	3.46
Mutual Aid Funds	0.20	0.19	0.16	0.25
Merchant, Savings & Finance	0.70	0.56	0.75	0.85
Banks	1.77	1.98	1.68	1.59
Investment Trust	6.73	8.56	6.29	4.61
Insurance	1.11	1.38	0.73	1.24
Stock	3.81	4.53	3.46	3.23

Fig. 7.3. Total transaction share (%) by type of investor

3.2. FEEDBACK TRADING

Three different ratios are estimated to see whether foreign investors follow positive feedback trading in the Korean stock market. Tables 7.5, 7.6, 7.7, and 7.8 summarize the results from the ratio analysis for the feedback trading by foreign investors for the whole period and before, during, and after the crisis, respectively. The tables report differences between the mean of the best

TABLE 7.3. Foreign Ownership Limit

Date	Limit (%)	Date	Limit (%)
January 1992	10	May 1997	23
December 1994	12	November 1997	26
July 1995	15	December 12, 1997	50
April 1996	18	December 30, 1997	55
October 1996	20	May 1998	100

Source: Bank of Korea, *Financial Market in Korea,* July 1999.

TABLE 7.4. Buy and Sell Shares (%) by Type of Investor

		Domestic Investors								
	Foreign Investors	All	Stock	Insurance	Investment Trust	Banks	Merchant Banks and Savings and Finance	Mutual Aid Funds	Government-Funded Institutions	Individuals
Buys										
All	7.4	92.6	3.5	1.1	6.5	1.3	0.7	0.2	2.5	76.7
Before crisis	6.0	94.0	4.2	1.5	8.5	1.8	0.6	0.2	2.1	75.2
In crisis	9.1	90.9	3.0	0.7	5.7	1.1	0.7	0.2	2.2	77.3
After crisis	7.0	93.0	3.1	1.0	4.9	1.1	0.8	0.2	3.5	78.3
Sells										
All	6.6	93.4	4.1	1.2	6.9	2.2	0.7	0.2	2.3	75.9
Before crisis	5.9	94.1	4.8	1.3	8.6	2.2	0.5	0.2	1.9	74.5
In crisis	8.0	92.0	3.9	0.8	6.9	2.3	0.8	0.2	1.9	75.4
After crisis	5.4	94.6	3.3	1.5	4.3	2.1	0.9	0.3	3.4	78.8

TABLE 7.5. Feedback Trading by Foreign Investors during the Whole Period

	All Investors		Individual Investors		Institutional Investors	
	Highest 20% −Lowest 20%	*t*-value	Highest 20% −Lowest 20%	*t*-value	Highest 20% −Lowest 20%	*t*-value
All						
S-ratio	0.032	6.04	0.065	4.11	0.028	5.32
D-ratio	0.054	11.30	0.033	1.47	0.054	11.34
N-ratio	0.011	6.04	0.029	3.18	0.009	5.05
USA						
S-ratio	0.032	3.05	−0.111	−2.78	0.032	3.03
D-ratio	0.048	5.23	0.014	0.43	0.052	5.47
N-ratio	0.012	0.51	0.022	1.63	0.011	3.06
UK						
S-ratio	0.012	1.03	−0.087	−0.74	0.015	1.29
D-ratio	0.059	5.31	−0.067	−0.60	0.062	5.52
N-ratio	0.001	0.14	−0.069	−1.53	0.002	0.48
Japan						
S-ratio	0.100	3.82	0.057	1.25	0.020	0.79
D-ratio	0.111	5.06	0.175	3.50	0.077	3.49
N-ratio	0.034	3.49	0.110	4.63	−0.003	−0.37
Germany						
S-ratio	−0.073	−0.95	−0.453	−1.56	0.004	0.07
D-ratio	0.086	1.35	−0.048	−0.29	0.074	1.34
N-ratio	0.014	0.72	−0.062	−0.92	−0.522	−35.89
Rest of America						
S-ratio	0.044	1.75	−0.014	−0.09	0.041	1.67
D-ratio	0.043	2.02	−0.217	−1.79	0.058	2.70
N-ratio	0.021	2.37	0.021	0.33	0.018	2.21
Rest of Europe						
S-ratio	0.032	3.00	0.544	1.66	0.032	2.93
D-ratio	0.039	4.25	−0.230	−0.57	0.040	4.39
N-ratio	0.011	3.08	0.186	1.47	0.011	3.02
Rest of Asia						
S-ratio	0.036	2.62	0.102	2.11	0.020	1.49
D-ratio	0.065	5.15	0.072	1.54	0.061	4.81
N-ratio	0.013	2.73	0.028	1.66	0.009	1.95
Others						
S-ratio	0.038	1.78	−0.316	−2.51	0.053	2.47
D-ratio	0.057	3.07	−0.091	−0.95	0.063	3.34
N-ratio	0.008	1.14	−0.040	−1.01	0.010	1.41

Note: Stock-months are divided into five groups according to prior-month return. For each group, *S*-ratio (the mean value of net purchase), *D*-ratio (the dollar mean value of net purchase), and *N*-ratio (the mean value of buyers' ratio) are calculated. Then we do a formal *t*-test on the difference between the mean purchase of the best-performing portfolio (group of highest 20 percent) and that of the worst-performing portfolio (group of lowest 20 percent).

performing portfolio (highest 20 percent) and that of the worst performing portfolio (lowest 20 percent) with *t*-values based on the *S*-ratio, *D*-ratio, and *N*-ratio. The classification of portfolio performance is determined by the previous month's dollar rate of return on each stock in the market.

For the whole period in table 7.5, we find strong evidence of positive feedback trading by all groups of foreign investors, with the exception of the in-

TABLE 7.6. Feedback Trading by Foreign Investors before the Crisis

	All Investors		Individual Investors		Institutional Investors	
	Highest 20% −Lowest 20%	*t*-value	Highest 20% −Lowest 20%	*t*-value	Highest 20% −Lowest 20%	*t*-value
All						
S-ratio	−0.020	−1.75	0.090	1.74	−0.028	−2.37
D-ratio	−0.018	−1.80	0.056	1.28	−0.023	−2.26
N-ratio	−0.007	−1.79	0.048	2.91	−0.011	−2.69
USA						
S-ratio	−0.021	−0.90	0.093	1.25	−0.036	−1.48
D-ratio	−0.017	−0.83	0.039	0.67	−0.023	−1.10
N-ratio	−0.002	−0.29	0.047	1.92	−0.009	−1.06
UK						
S-ratio	−0.021	−0.79	−0.297		−0.026	−0.95
D-ratio	0.007	0.26	−0.299		0.002	0.10
N-ratio	−0.017	−1.96	−0.121		−0.020	−2.23
Japan						
S-ratio	−0.048	−0.82	−0.056	−0.42	−0.044	−0.79
D-ratio	−0.032	−0.75	−0.108	−1.15	−0.003	−0.07
N-ratio	−0.016	−0.90	0.020	0.47	−0.030	−1.75
Germany						
S-ratio	−0.079	−0.85	−0.165	−1.08	0.007	0.28
D-ratio	−0.063	−0.38	−0.083	−0.27	−0.044	−0.28
N-ratio	0.043	1.03	0.081	2.07	0.004	0.28
Rest of America						
S-ratio	0.030	0.66	−0.109	−0.45	0.033	0.70
D-ratio	−0.013	−0.34	−0.255	−1.17	0.000	0.00
N-ratio	−0.019	−1.13	−0.027	−0.25	−0.019	−1.15
Rest of Europe						
S-ratio	−0.020	−0.91	0.000		−0.021	−0.91
D-ratio	−0.028	−1.49	0.000		−0.028	−1.49
N-ratio	−0.005	−0.63	0.000		−0.005	−0.63
Rest of Asia						
S-ratio	−0.019	−0.72	0.141	1.34	−0.035	−1.27
D-ratio	−0.026	−1.13	0.153	1.61	−0.045	−1.85
N-ratio	−0.002	−0.22	0.049	1.43	−0.008	−0.85
Others						
S-ratio	−0.019	−0.43	0.071	0.28	−0.025	−0.56
D-ratio	0.023	0.53	0.052	0.28	0.019	0.44
N-ratio	−0.019	−1.29	0.002	0.28	−0.019	−1.31

Note: Missing data are the result of a small sample problem.

dividual investor groups. In particular, all three ratios of British, German, and other foreign individual investors indicate that they follow negative feedback trading, although the *t*-values of the ratios are not significant.

From table 7.6, we see that foreign institutional investors and most of the individual investors from the United Kingdom, Japan, Germany, and the United States were negative feedback traders in the Korean stock market

TABLE 7.7. Feedback Trading by Foreign Investors during the Crisis

	All Investors		Individual Investors		Institutional Investors	
	Highest 20% −Lowest 20%	*t*-value	Highest 20% −Lowest 20%	*t*-value	Highest 20% −Lowest 20%	*t*-value
All						
S-ratio	0.745	76.01	0.500	7.02	0.138	6.24
D-ratio	0.268	18.45	0.300	6.20	0.252	16.30
N-ratio	0.054	6.55	0.184	6.21	0.031	3.84
USA						
S-ratio	0.192	4.59	0.521	4.48	0.140	3.22
D-ratio	0.256	9.28	0.229	3.82	0.254	8.38
N-ratio	0.074	4.61	0.235	4.62	0.049	3.07
UK						
S-ratio	0.113	2.64	−0.357	−2.21	0.119	2.75
D-ratio	0.228	7.41	0.104	0.47	0.130	4.17
N-ratio	0.016	0.99	−0.266	−3.71	0.019	1.20
Japan						
S-ratio	0.370	4.07	0.627	4.60	0.073	0.69
D-ratio	0.344	6.23	0.360	3.57	0.277	4.24
N-ratio	0.124	3.44	0.244	4.62	0.020	0.54
Germany						
S-ratio	1.067		1.059			
D-ratio	0.370		−0.516			
N-ratio	0.431		0.324			
Rest of America						
S-ratio	0.295	2.76			0.296	2.77
D-ratio	0.302	4.80			0.302	4.79
N-ratio	0.075	1.56			0.077	1.60
Rest of Europe						
S-ratio	0.150	3.40	1.132		0.144	3.27
D-ratio	0.252	8.35	0.536		0.250	8.25
N-ratio	0.034	2.07	0.447		0.031	1.92
Rest of Asia						
S-ratio	0.294	4.53	0.428	2.53	0.071	0.96
D-ratio	0.330	7.40	0.343	2.67	0.227	4.03
N-ratio	0.081	3.28	0.120	1.90	0.004	0.14
Others						
S-ratio	0.206	2.01			0.211	2.06
D-ratio	0.275	3.95			0.282	4.07
N-ratio	0.024	0.60			0.023	0.57

Note: Missing data are the result of a small sample problem.

before the crisis, but once again the ratios are not statistically significant. During the crisis period, the negative feedback trading of foreign investors became more pronounced, with the statistically significant *t*-values of the ratios. Foreign investors, irrespective of their nationality, bought winners and sold losers during the crisis (see table 7.7).

For the period after the crisis, we do not find any consistent result from

TABLE 7.8. Feedback Trading by Foreign Investors after the Crisis

	All Investors		Individual Investors		Institutional Investors	
	Highest 20% −Lowest 20%	*t*-value	Highest 20% −Lowest 20%	*t*-value	Highest 20% −Lowest 20%	*t*-value
All						
S-ratio	0.616	77.69	−0.138	−1.28	−0.178	−6.99
D-ratio	0.064	2.95	−0.251	−3.59	0.088	3.90
N-ratio	−0.012	−1.45	0.018	0.38	−0.013	−1.62
USA						
S-ratio	−0.189	−3.89	−0.209	−1.10	−0.180	−3.59
D-ratio	0.085	1.99	−0.131	−0.91	0.106	2.35
N-ratio	−0.025	−1.46	−0.017	−0.23	−0.021	−1.28
UK						
S-ratio	−0.173	−3.33	−0.855	−5.46	−0.155	−2.94
D-ratio	0.035	0.79	−0.727	−6.77	0.044	0.96
N-ratio	−0.025	−1.55	−0.485	−5.59	−0.018	−1.09
Japan						
S-ratio	−0.163	−1.34	−0.171	−0.79	−0.071	−0.50
D-ratio	0.005	0.05	−0.354	−4.27	0.344	2.68
N-ratio	0.057	1.25	0.107	1.12	0.010	0.24
Germany						
S-ratio	−0.618	−1.78			−0.298	
D-ratio	−0.025	−0.09			0.145	
N-ratio	−0.067	−0.42			0.005	
Rest of America						
S-ratio	−0.020	−0.20	0.775	2.83	−0.048	−0.50
D-ratio	0.086	0.89	−0.512	−1.73	0.127	1.26
N-ratio	0.016	0.40	0.475	3.06	−0.006	−0.19
Rest of Europe						
S-ratio	−0.195	−3.79	0.831		−0.196	−3.80
D-ratio	0.082	1.77	−0.884		0.093	2.00
N-ratio	−0.003	−0.19	0.466		−0.002	−0.15
Rest of Asia						
S-ratio	−0.150	−2.38	0.081	0.43	−0.194	−2.95
D-ratio	0.048	0.91	−0.100	−0.79	0.089	1.54
N-ratio	−0.007	−0.35	0.060	0.75	−0.023	−1.16
Others						
S-ratio	−0.210	−1.75			−0.205	−1.65
D-ratio	0.140	1.33			0.147	1.29
N-ratio	0.023	0.56			0.030	0.78

Note: Missing data are the result of a small sample problem.

our ratio analysis. Whether foreign investors follow positive feedback trading or not depends on the methodology we choose. Our results are only partially consistent with Kim and Wei (1999). We find that foreign investors were positive feedback traders during the crisis period but were not during the period both before and after the crisis.

3.3. INVESTORS' PORTFOLIO DECISIONS AND MARKET RETURNS

If average foreign investors bought winners and sold losers during the crisis period, it follows that average domestic investors must sell winners and buy losers because there are only two groups of investors. The positive feedback trading by foreign investors implies a causal relationship in which foreign investors' net buys are influenced by changes in the rates of return on stocks. The evidence of positive feedback trading in terms of the three ratios does not prove that the engagement of a particular investor group in positive feedback trading necessarily increases stock prices or market volatility. In order to test a causal linkage between stock prices and investors' excess demand for stock measured by net buys, we therefore turn to the Granger causality test and the VAR estimation in this section.

Causality Test

From the Granger causality tests,[7] we find that both average foreign and domestic investors respond to changes in the rate of return on the listed stocks in the Korean stock market. On the other hand, changes in stock prices are not significantly affected by the excess demand by either foreign or domestic investors. However, during the crisis we find that net buys for stocks by domestic investors had a significant effect on the rate of return on stocks (at the 5 percent level of significance). This means that the dramatic fall in Korean stock prices during the crisis period was caused largely by domestic investors, not foreign. This result is consistent with the evidence that domestic investors were net sellers during the crisis period.

When we divide domestic investors into eight groups, the causal relationship between investors' portfolio decisions and the market price varies over time. During the period before the crisis, only domestic insurance companies and individual investors responded to the market return, and their response in turn led to changes in stock prices. However, during the crisis period the excess demand for stocks by insurance companies, investment trust companies, mutual aid funds, and individual investors brought about changes in stock prices. This pattern of behavior destabilized the market at the time of the crisis. This causal linkage between domestic investor groups' trading and the market became insignificant after the crisis.

VAR Analysis

In order to substantiate further the Granger causality test, we also estimate the impulse response of net buys to the rate of return in terms of a two-variable VAR equation—the net buys of the Korean stocks by a particular investor group and the dollar rate of return. Prior to estimating the VAR model for causality, we perform a unit root test to check whether the two variables are stationary. The results indicate that they are stationary (see Park and Park 1999).

For a test of optimal lags in the VAR equation, we use the Akaike information criterion (AIC) and the Schwarz criterion (SC). In our test, we do not find any significant differences in VAR equations with different lags from 1 to 5. We therefore arbitrarily include five lags in the VAR equation.

The VAR model is then used to estimate impulse responses. Figures 7.4 and 7.5 represent changing patterns of the impulse response of the net buys by foreign as well as domestic investors to the rate of return for the four different periods. The impulse response patterns show that foreign investors are positive feedback traders while domestic investors are negative feedback traders for all the periods, but statistically this pattern of trading is less significant during the period before the crisis than during other periods. This finding confirms the earlier results we obtained from the ratio analysis.

The impulse responses of the rate of return to the net buys by both foreign and domestic investors are not significant at the 5 percent level when the period after the crisis is excluded. For the period after the crisis, the net buys by foreign investors immediately raise the dollar rate of return. This effect disappeared rather quickly, however.

In summary, the VAR experiments with the daily data support our earlier findings on positive feedback trading by foreign investors in the Korean stock market. For domestic investors, their trading pattern is a mirror image of that of the foreign investors. One interesting finding from the impulse response pattern in figures 7.4 and 7.5 is that the causal linkage between net buys and the rate of return for both foreign and domestic investors has been getting more sensitive and significant over time, especially during the period after the crisis. This development may be related to liberalization of the domestic financial market and the recovery of global capital movements.

Table 7.9 summarizes the immediate impulse responses together with the results from the Granger causality test. Overall, foreign investors positively responded to the price change. In contrast, banks, merchant banks, savings and finance companies, and individual investors in Korea respond negatively

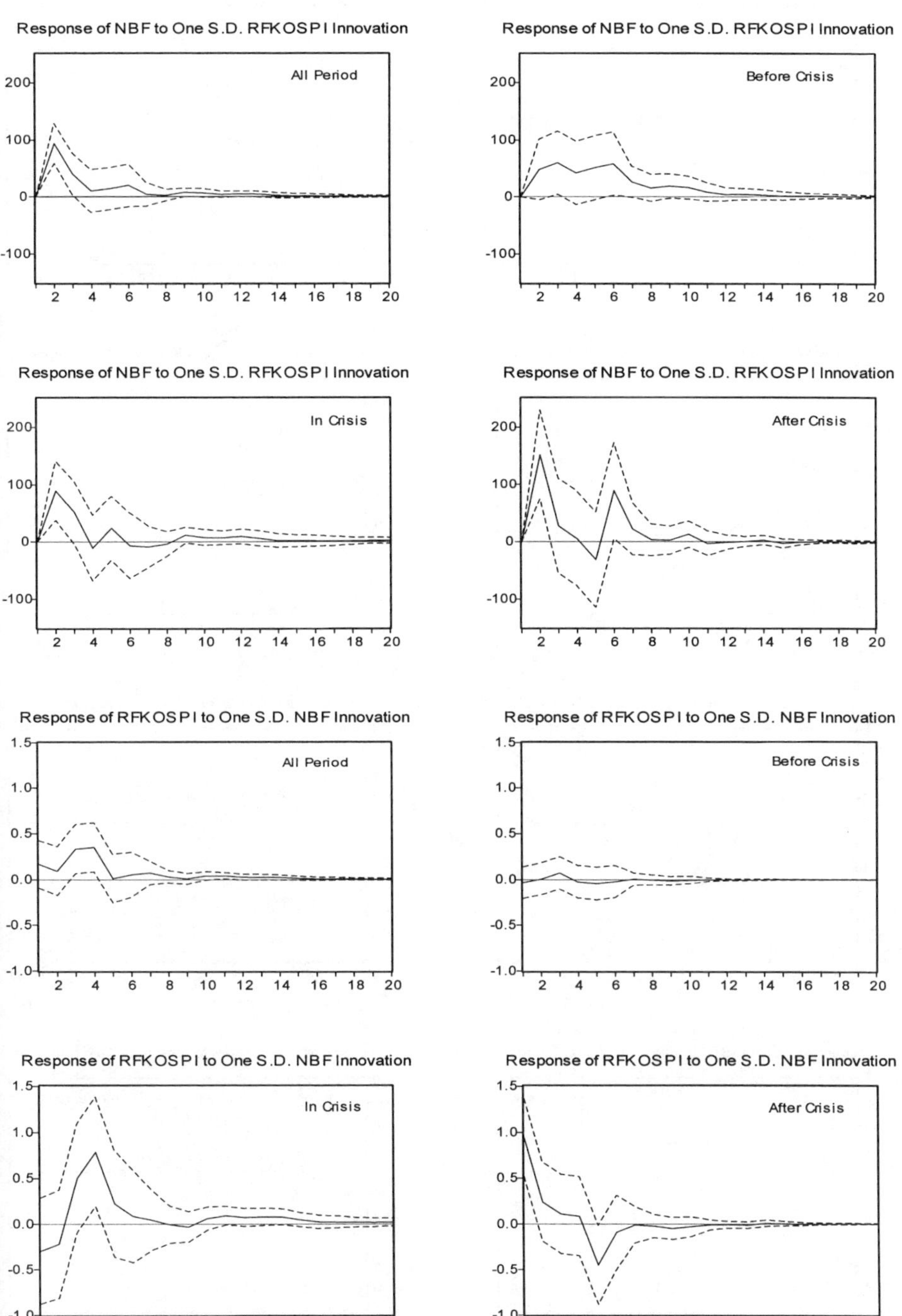

Fig. 7.4. Impulse responses of net buys by foreign investors (NBF, 100 million won) and dollar rate of return (RFKOSPI, %). Dotted lines indicate the significance range at the 95 percent level.

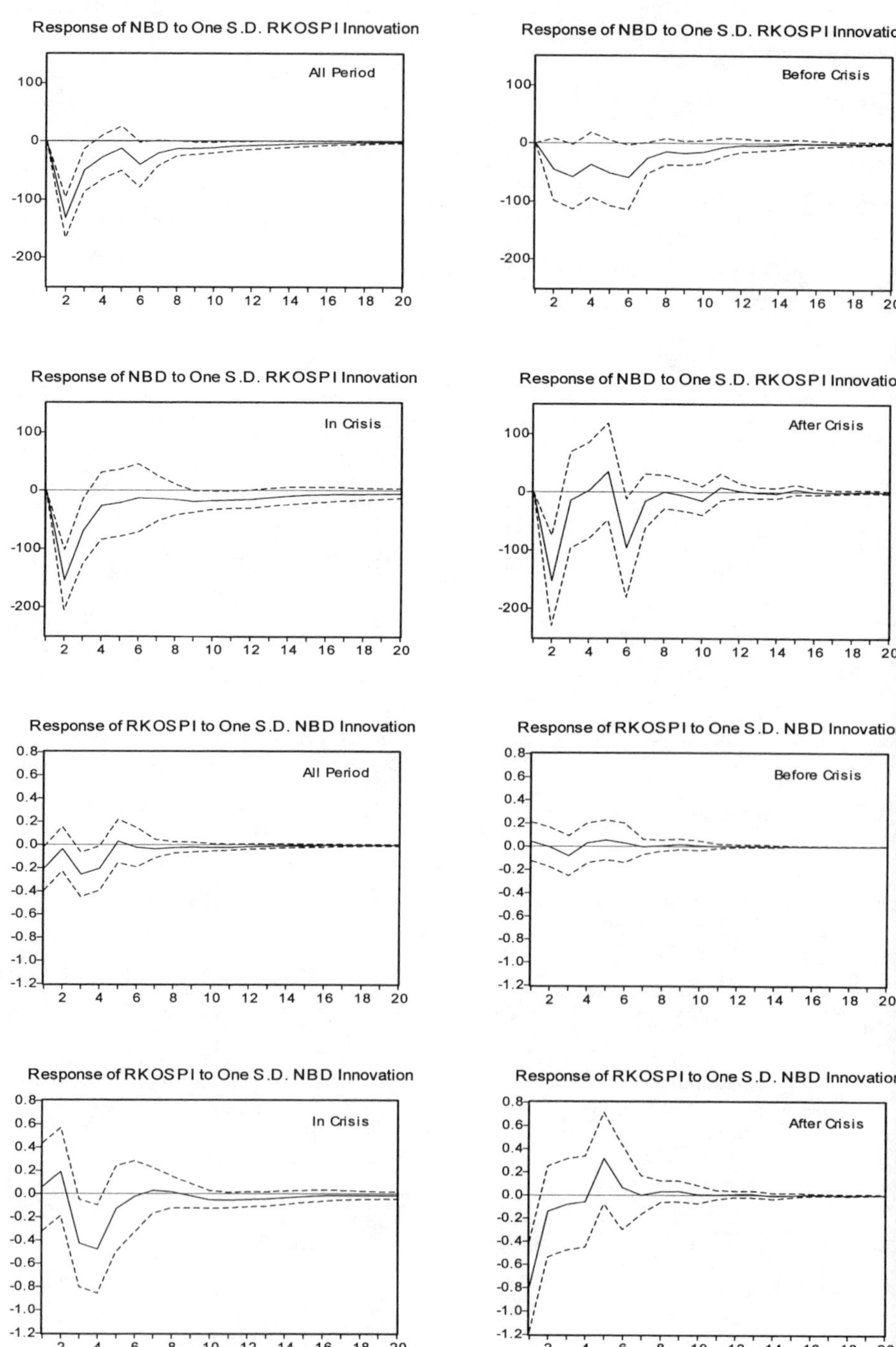

Fig. 7.5. Impulse responses of net buys by domestic investors (NBD, 100 million won) and rate of return (RKOSPI, %). Dotted lines indicate the significance range at the 95 percent level.

TABLE 7.9. Evaluations of the Relationship between Net Buys and Rate of Return by Type of Investor

Type of Investor (transaction share, %)	Granger Causality Test		Immediate (1 to 2 days) Impulse Response	
	Return □ Buys	Buys □ Return	Return □ Buys	Buys □ Return
Total period				
Foreign (7.0)	***	**	Positive**	Positive
Domestic (93.0)	***	**	Negative**	Negative
Stock (3.8)			Negative	Positive**
Insurance (1.1)	***		Negative	Negative
Investment trust (6.7)		***	Positive	Positive**
Banks (1.8)	***		Negative**	Negative**
Merchant and savings and finance (0.7)	***		Negative**	Positive
Mutual aid funds (0.2)	***		Negative	Negative
Government-funded institutions (2.4)			Negative	Negative**
Individuals (76.3)	***	***	Negative**	Negative**
Before crisis				
Foreign (6.0)	**		Positive	Positive
Domestic (94.0)	**		Negative	Negative
Stock (4.5)			Negative	Positive
Insurance (1.4)	**	**	Negative**	Positive
Investment trust (8.6)			Positive	Negative
Banks (2.0)			Negative	Negative
Merchant and savings and finance (0.6)			Positive	Negative
Mutual aid funds (0.2)			Negative	Negative
Government-funded institutions (2.0)			Negative	Negative
Individuals (74.9)	***	***	Negative**	Positive**
In crisis				
Foreign (8.6)	***		Positive**	Negative
Domestic (91.4)	***	**	Negative**	Positive
Stock (3.5)			Negative	Positive
Insurance (0.7)	**	***	Negative**	Negative
Investment trust (6.3)		***	Negative	Positive**
Banks (1.7)	**		Negative**	Negative**
Merchant and savings and finance (0.8)	***		Negative**	Negative
Mutual aid funds (0.2)		***	Negative	Positive
Government-funded institutions (2.1)	*		Negative**	Negative**
Individuals (76.3)	***	***	Negative**	Positive
After crisis				
Foreign (6.2)	***		Positive**	Positive**
Domestic (93.8)	***		Negative**	Negative**
Stock (3.2)			Negative	Positive**
Insurance (1.2)			Negative	Positive
Investment trust (4.6)			Positive	Positive
Banks (1.6)	*		Positive	Negative
Merchant and savings and finance (0.9)			Positive	Positive
Mutual aid funds (0.3)	*		Negative	Negative
Government-funded institutions (3.5)			Positive	Negative**
Individuals (78.5)	**		Negative**	Negative**

*, **, and *** indicate significance at the 10%, 5%, and 1% levels, respectively.

to the change. On the other hand, net buys by securities firms and investment trust companies increase the market price, but net buys by merchant banks, savings and finance companies, and government-funded institutions have a negative effect on the price.

Before the crisis, insurance companies and individual investors negatively responded to price changes, and net buys by individual investors caused a significant increase in the price, but this positive effect did not last long and the largest drop in the price followed. During the crisis period, all of the domestic investors engaged in negative feedback trading in contrast to the positive feedback trading by foreign investors. Net buys by banks and government-funded institutions decreased the price, whereas those by investment trust companies raised the price. After the crisis, foreign investors bought winners and sold losers, but domestic individual investors moved in the opposite direction. In general, the stock price is pushed up by foreign investors' purchases and pulled down by domestic individual investors' net buys.

The impulse responses, especially during the crisis period, show that most domestic investors, especially domestic individual investors, reacted sharply to the price changes and that their trading behavior was the main source of market turmoil, which in the end contributed to the market crash at that time of the crisis.

3.4. THE GARCH MODEL FOR VOLATILITY TEST

As we can see from figure 7.6, the volatility of the Korean stock returns has increased since the crisis. In this section, we attempt to explain the factors behind the extremely high volatility during and after the crisis period by estimating a GARCH model. The mean equation of GARCH(1,1) for the rate of return includes a constant; own lagged variables; exogenous variables, including two dummies for the periods during and after the crisis; investors' excess demand for Korean stocks; and an error term. The conditional variance equation of the model includes a constant, exogenous variables (dummies and square of the excess demand by investors), news about volatility from the past periods measured by the lagged squared residuals from the mean equation (the ARCH term), and past periods' forecast variance (the GARCH term).

In the GARCH(1,1) model estimation, the ARCH and GARCH coefficients are both significant in equations (1) to (8) (see Park and Park 1999). In most of the equations, the sum of the ARCH and GARCH coefficients is very close to one, indicating that volatility shocks are quite persistent. This means that the disturbance of the Korean stock prices is a linear function of one lagged squared disturbance and one lagged conditional variance.

This result is also supported by equations (2), (3), and (4), which include

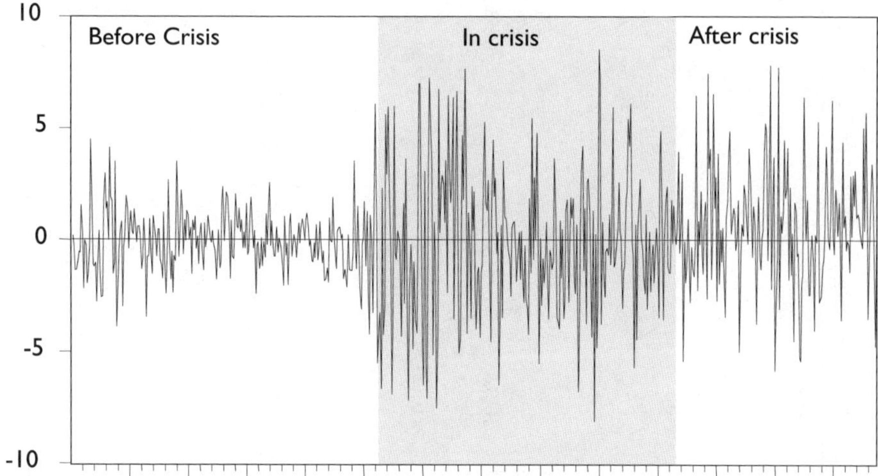

Fig. 7.6. Volatility of the rate of return (RKOSPI, %) on Korean stock

dummies to the GARCH model. The values of the GARCH coefficients are reduced when the dummies are included. However, the value of log likelihood without dummies (equation (1)) is higher than that with dummies (equations (2), (3), and (4)). This suggests that the model without dummies is more suitable, even though dummy variables are statistically significant for explaining the high volatility since the crisis.

In equations (5), (6), (7), and (8), the net buys by foreign investors explain the changes in the rate of return but the conditional variance is not statistically significant. This means that the excess demand by foreign investors affects the rate of return but does not explain the increased volatility. Foreign investors do not appear to have destabilized stock prices during the crisis.

In order to identify the groups that did, we perform the GARCH(1,1) estimation for different groups of domestic investors and find results similar to those of foreign investors. One significant finding is that the stabilizing effect of the trading by domestic investment trust companies is relatively strong at the 10 percent level of significance.

4. WHO TRIGGERED THE KOREAN CURRENCY CRISIS?

If the foreign portfolio investors did not trigger the Korean currency crisis, as we find in this study, who did? Table 7.10 clearly shows that 10.9 billion U.S. dollars' worth of huge capital outflows at the end of 1997 were mainly caused

TABLE 7.10. Capital and Financial Accounts from 1996 to 1998 (millions of U.S.$)

	1996	1997	1998	1997.9	1997.10	1997.11	1997.12	1998.1	1998.2	1998.3	1998.4	1998.5
Capital and financial account	23,326.8	1,314.4	−3,253.3	446.4	939.3	−4,470.9	−6,415.1	−488.3	−293.2	−220.6	2,385.8	−418.2
Financial account	23,924.4	1,922.0	−3,424.4	497.5	984.5	−4,408.3	−6,359.0	−476.8	−288.8	−212.4	2,422.4	−509.1
Direct investment	−2,344.7	−1,605.2	616.2	−137.4	−102.2	52.9	−162.5	−18.7	−132.3	−183.8	−72.9	331.2
Portfolio investment	15,184.6	14,295.3	−1,878.2	1,949.5	413.7	−815.1	829.6	370.6	2,169.8	1,265.5	3,667.7	−1,200.0
Equity securities	5,300.8	2,205.5	3,897.8	−503.7	−764.4	−1,074.4	459.7	851.6	1,493.1	545.5	266.0	38.5
Debt securities	9,883.8	12,089.8	−5,776.0	2,453.2	1,178.1	259.3	369.9	−481.0	676.7	720.0	3,401.7	−1,238.5
Other investment	11,084.5	−10,768.1	−2,162.4	−1,314.6	673.0	−3,646.1	−7,026.1	−828.7	−2,326.3	−1,294.1	−1,172.4	359.7
Loans	13,791.0	−8,081.4	2,096.4	−593.6	257.5	−3,323.2	−7,986.1	−3.6	490.5	373.5	563.3	1,640.6
Long-term	4,502.6	21,517.9	15,579.9	674.5	1,886.9	529.4	14,969.8	2,026.9	1,781.2	1,107.2	6,082.8	555.8
Monetary authorities	5.2	11,112.1	5,013.3	−0.2	−1.0	−10.5	11,118.5	2,006.1	2,023.9	0.7	−1.3	1,251.0
General government	−571.9	4,601.3	4,547.5	−24.6	−48.4	−36.1	4,951.8	1,015.5	−12.1	2,031.5	−37.9	58.7
Deposit money banks	2,448.2	2,433.1	1,507.2	716.2	1,522.7	382.2	−1,190.1	−1,170.8	−517.1	−1,062.0	3,466.9	−1,555.7
Other sectors	2,621.1	3,371.4	4,511.9	−16.9	413.6	193.8	89.6	176.1	286.5	137.0	2,655.1	801.8
Short-term	9,288.4	−29,599.3	−13,483.5	−1,268.1	−1,629.4	−3,852.6	−22,955.9	−2,030.5	−1,290.7	−733.7	−5,519.5	1,084.8
Monetary authorities	0.0	0.0	0.0	0.0	0.0	0.0	0.0	0.0	0.0	0.0	0.0	0.0
General government	0.0	0.0	0.0	0.0	0.0	0.0	0.0	0.0	0.0	0.0	0.0	0.0
Deposit money banks	3,852.3	−23,258.9	−4,417.1	−638.9	−519.1	−2,396.4	−19,693.5	−914.3	−791.8	−442.5	−2,252.1	1,466.1
Other sectors	5,436.1	−6,340.4	−9,066.4	−629.2	−1,110.3	−1,456.2	−3,262.4	−1,116.2	−498.9	−291.2	−3,267.4	−381.3
Trade credits	3,725.0	−5,602.2	−6,180.3	−519.0	−548.1	−919.3	−3,887.2	−2,486.6	−2,624.2	−1,697.8	−947.7	−631.5
Long-term	−148.7	−1,016.4	1,389.7	−119.5	−329.4	−13.0	−648.3	−63.9	−262.2	−103.5	−122.4	6.5
Short-term	3,873.7	−4,585.8	−7,570.0	−399.5	−218.7	−906.3	−3,238.9	−2,422.7	−2,362.0	−1,594.3	−825.3	−638.0
Currency and deposits	−2,609.4	166.2	1,564.2	−96.2	123.3	−555.2	1,733.5	234.9	−200.3	409.1	−650.6	479.2
Monetary authorities	0.0	0.0	0.0	0.0	0.0	0.0	0.0	0.0	0.0	0.0	0.0	0.0
Deposit money banks	−979.4	−454.1	695.5	−46.6	390.6	−856.8	579.1	−277.0	−13.5	440.4	−563.7	175.2
Other sectors	−1,630.0	620.3	868.7	−49.6	−267.3	301.6	1,154.4	511.9	−186.8	−31.3	−86.9	304.0
Other assets	−3,822.1	2,749.3	357.3	−105.8	840.3	1,151.6	3,113.7	1,426.6	7.7	−378.9	−137.4	−1,128.6
Capital account	−597.6	−607.6	171.1	−51.1	−45.2	−62.6	−56.1	−11.5	−4.4	−8.2	−36.6	90.9

Source: Bank of Korea, *Monthly Economic Bulletin,* various issues; Bank of Korea, *Monthly Balance of Payments,* various issues.

by the dramatic fall in short-term foreign loans to domestic deposit money banks. In 1997, the Korean capital and financial account recorded 1.3 billion U.S. dollars' worth of net capital inflows, but the net short-term foreign loans to deposit money banks and other sectors at that time were −30 billion U.S. dollars. The short-term capital outflows from deposit money banks were concentrated in November and December of 1997. The short-term capital outflows just before the crisis triggered the shortage of foreign exchange in the Korean banking sector. However, most of the capital outflows in 1997 were offset by long-term foreign loans and portfolio investment, especially to buy debt securities. The reversal of the capital account from positive in 1997 to negative in 1998 was deepened by the portfolio investment outflow not by net sells of equity securities but by net sells of debt securities after the crisis. These figures also support our earlier findings.

We divide the capital and financial accounts of table 7.10 into table 7.11 and table 7.12, in which changes in assets (capital outflows by domestic investors) and changes in liabilities (capital inflows by foreign investors) are shown. From those tables, we find that both 11.1 billion U.S. dollars' worth of increased short-term loans by Korean deposit money banks to borrowers abroad (see table 7.11) and 12.1 billion U.S. dollars' worth of withdrawn short-term foreign loans to Korean deposit money banks and other institutions (see table 7.12) mainly resulted in 6.4 billion U.S. dollars' worth of net capital outflows (see table 7.10) in December 1997. The huge short-term capital outflows at that time were partly covered by the inflows of long-term loans. We understand that the increased short-term loans by deposit money banks to borrowers abroad in December 1997 were mainly to help liquidity problems in their foreign branches.[8] From table 7.12, we also find that the withdrawal of short-term foreign loans to deposit money banks and other institutions had started in September 1997 and accelerated from November 1997 until the first half of 1998. Moreover, there were net sells of equity securities by foreign investors during the fourth quarter of 1997, but the volume was small and their portfolio decisions on the Korean stock market were quickly reversed after December 1997. These figures also support our earlier findings.

The sudden withdrawal of foreign loans to domestic financial institutions is also indicated in table 7.13.[9] Until the end of June 1997, there was no significant evidence of loan withdrawal by foreign investors, but it was noticed that foreign investors withdrew huge amounts of their loans from domestic financial institutions right before the crisis in October 1997. The total value of loan withdrawals at the end of December 1997 reached a peak of 19.4 billion U.S. dollars during that period. The Japanese and European investors equally share 34 percent of total withdrawals. The U.S. investors and other

TABLE 7.11. Changes in Assets (capital outflows by domestic investors from financial account) (millions of U.S.$)

	1996	1997	1998	1997.9	1997.10	1997.11	1997.12	1998.1	1998.2	1998.3	1998.4	1998.5
Financial account outflows	24,155.3	16,009.2	−306.7	−123.5	1,940.9	−2,075.9	6,054.4	−819.9	687.3	1,063.6	911.9	980.7
Direct investment outflows	4,670.1	4,449.4	4,799.4	180.2	247.8	233.4	549.5	131.1	339.8	368.5	267.4	177.7
Portfolio investment outflows	5,998.4	−2,008.1	1,586.7	−198.3	301.1	−747.2	−2,067.9	−335.3	−316.2	−562.9	−52.4	692.8
Equity securities	652.8	319.5	−41.6	22.1	5.1	90.3	−126.8	62.2	−78.4	−120.1	−107.2	41.3
Debt securities	5,345.6	−2,327.6	1,628.3	−220.4	296.0	−837.5	−1,941.1	−397.5	−237.8	−442.8	54.8	651.5
Other investment outflows	13,486.8	13,567.9	−6,692.8	−105.4	1,392.0	−1,562.1	7,572.8	−615.7	663.7	1,258.0	696.9	110.2
Loans	5,556.2	11,866.3	−3,604.3	−405.3	539.8	−1,129.1	10,958.0	202.0	64.6	1,044.0	−317.7	−1,055.7
Long-term	295.3	259.1	3,527.5	50.1	11.9	31.1	75.5	188.6	−233.2	449.6	789.5	1,149.2
Monetary authorities	−5.2	4.9	−0.1	0.2	1.0	10.5	−1.5	−0.5	−0.2	−0.7	1.3	−2.3
General government	79.3	69.3	80.6	3.9	12.5	3.5	15.6	6.8	−6.4	−25.2	1.3	3.1
Deposit money banks	44.2	−47.0	4,173.9	−39.9	0.1	−3.2	61.0	354.7	−130.0	370.5	915.1	1,117.9
Other sectors	177.0	231.9	−726.9	85.9	−1.7	20.3	0.4	−172.4	−96.6	105.0	−128.2	30.5
Short-term	5,260.9	11,607.2	−7,131.8	−455.4	527.9	−1,160.2	10,882.5	13.4	297.8	594.4	−1,107.2	−2,204.9
Monetary authorities	0.0	0.0	0.0	0.0	0.0	0.0	0.0	0.0	0.0	0.0	0.0	0.0
General government	0.0	0.0	0.0	0.0	0.0	0.0	0.0	0.0	0.0	0.0	0.0	0.0
Deposit money banks	3,339.4	11,173.6	−7,833.1	−279.9	436.8	−751.6	11,143.5	−134.6	573.0	510.2	−1,493.8	−1,912.1
Other sectors	1,921.5	433.6	701.3	−175.5	91.1	−408.6	−261	148.0	−275.2	84.2	386.6	−292.8
Trade credits	821.5	3,306.2	−915.2	123.3	574.0	422.5	1,879.9	596.3	610.1	295.2	141.5	331.9
Long-term	671.4	1,283.3	−1,352.7	84.3	329.5	21.1	651.5	56.7	264.2	196.8	245.8	63.6
Short-term	150.1	2,022.9	437.5	39.0	244.5	401.4	1,228.4	539.6	345.9	98.4	−104.3	268.3
Currency and deposits	2,630.8	−762.2	−885.9	−15.4	−89.1	43.0	−2,145.4	−217.8	94.5	−426.5	679.3	−461.9
Monetary authorities	0.0	0.0	0.0	0.0	0.0	0.0	0.0	0.0	0.0	0.0	0.0	0.0
Deposit money banks	810.9	55.9	−188.5	69.7	−330.2	493.9	−921.5	320.1	−78.5	−411.1	605.8	−123.7
Other sectors	1,819.9	−818.1	−697.4	−85.1	241.1	−450.9	−1,223.9	−537.9	173.0	−15.4	73.5	−338.2
Other assets	4,478.3	−842.4	−1,287.4	192.0	367.3	−898.5	−3,119.7	−1,196.2	−105.5	345.3	193.8	1,295.9

Source: Bank of Korea, *Monthly Economic Bulletin,* various issues; Bank of Korea, *Monthly Balance of Payments,* various issues.

TABLE 7.12. Changes in Liabilities (capital inflows by foreign investors to financial account) (millions of U.S.$)

	1996	1997	1998	1997.9	1997.10	1997.11	1997.12	1998.1	1998.2	1998.3	1998.4	1998.5
Financial account inflows	48,079.7	17,931.2	−3,731.1	374.0	2,925.4	−6,484.2	−304.6	−1,296.7	398.5	851.2	3,334.3	471.6
Direct investment inflows	2,325.4	2,844.2	5,415.6	42.8	145.6	286.3	387.0	112.4	207.5	184.7	194.5	508.9
Portfolio investment inflows	21,183.0	12,287.2	−291.5	1,751.2	714.8	−1,562.3	−1,238.3	35.3	1,853.6	702.6	3,615.3	−507.2
Equity securities	5,953.6	2,525.0	3,856.2	−481.6	−759.3	−984.1	332.9	913.8	1,414.7	425.4	158.8	79.8
Debt securities	15,229.4	9,762.2	−4,147.7	2,232.8	1,474.1	−578.2	−1,571.2	−878.5	438.9	277.2	3,456.5	−587
Other investment inflows	24,571.3	2,799.8	−8,855.2	−1,420.0	2,065.0	−5,208.2	546.7	−1,444.4	−1,662.6	−36.1	−475.5	469.9
Loans	19,347.2	3,784.9	−1,507.9	−998.9	797.3	−4,452.3	2,971.9	198.4	555.1	1,417.5	245.6	584.9
Long-term	4,797.9	21,777.0	19,107.4	724.6	1,898.8	560.5	15,045.3	2,215.5	1,548.0	1,556.8	6,872.3	1,705.0
Monetary authorities	0.0	11,117.0	5,013.2	0.0	0.0	0.0	11,117.0	2,005.6	2,023.7	0.0	0.0	1,248.7
General government	−492.6	4,670.6	4,628.1	−20.7	−35.9	−32.6	4,967.4	1,022.3	−18.5	2,006.3	−36.6	61.8
Deposit money banks	2,492.4	2,386.1	5,681.1	676.3	1,522.8	379.0	−1,129.1	−816.1	−647.1	−691.5	4,382.0	−437.8
Other sectors	2,798.1	3,603.3	3,785.0	69.0	411.9	214.1	90.0	3.7	189.9	242.0	2,526.9	832.3
Short-term	14,549.3	−17,992.1	−20,615.3	−1,723.5	−1,101.5	−5,012.8	−12,073.4	−2,017.1	−992.9	−139.3	−6,626.7	−1,120.1
Monetary authorities	0.0	0.0	0.0	0.0	0.0	0.0	0.0	0.0	0.0	0.0	0.0	0.0
General government	0.0	0.0	0.0	0.0	0.0	0.0	0.0	0.0	0.0	0.0	0.0	0.0
Deposit money banks	7,191.7	−12,085.3	−12,250.2	−918.8	−82.3	−3,148.0	−8,550.0	−1,048.9	−218.8	67.7	−3,745.9	−446
Other sectors	7,357.6	−5,906.8	−8,365.1	−804.7	−1,019.2	−1,864.8	−3,523.4	−968.2	−774.1	−207.0	−2,880.8	−674.1
Trade credits	4,546.5	−2,296.0	−7,095.5	−395.7	25.9	−496.8	−2,007.3	−1,890.3	−2,014.1	−1,402.6	−806.2	−299.6
Long-term	522.7	266.9	37.0	−35.2	0.1	8.1	3.2	−7.2	2	93.3	123.4	70.1
Short-term	4,023.8	−2,562.9	−7,132.5	−360.5	25.8	−504.9	−2,010.5	−1,883.1	−2,016.1	−1,495.9	−929.6	−369.7
Currency and deposits	21.4	−596.0	678.3	−111.6	34.2	−512.2	−411.9	17.1	−105.8	−17.4	28.7	17.3
Monetary authorities	0.0	0.0	0.0	0.0	0.0	0.0	0.0	0.0	0.0	0.0	0.0	0.0
Deposit money banks	−168.5	−398.2	507.0	23.1	60.4	−362.9	−342.4	43.1	−92.0	29.3	42.1	51.5
Other sectors	189.9	−197.8	171.3	−134.7	−26.2	−149.3	−69.5	−26.0	−13.8	−46.7	−13.4	−34.2
Other assets	656.2	1,906.9	−930.1	86.2	1,207.6	253.1	−6.0	230.4	−97.8	−33.6	56.4	167.3

Source: Bank of Korea, *Monthly Economic Bulletin,* various issues; Bank of Korea, *Monthly Balance of Payments,* various issues.

nationals share 12.4 percent and 19.6 percent of total withdrawals of foreign loans, respectively. Since then, all the foreign investors have behaved as a group in the loan market. The herding behavior of foreign investors deepened the shortage of dollar-denominated liquidity in the Korean financial market and contributed to the currency crisis.

With the acceleration of financial liberalization during the 1994–97 period, it was very popular for foreign investors to supply funds through domestic foreign exchange institutions like depository institutions, development institutions, and merchant banks. The increase in capital flows through those domestic financial institutions helped maintain a relatively strong won before the crisis occurred. However, the sudden withdrawal of foreign capital from capital and financial accounts in those institutions made the Korean economy highly vulnerable to the speculative currency attack and liquidity crisis after the Thai baht stopped floating on June 2, 1997.

The liquidity crisis was ignited by the mismanagement of assets and liabilities (short-term foreign credit abused as a means of financing long-term domestic investment; see table 7.14) in those domestic financial institutions and was deepened by the foreign financial institutions' decision to stop rolling over their short-term loans. As we can see from figure 7.7, which illustrates the monthly rollover rates of Korean foreign exchange banks in 1997, those domestic financial institutions encountered serious liquidity problems created by the loss of foreign investors' confidence during the second half of 1997. The domestic banks' huge demand for foreign exchange was caused by the termination of foreign bank loans. From 1996 to 1997, there was no distinguishable change in their balance sheets except (1) a 430 percent increase in interoffice asset transfers (3.3 billion U.S. dollars to 14.1 billion

TABLE 7.13. Outstanding Foreign Loans to Domestic Financial Institutions by Country of Origin (billions of U.S.$, %)

	1996.12	1997.3	1997.6	1997.9	1997.12	1998.3	1998.6	Total Withdrawal
Total	62.6	59.9	59.0	51.3	31.9	27.1	28.0	
Change		−2.7	−0.9	−7.7	−19.4	−4.8	0.9	−34.6
Japan	26.0	21.3	22.1	20.6	14.0	12.6	13.1	
Change		−4.7	0.8	−1.5	−6.6	−1.4	0.5	−12.9
Europe	18.8	20.5	18.6	17.3	10.7	9.3	9.8	
Change		1.7	−1.9	−1.3	−6.6	−1.4	0.5	−9.0
United States	7.0	8.8	8.6	7.0	4.6	3.6	3.7	
Change		1.8	−0.2	−1.6	−2.4	−1.0	0.1	−3.3
Others	10.9	9.2	9.7	6.4	2.6	1.6	1.5	
Change		−1.7	0.5	−3.3	−3.8	−1.0	−0.1	−9.4

Source: Ministry of Finance and Economy.

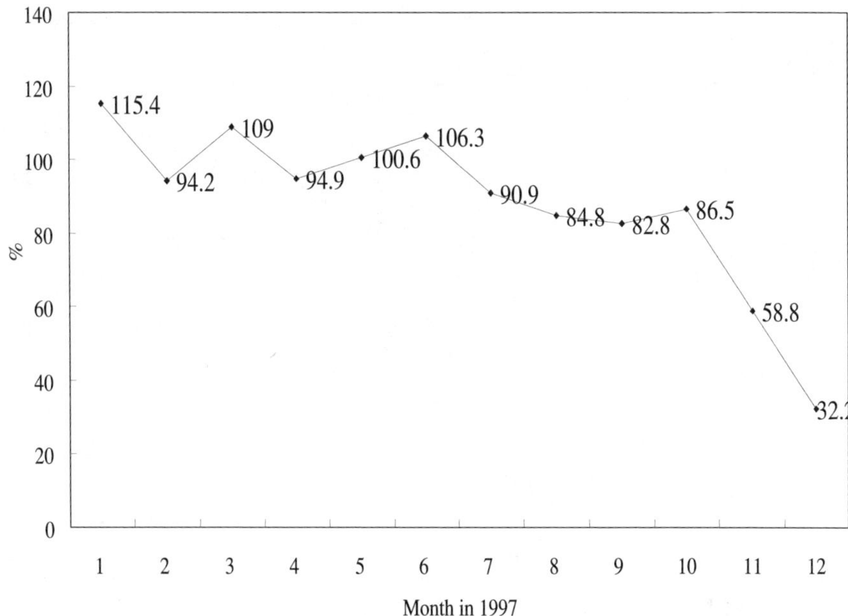

Fig. 7.7. Rollover rates of short-term credit to Korean foreign exchange banks in 1997

U.S. dollars), (2) a 39 percent fall in foreign borrowing (24.7 billion U.S. dollars to 15.1 billion U.S. dollars), and (3) a 21 percent increase in trust money from the central bank (32.2 billion U.S. dollars to 38.9 billion U.S. dollars). This means that the interoffice transfer cleared the sudden withdrawal of foreign bank loans from domestic banks and the interoffice transfer was financed by borrowings from the Bank of Korea.

In figure 7.8, we illustrate the monthly changing pattern of the three items mentioned earlier to find more detailed information about the liquidity position of domestic foreign exchange banks during the crisis period. From the figure, we find that the liquidity shortage was caused by foreign investors'

TABLE 7.14. Term Structure of Fund Management in Merchant Banks (end of October 1997, billions of U.S.$)

	Source of Funds	Use of Funds
Short term (shorter than 1 year)	12.9 (64.4%)	3.2 (16.3%)
Long term (longer than 1 year)	7.1 (35.6%)	16.8 (83.7%)
Total	20.0 (100.0%)	20.0 (100.0%)

Source: Ministry of Finance and Economy.

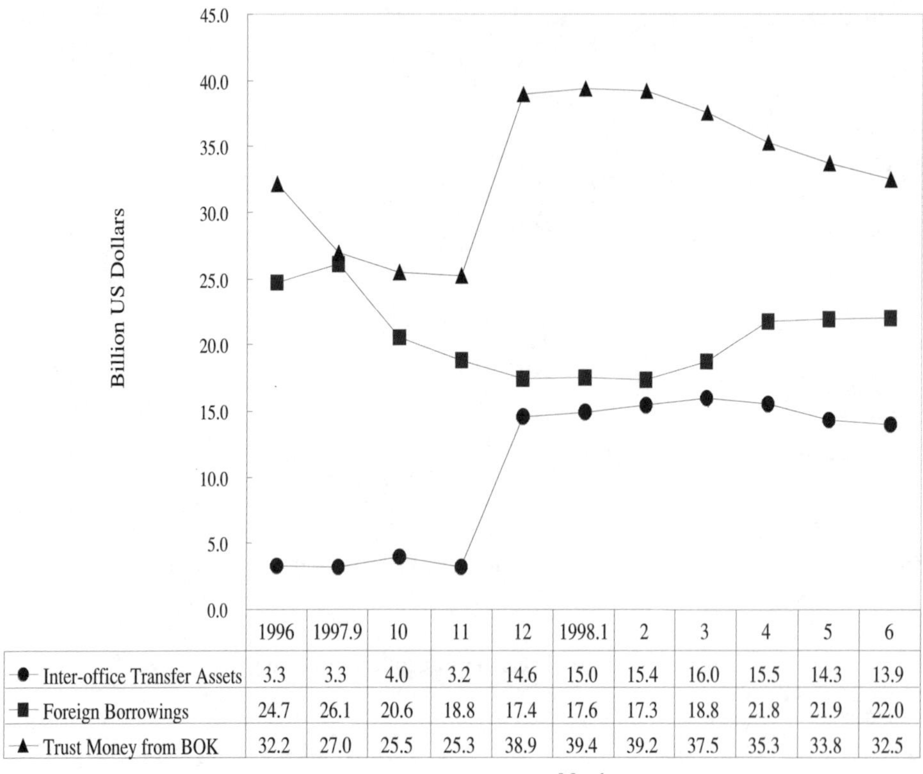

	1996	1997.9	10	11	12	1998.1	2	3	4	5	6
● Inter-office Transfer Assets	3.3	3.3	4.0	3.2	14.6	15.0	15.4	16.0	15.5	14.3	13.9
■ Foreign Borrowings	24.7	26.1	20.6	18.8	17.4	17.6	17.3	18.8	21.8	21.9	22.0
▲ Trust Money from BOK	32.2	27.0	25.5	25.3	38.9	39.4	39.2	37.5	35.3	33.8	32.5

Fig. 7.8. Interoffice transfer assets, borrowings, and trust money from BOK in domestic foreign exchange banks' balance sheets

withdrawal of bank loans, which started in September 1997 and continued until the end of the first quarter of 1998. The decline in foreign borrowings was met by interoffice transfers that were financed by the central bank beginning in December 1997. Figure 7.9 also highlights the sudden shift of foreign short-term capital from those domestic institutions to institutions abroad. This liquidity problem in the Korean capital account would invite speculators to foreign exchange markets and contribute to the Korean currency crisis.

5. CONCLUDING REMARKS

Who destabilized the Korean stock market? We carried out a number of empirical tests to find an answer to this question. Our tests confirm some, but

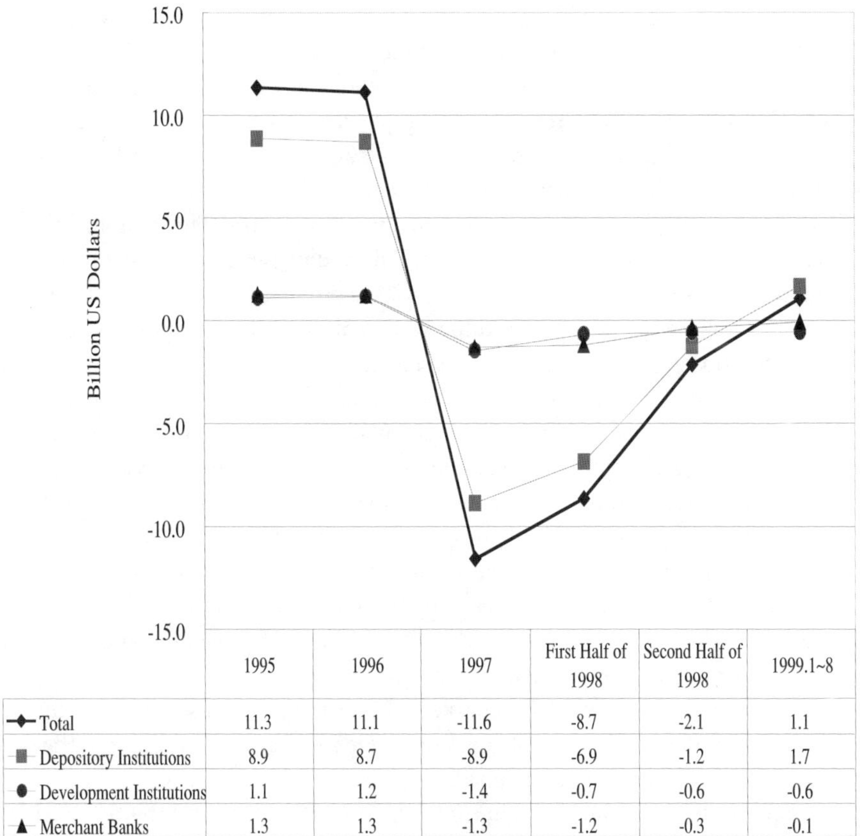

	1995	1996	1997	First Half of 1998	Second Half of 1998	1999.1~8
Total	11.3	11.1	-11.6	-8.7	-2.1	1.1
Depository Institutions	8.9	8.7	-8.9	-6.9	-1.2	1.7
Development Institutions	1.1	1.2	-1.4	-0.7	-0.6	-0.6
Merchant Banks	1.3	1.3	-1.3	-1.2	-0.3	-0.1

Fig. 7.9. Net short-term capital inflows to Korean foreign exchange banks

not all, of the earlier findings.[10] From our experiments, we find that foreign investors generally followed positive feedback trading during the crisis period, but we do not find any evidence that this destabilized the Korean stock market.[11]

From our historical data set, it can be seen that foreign investors actively increased their holdings of Korean stocks even during the crisis period, although they were net sellers immediately after the crisis occurred. In contrast, most domestic institutional and individual investors reduced their share holdings after the crisis broke out. Interestingly, domestic individual investors' responses to the market change were quite passive and perhaps irrational. When foreign and most domestic institutional investors left the market just after the crisis began, individual investors stayed on and increased their stockholdings. Similarly, when foreign investors and domestic investment trust companies returned to the market after market stability was restored, individual investors reduced their stockholdings and only gradually returned to the market.

We examined the effects of different investors' portfolio decisions on the volatility of Korean stock returns. The simple data analyses based on *S*-ratios, *D*-ratios, and *N*-ratios show that foreign investors followed positive feedback trading during the crisis period. However, before the crisis there is no strong evidence of positive feedback trading by foreign investors. Their trading behavior after the crisis is unclear, however. This finding is partly consistent with, but does not support the results of, the studies discussed in the introduction.

The Granger causality test and the VAR analysis also confirm the positive feedback trading by foreign investors and the negative feedback trading by most of the domestic investors. Both foreign and domestic investors became more sensitive to changes in market return after the crisis, contrary to what the ratio analysis suggests. The causality tests reveal that foreign investors did not have enough influence to change the market price but domestic investment trust companies and individual investors did, especially during the crisis period. This means that net sells by these two domestic investor groups exacerbated the crisis. We also find that the portfolio decision made by any particular investor group could not affect the market price after the crisis. This development may be related to efficiency gains from enhanced competition since the opening of the market. The VAR analysis also supports the view that domestic individual investor groups in particular exhibit rather passive and irrational trading behavior.

The results from the VAR impulse response estimation and the GARCH analysis suggest that the net buys by both foreign and domestic investors, excluding insurance companies, merchant banks, and savings and finance companies, affect the mean of the market return but none of the investor groups can explain the increase in market volatility. These findings indicate that foreign investors rationally responded to information on the economic fundamentals available rather than overreacting to disturbing factors in the market even during the crisis period. Since foreign investors account for a small share of trading, less than 7 percent for the whole period, our results are not surprising.

We also find from the experiment with the GARCH model that high volatility is quite persistent since the crisis occurred. What does explain, then, the increased volatility of the rate of return on Korean stocks? Based on the result from the Granger causality test and the VAR estimation, we conclude that domestic investors, especially individual investors, were the major source of the increased volatility. However, they are not solely responsible. Further research on trading patterns of domestic individual investors with disaggregated trade data may give us a better clue.

One more interesting finding from the impulse response estimation is that net buys and the rate of return on local stocks have become more sensitive to each other since the crisis occurred. The increased sensitivity is related to capital market liberalization through the relaxation of regulations and the abolishment of the foreign ownership limit, which has in turn improved the competitiveness and efficiency of the Korean stock market.

Finally, we show that the massive capital outflows from Korea at the end of 1997 were caused by the dramatic drop in short-term foreign loans to domestic deposit money banks. Until the end of June 1997, no significant evidence of loan withdrawal by foreign lenders was found. However, such a withdrawal occurred on a massive scale just before the crisis erupted in October 1997, indicating that foreign lenders, particularly bank lenders, triggered the Korean currency crisis. Moreover, from the data gathered it is also possible to note that foreign lenders exhibited herdlike behavior, as they acted as a group in the loan market. It is also interesting to note that the massive capital outflows that took place just before and during the crisis can also be explained by Korean bank lending abroad, apparently in an attempt to help their foreign branches cope with liquidity problems.

NOTES

An earlier version of this chapter was presented at the Workshop on Capital Flows organized by the Institute of Development Studies at the University of Sussex, Brighton, United Kingdom, September 13–14, 1999.

1. If positive feedback trading is a rational response to the market signal, the foreign investors' rational behavior will enhance market efficiency and reduce the possibility of sudden changes in the market.
2. The Korea Securities Computer Corporation (KOSCOM) kindly provided this data set.
3. This limitation will not be a big problem for analysis of the feedback trading of foreign investors in the KSE, but it will not be adequate in evaluating their herding behavior. This is the reason why we do not analyze herding behavior. In addition to the feedback trading analysis, we add VAR analysis by using the daily data set to increase our confidence in the results.
4. The Korea Stock Exchange kindly provided this data set.
5. For foreign investors, changes in the exchange rate will be compared to changes in the KOSPI to calculate the dollar rate of return.
6. For the variance equation, we use the square of the excess demand for stocks because the net buys have both positive and negative signs over time and changes in either direction will equally affect the forecast variance.
7. Results of the Granger causality test can be found in a more complete version of this chapter, Park and Park 1999. It is available at <http://www.ids.ac.uk/ids/global/intfin.html>.

8. This situation is discussed further in the analysis of figure 7.8.

9. The figures showing total changes in outstanding foreign loans to domestic financial institutions in table 7.13 are approximately the same as the sum of long- and short-term foreign loans to deposit money banks and other sectors in table 7.12.

10. See, for example, De Long, Shleifer, Summers, and Waldman 1990; Tesar and Werner 1993, 1995; Bohn and Tesar 1996; Brennan and Cao 1997; and Kim and Wei 1999.

11. Choe, Kho, and Stulz (1998) also indicate this fact.

REFERENCES

Aggarwal, Reena, Carla Inclan, and Ricardo Leal. 1999. "Volatility in emerging stock markets." *Journal of Financial and Quantitative Analysis* 34, no. 1 (March): 33–55.

Bank of Korea, 1999. "Financial Market in Korea." July.

Bekaert, Geert, and Campbell R. Harvey. 1995. "Emerging equity market volatility." NBER Working Paper 5307, October.

Bohn, Henning, and Linda L. Tesar. 1996. "U.S. equity investment in foreign markets: Portfolio rebalancing or return chasing?" *American Economic Review* 86, no. 2 (May): 77–81.

Brennan, Michael J., and H. Henry Cao 1997. "International portfolio investment flows." *Journal of Finance* 52, no. 4 (December): 1857–80.

Choe, Kyuk, Bong-Chan Kho, and Rene M. Stulz. 1998. "Do foreign investors destabilize stock markets? The Korean experience in 1997." NBER Working Paper 6661, June.

De Long, J. Bradford, Andrei Shleifer, Lawrence H. Summers, and Robert J. Waldmann. 1990. "Positive feedback investment strategies and destabilizing rational speculation." *Journal of Finance* 45, no. 2 (June): 379–95.

Froot, Kenneth A., Paul G. J. O'Connell, and Mark Seasholes. 1998. "The portfolio flows of international investors, I." NBER Working Paper 6687, August.

Kim, Woochan, and Shang-Jin Wei. 1999. "Foreign portfolio investors before and during a crisis." NBER Working Paper 6968, February.

Lakonishok, Josef, Andrei Shleifer, and Robert W. Vishny. 1992. "The impact of institutional trading on stock prices." *Journal of Financial Economics* 32, no. 1 (August): 3–22.

Park, Y. C., and I. Park. 1999. "Who destabilised the Korean Stock Market?" Presented at the *Workshop on Capital Flows,* organized by the Institute of Development Studies at the University of Sussex, Brighton, U.K., September 13–14.

Tesar, Linda L., and Ingrid M. Werner. 1993. "U.S. equity investment in emerging stock markets." *World Bank Economic Review* 9, 109–29.

———. 1994. "International equity transactions and U.S. portfolio choice." In *The internationalization of equity markets,* ed. J. Frankel. Chicago: University of Chicago Press.

———. 1995. "Home bias and high turnover." *Journal of International Money and Finance* 14, no. 4: 467–92.

CHAPTER 8

The Currency Shake-up in 1997: A Case Study of the Czech Economy

Oldrich Dedek

The last decade of the departing twentieth century will enter the history of the world economy as a period of increased instability of financial markets, contributing to major declines in the output of emerging market economies. Observers or analysts may find the truly global nature of the mentioned phenomena fascinating. While formerly located mostly in the Latin American region, the virus of currency crisis gradually shifted and affected with the same destructive effects the opposite part of the globe, the countries of the former Asian tigers. The collapse of the ruble in August 1998 added to the range of affected countries the most significant representative of transition economies.

Against the background of these spectacular events, which have triggered extensive considerations of the reform of the world financial architecture, the history of causes and consequences of the currency turbulence that hit the Czech economy in 1997 is of somewhat marginal interest. Nevertheless, from a purely professional viewpoint the example of the Czech economy is interesting in a number of ways.

First, the Czech Republic at that time had gained the image of a transition economy with a highly progressive reform program oriented toward an extensive liberalization of economic activities. The currency turbulence that dragged the country into a political crisis and economic recession could therefore be easily interpreted not only as a consequence of mistakes in the Czech economic policy but also as a failure of a more general transformation philosophy supported by the International Monetary Fund (IMF) and other prominent financial institutions.

Second, measured in absolute terms of key economic variables (e.g., the volume of capital movements, the volume of foreign exchange reserves, and so on), the Czech case can hardly be compared to cases of big countries affected by big crises. On the other hand, measured in relative terms, the Czech economy ranked first several times, be it due to an unprecedented high share of capital inflow to GDP shortly before the currency crisis or an alarming share of deficits of the current account in GDP, which set off the currency crisis. These relative values ultimately determine the degree of the absolute relevance of the problem.

Third, the aftermath of the currency crisis in the form of political instability and declining economic performance had many traumatic effects. However, in the light of international comparison, the impact of the crisis was far from that dramatic. The Czech authorities did not have to ask for IMF or other official loans, the withdrawal of foreign investors did not reach the stage of uncontrolled panic, and the exchange rate did not record a dive. The scope of losses caused by the crisis would have to be further cut down, if we admit a confluence of the postcrisis period with the cumulative consequences of incomplete structural and institutional reforms. Thus, a useful lesson may be drawn from the Czech experience as to how to handle difficult situations once they arise.

The more detached the view we take when investigating the currency crisis of 1997 the more common and the less original may seem the reasons that caused this event. It can be stated that the Czech economy underwent a standard shake-up caused by a gradualist accumulation and a shock-type solution to external imbalance.[1] There exists sufficiently conclusive evidence that the current account deficit gradually exceeded a sustainable limit. Simultaneously, the resistance of the economy was weakened partly by the reluctant implementation of a number of important reforms. In this hotbed, the market forced a fast and vigorous solution of external imbalance, with all negative consequences brought about inevitably by any sharp swing.

1. THE DEBATE ABOUT A SUSTAINABLE EXTERNAL IMBALANCE

A close look at the data describing economic development in the years 1993–96 (see table 8.1) reveals an evident tendency toward deepening external imbalance manifested by the widening deficits of the balance of payments' current account. The values of this variable ultimately brought—in the negative sense of the word—the Czech Republic the "leading position" in the group of emerging economies. However, quite a number of examples from other parts of the world warn that this growth of the current account deficit may end up causing serious problems. An unbiased observer may therefore ask why the Czech economy followed this dangerous path. Why did economic policy not pay greater attention to the growing deficits when the significance of this phenomenon for triggering currency turbulence is generally understood?

1.1. THE OBJECTIVE INCLINATION TOWARD DEFICITS

The tendency toward deficits on the balance of payments' current account is common to almost all transition economies regardless of often substantial differences applied in the economic policies. This fact is substantiated by several objective reasons: the transition economies were forced to undergo a deep restructuring, which irreversibly increased imports of investment goods; liberalization of trade flows brought the essential element of foreign competition, which in the short run contributed to the inability of the domestic supply side to satisfy the growing requirements of aggregate demand; the growth of consumer demand for imported goods reflected extended possibilities of satisfying the needs of households; and synchronization with the business cycle of the European Union was getting closer.

However, current account deficits by themselves are not an undesirable feature of the economic development of transition economies. On the contrary, their presence also has its positive interpretation. The current account deficit can bridge the bottleneck of domestic savings, that is, by using foreign savings to finance domestic restructuring. If such use of foreign savings serves predominantly to generate higher future export revenues, only a time lag may be expected between the present external financing of investments and the future repayment of the debt to the external sector. In this sense, current account deficits may have a self-liquidating nature and therefore they are sustainable. However, there is a crucial issue of timing, as it would be necessary for foreign

TABLE 8.1. Basic Indicators of Economic Development

	1990	1991	1992	1993	1994	1995	1996	1997	1998
Real GDP (1995 constant prices, %)		−11.6	−0.5	0.1	2.2	5.9	3.8	0.3	−2.3
Inflation (average CPI, %)	9.9	56.6	11.1	20.8	10.0	9.1	8.8	8.5	10.7
Unemployment (%)	1.0	6.6	5.1	3.5	3.2	2.9	3.5	5.2	7.5
Government budget balance (% GDP)	0.6	−2.3	−2.0	0.1	0.9	0.5	−0.1	−0.9	−1.6
Central government debt (% GDP)				15.6	13.3	11.2	9.9	10.3	10.7
Current account deficit (% GDP)				1.3	−1.9	−2.6	−7.4	−6.1	−1.9
Gross external debt (% GDP)				24.9	25.4	31.9	36.2	44.0	39.4
External reserves (U.S.$ billions)		1.4	0.8	3.9	6.2	14.0	12.4	9.8	12.6
Exchange rate, CZK/U.S.$	17.9	29.5	28.3	29.2	28.8	26.5	27.1	31.7	32.3
Exchange rate, CZK/DEM	11.1	17.8	18.1	17.6	17.8	18.5	18.1	18.3	18.3
Nonstate sector (% GDP)	12.3	17.3	27.7	45.1	61.3	66.5	71.9	76.8	77.3

Source: Czech National Bank, Czech Statistical Office, Ministry of Finance.

investors to be willing to finance the current account deficit for a sufficiently long time.

1.2. CONTROVERSIAL EVIDENCE

In no way can we claim that inadequate attention was paid to the issue of the sustainability of current account deficits. On the contrary, this issue had been attracting the significant attention of both analysts and politicians in the Czech Republic. As often happens when working with economic data, however, the knowledge acquired was a mixture of contradictory moments rather than unambiguous answers.

Favoring the self-liquidating hypothesis were the following facts. The indicator of the national propensity to save was exceeding the international average and consequently the issue of current account deficits could not be primarily connected to the insufficient creation of domestic savings.[2] The government strove for a balanced state budget, and as a result the generator of deficits was predominantly the private sector, which was thought to know how to better allocate resources efficiently. A high share of imports corresponded to imports for investments, and the gross formation of fixed capital constituted the most dynamic component of aggregate demand (see table 8.2). For a relatively long period, there were no problems with the financing of current account deficits by means of surpluses on the capital account of balance of payments and within this account by means of inflows of long-term capital.

On the other hand, there were still a number of counterarguments about the factual robustness of the self-liquidating hypothesis. First, a comparatively high share of investment was directed toward infrastructural industries and environmental projects. Second, experience from other countries in general does not prove the optimism of the so-called Lawson doctrine of the sustainability of deficits in case they are generated by the private sector. In addition, in the Czech Republic quite a large proportion of the private sector was of a quasi-private nature. Third, the sustainability of current account deficits was ever more doubtful, given their growing magnitude.[3]

TABLE 8.2. Structure of Imports (%)

	1995	1996	1997	1998
Total imports	100.0	100.0	100.0	100.0
Investment	38.9	39.2	39.0	40.8
Intermediate consumption	36.5	35.6	35.8	34.9
Personal consumption	24.6	25.2	25.2	24.3

Source: Czech National Bank.

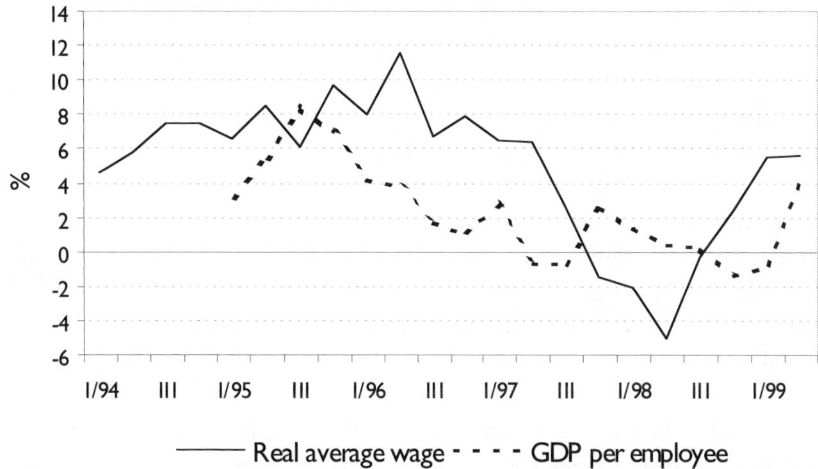

Fig. 8.1. Excess growth of real wages over labor productivity. (Data from Czech National Bank.)

1.3. RELUCTANCE TO COOL DOWN THE ECONOMY

The discussion on a sustainable external imbalance among Czech economists and politicians was very lively and stimulated extensive analytical research. The question is therefore why this discussion was ultimately sterile in the sense that it allowed the problem to develop into currency turbulence.

A reasonable explanation may be looked for in the logic of the political cycle, the unwillingness to accept the bitter truth as concerns both the causes of and the solution to excessive external imbalance. As regards the causes, it was observed that as a result of many institutional bottlenecks the supply side of the economy had failed to keep up with an expanding domestic demand. The excess pressure of demand over supply culminated in growing deficits of the current account. The economy thus suffered from symptoms of overheating as soon as it achieved moderate growth rates. To admit these constraints of growth potential would, however, be a major critique of the architects of economic transformation.

There was a firm link between the external imbalance and marked manifestations of internal imbalances. However, to address efficiently the internal imbalances would mean putting an end to the disproportionately high growth of real wages, which markedly exceeded the growth of labor productivity (see fig, 8.1) and thus slowing down the increase unit labor costs. Similarly, it was inevitable that credit expansion must be curbed, given the conditions of semistate banks and the nonrestructured corporate sector, as the established trends led to excessive indebtedness of companies and deterioration of the credit portfolios of banks. The "heretic" idea of a stabilization program that would aim at dampening aggregate demand even at the cost of a temporary slowdown in growth performance was, however, in contradiction to the then rhetoric of the Czech government.[4]

The answer to the question of why economic policy did not face the widening external imbalance should also include an evident underestimation of the already accomplished integration of domestic financial markets with world structures and underestimation of the role of expectations as an important driving force of capital movements. Had this awareness been stronger the discussion on the sustainability of deficits would have most probably far more seriously emphasized the approach based on vulnerability indicators. Instead of making apologies for specific needs of the transition economy and referring to the examples of countries that had also sustained large deficits, a vigorous and convincing response of the economic policy should have been called for by the concern that there might occur a turnover in the perception of the Czech economy by foreign investors.

2. LIBERALIZATION OF CAPITAL MOVEMENTS

Some economists include in the list of causes of the speculative attack the high speed in opening up the Czech economy in the capital account of the balance of payments. Indeed, in this respect the Czech currency assumed a unique position among other currencies of the reforming Central European economies. The attractiveness of the koruna was grounded in the degree of convertibility achieved, and a relatively advanced infrastructure of trading was reflected in a high turnover of the foreign exchange market.[5] An important circumstance in the speculative attack was also the existing minimum of restrictions allowed to assume classic speculative positions (so-called short selling) and the fact that a prevailing part of trading had for some time already been transferred to offshore centers (London in particular). Dynamically developing was the market in derivatives (mainly the segment of forward and swap operations).

Whereas the unsustainable current account deficits may be considered a phenomenon economic policy should consistently try to avoid, the high extent of external openness belonged to undisputed requirements dictated by the Czech Republic's ambitions of achieving integration with the European Union. Therefore, doubts should not be cast upon the objective of extensive liberalization as such, and reservations, if any, can relate at most to the applied sequence of liberalization steps and their synchronization with the progress in other fields of economic transformation.

2.1. THE INITIAL REGIME OF INTERNAL CONVERTIBILITY

After one year of intensive discussions, on January 1, 1991, a program of radical economic reform was launched. It was structured on five basic pillars: price liberalization, liberalization of foreign trade, macroeconomic stabilization, privatization, and creation of a safety net. The aim of this program was to implement a critical volume of reform measures in order to eliminate various aspects of the deeply rooted practices of forty years of a centrally planned economy. The backbone of the reform of external economic relations was the introduction of so-called internal convertibility.

The basic features of the regime may be described as follows: the domestic corporate sector was for the purposes of trade payments provided with free access to convertible currencies; free access to foreign exchange on the demand side was accompanied by a surrender duty on the supply side; and the access of the household sector to foreign currencies was regulated by foreign exchange limits.[6]

In contrast to the emphasis put on a liberal treatment of current account transactions, the approach of the internal convertibility to the capital account transactions was much more prudent. The aim was to develop an environment that would stimulate the inflow of foreign direct as well as portfolio investments in compliance with restructuring and privatization of the corporate sector and also in relation to the development of the capital market. For this purpose, the protection of foreign investments was guaranteed by the Constitution.[7]

The Foreign Exchange Act subsequently guaranteed free repatriation of investment revenues (i.e., profits, dividends, and interest) as well as invested capital. Excluded from the guarantee of free outflow were short-term portfolio investments (maturing in less than one year). The remaining transactions on the side of both capital inflow and outflow were either expressly forbidden by the Foreign Exchange Act or subject to approval procedures.

2.2. THE CONTROLLED AND SPONTANEOUS DEEPENING OF LIBERALIZATION

It would be highly misleading to judge the actual functioning of the internal convertibility regime only by sections of the Foreign Exchange Act. While on the one hand the language of this act did not change at all, or only slightly, on the other hand the general legislative environment and everyday practice were rapidly gearing the Czech economy for a higher mobility of capital flows.

From the legislative viewpoint, a significant breakthrough was the bilateral agreements on the promotion and protection of foreign investment. These agreements, which as a matter of fact treated investments only on a general level, implicitly constituted the right to the same treatment for the repatriation of revenues of long-term forms of investing as well as revenues from the short-term presence in the Czech capital or money market.

An important channel that was allowed to circumvent capital regulations was the banking sector. While the Foreign Exchange Act specified a list of nonpermitted capital transactions or transactions subject to approval procedures, many items on this list could be performed by banks with a foreign exchange license (granting credits to nonresidents, derivatives, purchases of foreign securities, and so on). Thus, many regulatory measures actually applied only to nonbank entities, that is, from the viewpoint of volume in general to a marginal set of potential transactions. Erosion of the existing regulatory framework by means of the banking sector was accelerating with the growing presence of foreign banks and foreign bank agencies.

Changing also was the approach to those regulated items that allowed a certain discretion in decision making. The approval procedure for credits received from abroad was an important example. It was evident that it was beyond the ability of the regulatory body to make a responsible assessment of applications. As a result, this regulation was soon deliberately limited to the registration of incoming foreign credits. The criterion for rejection or approval was as a rule a suspicion of money laundering or the legalization of other criminal activities.

2.3. THE INTRODUCTION OF EXTERNAL CONVERTIBILITY

After about three years of functioning, the regime of internal convertibility reached a stage that left itself open to a number of reservations. First, a visible contradiction developed between the actually achieved degree of liberalization of capital flows and the form of liberalization described by the Foreign Exchange Act. For the most part, this was caused by the deliberate unwillingness of regulatory bodies to intervene in the entrepreneurial activities of economic agents. In addition, existing conditions were taking their final shape through extensive opportunities to circumvent the regulations.

Second, the preferred asymmetry of the regulator with regard to inflow and outflow items, that is, support of capital inflows while controlling capital outflows, in practice discriminated against domestic entities. While foreign investors had freedom of movement in both directions, deriving from the guarantees not to limit the repatriation of invested funds, domestic investors were denied the effects of diversification of investment risks and integration with global financial markets.

It seemed that conditions were also favorable for a further shift in the financial opening of the economy. In the mid-1990s, the Czech Republic was basking in admiration for the achieved results of transformation: economic growth was restored with the prospect of its acceleration, inflation had been stabilized on a one-digit level, the government subscribed to a balanced budget, foreign exchange reserves were growing admirably, institutions of the money and capital markets were developing dynamically, and privatization and restructuring of the corporate sphere were progressing at a steady pace. These positive indicators were finding their reflection in the rating of the Czech Republic and in a massive inflow of foreign capital.[8]

The belief that the results achieved warranted a higher status of convertibility of the Czech currency resulted in the adoption of a new Foreign Exchange Act.[9] From the formal viewpoint, an important feature of the new legislation was compliance with the terms of Article VIII of the Agreement on International Monetary Fund, which required a full liberalization of so-called current international transactions. But most discussed were the issues going beyond the framework of requirements of Article VIII, namely, the issue of whether to allow the so-called external circulation of the Czech currency. There were those who argued that after lifting the ban on the use of the Czech currency in payments directed abroad and after the formation of offshore markets monetary policy would lose control over the portion of the money supply held abroad and thus would expose the domestic economy to higher risks. The argument highlighting the destabilizing effects of external convertibility was confronted with numerous counterarguments. First, the existence of a money supply in the form of money in circulation that is beyond the direct jurisdiction of the domestic monetary authority had already become a reality. Czech banknotes were regularly purchased and sold by many Austrian and German banks, with the so-called Viennese unofficial (also called the parallel) exchange rate even providing important feedback information on the credibility of the monetary policy of the Czech National Bank (CNB).

As far as noncash circulation is concerned, the regime of external convertibility in fact functioned between resident banks, whose nonresident clients could use them for payment purposes. Therefore, it would be only the technique of flight from the koruna that would make some difference. After all, it is irrelevant whether such a flight is triggered only by clients of domestic banks or also by clients of foreign banks, which of course must themselves be clients of some domestic bank.

In the clash over excessively fast liberalization, on the one hand, and the effects of financial opening on the other, the balance was held by the issue of what was seen as prestigious membership of the Czech Republic in the club of Organization for Economic Cooperation and Development (OECD) countries.[10] Such recognition for the success of the transformation acted as a catalyst for liberalization efforts.

Consequently, the new Foreign Exchange Act canceled a number of controls of capital movements, even though in many cases it merely codified the existing liberal environment (direct investments abroad, purchase of real estate abroad, borrowing from abroad, trading in securities with foreign entities, and so on).

Added to the general characteristics of the new Foreign Exchange Act may also be the fact that, in response to a powerful wave of capital inflows in the years 1994–95 the act incorporated authorization for the Central Bank to introduce, if need be, so-called deposit requirements. This measure would establish the obligation to deposit a certain portion of external funds interest free in an account with the Central Bank for a certain period. A potential imposition of this implicit form of taxation was, following the Chilean example, motivated exclusively by protection from excessive inflows of short-term capital. The later environment of monetary instability initiated considerations on the use of deposit requirements as a tool to prevent capital outflows. In spite of these circumstances, the authorities did not implement this measure in practice.

With the benefit of hindsight, it may be concluded that the speed of financial opening may seem rather excessive; similarly excessive was the optimism relating to the advancement of microeconomic and institutional reforms as a pillar for anchoring external convertibility. Nevertheless, the sequence of external sector liberalization was based on the logic of a selective and gradual lifting of capital controls. However, it was the pressure of real developments that moved regulatory practices ever farther from the initial arrangement. Therefore many liberalization provisions of the new Foreign Exchange Act reflected the existing reality only with delay.

3. THE PERIOD OF AFFLUENT CAPITAL INFLOWS

If there is any place to look for a boom and bust pattern, the data on capital flows, first to and then from the Czech economy, offer a unique spectacle. In the years 1994–95, the economy experienced the phase of boom, the period of the "wonderful years" of the Czech transformation. The economic policy at that time was pleasantly worried about opulence when a major concern was how to handle the quantities of incoming capital. Were the challenges of that time managed adequately? Or was it in this period that also rudiments of the future currency crisis were laid?

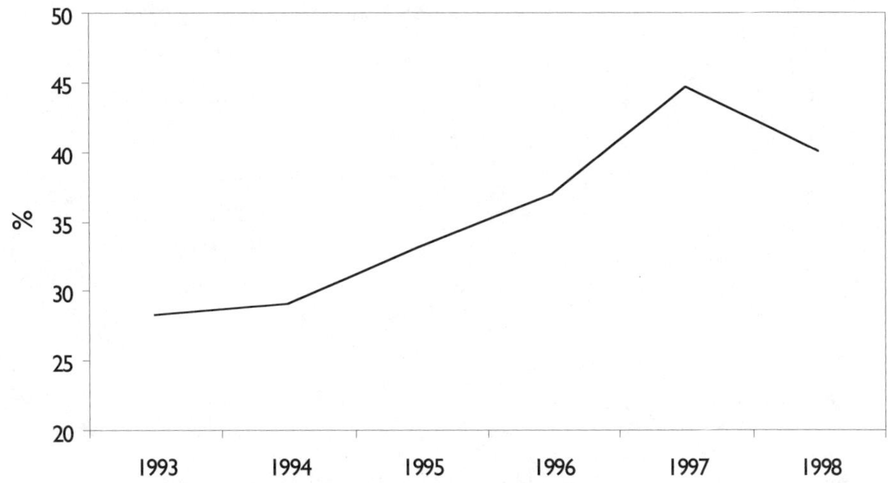

Fig. 8.2. Gross foreign indebtedness (% GDP). (Data from Czech National Bank.)

3.1. PARAMETERS OF THE INFLOW WAVE

Data on the intensity of capital inflow achieved are impressive. In 1994, the share of net inflow in GDP accounted for 8.5 percent; in the following year the same indicator increased to a record level of 16.6 percent.[11] Contributing largely to the acceleration of inflows was a declaration of a broader convertibility of the Czech currency and improvement of the rating of the Czech Republic.

The most significant inflow item quite quickly became financial loans granted by foreign banks to companies, later also indirectly in the form of drawing funds from abroad by domestic banks and their onlending in the form of foreign exchange loans.[12] On the one hand, such a structural shift positively contributed to the maintenance of the prevailing share of long-term capital; on the other hand, it negatively contributed to the growing significance of debt capital, the increase of foreign indebtedness (see fig. 8.2).

TABLE 8.3. Volume and Structure of Capital Flows (in CZK bil)

	1993	1994	1995	1996	1997	1998
Financial account	88.2	97.0	218.3	113.6	34.3	89.3
Direct investment	16.4	21.6	67.0	34.6	40.5	80.2
Portfolio investment	46.7	24.6	36.1	19.7	34.4	34.5
Other long-term investment	23.4	31.9	89.4	84.4	12.9	−29.4
Other short-term investment	1.6	19.0	25.8	−25.2	−53.5	4.0

Source: Czech National Bank.

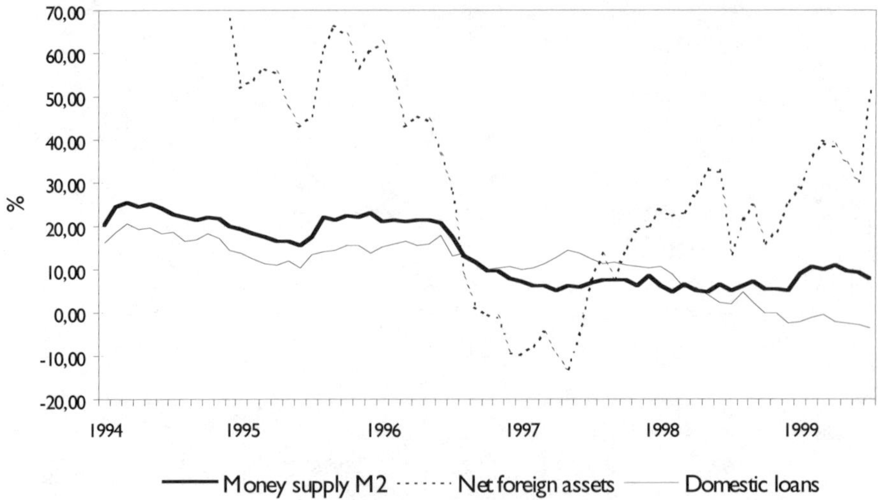

Fig. 8.3. Development of the money supply and its structure (y-o-y changes) (Data from Czech National Bank.)

The ongoing privatization, the product of which was also trading in shares from the voucher scheme, stimulated the growing inflow of portfolio investments. Quite a significant portion of these investments increased the presence of short-term volatile capital. A strong impetus to the inflow of hot money resulted equally from the interest rate differential existing in the money market instruments (its value ranged between 5 and 7 percentage points). In 1995, under the influence of these factors, short-term capital already accounted for almost 30 percent of the total inflow.

3.2. THE RESPONSE OF MONETARY POLICY

Due to enormous surpluses on the capital account of the balance of payments, monetary policy had to face many dilemmas. A powerful inflow wave was threatening to overheat the economy and triggering various bubbles. These concerns were based on high growth rates of the money supply, which markedly exceeded the limits of the set corridor. A dominant factor behind the growth of the money supply was capital inflow, which was reflected in the behavior of net foreign assets (the share of this component rose from 45 percent in 1993 to 80 percent in the last quarter of 1995). The domestic loan expansion, pushed and pulled by the excess of liquidity in the banking sector, was not lagging behind, either (see fig. 8.3).

What was the response of monetary policy to inflation risks and what were

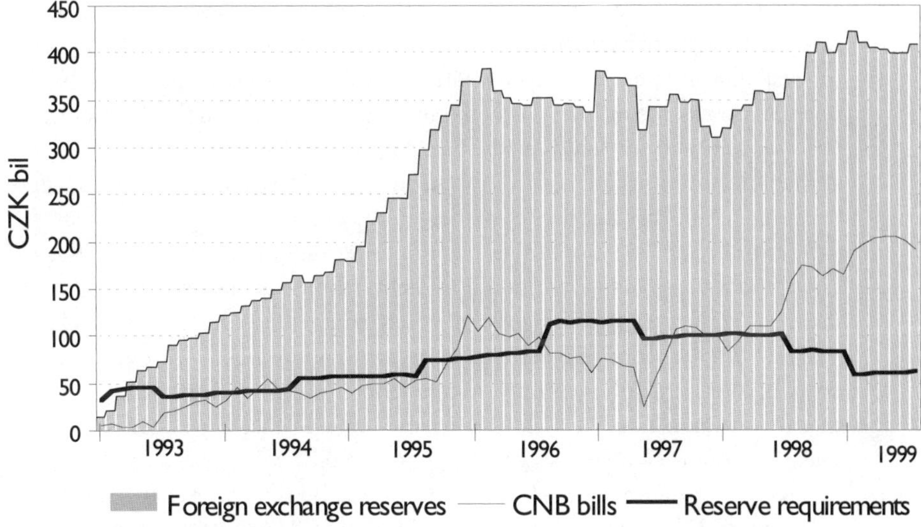

Figure 8.4. Sterilization and the growth of foreign exchange reserves

its outcomes? At a first level, transfers were used that could in a single step contribute to neutralization of monetary effects of the capital inflow. Included in this group of measures were prepayment of all loans accepted from the International Monetary Fund. Also an agreement was concluded with the government on withdrawing the privatization receipts from commercial banks to the central bank accounts.

One of the first steps of the application of direct instruments of monetary policy consisted of the closing of some credit facilities used by the Central Bank to lend funds to commercial banks. A more significant position was taken by non-interest-bearing minimum reserve requirements, the amount of which at the time of the culminating inflow were on the level of 8.5 percent. But the core response of the Central Bank to the massive inflow of capital was in open market operations, in the so-called sterilized interventions. As a result, foreign exchange reserves rose from almost zero after the monetary separation from Slovakia in February 1993 to approximately U.S.$14 billion by the end of 1995. Mirroring the buildup of foreign exchange reserves was an increase in the holding of short-term Central Bank debt in the portfolios of commercial banks from the average level of CZK14 billion in 1993 to 56 billion in 1995 (see fig. 8.4).

It is a general wisdom that sterilized interventions have a two-edged effect. The positive impacts include, among others, maintenance of exchange rate stability and immediate reduction of inflation pressures. On the other hand, since it is necessary to stimulate commercial banks to hold ever greater quantities of debt issued by the Central Bank, interest rates tend to go up. A higher interest rate differential in combination with a fixed exchange rate subsequently attracts the inflow of new hot money.[13] The enlarging pool of short-term securities in the hands of the banking sector also creates a reservoir of available liquidity, which may complicate the objectives of monetary policy in the future. And, last but not least, there is the cumulated accounting loss of the Central Bank, which is the recipient of lower interest on foreign exchange assets and a payer of higher interest on debt liabilities. This loss significantly increases with every percentage point of exchange rate appreciation.

The CNB was continuously confronted with all of these controversial aspects of sterilized interventions. A conviction was gradually strengthening that it was impossible to stick to the same line and that it was necessary to make a systemic change that would put an end to the everyday stereotype of inflating the balance sheet of the Central Bank by foreign exchange on the asset side and short-term debt on the liability side. This systemic change was meant to be the abandonment of the rigidly fixed exchange rate.

The list of measures responding to the inflow wave included several attempts at administrative regulation. This category included the so-called limits on open, short-term, nonresident positions introduced in August 1995. A common manifestation of the capital inflow was the fact that commercial banks accepted deposits from nonresidents that they subsequently lent to residents. As a result, the mismatch between nonresident assets and liabilities was growing. Short-term nonresident liabilities of banks were not allowed to exceed nonresident assets by more than 30 percent, with an absolute ceiling of CZK500 million. However, these limits did not meet with much success, as it was not difficult to find ways to circumvent them. Very simply, it could be done by means of the reclassification of short-term contracts (due in less than one year) to long-term ones (with, e.g., a maturity of one year plus one day).[14] It was also possible to place a domestic nonbank financial institution between the foreign lender and the domestic bank. In this case, the bank established the business contact with a resident and was no longer affected by the limits.

The growing problems with the inflow wave raised the issue of throwing bigger grains of sand into the wheels of capital flows. Particularly analyzed was the Chilean experience, in which a deposit requirement allowed a selective approach along the maturity spectrum of the incoming capital. Legislative support for the creation of obligatory deposits in the Central Bank was even incorporated into the new Foreign Exchange Act. However, in the end this measure was not applied. The prevailing liberal atmosphere was undoubtedly one of the explanations for this, though not the main one. More prevalent was the desire to keep the deposit requirement as a reserve and impose it only if other measures, in particular the change in the exchange rate regime, failed.

The episode of capital inflow in the years 1994–95 entered the history of the Czech economy as a period of abundance. The banking sector was flooded with liquidity, and the household sector enjoyed rapid growth of real wages. The prevailing optimistic climate was fostered by a swift pace of economic growth with extremely low unemployment. Unfortunately, the period of abundance did not last long. The inflow of capital lost its intensity, and a latent tendency toward overheating was taking an ever clearer shape. The party was over, but the company wished to go on enjoying themselves.

4. THE PHENOMENON OF A STRONG KORUNA

If we look for specific features in the approaches to economic transition that single out one country vis-à-vis the others, then the Czech method of transformation was unique due to its long-term exchange rate stability. It is really amazing that during the nine-year history of the economic reform the exchange rate of the Czech koruna with regard to the American dollar nominally weakened by approximately 18 percent and with regard to the German mark by 9 percent. In comparison, in the same period the Hungarian forint weakened with regard to the given currencies all the way up to 210 and 190 percent, respectively. In the case of the Polish zloty it was 270 and 240 percent, respectively.[15]

However, are we entitled to interpret this raw information on the unique external stability of the Czech currency as a success of the Czech economic policy?

4.1. ANCHOR, CUSHION, AND CORSET

The exchange rate applied at the beginning of the economic transformation has been evoking the association of two terms: an anchor and a cushion. The first of them—the anchor of macroeconomic stabilization—expressed the intention of reformers to use the policy of a fixed exchange rate as a sort of fixed point for all sweeping liberalization changes.[16] As a result, considerations of the beneficial effects of the exchange rate anchor led to the choice of a highly rigid exchange rate regime, which offered the monetary authorities a minimal space for discretion.

However, there was also the exchange rate cushion in the form of a sequence of initially very large devaluations. While at the inception of economic reform the exchange rate was unified at the level of 28.0 koruna per U.S. dollar, a year before it was still 14.3 for trade-related transactions. Even though a significant part of this movement of the domestic currency had the nature of a rectification of one of the most blatant price distortions taken over from the planned economy, it is a fact that the environment of an undervalued exchange rate was one of the intentions of the package of initial reform measures.

To complete the description of the exchange rate policy in the initial stage of reform, it will be useful to add to the terms *anchor* and *cushion* another term, *corset*. It was necessary to place the exchange rate cushion in the corset of restrictive policies and thus prevent a rapid depletion of the cushion, which would occur had galloping inflation pressed upon rapid real appreciation. After all, the initial weakening of the exchange rate initiated a marked inflation spike. In this respect, it is also necessary to take into account that corseting of the exchange rate was possible only due to the embryonic state of the financial markets. Initially, the economy was closed on the capital account. The Central Bank could regulate credit extension by means of credit and interest rate ceilings and also unofficially influence a handful of state banks that were singled out from the original arrangement of a monobank. Nothing similar could have been repeated later.

However, the policy of undervaluing the exchange rate was ever more clearly problematic. Many enterprises did not take advantage of the exchange rate cushion for the necessary restructuring but fell asleep on it and woke up only when the exchange rate "began to bite." The soft exchange rate did not stimulate nonprice forms of competition.

4.2. THE LEADING ROLE OF THE EXCHANGE RATE

By placing a padded anchor in the corset of restrictive policies, the unleashed devaluation stimulus did not turn into galloping inflation. On the contrary, the depletion of the exchange rate cushion took place gradually with the stabilization of inflation and its rapid downturn to one-digit values. Nevertheless, even with moderate values of inflation the inflation differential that brought about a real appreciation of the Czech koruna could not be neglected (see fig. 8.5).

But the decision-making problem consisted of something other than in finding out whether and to what extent the actually observed real appreciation exceeded the sustainable limit. The question was rather whether the conclusions on an excessive real appreciation were robust enough to strike a consensus of opinion in the sense that the policy of a fixed exchange rate had to be replaced with another regime. In practice, this would mean sacrificing the

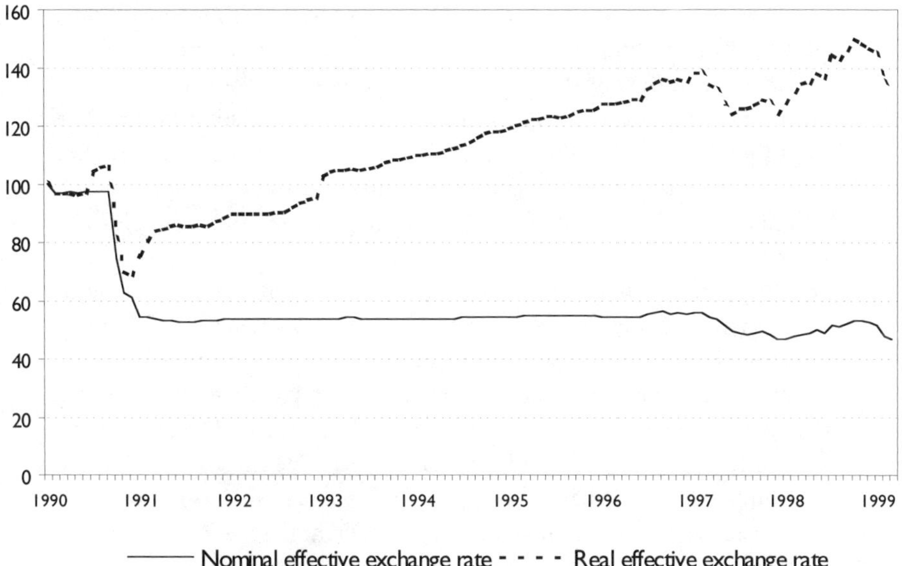

Fig. 8.5. Behavior of the nominal and real exchange rate. (Data from Czech National Bank.)

disciplinary function of the fixed exchange rate in favor of some regime of controlled devaluations. The reluctance to do this, nevertheless, was uniting all major economic policymakers. Benefits of a fixed exchange rate to macroeconomic stability, a low inflationary environment, and efficient restructuring had explicitly placed this exchange rate arrangement in the role of a clear prize winner.

4.3. FLOATING WITHIN THE BAND

The fixed exchange rate was abandoned after all. A primary impetus to change was the progressive liberalization of capital flows. This process ever more clearly laid bare the incompatibility of the magic triangle, the sides of which are the interest rate differential, the fixed exchange rate, and free movement of capital. This arrangement was producing a simple money machine, allowing the foreign investor to collect the difference between the domestic and foreign interest rates at an almost zero exchange rate risk.[17] A logical consequence was a vicious spiral of the growing inflow of hot money and costly sterilized interventions.

The new exchange rate regime first had to address this incompatibility. However, hardly anything could be done with the setting of domestic interest rates that reflected the domestic monetary conditions. The way back to closing the economy on the capital account was out of the question as well. The solution therefore consisted of undertaking a higher exchange rate risk. On this basis, in February 1996 the idea of a fluctuation band was implemented, with limits set in the vicinity of ±7.5 percentage points from the old-new central parity.

The question is how the new exchange rate regime handled the issue of real appreciation. Some commentators argued that a greater space for free functioning of market forces would take into account the fundamental interests of the current account. They expected that the growing deficits of the current account would lead spontaneously to a weaker exchange rate and consequently to the restoration of external balance. The chosen width of the fluctuation band provided adequate space to implement this scenario. However, the behavior of the exchange rate in general ignored these assumptions. As in all other financially open economies, the dominant position of the capital account over transactions of the current account prevailed. And, as capital flows had strong motives encouraging the inflow against which, "due to the lack of bad news," there were no significant motives promoting the outflow, the way was open to nominal appreciation.

At that time, there was no unity of opinion in the CNB itself in terms of whether to face nominal appreciation by means of foreign exchange interventions. In the end, though, the conviction prevailed that the CNB alone could hardly do anything to fight the trend. The trend was powerful, indeed, and later it even strengthened. The CNB thus wanted to avoid the risk that unsuccessful interventions would harm its credibility and again trigger the sterilization cycle. So it decided not to incur such risks.

And yet another substantial circumstance upsets the simple scheme, for by doing nothing, that is, by not intervening against nominal appreciation, the CNB hastened the currency crisis. The beginning of 1997 brought a positive breakthrough in the statistics of trade balance (see fig. 8.6). Its deficits fell, which supported the hypothesis that a combination of monetary restrictions and the preceding wave of export-oriented investments was beginning to bear fruit. Therefore, it would be proper to complain of bad luck, a sort of rashness of financial markets that did not offer time enough for the proving of the self-liquidating nature of external imbalance. In other words, had the external triggers to currency crisis come a little later they might not have been strong enough to kindle the crisis. Nevertheless, this conclusion would be too much like an alibi, as economic policymakers must never forget that unlucky days follow the lucky ones and a surprise may come at the least suitable moment.

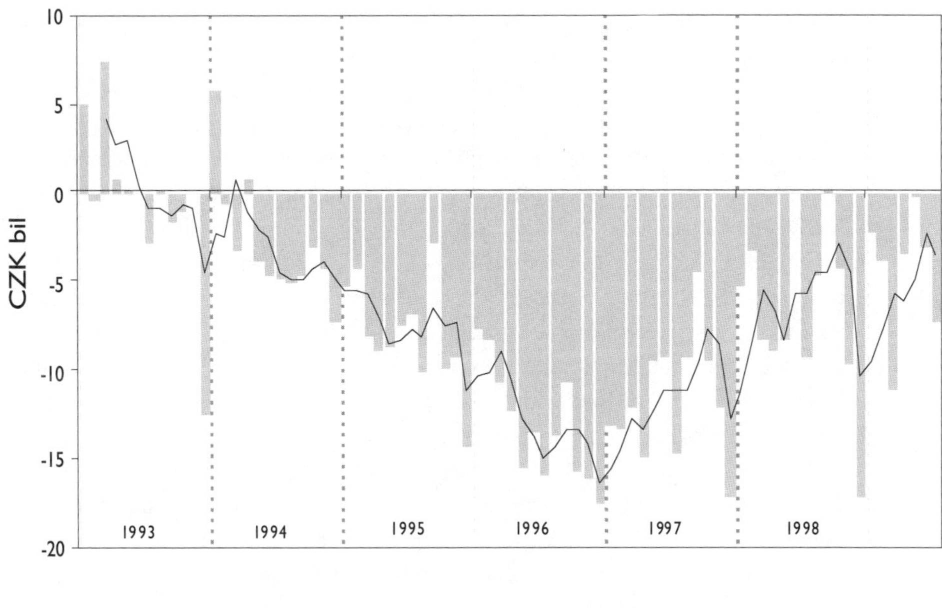

Fig. 8.6. Trade balance development. (Data from Czech National Bank.)

5. THE IMPENDING STORM

No war breaks out from one day to another. As a rule, we witness a gradual buildup of tension, borderline skirmishes, the exchange of diplomatic notes, and so on. In other words, there usually is enough time to become aware of an aggravating situation as well as a space for political settlement or at least for taking the edge off the conflict. It depends only on how well the main players are able to use the opportunity to avert the impending conflict. In this sense, 1996 and the first months of the following year may be considered a period of escalating tension. There were enough "red flags" signaling an exacerbating economic situation that were not spotted and used to find an efficient measure to prevent the increasingly large external imbalance.

5.1. THE FADING IMAGE OF SUCCESSFUL TRANSFORMATION

The beginning of 1996 was still marked by the offensive taken against the inflow wave. As pointed out earlier, substantial change was recorded by the exchange rate regime: starting on February 28 the fluctuation band was extended from the existing ±0.5 to ±7.5 percent with the preservation of central parity as well as the structure of the currency basket. The Central Bank was prepared to suppress excessive exchange rate fluctuations that could be triggered by the shift to the new exchange rate regime. Therefore, it intervened in response to the immediate outflow of short-term capital. The total extent of foreign exchange sales reached U.S.$660 million (approximately 5 percent of foreign exchange reserves) in three days. The interventions quickly smoothed out the turbulence ripple. Part of the short-term capital ebbed away, whereas the inflow of long-term capital (foreign direct investments and corporate loans in particular) went on with a constant speed.

However, stabilization in the foreign exchange market had not brought conditions back to the atmosphere of the preceding "wonderful years." On the contrary, the Central Bank became increasingly aware of forces that were pushing the economy into deepening imbalances. The money supply was markedly overshooting the upper limit of the set corridor, thus signaling potential problems with future inflation. Credit expansion went on at a galloping rate. Another concern related to the extent of deficits on the balance of payments' current account. The analysis of causes of these undesirable trends revealed an excess growth of real wages, leaving the growth rates of productivity of labor hanging behind. The state budget was sliding into a position of permanent deficits replacing the preceding surpluses.

A change for the worse could be spotted not only in the field of macroeconomic stability but also on the microeconomic level:

The accumulation of problems among the small banks, which threatened to turn into a systemic crisis, resulted in the introduction of a rescue package. For the period January–July 1996, seven small institutions were affected by forced administration, withdrawal of license, or liquidation.

The first big frauds took place in the sector of barely regulated investment funds. The accompanying scandals hinted at deeply nontransparent and unethical practices plaguing the domestic capital market. They were encouraged by the official rhetoric of the government on the harmfulness of excessive regulations.

A series of bankruptcies was experienced by the sector of health insurance companies, leaving behind many unsettled debts and a bitter taste of failure of the liberally conceived reform of health care financing. The biggest insurance company did not escape financial problems, either.

Public opinion was critical of failed privatization projects and speculative cases of "tunneling" (extracting funds) of both companies and banks by new owners. This was the toll paid for the chosen approaches to restructuring, which emphasized speed of privatization as the highest priority.

The suspected risks of the voucher privatization began to emerge in the form of a diluted and nontransparent ownership structure as well as a zero contribution to the capital strengthening of the corporate sector.

The general picture would not be complete without mentioning the parliamentary elections of May 1996, which added to the existing problems another dimension of the political cycle. In the preelection atmosphere, promises were made that were in contradiction to the view that the overheating economy needed cooling in the interest of the correction of deepening imbalances. The results of the elections led to the formation of an old-new coalition, which was, however, only a minority government affected by strained relations between coalition partners and, with regard to the distribution of political forces, also by doubts relating to the ability to maintain the continuity of the reform program.

5.2. OVERBURDENED MONETARY POLICY

In the atmosphere induced by the political cycle and the evident reluctance of the government to accept the signals of the creeping erosion of macroeconomic stability, the Central Bank set off on the race of a lonely runner. The monetary authority chose this option even though it was aware that an isolated application of monetary tightening was not the best response to the situation when the prevailing manifestation of the inflation gap (i.e., an overhang of aggregate demand over aggregate supply) was not the increase in prices but the increase in the external imbalance. In other words, one could expect that monetary tightening resorted to for the sake of dampening aggregate demand would much more severely affect investment than household consumption would. To reduce investment means to limit future growth potential. Higher interest rates also entice into the economy more short-term capital. As a result, the exchange rate is appreciated and export performance undermined.

It was evident that the optimal policy mix would have required a greater involvement of fiscal and incomes policies. The state budget, instead of sliding into deficits, should strive for surpluses, thus contributing to a decrease in aggregate demand along with a decrease in interest rates. The development of real wages should be more closely linked to the development of productivity of labor. Nevertheless, these requirements did not fall on fertile soil. There were arguments that the fiscal policy was doing its best within the given political constellation. As for wages, it was stated that the government did not have at its disposal instruments for influencing wage bargaining in the private sector and after all the observed growth of real wages was only offsetting their fall during the onset of the economic reform. Monetary policy was left lonely in its efforts to face the loosening of macroeconomic discipline.

First, a policy of minor steps was chosen, that is, the method of increasing the interest rate by small steps. This was insufficient. Therefore, in June 1996 a decision was made on a somewhat more vigorous tightening of monetary policy. The adopted decision of the CNB, at that time considered a legitimate response to higher inflation risks, became fatal in one respect. The CNB was blamed for insensitively stepping on the brakes without consulting anybody. Subsequently, this accusation increased the tension in the relations between the government and the Central Bank, which complicated the preemptive action against the impending currency crisis.

What was the reaction of foreign capital? Certainly it was not too logical when at the beginning of 1997 it was surprised by an explosion of Eurobond issues denominated in korunas (see fig. 8.7).[18] It may be called a surprise mainly because the phenomenon culminated at the moment when foreign analysts were extensively informed about the higher risks of investing in Czech assets (the external imbalance was deepening, economic growth was slowing down, and political stability was fizzling out). In any case, the wave of Eurobond issues arrived during an utterly unsuitable period, as it contributed to a strong appreciation of the domestic currency at the moment when the problem of the deficit of the current account culminated.

Nevertheless the Eurobond issues reminded us of how far the integration of the Czech economy with world financial markets had already progressed. It pointed out that the domestic monetary environment had become part of a greater whole, standing out of the reach of the domestic legislative and regulatory bodies.

5.3. TOO LITTLE, TOO LATE

A globally diversifying foreign investor for whom the Czech Republic was only one of many alternatives for the allocation of capital had to be confronted in the first quarter of 1997 with the following facts:

A look through the prism of indicators of external vulnerability showed one of the worst deficits of the current account with regard to GDP (estimates for the beginning of 1997 were above 10 percent) not covered by an inflow of long-term nondebt capital. The gross foreign indebted-

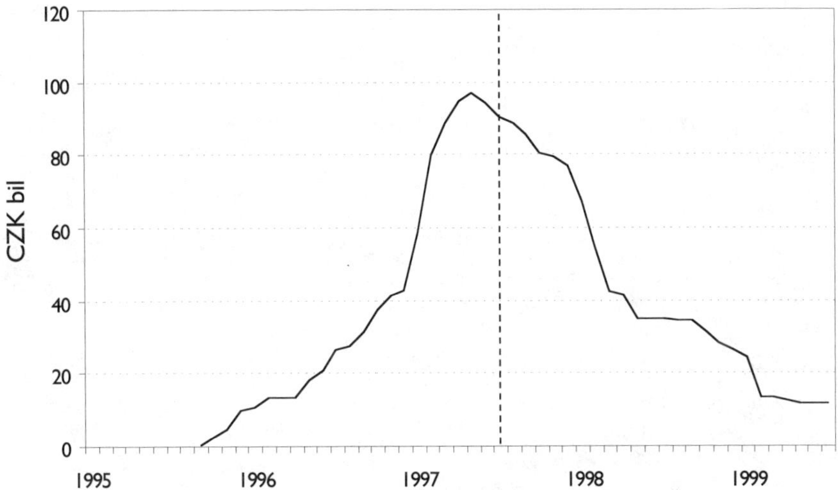

Fig. 8.7. Volume of outstanding Eurobonds (as of July 29, 1997). (Data from Czech National Bank.)

ness as a proportion of GDP was getting close to the safety limit of 40 percent (see table 8.1). Prolongation of trends signaled a rapid decline of foreign exchange reserves toward the safety constant of three-month imports (a comparison of 1996 and 1995 year end data showed a decline of foreign exchange reserves from the value of 6.2 to 4.3 for monthly imports). It should be emphasized also that the three-month rule does not take account of the impact of capital flows.

The analysis of the macroeconomic situation revealed symptoms of weakening economic growth with a simultaneous deepening of the external imbalance (an increase in current account deficits) as well as the internal imbalance (the growth of real wages over and above the growth of labor productivity and a strained state budget). The microlevel indicated an evident loss of transformation momentum (postponed privatization of banks, sluggish restructuring, and a feeble exercise of ownership rights, insignificant price deregulations, a highly nontransparent capital market, poor law enforcement, and so on).

The political scene was heading for ever greater instability nourished by bad news from the economy as well as by the stalemate result of the parliamentary elections.

There was tension between the two major policymakers, that is, the government and the Central Bank, marked by the dispute over who was to be blamed for slowing economic growth.

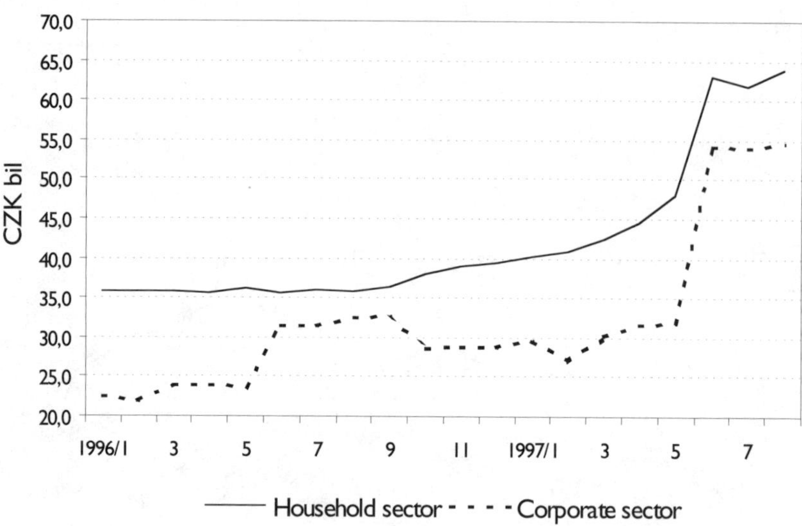

Fig. 8.8. Flight from the koruna (increase of foreign exchange deposits). (Data from Czech National Bank.)

A concern about the behavior of households was growing in connection with the accelerating currency switch in this sector (see fig. 8.8). The CNB was receiving signals from the market that important players (hedge funds) had invested, reckoning on a rapid depreciation of the exchange rate.[19]

All in all, the mosaic of news from the Czech Republic caused an abrupt change in the perception of this country as a territory exposed to potential turbulence. This unpleasant fact was also pointed out in the final report of the mission of the International Monetary Fund of the end of March 1997, which contained an explicit warning that the economy was running the risk of speculative attack.

In this atmosphere, in April 1997 the government adopted a document called the "Correction of Economic Policy and Additional Transformation Measures" and subsequently asked the Parliament for a vote of confidence. The aim of the package was to demonstrate the determination of the government to prevent further aggravation of both external and internal imbalances and to maintain the confidence of foreign investors. The steps that were supposed to lead to the achievement of this objective were the following: budgetary cuts in the amount of CZK25.5 billion (4.6 percent of projected budgetary expenditures); a decrease in wage growth in the public sector (instead of the promised yearly growth of 11.9 percent, it was only 7.3 percent); and the introduction of so-called import deposits.[20]

The package contained a number of suggestions that were meant to restore the earlier vigor of the economic reform. As a result, it was suggested that the government should establish an independent Securities and Exchange Commission and a special team for fighting financial criminality, should accelerate the privatization of banks, and should pursue the more consistent exercise of ownership rights in state enterprises.

The CNB welcomed and supported the adoption of the governmental package based on the consideration that the top priority had to be a rapid and efficient solution to the external imbalance. The achievement of this objective dictated the adoption of restrictive measures, though at the cost of short-term stagnation in growth. Nevertheless, a restriction may be optimized by a suitable mix of policies. The fiscal restriction could effectively and immediately impact the volume of consumption and imports as well as the behavior of wages in the still quite large state and semiprivate sectors. Another side effect could be the inclination of interest rates to decline. Thus, the CNB perceived the correction of economic policy as a certain kind of barter trade in the sense that if the government enforced a sufficient fiscal restriction that led to the slowdown of wage growth the Central Bank might consider a prudent loosening of monetary policy. As a gesture confirming this logic, a decision was made on the eve of the introduction of the stabilization package to decrease minimum reserve requirements.

5.4. THE DISPUTE OVER CONTROLLED DEVALUATION

To the credit of all parties involved in the formulation of the stabilization package, the sharp dispute over the so-called controlled devaluation did not leak out in the critical days, requiring the utmost pacification of exacerbated expectations. Only later was the public informed that economic ministers of the government intended to apply a demand restriction in conjunction with a purposeful depreciation of the exchange rate. However, such involvement of the exchange rate in the planned correction of economic policy was firmly opposed by the CNB.

There is nothing mysterious about the approach of the CNB if we take into account that the economy did not correspond to the textbook case of so-called expenditure switching in which the exchange rate would change the proportions between demand for the output of domestic and foreign sectors. On the contrary, the environment was already highly nonstandard and permeated with the feeling that the speculation attack might come quite soon. In other words, the exchange rate expectations had already become united in the devaluation direction. The recommendation to carry out a controlled devaluation could have easily become the outcry setting off an avalanche. Based on internal analyses of the potential force of the flight from the Czech currency, the mentioned concerns were taking quite a clear shape.[21]

Thus, the problem did not consist of some obsession over the role of the fixed exchange rate but rather over the timing of the exit from the declared commitments. The CNB wanted to prevent any massive speculation that could accompany the change of regime and could lead to costly overshooting. Therefore, it also required the government to create corresponding prerequisites for getting untied from its existing exchange rate obligations. This meant that fiscal policy would get more visibly involved in tackling the external imbalance. Also it was paramount to induce a U-turn toward sounder wage development. The argument was that only the environment of renewed macroeconomic discipline was suitable for implementation of the depreciation of the exchange rate. Due to the uncompromising position of the CNB, the controlled devaluation was not ultimately included in the governmental package.[22]

6. ANATOMY OF THE CURRENCY CRISIS

In the early morning hours of May 15, 1997 the exchange rate embarked on a breathtaking depreciation. Within one hour, the Czech koruna had lost 100 basic points and reached the 5 percent mark on the depreciation side of the fluctuation band. Two days before the Thai baht had been under the pressure of concentrated speculation. Thus, it might be assumed that the spark of contagion from Southeast Asia ignited in Central Europe, as both currencies had for some time been categorized as vulnerable. There was no doubt that the suspected risk of currency turbulence was beginning to take shape.

When describing and evaluating important events we are usually interested in what strategy the policymakers used in their approach to the challenges of a given period. Under the conditions of a currency crisis, such reasoning has, however, an evident stumbling block, as usually there is simply no time to consider, formulate, and evaluate strategic intentions. The situation develops hastily, new moments bring new surprises, and important decisions are often made under the stress of a time and information vacuum.

If we look for a suitable term to describe the behavior of the CNB, which in the first line of defense faced the feverish gusts of financial markets, it can be called an organized retreat. This implies that the strategic intention of the CNB was not an unconditional determination to resist the superiority of market players at any cost. The aim was rather to choose a suitable maneuver of retreat that would use all available weapons, thus minimizing the losses sustained because these losses could be formidably higher if the retreat turned into a stampede.

6.1. THE LIQUIDITY SQUEEZE

Among the salient features of the currency crisis in the Czech Republic was the fact that the contagion from Southeast Asia set the nonresidents in motion first. These players may be split into two groups: the disappointed investors and the eager speculators.

The so-called disappointed investor could be depicted as a person who had lost interest in the Czech stock and bond markets or more precisely one who was no longer willing to undergo the increasing risks of investing in Czech assets. Disappointed investors were in general determined to liquidate their positions, even at the cost of high losses, mainly for fear that hesitation in leaving could have consequences in the form of even higher losses. In contrast, the eager speculator impersonated the type of investor greedy for a big profit in case of a marked depreciation of the Czech currency. Therefore, this speculator was willing to invest a certain amount of capital and help the market forces to fertilize his or her investment.

Being aware of the spectrum of opponents, the CNB chose the tactic of the so-called liquidity squeeze. It consisted of the combination of nonsterilized interventions and withdrawal repo operations. In other words, the CNB intervened by means of the sale of foreign assets from its foreign exchange reserves, thus supporting the domestic currency.[23] In this way, the bank was withdrawing the koruna liquidity from the market, which it did not compensate for with open market operations. Quite a few observers perceived this activity as nothing more than a wasted attempt to protect the exchange rate band and a waste of foreign exchange reserves.

As mentioned earlier, the aim was not a victory but an organized retreat. Foreign exchange interventions have a pivotal role in this respect, as the sale of foreign exchange allows the disappointed investors to leave. These investors are out of play and do not nourish the psychosis of a mass rush. No one other than the Central Bank could give them the possibility of an orderly retreat as in the pandemonium of a speculation attack nobody else can sell foreign exchange.

Interventions had to be nonsterilized and supported by an additional drain on liquidity in order to save the Central Bank from financing a speculative attack against itself. As a result of the liquidity squeeze, the banks did not have enough cash to lend to speculators. The lack of liquidity undoubtedly caused the interest rates of the money market to soar. However, this was substantiated by the need to make borrowing Czech currency for speculation purposes more expensive. Higher rates also contributed to discouraging a headlong liquidation of the koruna positions.

The grip of the liquidity squeeze may be partially illustrated by the following data. The one-week Prague Interbank Offered Rate (PRIBOR), which the CNB used as an operational target, increased from the precrisis value of 12.5 percent during two weeks to a maximum of 85.6 percent. In the climax of the crisis, the one-week repo rate reached 75 percent. The Lombard rate, at which banks can borrow from the CNB against collateral, was increased from 14 to 50 percent, another necessary increase that was not carried out because the Lombard facility was discontinued. The difference between the short and long ends of the yield curve of the money market deepened from the original 0.65 to 42.18 percentage points. An absolute record was set by the overnight rate, which at one time reached 197.5 percent. The bid-ask spread in one-week PRIBOR ranged prior to the crisis around the value of 0.23 percentage points. The currency turbulence inflated this spread to the maximum of 50.33 percentage points.

The technique of liquidity squeeze had its evident costs and limits. First, the skyrocketing interest rates of the interbank money market started after some time to leak into the rates charged by banks to their clients. This was already having a direct impact on the real economy via the financial situation of the corporate sector. Second, the interventions against the depreciation of the currency are limited by the volume of foreign exchange reserves or the borrowing capacity of the monetary authorities.

Thus, the chosen retreat maneuver was an unpleasant optimization problem that offered a poor solution among even worse ones. A great mistake would be to resign at the very beginning of the currency turbulence and let the exchange rate overshoot at the time when there were some chances to calm down the situation and maintain the credibility of the band. An even greater mistake, however, would be to overestimate the Central Bank's abilities and not to spot the moment when a defensive tactic turns into bluffing in poker.

With the benefit of hindsight, it may be stated that the CNB was not driven to either of these two extremes and coped with its role relatively successfully. By means of well-timed and calibrated interventions, it prevented excessive volatility of the exchange rate from attacking the depreciation edge of the band. The disappointed investors got the chance for a relatively orderly withdrawal. Many eager speculators did not generate the intended exorbitant profits and began to lose interest. A certain part was played also by the consistent liquidity squeeze and an attempt at administrative separation of onshore and offshore markets.[24] Toward this end, the CNB consumed approximately 20 percent of its foreign exchange reserves (in terms of volume about U.S.$2.3 billion).[25]

It might seem that the achieved pacification of nonresident players would have brought the currency turbulence closer to its end. However, it was just the opposite. It was increasingly obvious that the hectic week full of news on a tense fate of the Czech koruna set in motion a huge mass of residents. The corporate sector engaged in all kinds of behavior symptomatic of devaluation expectations (acceleration of imports and postponement of exports, precautionary purchases of foreign exchange, and so on). The household sector engaged in a consumption binge, and a massive conversion of the domestic currency denominated accounts to foreign exchange ones. The psychosis of a threatened currency was further nourished by the comments of some domestic experts, who relentlessly predicted a deep dive of the Czech koruna.[26]

The situation began to take the shape of a meltdown, a marked loss of trust in domestic currency, and self-fulfilling expectations. This escalation of the crisis led to the revision in tactics. It was evident that the foreign exchange reserves of the Central Bank would never be extensive enough to cope with the mass rush on the domestic currency. And even if an end was put to this rush the decimated reserves would play into the hands of a recurring turbulence. The policy of prohibitively high interest rates was not sustainable in the long run as it posed the danger of a crisis of the banking sector and a deep recession in the real economy.

The topic of the day thus became the review of the exchange rate regime, namely, the contemplated exit from the declared obligation to intervene in defense of the threatened fluctuation band. In the evening hours of May 26, 1997, the twelfth day of the monetary crisis, the regime of managed floating was announced, with the German mark as the reference currency.

6.2. THE CRISIS SUBSIDES

The first days after the change of the exchange rate regime were critical. The repeal of the band posed the threat of an overshot drop of the currency, which had to be prevented. There were several interventions, including one that was verbal in the sense that the CNB expected in the short run the average exchange rate in the range of 17.0 to 19.5 Czech korunas for a German mark. Liquidity was further squeezed, and so the interest rates of the money market peaked. Wide spreads indicated a persistent nervousness in the financial markets. The combination of all these measures succeeded in preventing the overshooting of the exchange rate, as, after a fall of about eight percentage points in an immediate response to the repeal of the band, it stabilized at about 10 percent from the former central parity, measured in terms of the abandoned currency basket.

Thus, the Central Bank did not follow the commonly believed myth that a transition to floating would give market forces all the initiative in setting a new exchange rate level. On the contrary, it defended the exchange rate against overshooting by escalating the liquidity squeeze and increasing interest rates, even though at certain costs. But what would it mean to let the exchange rate excessively depreciate? The result would be the jump of import prices, bankruptcies of insufficiently hedged foreign exchange debtors, and unbearable stress in the banking sector. The inflation spiral could be stopped only by an uncompromising increase in interest rates. Consequently, the economy would not avoid even greater losses caused by irreversible effects of an overshot depreciation of the currency.

The first signs of calm came at the beginning of June when foreign exchange deposits ceased to grow. At the end of June, there even occurred slight pressures on appreciation of the exchange rate, which the CNB was subduing by means of interventions. It was possible to launch the strategy of the so-called landing of interest rates. The core of this maneuver was to reduce the reference rates of the Central Bank to levels that would already be adequate to meet the needs of ordinary policy making rather than the needs of liquidity squeezing. It was important to proceed prudently, that is, in small steps, in order to prevent the risk of a more marked depreciation of the Czech currency. In mid-June, the Lombard facility was reopened.

The process of reducing interest rates lasted approximately until the end of August, that is, less than three months. Measured against the basic reference rate of the CNB the newfound postcrisis level of interest rates was set approximately two percentage points higher compared to precrisis level. Also falling were spreads of interest rates in response to the general improvement in the situation. The CNB was testing the new exchange rate regime, which demonstrated an increased sensitivity to news about inflation, current account deficits, and other fundamental quantities. From the viewpoint of monetary decision making, the economy began to get back to normal. In fact, this was merely the beginning, as it was only the acute surgical procedure that had been accomplished and not the lengthy and equally painful convalescence.

7. EPILOGUE

The International Monetary Fund lists the Czech Republic among the countries that managed to cope successfully and solely on their own with the pitfalls of the monetary crisis. This institution has appreciated both the technique used to resist the speculative attack and the determination in the application of a broader stabilization program.

Nevertheless, with the extinction of the currency turbulence the problem was far from overcome. It was imperative to address the causes leading to this phenomenon and grapple with the consequences left behind. The Czech economy headed into a homemade recession, the only one in the group of reforming Central European economies, which intensified the debate about what made the behavior of the Czech economy stand out in this way.

There is no doubt that after the currency crisis faded away the economy remained in the grip of a sharp slowdown. After all, it was time for both governmental austerity packages to reverse the deeply rooted trend toward widening external imbalances. It was impossible to run away from the approved budgetary cuts, which caused the drop in the construction industry and a sharp decline of real wages in the public sector. Also monetary policy had to continue to be prudent for a number of reasons. The behavior of the exchange rate was under strong pressure due to the deepening political crisis accelerated by exacerbating problems of the domestic economy. The depreciated exchange rate started to manifest itself in increased inflation. These factors did not allow an immediate restoration of fiscal, wage, or monetary policies to precrisis levels.

With the knowledge of later developments and the depth of economic recession in particular, the question arises as to whether the screws of postcrisis restrictions were not tightened too much.[27] Fitting well into this interpretation was a marked decline in inflation, which started in the middle of 1998. The CNB significantly undershot its inflation target for that year. The application of a textbook theorem on the tradeoff between growth and inflation was misleading in the postcrisis period, however. The primary reason for the increased restriction of that time was not the fulfillment of overambitious disinflation targets but rather the efforts to restore external balance.

It would be incorrect not to admit that some decisions of the CNB might have been different had there been past experience of the behavior of an economy in recession. Had there been a more definite idea of the weakness of the growth performance and the proximity of deflation, the landing of interest rates would have most probably started sooner and the calibration of certain regulations of banking supervision would probably have been spread over a longer period of time.[28] Anyway a robust loosening of monetary policy was accomplished.[29] In spite of this, the response of the banking and corporate sectors remained at the freezing point. Attention started to concentrate on the so-called credit crunch.

Why did the granting of loans stagnate when both nominal and real interest rates reached their historically lowest values? Banks did not lend much, as they were hampered by high volumes of bad loans extended earlier and also by waiting for their long postponed privatization. The corporate clientele was crippled with debt and a lack of good projects. In other words, a credit crunch replaced the preceding credit euphoria, which had infested banks with bad loans.

More than two years after the currency turbulence of 1997 it is clear that the Czech economic policy succeeded in the treatment of external imbalance. Thus, it acquired the necessary immunity, which provided a shelter against the contagion spreading from Southeast Asia and Russia. The trust of foreign investors was recovered to such an extent that a new surge of foreign investments has come to the fore again. The cost of the elimination of external imbalances was economic recession. However, such a cost in a similar amount was paid by all countries affected by the monetary crisis. Never forgotten should be the experience gained that unsound expansion is sooner or later followed by a painful contraction, especially in a context of imperfections in international capital markets. The monetary shake-up of 1997 sent this message clearly. If economic policy grasps it in this way, it will be a message dearly paid for but not wasted.

NOTES

1. It is the type of monetary crisis the description of which at the model level is dealt with in, for example, Krugman 1979 and Obstfeld 1986.

2. The Czech national savings rate (calculated on the basis of national accounts as the ratio of gross national savings to gross disposable income) was ranging in the transformation period between 28 and 30 percent. In the neighboring Central European transition economies, it accounted for approximately 20 percent.

3. In 1996, there were growing concerns that the share of the current account deficit in GDP would exceed 8 percent, which provoked in the media numerous parallels with the Mexican crisis in 1994. The deficit estimate for the first quarter of 1997 was above 10 percent of GDP. According to this significant vulnerability indicator, the Czech Republic ranked among the first in the group of emerging economies, even ahead of Thailand, Mexico, and South Africa.

4. As an illustration, approximately two months before the currency crisis then prime minister V. Klaus announced that the country was entering the posttransformation phase of economic growth. There were promises to double wages and pensions by the year 2000 communicated in the course of the parliamentary preelection campaign. The Czech National Bank, which had to respond alone to the increase in imbalances by a gradual tightening of the monetary policy came in for sharp criticism for slowing down economic growth. This aspect of economic political debate will be further discussed below.

5. According to Citibank estimates, the total daily turnover with currencies of the transition economies amounted in April 1997 to U.S.$8.1 billion. Of this, the Czech koruna accounted for U.S.$5.5 billion, which represents almost 70 percent of the total sum (in March 1996 it was only U.S.$0.5 billion).

6. The volume of foreign exchange limits was continuously increased from the original approximately 70 dollars (2,000 korunas) in 1990 to about 3,570 dollars (100,000

korunas) in 1995. The extent to which households did not use these limits served as a significant indicator of trust in the domestic currency.

7. The declared interest in foreign direct investments for a long time contrasted with a clear reluctance to offer foreign investors a comprehensive program of investment incentives that had become a regular practice in many countries. The position of the Czech government took its toll in the lower inflow of foreign direct investment (FDI) in the Czech Republic compared to the neighboring transition economies.

8. The first rating of best speculative quality Baa1 was given by Moody's to the former State Bank of Czechoslovakia in January 1992. In March 1993, this agency increased its valuation to Baa3, by which the Czech Republic became the first postcommunist country to be granted an investment grade. In May 1994, it was further improved to Baa2 and in August 1995 to Baa1. This rating was not affected by the monetary crisis in 1997. Another well-known rating agency, Standard and Poor´s granted in July 1993 the BBB investment grade. In June 1994 this agency improved its rating to BBB+. In 1995, it even skipped one grade of its valuation by granting the investment grade A. The downgrade to level A− occurred in November 1998, that is, more than one year after the monetary crisis. The main reason was the statement of insufficient progress of restructuring of the banking sector and many enterprises. For details see Opravilova 1995.

9. The new Foreign Exchange Act came into effect on October 1, 1995. The time interval from the effective date of the preceding act, that is, the transition from internal to external convertibility, was less than five years.

10. The Czech Republic became a member of the OECD in December 1995 as the first among the postcommunist transition countries. Part of the admission procedure was the adoption of obligations contained in the so-called Liberalization Code. Further liberalization steps were scheduled, and their fulfillment has been regularly checked.

11. Through the prism of the figures of that time, the capital inflow looked even more dramatic (for 1994 and 1995 the share of GDP was reported in the amount of 9.4 and 18.4 percent, respectively). Only in the summer of 1997 did the Czech Statistical Office increase the estimates of GDP for the past years, which resulted in a partial decrease in a number of relative indicators.

12. Many times the banks granted foreign exchange loans in the form of Czech koruna deposits with a variable principal the amount of which depended on the given underlying volume of foreign exchange and on the exchange rate (as if a bank had lent foreign exchange that the client would immediately sell at the given exchange rate back to the bank). For enterprises, foreign exchange loans were interesting mainly because of lower interest. Banks then could, with their help, avoid the mismatch of foreign exchange assets and liabilities. On this basis, standard domestic currency loans were often reclassified into foreign exchange ones. However, another question was whether banks did not transform the exchange rate risk into a credit risk in case the company afflicted by foreign exchange loss ceased to meet its credit obligations.

13. The efficiency of sterilization is often measured by the estimate of the so-called offset coefficient. This coefficient takes values between zero and 1 and is interpreted in such a way that the closer the values are to 1 the lower is the ability of the Central Bank to execute autonomous management of the money supply (sterilization of the capital inflow only supports a new inflow). Repeated computations for the years 1994–95 showed the value of the offset coefficient in the interval of 0.3–0.6. The tendency toward higher values of this coefficient then corresponded with a widespread opinion that the efficiency of the ever more costly sterilization measures was gradually decreasing.

14. Instructive evidence is provided by Jilek (1996). Immediately prior to the introduction of the regulation of nonresident short-term positions the share of short-term and medium-term deposits in residential foreign banks amounted to 81 and 16 percent, respectively. After one month of the effect of the regulation, this relation between short-term and medium-term deposits amounted to 48 and 50 percent.

15. This is the ratio of the average value of March 1999 to the average value of 1991. Data are from the IMF's International Financial Statistics.

16. For a detailed discussion of exchange rate regimes in transition economies, see Dornbush 1994 and Sachs 1996.

17. This arbitrage opportunity was taken advantage of mainly by foreign banks and subsidiaries of foreign banks, which were offering the so-called nondeliverable forwards. The functioning of this product may be presented in a simplified way as follows. The bank concludes with a client a contract on a future purchase of foreign exchange at the forward exchange rate F and then upon maturity of the forward contract sells this foreign exchange immediately to the client at the spot exchange rate S. With regard to the technique of hedging a forward transaction (creation of a Czech koruna deposit against a forward purchase of foreign exchange and a dollar debt against a future dollar income), the forward dealing will be neutral for the bank on the condition that the forward rate is set in compliance with the condition of the so-called covered interest parity, $F = S(1 + r_D)/(1 + r_F)$. The symbols r_D and r_F stand for domestic and foreign interest rate levels, respectively. As a result, the bank neither gains nor loses; the positive interest differential $r_D > r_F$, however, implies that $F > S$ so that a simultaneous execution of both the spot and forward transactions generates for the client a koruna profit of $F - S$ per one dollar. And, as in both operations the client deals with the same bank, instead of a parallel performance of the two mentioned operations the client's account is simply credited with the arbitrage profit. The practical form of nondeliverable forwards had to take into account the volatility of foreign currencies within the structure of the currency basket and to respect also a certain sharing of the arbitrage profit between the bank and the client. Jilek (1996) estimated that, measured by the value of the underlying asset, the volume of nondeliverable forwards amounted to approximately CZK20 billion, which at the time was about U.S.$0.7 billion.

18. Whereas for the whole year 1996 there were 26 issues registered totaling U.S.$1.2 billion, the first quarter of 1997 recorded 35 issues in the amount of U.S.$1.7 billion. The upsurge of this market may be explained by the effort to use high interest rate differentials. Small investors who generated the decisive part of the demand were attracted by a high yield, and their concerns about the risk exposure were compensated by short maturity (mostly one to two years) as well as the reputation of the koruna as a stable currency with a strong link to the German mark. The issuers from the ranks of business, banking, and the public sector found these Eurobond instruments interesting mainly because by means of swap operations they opened the way to cheaper borrowing in other currencies (German marks or U.S. dollars).

19. The consolidated balance sheet of the banking sector reveals that from May 10 to May 20 (i.e., five days before and five days after the eruption of the speculative attack) koruna credits to nonresidents increased by less then CZK10 billion. This amount represents a negligible fraction of all credits extended. This piece of information tends to suggest the minor role of foreigners who speculated (i.e., practiced short selling) against the Czech currency.

20. This instrument required the importers of the selected commodity groups to

deposit in a non-interest-bearing account with a commercial bank 20 percent of the value of the imported goods for six months.

21. In-house CNB analyses signaled that in case of an abrupt change in the investor's climate, an outflow of capital in the range of U.S.$2 billion (16 percent of total foreign exchange reserves) might come in the course of several days. The outflow up to U.S.$4 billion (32 percent of total reserves) would take place in the course of several weeks, and the outflow of U.S.$8.8 billion (71 percent of total reserves) would threaten in several months. Identified were also the potential bottlenecks that would slow down the capital flight (the willingness of investors to liquidate their koruna positions even at the cost of high losses, the available liquidity of the money and capital markets, the elements of a passive resistance of the Czech banks, and so on). However, the frictional effect of these obstacles could be quantified only roughly.

22. The negative attitude of the CNB toward devaluation was based also on internal analyses, which did not confirm the comments on a fatal overvaluation of the Czech currency. This meant that the defense of the exchange rate against speculative attack was far from hopeless. Later events proved this attitude right in many respects, as in the course of the crisis the exchange rate depreciated with regard to the original central parity only by approximately 10 percent and at some points it even returned to the old fluctuation band. By refusing the controlled devaluation, the CNB unintentionally avoided the Mexican experience. As Griffith-Jones (1996) mentions, in the environment of jittery expectations the Mexican government decided to devalue the peso by 15 percent. But this step only provoked massive speculation, which forced the peso to float.

23. The CNB made an effort to intervene in the spot and forward foreign exchange markets. However, the intention to intervene through forward transactions was not very successful, as this market after some time ceased to be liquid. Only a fraction of the planned volume of forward transactions was accomplished.

24. By means of so-called moral suasion, the CNB made an attempt to put an end to lending domestic currency to nonresidents with the aim of paralyzing the speculative behavior of the offshore market. One group of banks expressed willingness to respect this recommendation; another one, in contrast, refused. The response of the majority was a cool reserve. However, despite a certain initial success, the efficiency of this informal limitation of external convertibility was quickly eroding. This was evident as early as after the first two weeks. It may be explained by the fact that the "obedient" banks were losing commissions on nonexecuted transactions and the measure itself was insensitive in the sense that it affected both purely speculative and hedging operations.

25. Under the pressure of the currency crisis, the so-called second governmental austerity package was adopted, which contained additionally approved budget cuts. The total reduction of budgetary expenditures thus reached 2.7 percent of GDP. Announced also was the promise to draw up the state budget for the next year, 1998, as a surplus one.

26. In the course of May, approximately CZK38 billion (U.S.$1.4 billion) was converted into foreign exchange by residents. The foreign exchange deposits of domestic enterprises rose by 72 percent; in the case of households, this increase amounted to 31 percent. If one takes into account that (1) the CNB injected into the economy via interventions CZK75 billion of foreign exchange reserves, (2) the foreign exchange position of the banking sector remained more or less balanced throughout the crisis, and (3) nonresidents increased their foreign exchange holdings by CZK1 billion, the capital flight from the country reached the value CZK36 billion (U.S.$1.3 billion).

27. The economy touched the bottom of economic recession in the first quarter of

1999 when the year-on-year drop in GDP reached −4.1 percent. For the preceding year, the decline in GDP was −2.3 percent.

28. In mid-1998, the CNB responded to the gloomy conditions in the field of secured loans with the adoption of a measure that required banks to replace within three years the real estate collateral in the worst category of bad credits by provisions in the full amount. This step was forced by a long-term unsatisfactory legal environment that more or less disqualified the function of real estate as quality collateral (consent of the debtor for the sale of collateralized real estate, lengthy litigation, a minimal yield from foreclosing proceedings, and so on). Stricter requirements for the creation of reserves affected quite severely the three biggest domestic banks, which were burdened with a high percentage of bad credits.

29. The CNB began to cut interest rates in July 1998 from the level of 15 percent. The basic operating rate declined subsequently in a total number of 17 steps during about one year to the level of 5.5 percent.

REFERENCES

Buch, C. M., and R. P. Heinrich. 1997. "The end of the Czech miracle?" Kiel Discussion Paper 301, Institute fur Weltwirtschaft, June.

Capek, A. 1997. "The real effective exchange rate: Problems of measuring" Working Paper 77, Institute of Economics. Czech National Bank. In Czech.

Dedek, O. 1995. "Currency convertibility and exchange rate policies in the Czech Republic." *Eastern European Economics,* November–December.

Dedek, O., and A. Derviz. 1996. "Exchange rate policies in a wider band." *Politicka Ekonomie* 5. In Czech: 583–605.

Dornbush, R. 1994. "Exchange rate policies in economies in transition." In *Approaches to exchange rate policy,* ed. R. C. Barth and Ch.-H. Wong. Washington, DC: IMF Institute.

Griffith-Jones, S. 1996. "The Mexican peso crisis." *CEPAL Review,* December. 60: 155–75.

Hrncir, M., and J. Klacek. 1991. "Stabilization policies and currency convertibility in Czechoslovakia." *European Economy* 2.

Jilek, J. 1996. "Foreign capital inflow and foreign exchange positions of the banks." *Politicka Ekonomie* 1. In Czech.

Krugman, P. 1979. "A model of balance-of-payment crisis." *Journal of Money, Credit, and Banking* 11 (August): 311–22.

Obstfeld, M. 1986. "Rational and self-fulfilling balance of payments crises." *American Economic Review* 76, no. 1 (March): 72–81.

Opravilova, R. 1995. "Development of the Czech Republic's rating." *Bankovnictvi* 20. In Czech.

Sachs, J. D. 1996. "Economic transition and the exchange-rate regime." *AEA Papers and Proceedings* 86 (May): 147–52.

CHAPTER 9

The Swings in Capital Flows and the Brazilian Crisis

Ilan Goldfajn

During the 1990s, Brazil experienced a complete cycle of capital flows. First, like many other developing countries Brazil experienced a surge in capital inflows that was initially praised for eliminating a decade of restricted borrowing. Second, the new flows seemed overwhelming and led to the introduction of a variety of controls over capital flows that were devised to modify their volume and composition. Finally, in the aftermath of the Russian crisis of August 1998, a series of events led to large outflows of capital that culminated in the Brazilian crisis and the floating of the real in January 1999.

The Brazilian crisis is interesting for several reasons. First, it is another instance in which one can analyze the role of capital flows in a currency crisis looking at different players—institutional investors, foreign banks, and domestic investors—and different types of flows—direct investment and portfolio and bank loans. Second, it is an interesting case of contagion. In academic and policy-making circles, the hypothesis is that there was an element of contagion from the Russian crisis to Brazil. If true, this fact is perhaps surprising. In contrast to the contagion from the Mexican and Thai crises, the Russian contagion to Brazil appears to have crossed regional borders. It is interesting to analyze the consequences of this fact in terms of our current understanding of crises and contagion. Third, the Brazilian crisis was milder than previous currency crises. It is interesting to examine the reasons for this performance.

Brazil's macroeconomic performance during the crisis year was better than expected. Inflation did not explode, GDP did not collapse, the government was not forced to restructure its public debt, and, slowly, both nominal and real interest rates have been going down. This performance is partly due to the fact that the private sector was largely hedged at the moment of the crisis and was insulated from the immediate effects of the devaluation. The reason for this "prudent" behavior is that the Brazilian crisis was anticipated by market participants. Following the Mexican crisis, the Brazilian economy was identified by analysts as vulnerable to crisis because of its large fiscal deficit and the short maturity of its public debt. The peg was sustained for several years based on high real interest rates and a comfortable level of reserves. However, when the Russian crisis occurred, large capital outflows quickly reduced what seemed to be a comfortable level of reserves. In October 1998, Brazilian authorities reached out to the International Monetary Fund (IMF) and a large-scale package ($41 billion) was provided, but that was not enough to calm markets. The crisis erupted in January 1999, and the real was allowed to float.

In this long process of preannouncing the crisis, the private sector slowly hedged its dollar liabilities by purchasing dollar-denominated securities and dollars in the futures markets, all provided by the government in its attempt to keep the peg. Therefore, in contrast to the Asian crises, there were mild balance sheet effects and almost no bankruptcies once the real floated and depreciation reached more than 80 percent.[1] Of course, this was no free lunch, given that the public sector bears most of the cost by increasing the public debt by 10 percent of GDP. A major fear during the crisis was the risk of an outburst of inflation fueled by the large depreciation and the return to a high inflation regime. This fear proved to be unfounded. The reasons for a low pass through of the exchange rate depreciation to inflation are related to: (1) a depressed level of demand after the crisis that discouraged the pass through, (2) a previous overvaluation of the exchange rate that was corrected by the nominal devaluation, and (3) low initial inflation at the end of 1998 (see Goldfajn and Werlang 2000). Another major fear that also fortunately proved to be unfounded was that output would decline significantly as a result of the crisis.

This chapter concludes that in the case of Brazil one cannot assert that a particular investor group had a predominant role in the crisis. If anything, the data suggest that while foreign investors (both banks and institutional investors) had long been in Brazil the speculation against the currency was not overwhelming. Once their position changed, the crisis erupted. The data do not seem to reflect a compensatory liquidation of assets story by foreign investors caused by the Russian crisis. Nor is it the effect of international interest rates. The econometric exercise on capital flows suggests that the push effects have a more long run effect, affecting capital flows only once large changes in international interest rates are factored in.

The chapter is organized in six sections. Section 1 describes the Brazilian crisis, looking at macroeconomic and financial variables. Section 2 analyzes the role of institutional investors, foreign banks, and domestic investors in the crisis. Section 3 examines the aftermath of the crisis and the reasons for its mild effect. Section 4 performs an econometric exercise, investigating the determinants of capital flows to Brazil in the 1990s. Section 5 formally tests the existence of contagion from the Russian crisis to Brazil. Finally, section 6 concludes, and the appendix describes the data.

1. THE BRAZILIAN CRISIS

This section examines the stylized facts regarding the Brazilian crisis. Brazil had had a history of very high inflation (hyperinflation at times) until the Real Plan of July 1994.[2] The latter was an ingenious scheme of changing numeraires. In March 1994, nominal prices, wages, and other contracts were allowed to be quoted in a unified reference value (URV) that would be replaced with a new currency, the real, in July 1994. Since prices were already indexed to several different references, the innovation of the URV was to coordinate a unified unit of account that would substitute for all other indexation mechanisms. In the interim period following the introduction of the URV and before its replacement with the real, it was expected that relative prices would converge to their equilibrium value. This was important to the second phase of the conversion, when the URV would be transformed into the real on a one-to-one basis and then pegged to the dollar. This pegging, in fact, caused inflation to plunge from 46 percent in June 1994 to 1.5 percent in September 1994.

The drastic reduction of inflation after July 1994 changed the inflationary scenario and, as a consequence, contributed to the delivery of two presidential mandates and several seats in congress to the people and parties perceived to be responsible for this change. Since then, low inflation has been considered a political asset. However, the fall in inflation was not fast enough to avoid a real appreciation of the exchange rate, which prompted the central bank to set an adjustable band for the dollar value of the real and maintain a continuing crawling peg within it from 1995 to 1999 (see fig. 9.1). Notwithstanding the crawling peg, which was set at approximately 7 percent per year, the real exchange rate remained clearly overvalued, as can be seen from the increasing current account deficits (from around 2 percent in 1995 to 4.5 percent in 1998). The overvaluation contributed to the lack of growth in the gross domestic product (GDP) (see table 9.1).

In addition to the lack of competitiveness and poor GDP growth, fiscal performance deteriorated in 1997 and 1998, which made the Brazilian economy vulnerable to external shocks. There were three major external shocks after the Real Plan, the Tequila effect in 1995, the Asian crisis in 1997, and the Russian crisis in 1998. The reaction to the crises was similar in all cases. Nominal interest rates were doubled (see fig. 9.2) and a fiscal package promised. This strategy was successful in averting a crisis after the Tequila and Asia shocks. However, after the Russian crisis this same strategy had a perverse effect. Instead of attracting capital, the strategy this time induced capital outflows. The reason was that the fiscal package was not credible and the higher interest rates increased nominal fiscal deficits and raised fears of a sovereign default. As a consequence, large withdrawals followed and the currency came under pressure.

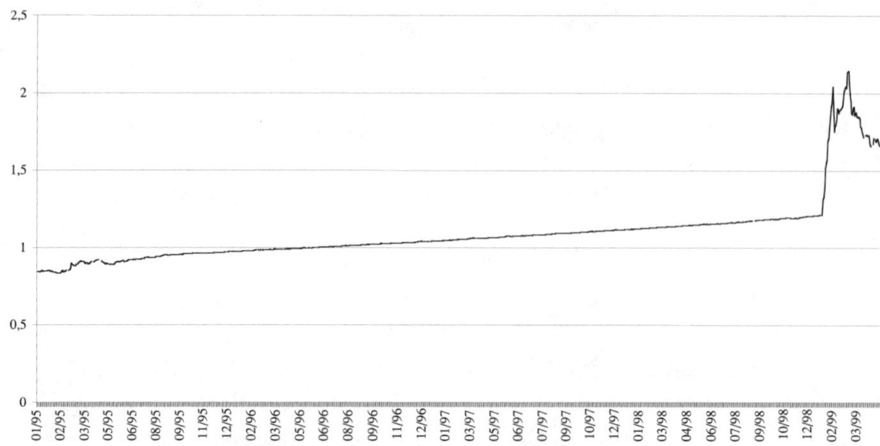

Fig. 9.1. Brazilian exchange rate

The crisis was triggered by foreign investors that were exposed to Russian risk and suffered major losses from both the restructuring of the Russian debt or/and the devaluation of the ruble. The effect on the exchange market in Brazil was extreme. In August and September alone, the excess demand for dollars in the foreign exchange market was 11.8 and 18.9 billion dollars, respectively. This obviously implied a huge loss of reserves during these months and the following one (see fig. 9.3).

Analyzing the composition of flows at that time is interesting. Table 9.2 and figure 9.4 show that the crisis hit net portfolio flows and debt securities very hard, whose fall deepened immediately after the Russian crisis and only recovered in late 1999. In contrast, the share of net direct investment increased

TABLE 9.1. Major Macroeconomic Indicators

	1995	1996	1997	1998	1999	2000
Current account deficit (%)	2.55	2.98	3.85	4.34	4.39	3.50
Non-FDI external* requirements (U.S.$)	12.50	12.80	13.80	7.70	−5.60	−4.00
GDP	4.22	2.66	3.60	0.20	0.90	4.00
Primary fiscal deficit (%)	−0.35	0.09	1.00	−0.02	−3.13	−3.20
Nominal fiscal deficit (GDP)	7.05	5.87	6.67	8.65	10.01	4.50
CPI	22.41	9.56	5.22	1.66	8.94	6.80
Unemployment	4.64	5.42	5.66	7.60	7.55	7.00
Real interest (accumulated)	25.50	16.80	19.60	25.80	15.80	10.50
Nominal interest (accumulated)	53.08	27.41	24.78	28.92	25.54	18.00

*Current account deficit minus FDI.

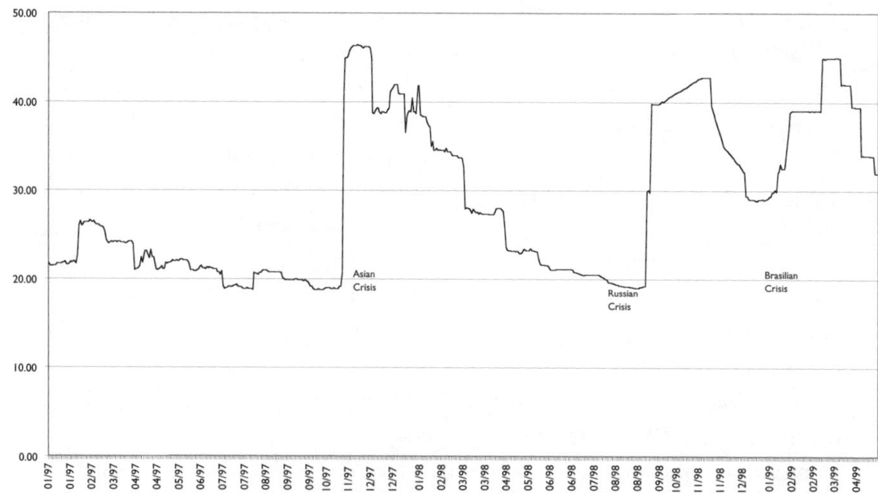

Fig. 9.2. Brazilian interest rates. (Data from author's calculations, Central Bank of Brazil, ECLAC, and Instituto Brasileiro de Geografia e Estatistica.)

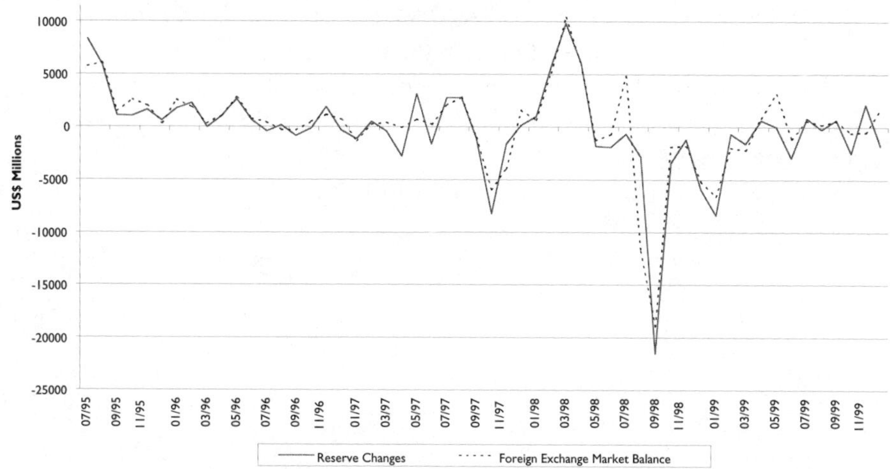

Fig. 9.3. Foreign exchange market and reserve movements. (Data from Central Bank of Brazil.)

steadily, surpassing $20 billion in 1998 and $25 billion in 1999. This would suggest that the crisis was driven (or at least validated) by outflows of equity and debt securities that are more volatile and react strongly during crisis, at least compared to direct investment flows. This gives support to the notion that policymakers should use caution when the economy's external accounts are financed by more volatile flows (this call for caution often includes support for capital controls in order to put some "sand on the wheels" and reduce the swiftness of these flows).

The effect of fast outflows can be observed on the movement of reserves and spreads on Brady bonds in figures 9.5 and 9.6. It is important to remember that in pegged regimes (or crawling pegs) the appropriate variables to infer pressure are indeed either reserve movements or interest rate levels. The latter are better used when looking at nonpolicy interest rates, which are more market determined and less influenced by the short-term objectives of policymakers.

With daily data, one can check the alternative hypothesis that it was the liquidity crisis in mature markets that timed the crisis in Brazil and not the Russian crisis. The Long-Term Capital Management (LTCM) crisis deepened in September 1998 (the rescue plan was announced on the twenty-third of the month) while the Russian default occurred a month earlier, on August 17. Figures 9.5 and 9.7 reveal that most of the action occurred immediately after the Russian crisis both in the foreign exchange market and the Brady bond market, although the spreads in the latter market suffered a new blow during the LTCM crisis, especially the shorter maturity Brazilian bond. Rather than concluding in favor of the LTCM effect on this market, the fact that the reaction occurred a couple of weeks before the LTCM crisis is revealed and the withdrawals lead us to favor instead the argument that Brazilian residents reinforced the speculation once they realized that the speculation now included foreign and institutional investors as well.

Other Brazilian financial variables reflect the Russian crisis with different

TABLE 9.2. Capital Flows

	1991	1992	1993	1994	1995	1996	1997	1998	1999
Net direct investment	−408	1,268	−481	852	2,376	9,519	15,364	22,988	25,946
FDI	505	1,156	397	117	5,475	10,349	17,086	26,134	27,109
Reinvestment	365	175	100	83	384	531	151	124	
NBI	−913	112	−878	−1,065	−1,560	77	−1,569	−3,212	−1,163
Net portfolio securities	578	1,704	6,651	7,280	2,294	6,040	5,300	−1,861	1,529
Debt securities	2,368	5,761	5,866	3,713	3,113	12,727	19,771	28,968	−7,982
Short-term capital and others	−7,406	−2,844	−4,432	−3,825	21,523	4,856	−15,517	−30,032	
Total	−4,868	5,889	7,604	8,020	29,306	33,142	24,918	20,063	
Reserve changes	−567	14,348	8,457	6,595	13,034	8,270	−7,937	−7,616	−8,214
Current account deficit	1,407	6,144	592	1,688	17,972	23,136	30,916	33,611	24,378

Source: Central Bank of Brazil.

Note: FDI and NBI stand for foreign and Brazilian direct investment, respectively. Portfolio investment is comprised of investment in equity securities and funds. Debt securities include medium- and long-term loans and financing. Short-term capital and others equals the International Financial Statistics "financial account" minus the sum of direct investment, equity securities, and debt securities.

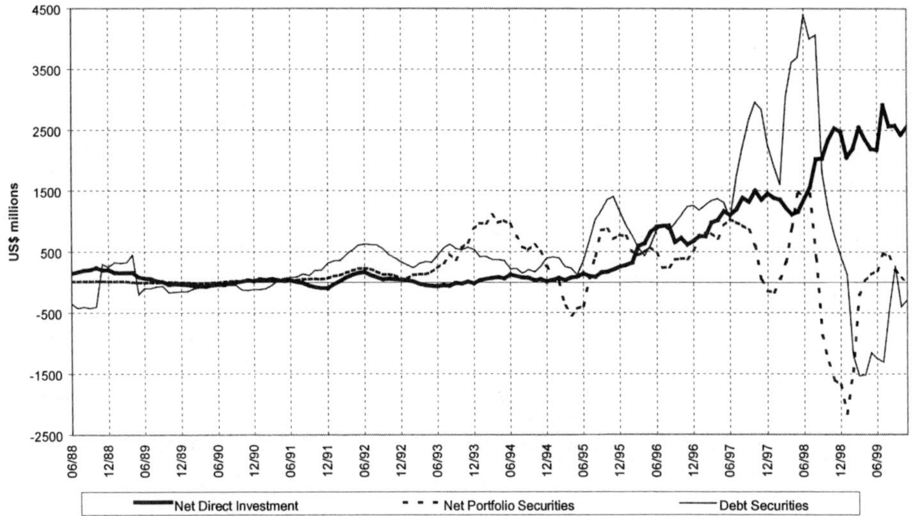

Fig. 9.4. Composition of capital flows (six-month moving average). (Data from Central Bank of Brazil.)

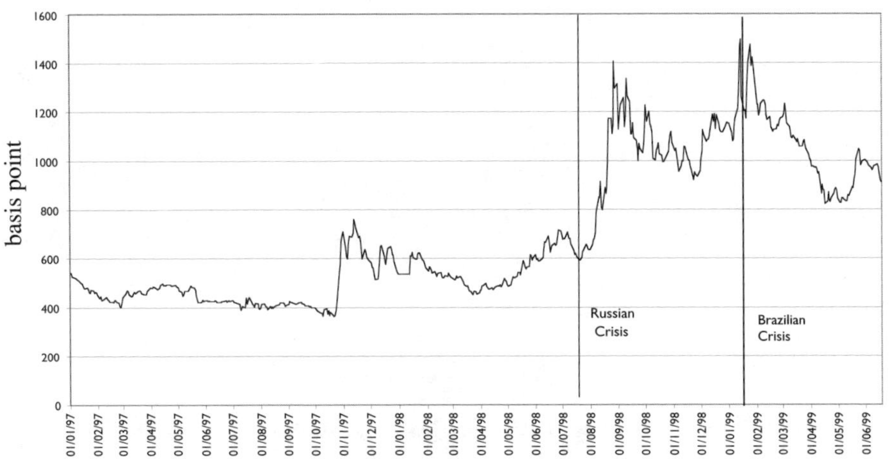

Fig. 9.5. Spreads (C-Bonds)

lags. The floating of the exchange rate occurred only in January 1999, five months after the Russian crisis. In the beginning, interest rate policy (the overnight rate on federal funds—Special Settlement and Custody System [SELIC]) was raised to levels close to the ones reached during the Asian crisis, but this time speculation forced the change in the exchange regime.

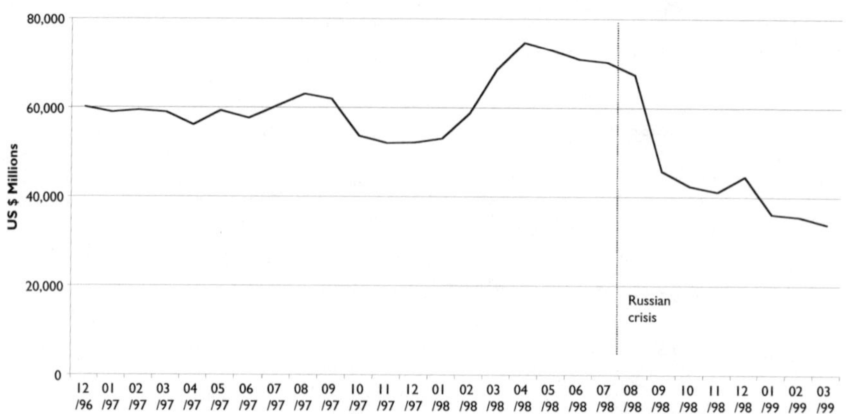

Fig. 9.6. Brazilian international reserves (U.S.$ millions).

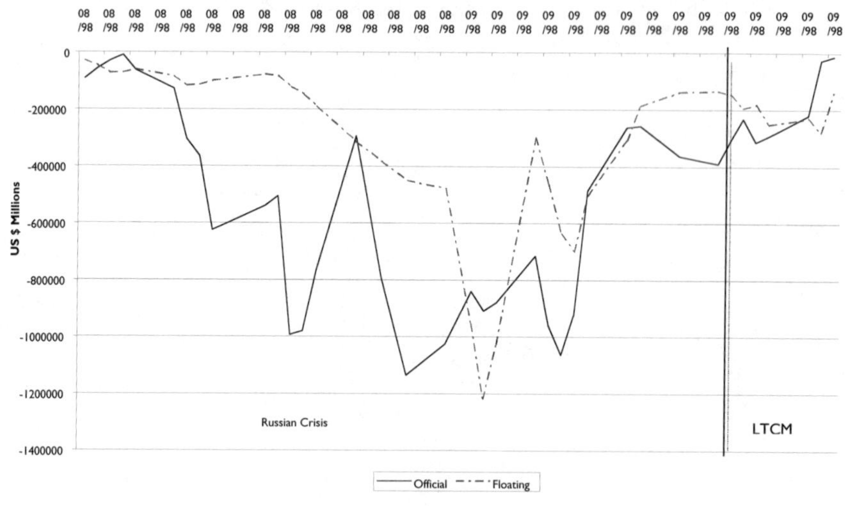

Fig. 9.7. Brazilian foreign exchange. (Data from Central Bank of Brazil.)

In sum, in this section I argued that Brazil was vulnerable to a crisis given its fiscal policy and overvalued exchange rate. The timing of the crisis was dictated by an external event, the Russian crisis, and triggered by large withdrawals of portfolio and debt securities assets by both domestic and foreign investors. The next section concentrates on the players involved as they tried to disentangle the relative roles of foreign, domestic, and institutional investors.

2. THE ROLES OF DOMESTIC, FOREIGN, AND INSTITUTIONAL INVESTORS IN THE BRAZILIAN CRISIS

Different agents have played different roles in other crises in the past. During the debt crisis of the 1980s, it is well known that the crisis predominantly involved traditional bank loans. Bank overborrowing and overlending were at the heart of the crisis. In contrast, in the more recent Mexican and peso crises, institutional investors had a predominant role. Here I investigate the players involved in the withdrawals of funds from Brazil during the crisis.

Table 9.3 is an attempt to disentangle the roles of domestic, foreign, and institutional investors in the various phases of the Brazilian crisis. One can observe large withdrawals from Brazil by all the agents involved, in particular after the Russian crisis and up to the Brazilian crisis, in the first quarter of 1999. The magnitudes are overwhelming. Institutional investors withdrew U.S.$13.1 billion, banks withdrew U.S.$10.9 billion, and Brazilian investors withdrew U.S.$7.0 billion. In addition, large withdrawals in the amount of U.S.$16 billion from the so-called CC5 accounts (accounts for non-resident individuals and corporate activities denominated in Brazilian reals) were observed during the same period.[3] Therefore, in the case of Brazil one cannot assert that a particular investor group had a predominant role in the crisis. If anything, Brazilians were responsible for a large share of the withdrawals, if one includes the CC5 accounts.

In table 9.3, one can observe the relative behavior of the players in the last few years. It is clear that institutional investors (and also foreign banks)

TABLE 9.3. Net Inflows to Brazil by Type of Investor (U.S.$ millions)

Period	Institutional Investors[a]	Brazilians[b]	Banks[c]	Companies	Other Foreign[d]	CC5 Operations[e]
Annual average, 1996–99	2,752	−2,598	−2,177	2,645	10,381	−17,356
Asian crisis	−1,725	−1,192	−271	1,616	−1,226	−12,445
Russian crisis	−10,601	−4,965	−6,889	815	5,502	−12,580
Brazilian crisis	−2,567	−2,025	−3,999	1,617	−6,398	−4,315
Dec 1998	−1,008	−175	−1,665	1,130	−629	−1,774
Jan 1999	−1,606	−1,367	−1,916	307	−706	−2,019
Feb 1999	47	77	−417	180	−5,062	−522
1999	1,522	−1,951	−1,990	1,398	1,520	−10,373

Source: Central Bank of Brazil.

Note: Asian crisis from August 1997 to December 1997; Russian crisis from August 1998 to October 1998; Brazilian crisis from December 1998 to February 1999.

[a]Portfolio investment.

[b]Portfolio investment plus medium- and long-term flows.

[c]Net medium- and long-term loans to banks and credit lines (short term).

[d]Includes medium- and long-term bonds, commercial papers, notes, securitization, and others.

[e]Operations with nonresident accounts.

exhibited very atypical behavior during the Russian crisis. It is interesting to compare this with what occurred after the Asian crisis. During that period, the speculation against the currency was concentrated in the CC5 accounts. The withdrawals by both institutional investors and foreign banks were rather modest, especially compared to the effects of the Russian crisis. This raises the hypothesis that while foreign investors (both banks and institutional investors) had long been in Brazil the speculation against the currency was not overwhelming and Brazilian policymakers could sustain withdrawals by Brazilian investors running from fear of devaluation. Once the position of foreign investors changed, the balance of forces was altered and the currency peg could no longer be sustained (although there were five months between the Russian crisis and the Brazilian devaluation).

Further information may be obtained from movements in the dual foreign exchange market. At the time of the crisis, the central bank was setting an adjustable band for the dollar value of the real and maintaining a continuing crawling peg within it. There were two foreign exchange markets, the "official" and the floating market. Their difference was in the type of transaction allowed. In the official market, mostly proceeds of exports and imports of goods and services were allowed but also a few capital account transactions. One important example is most of the portfolio investment by foreign investors, which was channeled either through two classes of fixed-income funds or through one of the five alternatives established under National Monetary Council Resolution 1289. In the floating market, most of the rest of the capital account transactions were transacted, in particular those made by Brazilian residents. The Brazilian government would keep the exchange rates on both markets aligned and would not allow big differences between them.

It is clear from table 9.4 that the extent of withdrawals in the official mar-

TABLE 9.4. Brazilian Foreign Exchange Market (U.S.$ millions)

		Floating Market Rate	Official Rate	Exchange Rate	Foreign Reserves Changes
Average, Jul 95–Jul 98		−1,322	2,670	1,348	992
Average, Aug 98–Dec 98		−3,601	−4,327	−7,928	−6,996
Average, Jul 95–Nov 99		−1,593	1,324	48	−198
Asian crisis	Sep 97	−1,651	613	−1,038	−1,125
	Oct 97	−4,912	−1,039	−5,951	−8,241
	Nov 97	−3,700	−292	−3,992	−1,655
Russian crisis	Jul 98	−1,839	6,693	4,855	−688
	Aug 98	−2,821	−8,989	−11,810	−2,877
	Sep 98	−8,578	−10,348	−18,926	−21,522
	Oct 98	−2,867	971	−1,896	−3,426

Source: Central Bank of Brazil.

ket during the Russian crisis was severe, reflecting withdrawals by foreign investors. This is in contrast to their behavior throughout the Asian crisis, when the withdrawals were about average for this market. On the other hand, the floating markets had already shown large withdrawals during the Asian crisis but were reversed a few months later. During the Russian crisis, the large withdrawals did not reverse and were fueled by fears of parallel withdrawals in the official markets. Therefore, the information obtained from the two separate exchange markets would suggest that in fact the withdrawals by foreign investors made the difference in terms of the effect of the Russian crisis relative to the Asian crisis. This contributes to the hypothesis that the contagion from Russia was triggered by foreign investors who were in panic during the Russian crisis. The floating market investors, including Brazilian residents, had jumped ship during the Asian crisis and repeated the pattern during the Russian crisis, which of course contributed to the pressure in the exchange markets.

Therefore, I am confirming in this section that, although the Brazilian economy was vulnerable to shocks and Brazilian investors were always prone to withdraw their funds from their country, the timing of the crisis was dictated by the Russian crisis and the withdrawals of foreign lenders and investors, in particular institutional investors.

2.1. THE ROLE OF INTERNATIONAL BANKS IN THE CRISIS

Throughout the crisis, foreign actors reduced their exposure to Brazil as maturing obligations came due. Tracking this process may give us information regarding the players involved in the crisis. The Central Bank of Brazil follows the maturing short-term external liabilities of its banking system on a weekly basis. The short-term obligations include interbank and credit lines. This survey-based monitoring system was introduced in October 1998, after the Russian crisis and during the negotiations with the IMF.

Table 9.5 shows the cumulative reduction in short-term exposure to Brazilian banks by nationality. Over the sample period, the rolled over portion was $4 billion out of the total $6.6 billion that was maturing, amounting to a rollover rate of around 62 percent. U.S. banks reduced their exposure by $931 million, with a rollover rate of 60 percent. Within the United States, the reduction in exposure was concentrated but widespread. Almost one-half of the reduction came from two banks, and 10 banks accounted for 84 percent of the total decline. As expected, many regional banks reduced their exposure.

The rollover rate for U.S. banks was well below the rollover rates of Germany (79 percent) and the United Kingdom (77 percent), although it was roughly in line with that of Japan (58 percent), France (54 percent), and Italy

TABLE 9.5. Changes in the Exposure of Short-Term Loans (interbank and trade) to Brazil (millions of U.S.$)

	Maturing	$ Rolled Over	Rollover Rate
United States	2,352	1,421	0.60
Canada	168	74	0.44
France	947	516	0.54
Germany	1,060	835	0.79
Italy	215	129	0.60
Japan	715	416	0.58
Netherlands	222	69	0.31
Portugal	97	90	0.93
Spain	350	145	0.41
United Kingdom	505	389	0.77
Total	6,630	4,082	0.62

Source: BIS.
Note: From October to December 1998.

(60 percent). This is interesting because it bears on our fundamental question regarding the contagion from Russia to Brazil and the hypothesis that liquidity needs and withdrawals were one of the channels of contagion. German banks had a larger exposure to Russia, were badly affected by the Russian crisis, and had the largest maturing amount of debt after the United States. Their rollover rate, however, does not reflect a compensatory liquidation of assets since it is far above average.

The fact that the data do not support a common lender channel through Germany does not contradict our previous finding that foreign investors triggered the Brazilian crisis. The common lender is just one of several possible channels of contagion. It could well be the case that foreign investors adjusted their probability of Brazilian default once they observed the Russian crisis (e.g., because of a default under an IMF program), or the Russian crisis could have triggered pure herding behavior by foreign investors.

The frequency of the data also allows us to follow the timing of the reduction of exposure, although with a lag, given that the first data are from the third week of October. Figures 9.8 and 9.9 show the net outflows per week and the rollover rate over time. The weekly changes in exposure have been volatile, with a particularly sharp deterioration in October and over the final two weeks of the year, which was end-of-year window dressing. The high rollover weeks occurred in April, after the Brazilian agreement with international banks to maintain short-term lines. For the 11-week monitoring period ending January 1, 1999, the aggregate rollover rate was 72 percent. The weekly observations, however, have been volatile, ranging from 50 to 90 percent. It is also interesting to note that the international banks have not increased their exposure to

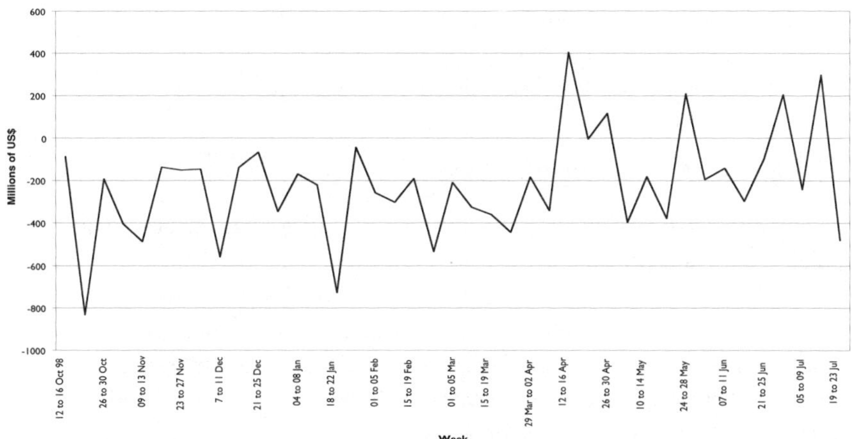

Fig. 9.8. Brazilian weekly short-term bank loans (short-term interbank and trade credit lines). (Data from Central Bank of Brazil.)

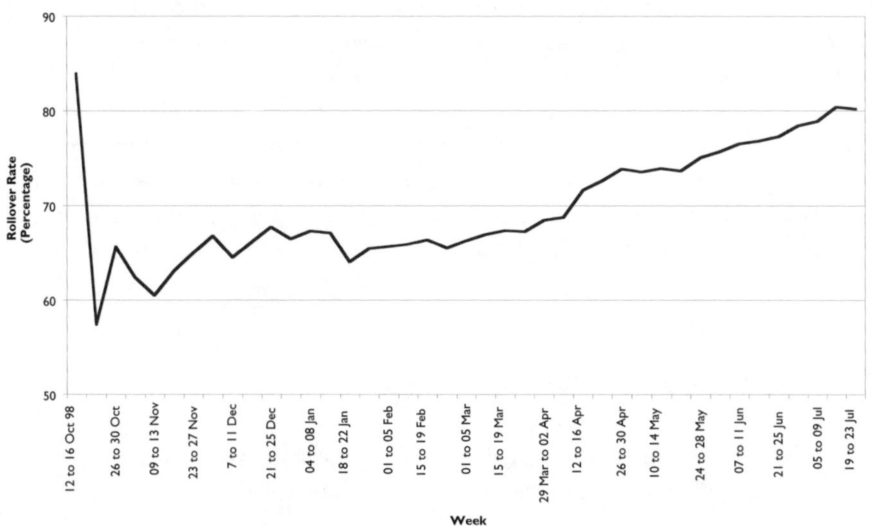

Fig. 9.9. Brazilian crisis and short-term rollover rates (accumulated rate). (Data from Central Bank of Brazil.)

the levels experienced before the Russian crisis. This is in part due to lack of demand for short-term borrowing by Brazilian banks after the floating of the exchange rate and the associated higher exchange rate risk.

2.2. BIS DATA AND OVERALL BANK EXPOSURE

The weekly monitoring by the Central Bank of Brazil has the advantage of a higher frequency, but the coverage is not universal and only short-term assets are included. In contrast, the reporting banks of the Bank of International Settlements (BIS) is only published twice a year but has a broader coverage. Table 9.6 and figure 9.10 show the overall exposure of reporting banks on Brazil and other emerging markets. The exposure in Brazil decreased by around $10 billion from the first semester of 1998 to the first semester of 1999, while the exposure in Russia decreased by almost $15 billion in the same period.

It is interesting to note the similar path for the banks' exposure to Russia and Brazil, in contrast to the rest of Latin America, in particular Mexico and Argentina. The reduction of the exposure to Asia diminished about a year earlier. The different paths for the exposure on Brazil and the rest of Latin America provide support for the fact that the contagion from the Russian crisis was not generalized, as it would be if it had been driven only by liquidity needs.

In this section, I analyzed in more detail the behavior of foreign investors. All the players reduced their exposure to Brazil after the Russian crisis. I concluded that, although there was contagion from Russia (more formal tests are described in section 5), the channel was probably not through a common lender. In the next section, I continue the analysis of the Brazilian crisis, focusing on its aftermath.

3. THE AFTERMATH OF THE CRISIS, 1999

Brazil's macroeconomic performance during the crisis year was better than expected. Inflation did not explode, GDP did not collapse, the government

TABLE 9.6. BIS Banks Holding (U.S.$) in Emerging Markets Data (U.S.$ billions)

	Brazil	Mexico	Russia	Argentina
97.1	71,862	62,161	69,081	44,844
97.2	76,292	61,794	72,173	60,413
98.1	84,585	62,892	75,853	60,222
98.2	73,313	64,962	58,594	61,517
99.1	62,310	63,776	55,424	66,683

Source: BIS.

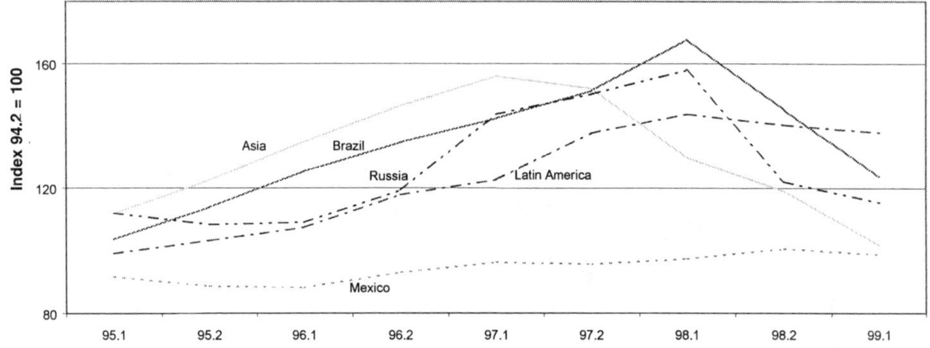

Fig. 9.10. Bank holdings in emerging markets. (Data from BIS.)

was not forced to restructure its public debt, and, slowly, both nominal and real interest rates have been going down (see table 9.1). This performance is partly due to the fact that the private sector was largely hedged at the moment of the crisis and was insulated from the immediate effects of the devaluation. In fact, the government carried most of the costs of the devaluation by having its public debt increased by around 10 percent of GDP. Since debts eventually have to be paid, or at least not allowed to explode, the better than expected performance has to be judged against the feasibility of generating current and future fiscal surpluses in a country where sustained growth is long overdue and fiscal consolidation is a novelty.

Brazil's better than expected macroeconomic performance had been achieved partly because of a more responsible fiscal policy. In the past, Brazil has inflated its way out of fiscal inconsistencies, using inflation as the means of financing deficits that otherwise could not be financed. The consequences of this are clear, for inflation reached more than 1,000 percent, growth stalled, and income distribution deteriorated substantially. This time Brazil had met the IMF-agreed target.

In contrast to the generalized expectation, inflation was extremely moderate in both 1999 (8.4 percent) and 2000 (5.5 percent), notwithstanding the large nominal depreciation that followed the floating of the exchange rate. Of course, exchange rate depreciation has a greater effect on wholesale prices, but even the general price index (IGP) did not exceed 20 percent in 1999. The reasons for such a low pass through of the exchange rate depreciation to inflation are related to: (1) a depressed level of demand after the crisis, which discouraged the pass through; (2) a previous overvaluation of the exchange rate, which was corrected by the nominal devaluation; and (3) low initial inflation at the end of 1998 (see Goldfajn and Werlang 2000).

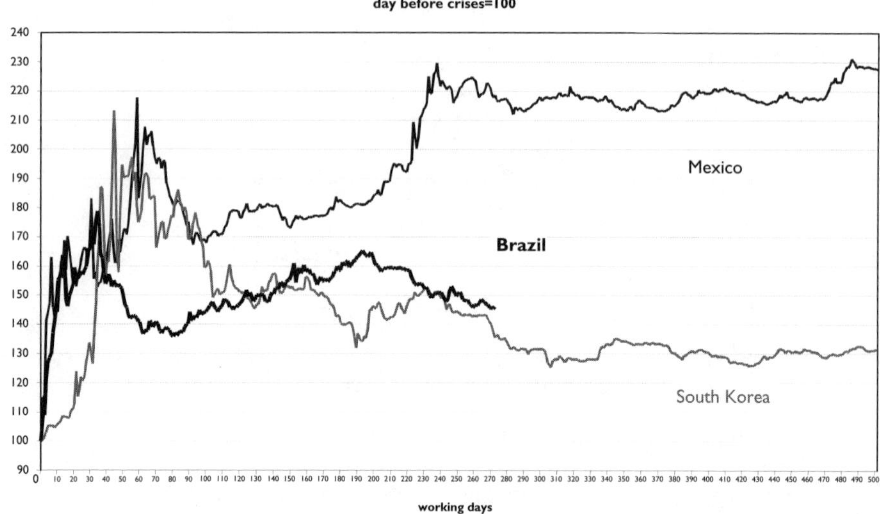

Fig. 9.11. Nominal exchange rate–selected (day before crisis = 100). (Data from Central Bank of Brazil.)

The combination of very large nominal depreciation (60 percent) and moderate inflation led to an impressive 50 percent real exchange rate depreciation (see fig. 9.11).

4. CAPITAL FLOWS TO BRAZIL IN THE 1990S: ECONOMETRIC ANALYSIS

I will now investigate the determinants of capital flows to Brazil. The ordinary least squares (OLS) regression controlling for heteroskedasticity and serial correlation is

$$nf = \frac{NF}{GDP} = \beta_0 + \beta_1(i - Ee) + \beta_2 i^* + \beta X + \varepsilon,$$

where nf, i, i^*, and Ee are the net capital flows as a percentage of GDP, the domestic interest rate, the foreign interest rate, and expected devaluation, respectively, and X is a group of variables that includes domestic variables such as inflation, government spending, the real exchange rate, and a series of dummies for the Real Plan, the Tequila effect, the Asian crisis, the Brazilian crisis, and the Russian crisis. The data are in monthly frequency (see the appendix for formal definitions of the variables). The results are summarized in tables 9.7 and 9.8.

As predicted by theory, the coefficient of the international interest rate is negative and significant. This result is consistent with evidence for Latin America provided in Calvo, Leiderman, and Reinhart 1993 and with evidence for developing countries in Fernández-Arias and Montiel 1995. The result is robust across specifications and in using either returns on U.S. Treasury bills or yields on 10-year Treasury bonds. The coefficient of the domestic interest rate adjusted for expected depreciation and the coefficients of other domestic factors do not help explain capital flows to Brazil. I interpret the results as evidence in favor of *push* as opposed to *pull* effects in explaining the surge in capital flows in the 1990s.

This result does not contradict our previous assertion that Brazil was vulnerable to a crisis and that the timing of the crisis was dictated by sudden large withdrawals of capital. The determinants of capital flows to Brazil in the long run are dominated by push effects (foreign interest rates), but the composition

TABLE 9.7. Dependent Variable: Ratio of Monthly Total Net Private Capital Flows to GDP, January 1988–November 1999

Constant	4.78	4.95	5.28
	(5.05)	(5.14)	(2.69)
i^*	−0.64	−0.68	−0.79
	−(4.60)	−(4.68)	−(3.13)
$i - Ee$	−0.01	−0.13	0.02
	−(0.62)	−(0.64)	(0.50)
Tequila dummy	−5.65	−5.96	−6.07
	−(5.60)	−(5.43)	−(5.33)
Real Plan dummy	2.47	2.78	2.49
	(2.98)	(2.99)	(2.46)
Asian dummy	2.73	2.41	2.42
	(2.99)	(2.42)	(2.42)
Russian dummy	—	−4.60	−4.86
		−(1.63)	−(1.54)
Brazilian dummy	—	−0.56	−0.09
		−(0.47)	−(0.06)
Inflation rate	—	—	0.01
			(0.28)
Ratio of government spending to GDP	—	—	2.38
			(0.24)
Real exchange rate (deviation from equilibrium rate)	—	—	−2.48
			−(0.55)
Adjusted R^2	0.24	0.26	0.25

Source: See the appendix at the end of this chapter.
Note: t-statistics in parentheses.

of the flows was determined by weak Brazilian fundamentals. In fact, the composition of capital flows was concentrated on short-term portfolio flows that are prone to sudden spikes in capital flows. A better macroeconomic environment would imply a larger proportion of foreign direct investment (FDI) in the overall capital flows (fig. 9.3 confirms that this has been the case since 1999).

The dummies for the Tequila and Real Plans are strong and significant. The Russian crisis has a strong negative coefficient, but it is not statistically significant. This lack of significance is a bit surprising, since in sections 1 and 2, in the higher frequency data, we observed a large withdrawal of capital during the Russian crisis. However, from a longer term perspective the Russian crisis did not in fact change the flows to the Brazilian economy. Capital inflows recovered, and there was an important change in the composition of capital flows to Brazil, with net foreign investment replacing other components of flows and partially dampening the effect of the Russian crisis.[4]

It is interesting to observe that in the period 1995–99, in table 9.8, the coefficient on international interest rates loses its significance. This suggests that the push effects have a long-run effect, affecting capital flows only after large changes in international interest rates are factored in.

TABLE 9.8. Dependent Variable: Ratio of Monthly Total Net Private Capital Flows to GDP, January 1995–November 1999

Constant	24.83	42.75
	(1.20)	(2.23)
i^*	−3.87	−7.04
	−(0.99)	−(1.86)
$i - Ee$	−0.62	−0.42
	−(3.19)	−(0.94)
Asian dummy	1.77	1.11
	(1.25)	(0.87)
Russian dummy	−6.50	−8.00
	−(1.29)	−(1.67)
Brazilian dummy	−2.83	3.03
	−(1.07)	(0.40)
Inflation rate	—	−0.27
		−(0.36)
Ratio of government spending to GDP	—	−26.38
		−(1.05)
Real exchange rate (deviation from equilibrium rate)	—	−26.29
		−(0.87)
Adjusted R^2	0.05	0.09

Source: See the appendix at the end of this chapter.
Note: t-statistics in parentheses.

5. TESTING CONTAGION

In the previous sections, I argued that the timing of the Brazilian crisis was a consequence of the contagion from Russia, but I had not offered formal tests of this proposition. This section fills this gap using primarily the sovereign spreads. Analyzing the currency market is not very useful, as for most of the sample period both the Brazilian real and the Russian ruble were fixed to the dollar. The currencies move about relatively freely only after January 1999 (when the real peg unraveled), but that period leaves out many important phases of the crisis.

In order to understand the transmission of shocks from Russia to Brazil, I carried out a series of tests. I begin by looking at rolling correlations (at three-month intervals) between the relevant variables. I use Granger causality tests and reduced form (VARs) to examine the direction of shocks between Russia and Brazil.

I then define crisis and tranquil periods and test for significant changes in correlations between the two periods. I apply the Forbes and Rigobon (1999)[5] methodology to adjust the crisis period correlations for sudden increases in variance (see appendix). The motivation for this approach is to control for the correlation bias associated with higher variances, that is, in the standard correlation formula, higher variances lead to higher correlations. Once the adjustment is performed, crisis period correlations can be tested for significant increases without the potential for this bias. I use the Forbes and Rigobon test with caution, as I am not sure a study of contagion ought to control for the increased variances that are an integral part of any crisis scenario. It could very well be that the factors behind the increased variances (thin markets, panic, institutional failures, and so on) are precisely what make up contagion, and controlling for these factors makes the test for contagion moot.

During the tranquil period, sovereign spreads correlations are substantially larger than what we saw in the stock market case. Using 106 observations from January to May 1997, the correlation was found to be 0.35. The spreads of both the bonds under discussion shot up even further in the crisis period. The correlation of the spreads also jumped and remained at very high levels till late 1998. The direction of the shock goes both ways, as at various periods the two markets appear to be Granger causing each-other.[6]

Impulse response function from the VARs show large and persistent shocks transmitting from both countries during the crisis period. The adjusted correlations for the spreads show significantly higher correlation during the crisis period subsamples compared to the tranquil period. All but two subsamples in the crisis period had significantly higher adjusted correlations.

This confirms the findings from previous work (Baig and Goldfajn 1998) that the correlations in the Brady markets are very high and increase significantly (even after the adjustment) during the crisis. This gives support to the fact that if there was contagion from Russia to Brazil the most likely location of the transmission was the offshore Brady markets.

6. CONCLUSIONS

The chapter has reached a few conclusions that are worth summarizing here. First, I argued that Brazil was vulnerable to a crisis given its fiscal policy and overvalued exchange rate. The timing of the crisis was determined by an external event, the Russian crisis, and triggered by large withdrawals of portfolio flows. In the case of Brazil, one cannot assert that a particular investor group had a predominant role in the crisis. If anything, the data suggest that, while foreign investors (both banks and institutional investors) had long been in Brazil, speculation by residents against the currency was not overwhelming and Brazilian policymakers could sustain withdrawals from Brazilian investors running from fear of devaluation. Once the position of foreign investors changed, the balance of forces was altered and the currency peg could no longer be sustained.

Second, using weekly data on foreign banks' exposure to Brazil from the Central Bank of Brazil, I checked the hypothesis that liquidity needs and withdrawals were one of the reasons that determined the timing of the Brazilian crisis. It was observed that German banks (which were known to have had a large exposure to Russia and to have been badly affected by the Russian crisis) had one of the highest rollover rates within the Group of Seven (G7) nations and therefore the data do not seem to reflect a common lender channel through Germany. This does not contradict the previous finding that foreign investors triggered the Brazilian crisis. The common lender is just one of several possible channels of contagion. It could well be the case that foreign investors adjusted their probability of Brazilian default once they observed the Russian crisis (e.g., because of a default under an IMF program) or the Russian crisis could have triggered pure herding behavior by foreign investors.

Third, using daily data on several financial variables from Bloomberg, one can check the alternative hypothesis that it was the liquidity crisis in mature markets, and not the Russian crisis, that timed the crisis in Brazil. However, most of the action occurred immediately after the Russian crisis both in the foreign exchange and the Brady bond markets, although the spreads in the latter market suffered a new blow during the LTCM crisis. Therefore, rather than concluding in favor of an LTCM effect on this market, this leads me to favor instead the argument that Brazilian residents reinforced the speculation once they realized that it now included foreign investors.

Fourth, Brazil's macroeconomic performance during the crisis year was better than expected. Inflation did not explode, GDP did not collapse, the government was not forced to restructure its public debt, and, slowly, both nominal and real interest rates have been falling. This performance is partly due to the fact that the private sector was largely hedged at the moment of the crisis and was insulated from the immediate effects of the devaluation. In addition, the reasons for such a low pass through of the exchange rate depreciation to inflation are related to: (1) a depressed level of demand after the crisis, which discouraged the pass through; (2) a previous overvaluation of the exchange rate, which was corrected by the nominal devaluation; and (3) low initial inflation at the end of 1998.

Fifth, the econometric exercise on capital flows suggests that there is evidence in favor of *push* as opposed to *pull* effects in explaining the surge of capital flows. However, the push effects have a longer run effect, affecting capital flows only once large changes in international interest rates are factored in. This result does not contradict the assertion that Brazil was vulnerable to a crisis and that the timing of the crisis was determined by sudden large withdrawals of capital. The determinants of capital flows to Brazil in the long run are dominated by pull effects (foreign interest rates) and the composition of flows were determined by weak Brazilian fundamentals.

Finally, the econometric test of contagion from Russia shows that the comovement between the variables is remarkable, especially with regard to the spreads on Brady bonds. This confirms the findings from previous work (Baig and Goldfajn 1998) that the correlations in the Brady markets are very high and increase significantly (even after adjusting for the bias) during the crisis. This gives support to the fact that if there was contagion from Russia to Brazil the most likely site of transmission was the offshore Brady markets.

APPENDIX 1: DATA USED IN THE CHAPTER

- For the Brazilian stock market, I take daily closing figures from the Bovespa index and convert them to U.S. dollars by the end-of-day exchange rate. For Russia, I do the same, using the Moscow index. Converting the indices in dollars allows me to keep the analysis uniform before and after the devaluation of the currencies. Source: Bloomberg.
- For sovereign bonds, we use the spreads on the Brazilian C-Bond and the Russian Eurobond. The spreads were calculated by subtracting the yield to maturity of treasury bills with same duration from yield to

maturity of the respective bonds: the Brazilian C-Bond, maturity April 15, 2014; coupon, 8 percent variable, six months; Russian Eurobond, maturity November 2001; and coupon, 9.25 percent fixed, six months. Source: Bloomberg.

- Financial flows are the balance of the foreign exchange transactions in the financial markets. Ultimately, the government would have to balance the market balance in order to keep the exchange rate crawling peg. However, the changes in reserves do not necessarily track down the exact financial exchange flows because some of the transactions are settled with a lag period (30 days or so). Source: Central Bank of Brazil.
- The Central Bank of Brazil follows the maturing short-term external liabilities of its banking system on a weekly basis. The short-term obligations include interbank and credit lines. This survey-based monitoring system was introduced in October 1998, after the Russian crisis and during the negotiations with the IMF.
- BIS exposure data were obtained from its semiannual reports.
- Daily interest rates and exchange rates are from Bloomberg.
- News dummies were created using news obtained from Bloomberg.

MONTHLY DATABASE USED IN THE ECONOMETRIC EXERCISE ON CAPITAL FLOWS

- International interest rates: U.S. three-month Treasury bill rates from the Federal Reserve Bank of Saint Louis.
- Domestic interest rates in dollars: short-term rates on public debt Treasury bills from the Central Bank of Brazil discounted by the expected devaluation implicit in dollar futures contracts (first day of the month) from Bolsa de Mercadorias e Futuros (BM&F).
- Government spending: federal government total expenditures, Central Bank of Brazil.
- Real exchange rate: deviations from equilibrium real exchange rates as calculated in Goldfajn and Valdés 1996.
- Inflation: changes in the general price index, Índice Geral de Preços (IGP-DI), Fundação Getúlio Vargas.
- Total net private flows: from the Central Bank of Brazil's monthly statistics on "capital movement." Monthly capital movement statistics do not include short-term capital flows and reinvested profits. See table 9.2 for the composition of total flows. Net direct investment corresponds to

row 1 in table 9.2, equity securities correspond to row 5, debt securities correspond to row 6, and total net private flows correspond to the sum of these three flows.

- Nominal monthly GDP: from the Central Bank of Brazil.

NOTES

This chapter is part of a United Nations Development Programme-Institute of Development Studies (UNDP-IDS) project. I would like to thank Jacques Cailloux, Ricardo Gottschalk, and Stephany Griffith-Jones for their comments and support; Rodrigo P. Guimaraes, Igor Bareboim, and Rafael Melo for excellent research assistance; and Daniel Gleizer for providing the weekly exposure data on banks. All remaining errors are my responsibility.

1. Another important factor that explains why the crisis in Brazil was milder than in other crisis countries is that the financial system had been strengthened in response to the Mexican crisis of 1994.
2. On the Real Plan, see Franco 1996 and Clements 1997.
3. These CC5 deposit accounts were created in the past to allow nonresidents to invest in Brazil. Their regulations are very lax, but they are subject to high taxes. In practice, they are owned predominantly by Brazilian residents disguised as residents of other countries. Foreign investment is mostly channeled through special fixed income and equity funds with lower tax incidence. Therefore, in the past few years there are only withdrawals from the stock of CC5 accounts.
4. The analysis and econometric regressions of the components of capital flows may be obtained directly from the author.
5. Details on their methodology can be found in a more complete version of this chapter, Goldfajn 1999. "The Swings in Capital Flows and the Brazilian Crisis." Mimeo, 1999.
6. Results of the Granger causality test can be found in ibid.

REFERENCES

Baig, T., and I. Goldfajn. 1998. "Financial markets contagion in the Asian crisis." *IMF Staff Papers* 46 (November): 167–95.

———. 1999. "The contagion from Russia to Brazil." Working Paper 420, Department of Economics, Pontificia Universidade Catolica (PUC), Rio de Janeiro.

Calvo, Guillermo, Leonardo Leiderman, and Carmen Reinhart. 1993. "Capital inflows to Latin America: The role of external factors." *IMF Staff Papers* 40 (March): 108–51.

Cardoso, Eliana. 1997. "Brazil's macroeconomic policies and capital flows in the 1990s. "In *WIDER Project on capital flows in the 1990s,* edited by S. Griffith-Jones, M. Montes, and A. Nasution.

Clements, Benedict. 1997. "The Real Plan, poverty, and income distribution in Brazil." *Finance and Development* 34, no. 3 (September): 44–46.

Fernández-Arias, Eduardo, and Peter Montiel. 1995. "The surge in capital inflows to developing countries." Policy Research Working Paper 1473, World Bank, Washington, DC.

Forbes, Kristin, and Roberto Rigobon. 1998. "Measuring stock market contagion: Conceptual issues and empirical tests." Mimeo, Massachusetts Institute of Technology, April.

Franco, G. B. F. 1996. "The Real Plan." Essays in International Finance 217, International Finance Section, Princeton University.

Goldfajn, Ilan, and Rodrigo Valdés. 1996. "The aftermath of appreciations." *Quarterly Journal of Economics* (March).

Goldfajn, Ilan, and Sergio Werlang. 2000. "The passthrough from depreciation to inflation: A panel study." Mimeo: Rio de Janeiro, Brazil.

CHAPTER 10

The Financial Crises of the Late 1990s: Summary and Policy Lessons

Ricardo Gottschalk and Stephany Griffith-Jones

This chapter summarizes the main empirical insights of the book. It draws particularly from the six case studies presented, which cover the East Asian countries most affected by the 1997–98 East Asian financial crisis (Indonesia, Malaysia, South Korea, and Thailand) plus the Czech Republic and Brazil, with a focus primarily on the role of international players in each crisis episode. The policy implications for a new international financial architecture will be drawn in chapter 11.

The chapter begins by looking at the role of macroeconomic fundamentals in the crisis episodes. It shows that even with good macroeconomic fundamentals, countries are still subject to costly currency and financial crises.

However, it should be stressed that, although—as we shall see—macroeconomic fundamentals were broadly sound in East Asia, there were important structural and policy weaknesses in these countries, especially in the domestic financial sector and its regulation. As we discussed in chapter 1, recent work surveyed by Dooley (1996) and Wyplocz (2001) argues that the negative effects of liberalization (and implicitly of large surges and reversals of capital flows) occur mainly in countries with poor institutions such as the lack of proper bank regulation and "poor law and order." This could help explain why liberalization has been far less costly in developed than in developing countries (even though developed countries have had their share of crises) and strengthens the case for prudence in the timing of total liberalization until a proper economic and possibly political infrastructure has been built, which may take a long time. However, we feel that blaming different and numerous crises largely on somewhat unclear country features is somewhat problematic. Clearly, institutional limitations and imperfections must be addressed by the countries themselves, but simultaneously the international community needs to manage imperfections in international capital markets in order to make crises less likely, given that such imperfections seem to have been a major cause of recent crises.

The chapter then examines the magnitude and nature of capital flows in the six countries for which studies were carried out. It shows that most of the countries had accumulated large stocks of short-term debt just before the crises, which made them vulnerable to sudden capital flow reversibility. It then discusses different vulnerability indicators, including the indicator that is proposed in chapter 1, which takes account of the degree of reversibility of each type of capital flow.

Next the chapter looks at the role of players, showing which sort of player triggered and deepened the crisis in each country and the extent to which there were contagion effects across countries due to herding behavior among players. It also looks at two aspects that help to explain why the major players differed across countries: the capital account liberalization path pursued in each country and the regional links with different source countries.

The chapter concludes with a summary of the main effects of the crises in each country. It shows that in all countries the costs were very high, but that the speed of recovery differed among them, this being partly explained by their underlying structural differences and policy responses to the crises.

1. THE ROLE OF FUNDAMENTALS

The suddenness with which the East Asian crisis unfolded and the fact that it was largely unanticipated, on the one hand, and the soundness of most of the region's macrofundamentals, such as balanced government budgets, low inflation rates, and high savings rates in a context of continued growth (see table 10.1), on the other hand, seem to show that macroeconomic fundamentals were not the main cause of the East Asian crises.

However, it is true that external imbalances in some countries had been large for a long time. By the end of 1996, Thailand and Malaysia were exhibiting a current account deficit of considerable magnitude—8 and 6 percent of their GDP—but such deficits were just moderate in Indonesia, around 4 percent of GDP, and were even falling in South Korea.

TABLE 10.1. Basic Macroeconomic Indicators, 1996

	Fiscal Balance (% GDP)	Inflation (annual %)	Savings Rate (% GDP)	GDP Growth (%)	Current Account Balance (% GDP)
Indonesia	no data	8.0	31.5	7.8	−3.5
Malaysia	0.7	3.5	42.6	10.0	−6.1
South Korea	0.1	4.9	34.5	6.8	−4.4
Thailand	0.9	5.8	35.9	5.5	−8.0

Source: IMF, World Economic Outlook 2000; World Bank, World Development Indicators 2000 CD-Rom; Global Development Finance Country Tables 1999; country studies in the book (Chapters 4, 5, 6 and 7).

In East Asia, such external imbalances invariably were linked to private investment being in excess of private savings in countries that had already established high savings and investment patterns in the 1980s (see table 10.2) and achieved sustained economic growth. This pattern of high savings and investment differed markedly from Latin America, a region with historically high consumption levels.

In the 1990s, the even higher investment levels in East Asia—and in the Czech Republic as well—were not perceived as a problem but were welcomed as a healthy trend, with the resulting external imbalance viewed as transitory. It was believed to reflect high levels of imports mainly of capital goods linked to large investment projects, which were expected to lead to higher exports and smaller current account deficits in the medium term. This argument is often used during surges, but it seemed more justified in the Asian case.

Once the crises hit the region, and strongly affected both the financial and corporate sectors, with nonperforming loans increasing rapidly due to insolvent borrowers, a less benign story gained prominence: it was suggested that much of the additional investment had been of doubtful quality and directed toward the service and property sectors and not to the tradable activities as initially thought.

However, statistical evidence from our country studies for the 1990–96 period, based on national sources, does not on the whole indicate a significant change over time in the distribution pattern of foreign capital flows or of domestic bank credit (a major intermediary of such flows) across different sectors of the economy.

This supports preliminary evidence reported by Radelet and Sachs (1998, table 8), based on information on outstanding debt for the East Asian crisis

TABLE 10.2. Investment and Savings, 1980–97 (% GDP)

Country	1980–84	1985–89	1990–94	1995–97
Indonesia				
Investment	23.7	25.0	27.0	28.8
Savings	31.4	29.8	32.3	30.6
Malaysia				
Investment	34.3	26.5	36.5	42.5
Savings	31.6	34.6	36.1	42.1
South Korea				
Investment	29.4	29.5	36.8	36.1
Savings	26.7	35.7	35.9	34.9
Thailand				
Investment	28.0	29.2	40.2	39.3
Savings	23.8	29.1	35.6	35.6

Source: World Bank, World Development Indicators CD-Rom, 2000.

Note: Investment and savings stand for gross domestic investment and gross domestic savings, respectively.

countries, which suggests for most East Asian countries only a modest shift in lending to the real estate sector.

From this, three lessons from the Asia crisis emerge. First, high savings and investment rates do not prevent a country from suffering a major balance of payments crisis. Indeed, if a country has high savings and investment, the net benefits of capital flows may be particularly doubtful. Additional investment may have limited benefits, as investment rates are already so high that they may have lower productivity than the average or may be speculative, as "good projects" may be scarce. The potential costs—due to the risk of crises—may not be lower than for other countries. This is really quite a new lesson in that most economists previously believed that high domestic savings rates would help protect countries from crises.

Second, a country does not need to experience a sharp deterioration in macroeconomic fundamentals for a crisis to occur; and, third, other countries praised for the soundness of their fundamentals and for their economic performance can be affected by such a crisis occurring elsewhere. We will see that contagion effects were caused by herding behavior.[1]

Today the new international financial architecture has been to a large extent marked by national measures intended to reduce country vulnerability and efforts to promote codes and standards in developing countries.

While these measures (particularly the former) are valuable and necessary, we believe they are not sufficient for crisis prevention. The insufficiency of this approach and the need for complementary measures in international financial architecture, which directly address the instability of international financial markets and their potential harmful effects on developing countries, are discussed in chapter 11.

2. CAPITAL FLOWS AND INTERNATIONAL RESERVES MANAGEMENT

As was reported in the country studies, as well as in chapter 1, all affected countries witnessed massive surges of capital inflows in the 1990s. In some instances, average annual net inflows amounted to over 10 percent of the countries' GDP. In Thailand and the Czech Republic, they reached 15 and 16.6 percent of GDP in 1995, respectively; and in Malaysia 20 percent in 1993. Most of such flows were in the form of bank loans and portfolio investments. In East Asia, such flows corresponded to 66 percent of total flows between 1989 and 1996, with bank loans having the largest share, most of which were of short maturity. Flows as a proportion of GDP were never as high in Latin America as they were in East Asia (see chap. 1). Furthermore, these high inflows in East

Asia had been large for a longer period than the surge in Latin America, implying very large accumulated stocks of easily reversible liabilities. This may have contributed to the greater severity of the Asian crisis than that of Mexico.

Given their potential reversibility, accumulated stocks of short-term capital can be seen as a crucial vulnerability indicator for potential crises. As Rodrik and Velasco (1999) have pointed out, to some extent the shortening of maturities can also be the effect of (anticipated) crises rather than the cause. From information provided in chapter 1, we can see that the accumulated stocks of short-term bank lending had by mid-1997 reached U.S.$101 billion in South Korea and U.S.$75 billion in Thailand. These values correspond to 3.0 and 2.4 times the size of the countries' foreign reserves at the time, respectively. These ratios are far beyond what is now considered safe—a ratio of about 1—which prevents the country from suffering liquidity problems.

It should be noted, however, that the numerator of such ratios does not include the stock of portfolio flows, which are even more easily reversible than bank lending. In order to address this problem, chapter 1 builds a more comprehensive vulnerability indicator in which the potential reversibility of all types of flows is accounted for. This indicator based on the stocks and past volatility of each type of foreign flow calculates the level of net reserves necessary to significantly reduce the likelihood of a crisis caused by capital outflows. According to such estimates, the levels of reserves that Indonesia, South Korea, and Thailand needed in order to prevent a crisis by mid-1997 were extremely high and well above existing levels at the time (see table 10.3).

It is worth noting that the ratio in column 3 of the table is probably underestimated, as the actual levels of reserves held by the countries were not net of forward positions, which actually hampered the availability of liquidity at the time of the crisis, while the required level in the first column is naturally net.

Such high levels of reserves are required for defending fixed, quasi-fixed, or narrow band exchange rates, which were the exchange rate regimes pursued by East Asian countries until 1997. However, even if countries adopt "flexible" exchange rates, the authorities are de facto broadly committed to stability, and for that they need similarly high reserves.

TABLE 10.3. Level of International Reserves in Mid-1997 (U.S.$ billions in current prices)

	Level Required for Crisis Avoidance (1)	Actual Level (2)	Ratio (1)/(2)
Indonesia	39.6	20.3	1.9
South Korea	109.6	34.1	3.2
Thailand	56.4	31.4	1.8

Sources: Chapter 1, table 1.11; and IMF.

The problem for countries of maintaining such high levels of net foreign exchange reserves to protect themselves from currency crises is their high financial cost; the question needs to be asked whether such large capital inflows are desirable, if such a high proportion cannot be used to finance higher investment or consumption, but has to be accumulated in high-cost foreign exchange reserves to protect countries from reversals and crises. The answer would seem to be linked to the creation of sufficiently large contingency credit lines, particularly from the International Monetary Fund (IMF) and possibly from private banks, to be easily available, so as to reduce the need in such large countries for self-insurance against crises, based on very high net foreign exchange reserves. The availability of sufficiently large contingency credit from the IMF not only reduces the significant cost of individual countries maintaining such high reserves; it also reduces the risk of crises occurring and, especially spreading via contagion, to other countries. Therefore, large amounts of contingency credit from the IMF (even though they may be used by a few or even no countries) will have important cross-country externalities; the reduction of crises risk would reduce the level of necessary reserves.

3. THE ROLE OF PLAYERS IN TRIGGERING THE CRISES

Our empirical research has pointed to the growing influence of international bank and portfolio investors in both surges and (sudden) reversals of capital flows. It is worth noting in particular the role they played in triggering and exacerbating the crises. In some cases, such as that of South Korea, even though international actors (banks in this case), played a major role, domestic actors (in this case in the stock market) were also important (see chap. 7). See table 10.4 for a listing of the major players in the crises.

In Thailand, where the crisis started in early July 1997, international bank lenders (by not renewing short-term loans), together with domestic debtors making prepayments, were the first to leave the country. This pullout began in the third quarter of 1996 (see chap. 4), several months before the crisis unfolded. This was followed by attacks on the currency by hedge fund speculators, which occurred intermittently throughout the first semester of 1997.

The other two crises that began in the same month occurred in Indonesia and Malaysia. In Indonesia, foreign banks were the first to leave the country, whereas in Malaysia foreign institutional investors were the first to pull out. The latter, although they were in the minority, had a big impact on the stock market due to their greater turnover vis-à-vis domestic institutional investors. Also in Malaysia hedge funds played an important role in the crisis.

TABLE 10.4. The Major Players

Brazil	Czech Republic	Indonesia	South Korea	Malaysia	Thailand
Foreign and domestic	Foreign banks and domestic investors	Foreign banks	Foreign banks; in stock markets domestic investors were major players	Foreign (institutional) investors	International investors and domestic debtors making prepayments

Source: Chapters (4–9).

In South Korea, the crisis was triggered and exacerbated by foreign banks, which withdrew short-term loans, made mainly to deposit-money banks, beginning in September 1997, just before the crisis broke out. But, as stressed in chapter 7, unlike the situation with bank lending, the stock markets were destabilized by domestic rather than foreign investors.

In the Czech Republic, foreign banks were also the first to leave the country, followed by domestic investors. Thus, both foreign lenders and domestic investors contributed to deepening the crisis. In the Brazilian study, it was pointed out that all sorts of investors—foreign (institutional and banks) and domestic—pulled out more or less at the same time, though detailed high frequency data on net flows provided by the study suggest that portfolio flow withdrawal preceded that of bank loans. As the author of the Brazilian study noted, the crisis in early 1999 contrasted with previous speculative attacks in Brazil, for example, associated with the East Asian crisis, when only domestic investors pulled out heavily. This indicates that only when international players changed their positions and the government no longer had the strength to counteract both them and domestic investors did the crisis finally occur. However, the data show that residents were responsible for a large share of the withdrawals.

The Brazilian study pays particular attention to the contagion effects of the Russian crisis, which had occurred months before. Based on econometric results and qualitative analysis on banks' behavior, it notes that neither fundamentals nor the common lender channel can explain contagion. The only remaining explanation for contagion between Russia and Brazil is therefore herding behavior caused by panic among lenders and investors (see chap. 9).

Chapter 3, on international bank lending, shows that in East Asia panicking along with the common lender channel story seem to explain herding among lenders, especially from Europe and the United States (as will be seen, the causes of withdrawal from Japanese lenders are more complex). This is an important conclusion to draw. It is also important to note that in East Asia herding occurred among different actors, thus denoting a high correlation between their investment and lending decisions. This was clearly the case of Thailand, where both lenders and institutional investors pulled out in a sequenced way.

This leads us to the important question of whether there really exist different motivations and incentives for different actors that make them prone to surges and reversals in a context of herding. If the answer is affirmative, then regulation should be targeted at specific groups and tailored to address their specific characteristics. For example, institutional investors seem to be particularly prone to herding given the incentive structure to which fund managers, for example, are subject. However, if the answer is negative and the fear of losses encourages different actors to rush to the exit door simultaneously, then curbing excessive volatility requires general regulation. This affects all actors who channel potentially reversible flows simultaneously.

The evidence assembled here and in other studies seems to indicate that there are both specific (to certain actors) and general (across actors) herding. As a result, both specific regulation—for different actors like banks and mutual funds—and broader criteria for general regulation (such as countercyclical elements) are important. To deal appropriately with the latter, it is crucially important to have global coordination of regulations, both across sectors and across countries. In this sense, the fairly recently created Financial Stability Forum is potentially a very important step toward dealing with the problems of volatility of capital flows through coordinated regulation.

The picture that emerges is that in East Asia and the Czech Republic it was international rather than domestic lenders who pulled out first. This can be contrasted with the Mexican crisis of December 1994, in which domestic investors began to pull out well before the crisis was triggered (although, as in Brazil in early 1999 and also in Mexico, only when foreigners also rushed to leave did a crisis occur). It is interesting to note that in Brazil, although domestic investors did not have the power to trigger the crisis, they did move out quickly and apparently ahead of their foreign counterparts.

This difference between Latin America and East Asia might be explained by the fact that in Latin America domestic investors were more used to crises and aware of their likely recurrence, whereas until 1997 crises were practically unknown in the East Asian emerging economies, which were used to continuous prosperity.

An additional, less noticeable fact that might also have had a part in explaining the more prominent role of international players in East Asia relative to Latin America is that, as reported in chapter 1, capital flows reached an average of 9.2 percent of GDP in the four Asian countries in the period just before the crisis (1995–96), a level two and a half times higher than those observed in Brazil, Mexico, and Argentina at the time and higher than the 6.7 percent observed in Mexico in 1989–94. Therefore, international players in East Asia had more weight and therefore more power to trigger and exacerbate a crisis.

Within the group of international players, banks pulled out first in Thailand, South Korea, Indonesia, and the Czech Republic. In Malaysia, it was institutional investors who were first to leave the country, whereas in Brazil banks and institutional investors pulled out at the same time.

The country studies have permitted us to identify the main players in spite of data limitations. In this context, it is very important to stress the urgent need to improve transparency of international market actors and flows, especially when information is limited or nonexistent, as is the case for hedge funds and over the counter derivatives. The differences regarding which players triggered the crises can be associated with, first, the ways in which capital account liberalization had been pursued in each country and, second, the regional links with different source countries and the different weights players have in each of these regions.

3.1. CAPITAL ACCOUNT LIBERALIZATION

Although all countries liberalized their capital accounts considerably, a closer analysis suggests that there were important differences, not just in speed but in the sequencing of such liberalization.[2]

Two broad groups can be initially identified: the first with many years' experience of an open capital account and the second in which liberalization was pursued mostly in the 1990s and in a gradual fashion. The first group includes Thailand, Malaysia, and Indonesia, while the second includes South Korea, the Czech Republic, and Brazil.

Among the first group, liberalization in Thailand can certainly be identified as being among the most aggressive, particularly in the early 1990s with the creation of the Bangkok International Banking Facility (BIBF), which through tax privileges greatly encouraged external flows, especially short-term ones. Restrictions were imposed to reduce the volume of such inflows, but, as argued in chapter 4, these always found ways to enter the country by taking a different form. Although it had been relatively open for years, Malaysia relied upon reserve requirements on foreign borrowing as a way to deter the large surges of the 1990s, with the coverage of this instrument becoming quite extensive during certain periods (see chap. 5).

Indonesia, in turn, greatly encouraged capital flows, especially direct foreign investment (FDI), from the start, although bank lending to the domestic banking sector also became prominent in the 1990s. In the mid-1990s, there was an effort to prioritize FDI over other types of flows, with ceilings on foreign lending being relied upon as an instrument, though with poor effectiveness.

In the second group, South Korea started out with gradual liberalization, with residents being permitted to issue securities abroad and foreigners being allowed to invest directly in the Korean stock market (though limits existed on the latter). From 1993 onward, the process of liberalization accelerated with the lifting of barriers on short-term borrowing. This change in the liberalization pattern reflected both domestic preferences and external pressures, the latter including pressures from the OECD as part of the negotiation process for South Korea's accession to the organization (Chang 1998; Griffith-Jones, Gottschalk, and Cirera 2001).

With regard to the Czech Republic and Brazil, liberalization in both countries, though speedy, had some elements of gradualism. In the Czech case, it was argued in chapter 8 that a logic of selective and gradual liberalization had been pursued but that this had been superseded by the inevitability of capital surges, forcing regulation to adapt to this reality in the mid-1990s. In Brazil, two factors should be mentioned: first, although portfolio flows were liberalized in the early 1990s, some restrictions remained in the way investors could operate; second, domestic bank accounts for nonresidents, or dollar accounts, had never been permitted. Furthermore, at times of large surges, tax-based restrictions were used in an attempt to reduce monetary pressures but also to influence the composition of flows in favor of portfolio flows so as to discourage potentially more reversible flows.

With large surges of capital flows, the challenges governments faced were to manage their macroeconomic impact and help reduce their pressure on the domestic financial systems, with most of them attempting to respond to such challenges by reimposing some sort of (generally temporary) restriction on the capital account at different points in time.

The patterns of liberalization can thus be seen as an important factor in explaining which sort of player had a major role in triggering the crisis in each country. Where short-term flows in the form of bank lending (South Korea) or BIBF (Thailand) were prioritized for capital account liberalization the crises were triggered by international bank lenders. And where short-term bank lending was more restricted and portfolio debt flows (e.g., in Brazil) and equity flows (in Thailand) were prioritized for liberalization, institutional investors played a more prominent role in both the inflows and the reversals during crises.

The policy lessons we can draw from this are that the traditional conventional wisdom on capital liberalization (which had been largely forgotten in the euphoria of liberalization in the early 1990s) was right in recommending that countries liberalize long-term capital flows first. Only when the country had achieved a sufficient level of institutional capacity was it to liberalize other sorts of flows. However, even a sequenced approach toward liberalization has problems, as in reality there are limitations to the control of massive inflows. This requires that regulation should be both national and international, with one complementing the other, as will be discussed in chapter 11. Naturally, regulation—both national and international—is not by itself a panacea, given that—like all other policies—it has limitations. Given the complexity of the determinants of crises, it is necessary to deploy a variety of policy measures—national and international, macroeconomic and regulatory—to try to prevent them.

3.2. THE SOURCE COUNTRIES

As has been seen, while institutional investors had a prominent role in the Brazilian and Malaysian crises, the nonrenewal of bank loans was a major factor behind the crises in the other countries, especially Thailand and South Korea but also Indonesia.

Chapter 3 shows that Japanese banks accounted for the largest share of total claims in East Asia and explains most of the loan reversals in the region. Interestingly, their behavior during and after the crises differed from that of the European and U.S. banks. The behavior of the latter seems to confirm the common lender channel and panic hypotheses. Indeed, U.S. and European bank loans fell similarly between banks and across borrowers during and after the Asian crisis. Elements of countercyclical regulation (see chap. 11 for more details), if they had been in place, would have helped moderate such boom and bust behavior by European and U.S. banks.

As for Japanese banks, the story appears to be more complex than can be explained by means of the common lender channel or panicking theories. Indeed, analysis of the data from individual banks does not permit us to detect any clear similarities in their behavior. A number of factors can explain this dissimilarity and why the ultimate outcome still took the form of a heavy pullout. First, Japanese banks' approach to customers differs according to their affiliation status. For example, in normal times both affiliates and nonaffiliates have continued to provide access to finance, but in times of crisis Japanese banks tend to treat affiliates better, as they are backed by their parent companies. However, as the crisis unfolded the impact of the devaluation on the level of bad loans interrupted the rollover of loans even to affiliates. Furthermore, the Japanese banking system crisis that deepened in the first semester of 1997 worsened the capital asset ratios of many banks, and the declining yen aggravated this. As a result, banks were forced to reduce their exposure. Finally, an underlying important factor is that a particularly large proportion of Japanese bank lending had been short term; indeed, by law a large proportion of Japanese banks—for example, the commercial banks—can only lend short term (see chap. 3).

In summary, although much of the behavior of international banks in the East Asian crises was herding prone, the behavior of Japanese banks, which were the major lenders, was dominated by their more peculiar approach to customers and by the banking crisis at home. Therefore, the crises in East Asia were to an important extent influenced by domestic developments in the source country and the peculiar behavior of its banks.

An important policy implication is that the regional dimension and peculiarities are important and therefore regional mechanisms need to play a significant role. In particular, these regional mechanisms need to take account of the business cycle, particularly in the main regional source country.

With regard to institutional investors, chapter 2 shows that in Malaysia, the country whose stock market was most open to foreigners among the four East Asian countries, foreigners accounted for half of the country's stock market capitalization. Moreover, foreign institutional investors were dominant in the "free float" segment (i.e., stocks readily available for public ownership). The major presence of foreign investors in the Malaysian stock market thus does much to explain their prominent role in the Malaysian currency crisis. This contrasts, for example, with the South Korean experience, in which a ceiling of 20 percent had been placed on foreign ownership in the domestic stock market, thus reducing the power of foreign institutional investors to influence events in the country in a major way.

Like Malaysia, Brazil was relatively more open to portfolio flows than, for example, South Korea, which explains why institutional actors played a major role in the Brazilian currency crisis of early 1999. However, a regional factor was also at play, as U.S. institutional investors have had a significant presence in the Latin American markets, particularly in countries like Brazil and Mexico, where capital markets are deeper and more liquid than most other Latin American markets.

U.S. mutual funds are particularly active in Latin America, having been major players in the Mexican peso crisis in 1994–95 and, according to Kaminsky, Lyons, and Schmucker (1999), were responsible for the spillover effects of the Mexican crisis on other Latin American countries. Likewise, they were responsible for the massive portfolio outflows Brazil witnessed during the country's 1999 currency crisis.

Thus, the differences between Latin American and Asian countries regarding the role of players can also be partly explained by regional factors. In the former case, the stronger trend toward institutionalization of savings in the United States implied that institutional investors have a greater presence in Latin America. In the latter case, the presence of Japanese banks, with their long-term lending strategies in Asia, explains the dominance of bank lending over other types of capital flows in the region.

4. THE MACROECONOMIC AND WELFARE EFFECTS OF THE CRISES

The macroeconomic and welfare effects of the crises were developmentally very costly. The speed of recovery, in turn, has been quick on the whole—but

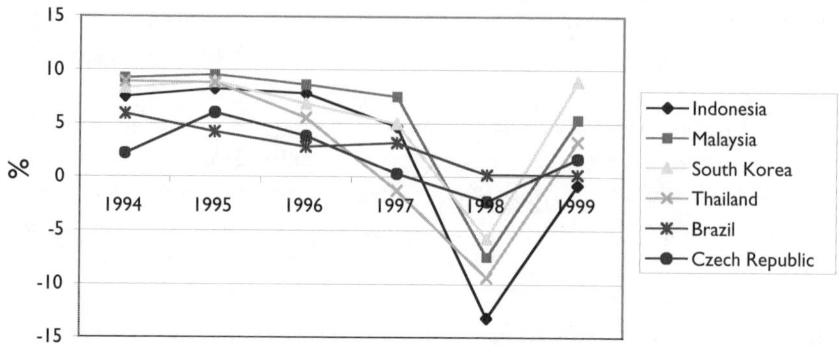

Figure 10.1. GDP growth. (Data from World Development Indicators 2000 and World Economic Outlook 2000.)

with differences among countries (see figure 10.1), especially compared to the pattern of recovery during the debt crisis of the 1980s.

Thailand, where the East Asian crisis began, witnessed huge outflows of capital and depletion of reserves. This resulted in the adoption of a floating exchange regime, leading to massive exchange rate devaluation. At the same time, interest rates shot up to the two-digit level. GDP fell by 8.5 percent in 1998, and unemployment rose sharply. A fiscal squeeze was pursued in the beginning under strong pressure from the IMF, but this policy was later relaxed. The financial sector generated a massive knock-on effect on the whole economy, with nonperforming loans reaching 47 percent of total loans and with the fiscal cost of the banking crisis estimated at 15 to 20 percent of the country's GDP.

In South Korea, similar patterns could be detected, with GDP falling by nearly 6 percent in 1998; however, recovery has been very rapid in South Korea, even though there are unresolved banking and corporate problems. In Indonesia, the economic and social consequences have been even more acute and particularly difficult to overcome given the political instability in the country. In 1998, GDP fell by nearly 14 percent and recovery has been far more sluggish relative to other crisis-hit countries. The country experienced massive devaluation, and inflation exploded. In Malaysia, on the other hand, the policy response was rather unconventional, in part, as argued in the study, because the country did not need to resort to the IMF for emergency facilities given its lower exposure to external indebtedness. Such policies included, for example, reimposing capital controls, though at a time when the economy had already started to recover.

In the Czech Republic, the government responded to speculative attacks by adopting a combination of fiscal and monetary tightening, which resulted in large interest rate increases. But as residents moved out, following non-residents, reserves fell and the currency was floated, with new rounds of liquidity squeezes and interest rate hikes taking place. Unlike the situation in East Asian countries, the country experienced only a mini–currency crisis, with the exchange rate stabilizing only 10 percent lower than the level experienced before the crisis. The biggest effects of the crisis were felt in the real economy, with an initial drop in the country's GDP, very slow recovery to date, and a sharp increase in unemployment levels.

In Brazil, notwithstanding the fairly sharp devaluation that followed the decision to float the currency, the effects of the currency crisis were far milder than in the East Asian countries, with a relatively quick recovery. A number of elements contributed to that. First, the financial system had been strengthened in response to the Mexican crisis of 1994. Second, unlike the other crisis-hit countries, in Brazil the currency was subject to attack when reserves were still high; additionally, the existence of a large IMF package before the crisis erupted seems to have helped to moderate the decline of reserves and the magnitude of the crisis. Furthermore, short-term foreign debt as a proportion of accumulated reserves was lower than that observed in the other countries. Third, the country still had large public assets to be privatized and, partly in connection with that, FDI continued to be high during and after the crisis. Fourth, the private sector had a low level of indebtedness and hedged against exchange rate risk. As Goldfajn notes (in chapter 9), widespread hedging was due to the crisis being anticipated by market participants. And, finally, the country had not liberalized the capital account completely and adopted taxes at times of capital flows surges in an attempt to interfere in their composition.

But it is important to note that if the private sector escaped mostly unhurt the crisis was still very costly, as public sector debt increased by more than 10 percent of GDP.

To summarize, all countries suffered a large negative developmental impact, in terms of output and unemployment, with the consequences in Brazil being concentrated in the public sector. But the speed of recovery differed across countries due to underlying structural differences between them and to the policy responses undertaken. Tables 10.5, 10.6, and 10.7 summarize the main features of the countries covered: fundamentals, the capital account, and the macroeconomic effects of the crises.

Because the costs of crises are so large, it becomes imperative to design a new international financial architecture that can make them less likely and less costly. Such a new financial architecture should not just aim to try to prevent crises and manage them better when they do occur; it should also

TABLE 10.5. Fundamentals

	Brazil (data for 1998)	Czech Republic (data for 1996)	Indonesia (data for 1996)	South Korea (data for 1996)	Malaysia (data for 1996)	Thailand (data for 1996)
Fiscal balance, % GDP	−8.65	0.1	balanced throughout	−0.1	−0.71	−0.9
Current account balance, % GDP	−4.34	−7.4, but at times 10%	−3.7	−4.4	−6.1; −8.0[a]	−8.0
Inflation, %	3.2	8.8	8.0	4.9	3.5	5.8
Savings rate, % GDP	18.6	28.5	31.5	34.5	42.6	35.9
Gross external debt, % GDP	30.6	35.0; 44.0[a]	58.3	22.3	42.0	51.4
International reserves, U.S.$ billions	43.9	13.1	19.4	34.2	28.0	38.7

Source: Chapters 1 and 4 through 9; World Bank, Global Development Finance 2000.

[a]1997.

TABLE 10.6. Capital Account

	Brazil	Czech Republic	Indonesia	South Korea	Malaysia	Thailand
Total net private flows, % GDP (maximum annual flow)	4.9%[a]	16.6%[a]	5.4%[a]	10%[b]	20%[c]	15.3%[a]
Composition of flows	Portfolio and bank loans; from 1995 on FDI picked up	Bank lending mainly; portfolio investment. Linked to privatization	Bank loans predominated	Bank loans (most of short-term maturity)	Portfolio flows predominated	Bank lending, corresponding to 58% of total inflows over 1993–96
Debt/exports ratio	359%[d]	64%[b]	219%[b]	74%[b]	42%[b]	120.4%[b]
Short-term debt/total debt	10.8%[d]	28.6%[b]	25%[b]	57.5%[b]	27.9%[b]	41.4%[b]
Major players	Foreign institutional, and domestic	Foreign investors	Foreign banks	Foreign banks; in stock markets domestic investors were major players	Foreign (institutional) investors	International investors and domestic debtors making prepayments

Source: Chapters 1 and 4 to 9; World Bank, Global Development Finance 2000.

[a]1995.

[b]1996.

[c]1993.

[d]1998.

TABLE 10.7. Macroeconomic Effects of the Crises

	Brazil	Czech Republic	Indonesia	South Korea	Malaysia	Thailand
Crisis date	Jan 1999	May 1997	July 1997	Oct 1997	July 1997	July 1997
Capital outflows	Equity and debt securities; bank loans as well; FDI poured in	Initially massive, but then contained	Bank loans	Bank loans	Portfolio flows	Bank loans and portfolio flows
Nominal devaluation[a]	41%	11%	84%	46%	45%	53%
GDP[b] %	0.2[c]	−2.3[d]	−13.2[d]	−5.8[d]	−7.5[d]	−9.4[d]
General points	Crisis effects were milder due to private sector enjoying strong hedging positions	Policy response: fiscal and liquidity squeeze (resulting in interest rate shock)	Inflation exploded. Sluggish economic recovery	Short-term loans were mainly responsible for the liquidity crisis	No need to go to the IMF for emergency credit facilities; responses included capital controls	Authorities let the currency float at a time when reserves were already depleted

Source: Chapters 4 to 9; IMF, International Financial Statistics CD-Rom.

[a]Maximum nominal devaluation observed over a period up to one year after the outbreak of the crisis, using IMF monthly data, end of period.

[b]GDP growth during the first calendar year when the effects of the crisis were fully felt (the year is indicated in superscript).

[c]1999.

[d]1998.

encourage sufficient and sufficiently stable private flows to different categories of developing countries. We turn to this in chapter 11.

NOTES

1. For a formal contribution on the role of contagion in causing currency crises, see Krugman 1999.

2. A more detailed account of how the capital accounts were liberalized and the sort of restrictions that were reimposed with time can be found in chapter 1.

REFERENCES

Chang, H. 1998. "Korea: The misunderstood crisis." World Development 26, no. 8:1555–61.

Corsetti, G., P. Pesenti, and N. Roubini. 1998. "What caused the Asian currency and financial crisis?" Mimeo available at <http:// www.stern.nyu.edu/~nroubini/asia/Asia-Homepage.htm>.

Dooley, M. 1996. "A survey of academic literature on controls over international capital transactions." *IMF Staff Papers* 43:639–87.

Griffith-Jones, S., R. Gottschalk, and X. Cirera. 2001. "The OECD experience with capital account liberalisation." Paper presented at the workshop Management of Capital Flows: Comparative Experiences and Implications for Africa, UNCTAD, Cairo, Egypt, March 20–21.

IMF. 2000. World Economic Outlook. Washington, DC: IMF.

———. 2000. International Financial Studies 2000. Washington, DC: IMF.

Kaminsky, G., R. Lyons, and S. Schmucker. 1999. "Managers, investors, and crises: Mutual fund strategy in emerging markets." Mimeo, World Bank.

Krugman, P. 1999. "Balance sheets, the transfer problem, and financial crises." Mimeo, Massachusetts Institute of Technology, January.

Radelet, S., and J. Sachs. 1998a. "The onset of the East Asian crisis." Mimeo, Harvard University.

———. 1998b. *The East Asian financial crisis: Diagnosis, remedies, prospects.* Brookings Papers on Economic Activity 1. Washington DC: Brookings Institution.

Rodrik, D., and A. Velasco. 1999. "Short-term capital flows." In Proceedings of the World Bank annual conference on development economics. Washington: World Bank.

World Bank. 2000. World Development Indicators. CD-Rom.

———. 2000. Global Development Finance. Washington DC: World Bank.

Wyplosz, C. 2001. "How risky is financial liberalization in the developing countries?" Paper presented at the seventh Conference on Current Issues in Emerging Market Economies, Dubrovnik, June 28–29.

CHAPTER 11

Key Elements for a New International Financial Architecture

Stephany Griffith-Jones and
José Antonio Ocampo

1. WHAT PROGRESS ON INTERNATIONAL FINANCIAL REFORM?

The recent wave of currency and banking crises that began in East Asia and then spread to many other emerging markets (as described in depth in previous chapters) and even threatened briefly to spill over to the United States in the wake of Russia and Long Term Capital Management (LTCM)—generated a broad consensus that fundamental reforms were required in the international financial system. More recent crises, as in Brazil, as well as critical situations in Turkey and Argentina, reiterate the need for additional changes in the eyes of many observers. Existing institutions and arrangements were widely seen as inadequate for dealing with very large and extremely volatile capital flows, in which an important part of the volatility was caused by serious imperfections in the financial markets themselves.

The seriousness of the situation is underlined by the fact that in the 1990s, out of 120 months, during 40 (that is 33 percent of the time) there have been important crises. This is particularly problematic for two reasons. First, currency and banking crises—which have recently occurred mainly in emerging markets—have extremely high development and social costs. Indeed, deep and frequent crises in developing countries could undermine the United Nations (UN) goal of halving world poverty by 2015. Second, there is always the very small—but totally unacceptable—risk that contagion and spillovers in an increasingly interdependent international financial system could lead to global problems. Both of these problems implied that urgent action was required to overcome the risk that the important benefits that globalization offers in other fields could be seriously undermined by international financial developments.

Several years after the Asian crisis, it is a good time to evaluate the progress achieved in reforming the international financial system. In this chapter, we will do so particularly from the perspective of developing countries' interests; our policy proposals will emphasize how to deal with problems originating in the supply of capital flows, which is the focus of both our empirical and policy concerns in this book. We will also review very briefly the vast literature and discussion on international financial reform, so as to place our policy analysis and recommendations in the context of this broader debate.

Some progress has been made on reforming the international financial system, but it is clearly insufficient. Important changes have been implemented. For example, lending facilities of the International Monetary Fund (IMF) for both crisis prevention and management have been quite usefully expanded and adapted, and the Fund's total resources were increased.

Important institutional innovations have been introduced, such as the creation of the Financial Stability Forum (FSF), to identify vulnerabilities and sources of systemic risk, to fill gaps in regulations, and to develop consistent financial regulations across all types of financial institutions. As capital and credit markets become increasingly integrated both among each other and between countries, it is essential for regulation to be efficient so that the domain of the regulator is the same as the domain of the market that is regulated. Given that regulation is still national and sectoral, an institution like the FSF is valuable to help coordinate regulation globally and across sectors. The creation of the Group of 20 (G-20), the body formed to discuss international financial reform, which includes both developed and developing countries, is also a positive development.

Developing countries have been asked to take a number of important measures to make their countries less vulnerable to crises; these include the introduction of a large number of codes and standards. Though introducing standards is very positive, there are concerns in developing countries that the number of standards (at more than 60) is too large; developing countries also are worried that the standards are too uniform in the assumption that "one size fits all." At a major conference organized with the IMF and the World Bank held at the Commonwealth Secretariat in June 2000, senior policymakers from developing countries called for greater selectivity and flexibility in the standards they are asked to implement. A more inclusive process is also necessary, whereby developing countries can participate in the development of these standards and codes, which at present they are asked to implement without having been involved in their design.

Even though there has been significant progress on reform of the financial architecture, it has suffered from two serious problems. First, it has been insufficient, given the magnitude of the changes required to create a financial system that supports—and does not undermine—growth and development in the dramatically changed context of the twenty-first century, which has been characterized by very large but extremely volatile and highly concentrated private capital flows. It is essential to develop a clear vision of an appropriate financial architecture under these new circumstances. Drawing parallels from the institutional mechanisms developed nationally as domestic credit and capital markets grew a new international architecture requires: (1) appropriate transparency and regulation of international financial loan and capital markets, (2) provision of sufficient international official liquidity under conditions of distress, and (3) standstill and orderly debt workout procedures at an international level. The mechanisms that exist and the adaptations made till now do not fully meet the new requirements.

Second, the progress made has been asymmetrical in three key aspects, in which a more balanced approach is urgently needed.

A first asymmetry in the reform process is that far more progress has been made on important measures taken by developing countries, which are being asked to introduce a very large number of codes and standards, so as to make them less vulnerable to crises. However, far less progress is being made on equally important and complementary international measures. As much of the literature has argued, crises—such as those in Asia—were not just caused by country problems but also by imperfections in international capital markets that lead to rapid surges and reversals of massive private flows. To deal with the problems in the international financial markets, it is thus essential that international measures both for crisis prevention and management are also taken.

As the Group of 24 (G-24), which represents developing countries, has pointed out, standards in the area of transparency are being pressed upon developing countries to improve information for markets without equal corresponding obligations for disclosure by financial institutions, including highly leveraged ones, such as hedge funds, which have no reporting obligation. Better information on financial markets would be of great value to policymakers, especially in developing countries. Transparency should not be a one-way street. Furthermore, while valuable progress is being made in the attempt to improve the regulation of domestic financial systems in developing countries, there has been painfully slow progress in filling important gaps in international regulation, of institutions such as mutual funds or hedge funds, or of modifying regulations, as of banks, where current regulations may have contributed—rather than prevented—greater short termism of flows (subsequently discussed in more detail). In the field of international regulation, valuable studies have been carried out, particularly by the Financial Stability

Forum Working Parties, but the recommendations made are being implemented very slowly.

Passing from crisis prevention to crisis management, it seems important that the IMF's own resources are large enough to meet the financing needs of a systemic crisis involving several economies simultaneously while also retaining sufficient liquidity to meet normal demands on the Fund's resources. Michel Camdessus and others—including the influential U.S. Council of Foreign Affairs—have suggested that this expansion of official emergency financing could be funded in part by temporary and self-liquidating issues of special drawing rights (SDRs). Such a mechanism would not add to total world liquidity except in a temporary manner during a crisis situation, when it would be compensating for reductions or a reversal of private flows. This proposal deserves serious analysis and consideration. Speedier progress on orderly debt workouts is also urgent.

A second source of asymmetry in the reform process that needs to be urgently overcome is the insufficient participation of developing countries in key forums and institutions. With regard to international financial institutions, more representative governance needs to be discussed in parallel with a redefinition of their functions. It is particularly urgent that developing countries (which are now only represented in a very limited way in the FSF working parties) are fully represented in the FSF itself, as the issues discussed there have very profound effects on their economies and as their insights can make an important contribution to the Forum's valuable work. It is important to note that after their 2000 annual meeting the Commonwealth Finance Meetings called for such developing country participation in the Forum. The inclusion of major developing countries in the G-20 is clearly a welcome step, but it might be of value to also include some smaller developing nations so as to reflect their specific concerns. Above all, it would be helpful if the agenda of the G-20 could be broadened to include more explicitly the key issues of international financial reform. (For a more detailed discussion of the issue see Griffith-Jones and Kimmis 2001 on the participation of developing countries in global financial governance).

A third asymmetry that has emerged in recent discussions on reform of the system is that we have all placed excessive focus on crisis prevention and management, mainly for middle-income countries. Important as this is, it may have led us to neglect the equally—if not more important—issues of appropriate liquidity and development finance for low-income countries. With regard to liquidity, it is important that existing IMF facilities for low-income countries—such as the Compensatory Financing Facility and the Poverty Reduction and Growth Facility—should be made more flexible in case terms of trade shocks affect such countries. More generally, the role of the IMF in providing liquidity to low-income countries is crucial. With regard to development finance, low-income countries need sufficient multilateral lending and official flows as well as speedy debt relief. It is a source of concern that multilateral lending to low-income countries, especially via the International Development Agency (IDA), has recently fallen sharply. Furthermore, in a world of rapidly increasing private flows, it is important that low-income countries, donors, and international organizations collaborate to help attract more significant private flows to them. Mobilizing sufficient and stable development finance, both private and official, to low-income countries is an essential precondition that can help ensure growth and poverty reduction in the poorest countries.

It is important that significant further progress on reforming the international financial system is accomplished quickly, as the risks and potential costs of not doing so are unacceptably large, especially for poor people in developing countries.

Given the focus of this book on the problems originating in the supply of capital flows, the policy discussion that follows in this chapter focuses on two aspects: (1) better international information on markets and financial regulation (these are international measures for crisis prevention, where there has been very little action and even little analysis) and (2) provision of sufficient international liquidity to developing countries in distress situations and of sufficient development finance to help support their growth and poverty reduction. We will not discuss here some very important issues, probably the main being private sector involvement and burden sharing, on which there is already a large amount of literature (for a seminal contribution, see Eichengreen and Portes 1995), even though again there has been relatively little action. Furthermore, the type of preventive measures—à la regulation—suggested here seem to us to be more appropriate than burden sharing measures to be taken mainly ex post, as the former seem more market friendly and therefore less likely to discourage excessively private flows to developing countries or to increase their cost too much.

We would like to stress that this chapter does not and could not attempt the Herculean task of reviewing the vast literature on international financial architecture.[1] This includes not just numerous books and articles but also major reports. Some of the most important ones include the so-called Geneva Report, written by de Gregorio, Eichengreen, Ito, and Wyplocz (1999); the Council of Foreign Relations Report (1999); Ahluwalia 2000; United Nations Task Force 1999; the so-called Meltzer Report (Meltzer 2000); IFIAC 2000; the so-called Zedillo Report (Zedillo 2001); and the Eminent Non–G-7 Report (2001). However, we would like to try to place our thinking in the context of this broad discussion.

At the risk of oversimplification, the positions on international financial architecture can be broadly grouped in three ways.

1. A first position holds broadly that most necessary changes have already been made and that only relatively marginal additional improvements (such as streamlining conditionality) need to be added. Great emphasis is placed in this position on improvements in domestic policies, with a rather large focus on improved transparency and implementing codes and standards. This broadly corresponds to the G-7 position (see, e.g., the G-7 finance ministers' statements at their annual summits).

2. A second position analytically emphasizes public failures and above all moral hazard. The solution to these problems is seen by this line of analysts to significantly reduce the role of the international financial institutions, for example, by restricting the role of lending by both the IMF and the World Bank. The IMF should only lend to the emerging markets; and World Bank finance to middle-income countries should be eliminated. Grants should be the preferred channel of official finance to low-income countries. Perhaps the clearest document representing this position is the so-called Meltzer majority report (Meltzer 2000). As Williamson (2001) neatly summarizes it, the "Meltzer Majority Report starts from a concern that IMF lending may promote moral hazard (a phenomenon whose importance cannot be overstated, according to the Meltzer Report) and concede only reluctantly—and to the dismay of two of their members—that there may after all be a limited role for the Fund" (101). The Meltzer majority report argues that the IMF should only focus on crisis management for emerging economies, should only lend very short term (a maximum of 120 days), and should increase the interest rates it charges. Although in the intellectual debate there was profound and widespread disagreement with the Meltzer majority report in most respects, this report and its position are potentially influential because they may possibly have an impact on the U.S. administration's position on financial architecture.

3. A third position emphasizes the need to deal with market failures and gaps that have arisen from the growth and changing nature of international capital flows. For this purpose, most supporters of this position emphasize the need to strengthen and significantly adapt the international financial institutions (IFI); they advocate increases of IFI lending and suggest new sources of funding for this lending such as SDR issues in the case of the IMF. This line of thinking believes that the IFIs should

provide both liquidity and development finance to different categories of developing countries. Some, though perhaps not that many, supporters of this position also stress the need for improved global and source country regulation (Eatwell and Taylor 2000). Others emphasize the need for orderly debt workouts and payment standstills. (It is interesting that the IMF Deputy Managing Director, Anne Krueger, also supports these.) This type of position is on the whole supported more by developing countries (see, e.g., recent statements of the G-24). Our policy proposals on the whole belong to this broad category.

There is also a fourth position, clearly not so intellectually well articulated as the previous three but very vocal, which can be called that of the "extreme antiglobalizers." Though views vary, there is a strand that is strongly against the IFIs and would even like to abolish them. Paradoxically, in this aspect the extremes meet, as the radical Right (the extreme moral hazard school) and the radical Left (the extreme antiglobalizers) agree;[2] we believe that both of these extreme positions are wrong on this subject and that large—as well as volatile and concentrated—capital flows require strengthened and adapted IFIs as well as—more broadly—better management of capital flows internationally, regionally, and nationally.

There is one final important point about the discussion of international financial architecture. This discussion arose mainly out of the Asian crises and concerns the excessive volatility and reversibility of private capital flows, especially but not only short-term bank lending. Many of the proposals have been dominated by those concerns. However, in the last three years the nature of the flows to emerging countries has changed in two fundamental ways. First, their level has fallen significantly, with net bank lending becoming negative. Second, their structure has changed dramatically, with foreign direct investment becoming not only the dominant flow but also the only significantly positive one. While the increased importance of FDI is on balance very positive, the sharp reduction of overall flows and the negative net flows for most categories are very problematic.

Should these new tendencies in capital flows continue, the discussion of international financial architecture must shift to include not just measures to prevent and manage excessive surges of capital flows to developing countries but also measures to encourage sufficient private flows to take place at all. In this context, care should be taken in designing measures for orderly debt workouts to prevent them from further discouraging private flows. Furthermore, as discussed below, in designing measures such as the new Basle Capital Accord, care must be taken not to design systems that could excessively discourage private bank lending to most developing countries.

2. BETTER INTERNATIONAL INFORMATION AND FINANCIAL REGULATION

2.1. ADDITIONAL INFORMATION ON MARKETS TO DEVELOPING COUNTRIES

As pointed out earlier, better information to markets on developing countries has to be complemented with better information on international financial markets available to policymakers, especially but not only in developing countries. Particularly during the crisis that started in Asia, emerging country policymakers have found important limitations in the essential information available on the functioning of international capital and banking markets. The type of information required is particularly on almost day-to-day changes in the functioning of markets—and their key actors—globally and regionally.

The IMF has led the way in improving information—and its dissemination—on emerging market economies, which is of particular use to markets. A parallel symmetric effort needs to be made to gather and provide timely information on market evolution to emerging markets' policymakers. This task should perhaps be led by the Bank of International Settlements (BIS) and coordinated by the newly created Financial Stability Forum. Inputs from other institutions would be very valuable, especially from the IMF and the private sector (e.g., from the Institute for International Finance [IIF]). These suggestions relate not just to better statistics on international banks' exposure but also on compiling data on international exposures of investment banks, hedge funds and other institutional investors. Furthermore, the growth of financial innovations such as over the counter derivatives, while designed to facilitate the transfer of market risk and therefore to enhance financial stability, have also made financial markets more complex and opaque. This has created difficulties in monitoring patterns of activity in these markets and the distribution of risks in the global financial system for market participants, regulators, central banks, and other authorities, including particularly those in developing countries. It would seem appropriate for major central banks and the BIS to attempt to improve the registration of derivatives and institutions like hedge funds by making it obligatory. Unfortunately, such initiatives to make reporting obligatory have until now been blocked, especially in the U.S. Congress.

Given the speed with which markets move, it seems particularly important that the frequency with which relevant data are produced is very high (and possibly higher in times of market turbulence, when it becomes particularly crucial) and that dissemination is instant to all countries' central banks. Indeed, a special additional service could be provided by the BIS in which it would play the role of a clearinghouse for information. For this purpose, it could not just draw on information it can gather directly from markets but could collect and centralize information on their markets that individual central banks have and where the aggregate picture is not easily available to any individual central bank. This could possibly include both quantitative and qualitative information. Via the Internet, the BIS could standardize the information requirements, collect the information, aggregate it, and disseminate it rapidly to all central banks as well as to other relevant institutions. Such a service would be of the greatest usefulness to developing country policymakers, especially immediately before and during crises; however, it would naturally also be very valuable to developed country policymakers and international institutions (including the BIS itself) in handling crisis prevention and management.

2.2. IMPROVED INTERNATIONAL FINANCIAL REGULATION

The Case for Regulation

A strong case can be made that international financial regulation is welfare increasing. At the domestic level, it is broadly accepted that financial markets, due to problems such as asymmetries of information, behave erratically at times and that the first best response to these problems is regulation and supervision (Greenwald, Stiglitz, and Weiss 1984; Wyplocz 2001). Major efforts are now being made to develop and improve financial regulation in developing countries. But, as financial markets have become globalized, similarly it is increasingly accepted that financial regulation also has to be globalized. Welfare-increasing effects of global financial regulation will be larger if—as we will discuss—such regulation has explicit countercyclical elements to compensate for inherent procyclical behavior by financial actors, which can also partly characterize traditional financial regulation.

Indeed, there is growing support for a view that the process of international financial intermediation has a second-best element in which welfare for both source and recipient countries can be increased by regulatory changes (through measures in source and/or recipient countries), which would reduce excessive lending or investing. It is noteworthy that Chairman Alan Greenspan proposed—for the case of interbank lending—that it could be appropriate for either borrowing countries or lending ones to impose reserve requirements to "deter aberrant borrowing: sovereigns could charge an explicit premium, or could impose reserve requirements, earning low or even zero interest rates, on interbank liabilities. Increasing the capital charge on lending banks, instead of on borrowing banks, might also be effective."[3]

There is growing recognition that it may often be desirable to regulate excessive surges of potentially reversible capital flows in recipient countries. Indeed, an important part of the responsibility for discouraging excessive reversible inflows—as well as managing them—lies with the recipient countries. However, the experience of the 1990s, with very large international funds—compared to the small size of developing country markets—leads to the question of whether measures intended to discourage excessive short-term flows by recipient countries are sufficient to deal with capital surges and the risk of their reversal.

Aizenman and Turnovsky (1999) have formalized such analysis by developing a rigorous model that analyzes the impact via externalities of reserve requirements on international loans (both in lending and recipient countries) on the welfare of both categories of countries. Aizenman and Turnovsky thus evaluate the macroeconomic impact of reserve requirements in a second-best world where there is moral hazard due to likely bailouts on the lender's side and sovereign risk on the borrower's side; both generate large negative externalities on welfare.

The broad theoretical rationale for such measures is that, unlike the case of trade in goods and services, where most mainstream economists agree that free trade is beneficial, there is no such consensus with regard to capital flows. Indeed, many mainstream economists have identified circumstances in which unlimited capital mobility may be suboptimal; such views have become more widespread as currency crises have become more frequent. This does not imply advocating closed capital accounts, as many flows are beneficial. However, it does lead to the conclusion that—globally as well as nationally—the optimum result may be appropriate regulation.

The general conclusion of the Aizenman and Turnovsky model is that the introduction of a reserve requirement in either source or recipient country reduces the risk of default and raises the level of welfare in both the source and the emerging market borrowing country. More specifically, they show that: (1) the introduction of a reserve requirement by the lending country will increase welfare in both economies (this is particularly strong when there is no reserve requirement in the borrowing nation); (2) starting from a situation in which there are no reserve requirements, the introduction of a reserve requirement by the borrowing country will increase welfare in both economies; and (3) more generous bailouts, which encourage borrowing and increase default risk, increase as a consequence the need and level of the lender's optimal reserve requirement. If such higher reserve requirements are applied, world welfare is unchanged by larger bailouts; (4) on the other hand, more generous bailouts in the absence of reserve requirements will reduce welfare due to the increase of default risk; (5) given that it is unlikely that a "nonbailout policy" can be totally credible, reserve requirements—particularly in source countries—are clearly welfare-enhancing; and (6) comprehensive reserve requirements—independently of their size—will most probably improve information about countries' exposure (this may improve the supply of credit to them and especially its stability).

The aim of such regulatory changes is to help smooth capital flows to emerging markets without discouraging them excessively. This is in contrast to views based on a belief that crises in emerging markets are due only to moral hazard and that the appropriate way to combat such moral hazard is by scaling down the role of the IMF in providing financial packages before and during crises. The latter view has acquired some prominence in developed countries, particularly but not only in the United States. In particular, the majority Meltzer report (Meltzer 2000) took such views to the extreme. However, such a reduction of the role of the IMF could either make crises even more costly (as can be seen in the case of Argentina) and/or lead to a sharp reduction in private flows to developing countries. These are both highly undesirable effects, which could significantly diminish welfare, particularly but not only in the developing economies, as well as undermine support for open economies and market-based economic policies in developing economies. Therefore, an approach based on better regulation is clearly better and more welfare enhancing than one that cuts back the IMF.

Filling Gaps

The broad welfare case for applying reserve requirements in both source and recipient countries can also be applied to institutional investors and in particular to mutual funds, which became increasingly important in relation to banks in the 1990s. This growing importance occurred both within the developed countries and particularly within the United States—where mutual funds receive more than 50 percent of total deposits in the financial system—and in capital flows from developed to developing countries (see d'Arista and Griffith-Jones 2000; for their importance in recent crises, see chapter 2). The narrowing of differences between banks and institutional investors like mutual funds, and the fact that securities markets and thus mutual funds also have access to the lender of last resort, nationally in the United States but more importantly in our context also internationally due to the frequent rescue packages put together by the IMF in recent serious currency crises, suggests the importance of improving prudential standards for institutional investors such as mutual funds.

It is also important to stress that the risks being borne by institutional investors, such as mutual funds, are increasingly similar to those facing banks, including both liquidity management problems and a greater exposure to macroeconomic problems and macroeconomic effects. With regard to the latter, institutional investors seem up to now to be insufficiently aware of the risks that macroeconomic problems and developments can have on their investments, which would seem to justify regulatory actions such as those we will suggest below to help take account of macroeconomic risks when investment decisions are made.

Another source of concern is liquidity management by international institutional investors; such liquidity management in the face of heavy redemptions—for example, as currency crisis threatens or explodes—may become an issue not just for the mutual funds concerned but for the countries in which they are invested. As institutional investors attempt to meet redemptions—or even accumulate cash for possible large redemptions—this will encourage them to liquidate their investments very quickly, sometimes even more quickly than their liquidity needs warrant. This will contribute to short-term excessive and rapid outflows from developing countries' securities markets. Better arrangements for managing mutual funds' liquidity—such as the cash requirements we will suggest—would, by reducing the need for mutual funds to liquidate their cash holdings, dampen the reversibility of investment flows out of developing markets. Equally important, such cash requirements would also boost investors' confidence in the financial strength of such funds, lowering the trend toward large redemptions in unfavorable circumstances.

Both aspects promote more gradual changes in investment holdings and thus smooth international capital flows overall.

With regard to portfolio flows to emerging markets, there is an important regulatory gap, as at present there is no regulatory framework internationally, for taking account of market or credit risks on flows originating in institutional investors such as mutual funds (and more broadly for flows originating in nonbank institutions). This important regulatory gap needs to be filled, both to protect retail investors in developed countries and protect developing countries from the negative effects of excessively large and potentially reversible portfolio flows.

The East Asian crisis (see chap. 2) and even more the Brazilian experience (see chap. 9) confirm what was particularly clearly visible in the Mexican peso crisis (Griffith-Jones 1998). Institutional investors, like mutual funds, given the very liquid nature of their investments, can play an important role in contributing to developing country currency crises (for more evidence, see Kaminsky, Schmukler, and Lyon 2000). It seems important, therefore, to introduce some regulation to discourage excessive surges of portfolio flows; this should not affect normal portfolio flows to emerging markets, which play an important role such as helping to deepen domestic financial markets. This could perhaps best be achieved by a variable risk-weighted cash requirement for institutional investors such as mutual funds. These cash requirements would be placed as interest-bearing deposits in commercial banks. Introducing a dynamic risk-weighted cash requirement for mutual funds (and perhaps for other institutional investors) is in the mainstream of current regulatory thinking and would require that standards be provided by relevant regulatory authorities or agreed on internationally. The guidelines for macroeconomic risk, which would determine the cash requirement, would take into account such vulnerability variables as the ratio of a country's current account deficit (or surplus) to GDP, the level of its short-term external liabilities to foreign exchange reserves, the fragility of the banking system, and other relevant country risk factors. It is important that quite sophisticated analysis is used to prevent simplistic criteria from stigmatizing countries unnecessarily; this could be based on the extensive literature on vulnerability indicators. The views of the national central banks and treasuries in the source countries and of the IMF and the BIS should be helpful in this respect. The securities regulators in source countries would be the most appropriate institutions to implement such regulations, which could be coordinated internationally by International Organization of Securities Commissions (IOSCO), probably best in the context of the Forum for Financial Stability.

The fact that the level of required cash reserves would vary with the level of countries' perceived "macroeconomic risk" would make it relatively more profitable to invest in countries with good fundamentals and relatively less profitable to invest in countries with more problematic macro- or financial sector fundamentals. If these fundamentals deteriorate, investment would decline gradually, which hopefully would force an *early correction* of policy and a resumption of flows. Although the requirement for cash reserves on mutual funds' assets invested in emerging markets could increase somewhat the cost of raising foreign capital for them, this would be compensated for by the benefit of a more stable supply of funds at a more stable cost. Furthermore, this countercyclical smoothing of flows would hopefully discourage the massive and sudden reversal of flows that sparked both the Mexican and the Asian crises, making such developmentally costly crises less likely.

Given the dominant role and rapid growth of institutional investors in countries such as the United States, the United Kingdom, and France, this proposal—for a risk-weighted cash requirement on mutual funds—could possibly be adopted first in those countries, without creating significant competitive disadvantages. Soon after international harmonization would have to be introduced. However, an alternative route would be for such measures to be studied and implemented internationally, being discussed initially within IOSCO and/or in the broader context of the Forum for Financial Stability. International coordination of such a measure would prevent investments by mutual funds from being channeled through different countries, and especially offshore centers, that did not impose these cash requirements (the latter point draws on communication with the Federal Reserve Board).

Such IOSCO international guidelines would be formulated through international guidelines similar to those employed by the Basle Committee in developing the "Core Principles for Effective Banking Supervision" (see www.bis .org). The guidelines could be developed by a working group consisting of representatives of the national securities' regulatory authorities in source countries together with some representation from developing countries, in the context of IOSCO. Due account should be taken of relevant existing regulations such as the European Commission's Capital Adequacy Directive.

Finally, it is important to stress that additional regulation of mutual funds should be consistent with regulation of other institutions (e.g., banks) and other potentially volatile flows.

It is encouraging that the September 1998 emerging markets IOSCO report *Causes, effects, and regulatory implications of financial and economic turbulence in emerging markets* (IOSCO 1998) has in fact described in some detail and evaluated rather positively this proposal. This report emphasized that "there appears to be scope—and an urgent need for further work. This is very likely to require a multilateral effort—i.e. by regulators from both source and recipient countries in collaboration with the industry" (10). It is therefore to be hoped that this type of proposal will be analyzed in further detail, with a view toward possible implementation, either within IOSCO or within the Financial Stability Forum.

With regard to HLIs, the Financial Stability Forum working group on Highly Leveraged Institutions (HLIs) rightly focused on two problems: systemic risk linked to high leverage and reduction of the market and economic impact of the collapse of unregulated HLIs (FSF, 2000a). Particular emphasis was placed on HLI activities in small and medium-sized open economies, where the potential damage that can be caused by large and concentrated positions can seriously amplify market pressures.

With regard to HLIs, the FSF Working Group considered formal direct regulation of currently unregulated institutions. This would include a licensing system, minimum capital and liquidity standards, large exposure limits, minimum standards for risk management, and even an enforcement regime with fines for transgressions.

Such regulation was seen to have several very desirable effects (such as regular oversight over HLIs and reducing the likelihood of disruptive market events), but due to what were seen as both philosophical and practical problems the working group did not recommend applying a system of direct regulation to currently unregulated HLIs at this stage, though it did not reject the possibility of establishing such a regime at a later stage. It emphasized that the failure to carry out its recommended measures would prompt such a reconsideration (FSF, 2000a, op. cit.).

The philosophical objection relates to the fact that direct regulation would not be aimed at investor protection (as investors are sufficiently wealthy or sophisticated enough to exercise their own due diligence) but on the mitigation of systemic risk. However, it could be argued that mitigation of systemic risk is also an increasingly valid regulatory aim. There were also practical objections, including how to avoid leakage through offshore centers. However, current efforts to improve and complete regulation in offshore centers should help overcome those problems (see discussion of the FSF Working Group report on offshore centers, FSF 2000b, 10–15). Other practical issues are more technical and more valid, including the need to adapt capital adequacy and large exposure rules to the specific risk profile of HLIs. This should be done in such a way that any regulatory capital requirement would not adversely affect the efficiency and liquidity of markets in which HLIs are significant participants. This seems particularly important in a context in which several large hedge funds have been wound down, which may diminish some of the negative impacts they have had in recent crises, but could according to some observers deprive markets of contrarian actors, who have some useful roles to play in stopping deepening crises.

Removing Regulatory Distortions and Dampening the Exuberance of Bank Lending

With regard to bank lending, there has first been concern that the 1988 Basle Capital Accord contributed to the buildup of short-term bank lending and its reversal in East Asia and elsewhere due to significantly lower capital adequacy requirements for short-term than for long-term lending. The new proposal, published in January 2001, attempts to address this distortion by reducing somewhat (though perhaps not sufficiently) the differential between capital adequacy for short-term and other lending (Basle Committee 2001). However, the proposed Basle Capital Accord, although it includes many positive elements, also has suggestions that are widely seen as problematic, particularly for developing countries (see Griffith-Jones and Spratt 2001 and Reisen 2001). Some of these problems are *partly* addressed in the November 2001 consultation documents.

In recent years, criticisms from many quarters have been leveled at the functioning of the 1988 accord, with critics arguing that the regulatory requirements do not correspond to actual levels of risk. The consequences of this have been distortions and biases in the practices of the banking industry. Consequently, the proposals aim to increase the risk sensitivity of capital requirements and thereby more closely align these requirements with actual risks. To this end, a major proposal is to move toward ever greater use of banks' own internal risk management systems. However, although the focus of the proposals is aimed at the needs of major banks from the Group of 10 (G-10), it is likely that the *new accord, when implemented, will have significant, and broadly negative, repercussions for the developing world.*

Developing sovereigns, corporates, and banks wishing to borrow in international markets will find the lending environment greatly worsened, as the major banks' lending patterns have been significantly changed by the adoption of internal-ratings-based (IRB) approaches. The outcome of these changes is likely to be a significant reduction of bank lending to the developing world and/or a sharp increase in the cost of international borrowing for many developing countries. According to estimates by Reisen (2001), based on estimates by Deutsche Bank, we can see in table 11.1 that the adoption of the IRB approach as currently proposed could result in speculative-grade borrowers (with a rating of BBB- or lower) being effectively excluded from international bank lending (the median sovereign rating for nonmembers of the Organization for Economic Cooperation and Development [OECD] countries in 2001 was BB, with 31 of the 53 rated non-OECD countries being rated below BBB-). We believe that the proposed changes will be neutral or broadly positive for sovereigns rated BBB or higher. However, for sovereigns rated below that, the situation is very problematic. For example,

TABLE 11.1. Sovereign Borrowers

	Risk Weight	Capital Required per U.S.$100	Estimated Breakeven Spread Change bp.[a]	Examples of Countries in Category	
Double-A (OECD)					
Current	0	0	—	Belgium	Bermuda
Standardized	0	0	—	Canada	Italy
IRB approach	7	0.6	+3	Italy	Portugal
Triple-B (non-OECD)					
Current	100	8.0	—	China	Malaysia
Standardized	50	4.0	−50	Korea	Tunisia
IRB approach	40	3.2	−60	Egypt	Latvia
Double-B (non-OECD)					
Current	100	8.0	—	Brazil	Costa Rica
Standardized	100	8.0	—	Colombia	Morocco
IRB approach	379	30.3	+1,115	India	Kazakhstan
Single-B (non-OECD)					
Current	100	8.0	—	Argentina	Mongolia
Standardized	100	8.0	—	Jamaica	Paraguay
IRB approach	630	50.4	+3,709	Pakistan	Venezuela

Source: Reisen 2001 and Standard and Poor's sovereign ratings, June 6, 2001.
[a]Estimated base points.

for sovereigns such as Brazil and India, rated BB under the current accord, each $100 lent requires an $8 capital requirement. Under the new standardized approach, this would be unchanged; however, under the IRB approach (and based on the calculations by Reisen, op. cit. reflected in table 11.1) it can be seen that the capital required for the same $100 could rise to $30.30 and spreads could increase by 1,115 bp (11 percent). Even more dramatically, for countries such as Argentina and Pakistan, which are rated B, spreads could increase by 3,709 bp (37 percent) under the IRB approach to produce an equivalent level of risk adjusted return as under the existing accord.[4] The implications of this are clear: *large parts of the developing world would no longer be able to access international bank lending on terms likely to be acceptable.* The impact of this is likely to be felt most severely in the lowest-rated countries—such as those of sub-Saharan Africa, the very countries most in need of such access. The revisions to the proposed Capital Accord issued in November 2001 significantly reduced, but by no means eliminated this problem.

The effect was this extreme because the Basle Committee proposed a strongly exponential, rather than a linear, rise in risk weightings along the spectrum of probability of default. Thus, once ratings fall below BBB the capital requirements increase sharply, implying that for the lowest-rated borrowers the cost of loans from banks operating on the IRB approach is likely to be prohibitively high. Therefore, it is not the principle that increased riskiness should be reflected in higher-risk weightings that is being challenged but a concern that the IRB approach increases the weights far more rapidly than is objectively justified as one moves to lower creditworthiness ratings.

A second highly problematic likely effect of the new Basle Capital Accord would be sharply increased procyclicality. This would imply that for both developed and developing countries in periods of slowdown or recession, perceived riskiness of loans would increase. This would imply far higher capital requirements, which would lead to sharp reductions in bank lending and would in fact deepen any slowdown or recession.

It is ironic and particularly problematic that these proposals (which would imply less and more costly lending to developing countries, as well as more procyclical lending, which is particularly damaging for developing countries) have emerged at the same time as developing countries are being urged to make greater use of private capital flows and as these flows—especially bank lending—are not only slowing down but are negative in net terms.

Countercyclical Elements in Regulation

The answer thus may lie in the implementation of an explicit countercyclical mechanism that would, in boom periods and in contrast to ratings, dampen excess bank lending. Countercyclical elements can also be introduced in regulating other actors (see the earlier discussion of mutual funds). On the contrary, in periods of slowdown and scarcity of finance the new mechanism should not further accentuate the decline in lending, as exemplified by the 1997–98 Asian crisis, and to a lesser extent the 1999–2001 period. Rather, it should encourage such lending. (For an excellent discussion of countercyclical issues in regulation, see BIS 2001).

There would be two linked objectives for introducing elements of countercyclical regulation. One would be to help smooth capital flows, and the other would be to smooth the domestic impact of volatile capital flows on the domestic financial system and therefore on the real economy. Introducing countercyclical elements into regulation would help build a link between the more microeconomic risks on which regulators have tended to focus till recently and the macroeconomic risks that are becoming increasingly important, both nationally and internationally.[5] Countercyclical elements in regulation related to bank lending could be applied internationally, nationally, or at both levels.

Several mechanisms could be used to introduce a countercyclical element into the regulation of bank lending. One mechanism would be to raise the required capital ratio in times of boom and to allow banks to use the additional cushion provided by the higher capital ratio so they could sustain lending in times of recession at a lower capital asset ratio (when increased bad loans are likely to be reducing their capital). Some practical difficulties may arise in implementing such a mechanism, of which the most serious one may be getting international agreement on a general formula for cyclically adjusted capital asset ratios.

A second mechanism for introducing countercyclical elements in bank lending regulation is for regulators to suggest that higher general provisions be made for possible loan losses (i.e., subtracted from equity capital in the books of the bank) to cover normal cyclical risks (Turner 2000). This would allow for provisions built up in good times to be used in bad times without affecting reported capital. The way to ensure this would be to maintain higher general provisioning that applies to all loans. The main problem for this mechanism, according to Turner, may be that tax laws often limit the tax deductibility of precautionary provisioning; however, it is possible to change such tax laws, as indeed was done in the late 1980s in the United Kingdom. It is encouraging that the Spanish Central Bank has already introduced such a "forward-looking" provision and that other central banks and regulators are beginning to evaluate provisioning, that would attempt "to see though the cycle."

A third relevant mechanism, particularly for domestic bank lending, is for regulators to place caps on the value of assets (such as real estate or stocks and shares) to be acceptable as collateral when the value of such assets has risen sharply in a boom and is at risk of declining sharply in a recession. Rules could be used such as averaging values for the last five years or accepting only 50 percent of current prices in the peak period of a boom. The latter mechanism seems to have the fewest implementation problems (indeed, reportedly it has already been applied in jurisdictions such as Hong Kong).

A fourth possible countercyclical mechanism is that monetary authorities could monitor and try to limit or discourage lending for property, construction, and personal consumption, as these items tend to increase substantially—and often even are a major factor—in booms. A possible implementation problem would be that it may be difficult to verify the final use of credit and such measures could be partially evaded.

Furthermore, regulators should be flexible in downturns, particularly in allowing banks to easily use cushions (e.g., of capital or provisioning) in times of recession; it may even be advisable, if a recession is very serious, to allow ratios to fall below normally required levels (to help sustain lending), with the understanding that they will be rebuilt as soon as the economy begins to recover. Some tension may arise here between the regulatory concerns about individual bank liquidity and solvency and the macroeconomic externalities of their actions, particularly during recessions.

Specific issues seem to require further study. How best can the distinction between a temporary boom and a permanent increase in growth be made? After what period of "boom" should regulatory changes be introduced? How large should such changes be? What are the best mechanisms through which countercyclical measures should be introduced (flexible capital adequacy ratios, higher provisioning against losses, more "realistic" pricing of collateral)? Should such measures be introduced for both international and domestic lending or preferably for one of them? This chapter provides only initial thoughts on these important issues. We suggest that further research in this area is important, and we are initiating some work ourselves at the time of writing.

2.3. EMERGENCY AND COUNTERCYCLICAL FINANCING

The enhanced provision of emergency financing during crises is another pillar of the system to prevent and manage financial crises. Indeed, although the direct focus of emergency financing is crisis management, it also has crisis prevention effects, as it plays an essential role in avoiding the destabilizing expectations that are responsible for deepening and spreading crises (contagion) and ultimately for systemic failures. This has been, in fact, the essential defense for the role that central banks play at the national level as lenders of last resort. Current international arrangements are weaker in this regard. Indeed, the IMF provides "emergency financing" but certainly not *liquidity,* a fact that is reflected in the lack of automaticity in the availability of financing during crises.[6] Although the International Monetary Fund has the capacity to create fiat money through the issue of SDRs, it was used only in the past and in a very limited way.

It is important to emphasize that in this regard emergency financing is not a substitute for, but a complement to strong regulation and debt workout procedures. Regulatory changes help smooth capital flows to emerging markets. Together with private sector involvement in crisis resolution, through adequate debt workouts, they are essential to avoiding moral hazard. However, the view that the appropriate way to combat such moral hazard is by scaling down the role of the IMF in providing financial packages during crises would make them even more costly and/or would lead to a sharp reduction in private flows to developing countries. Indeed, as discussed, there may be a case in the current context of large and volatile private flows even for significantly larger official emergency financing than currently exists. The great majority of recent reports support this view (Williamson 2001), with the major exception being the majority Meltzer report (Meltzer 2000), although the minority view in Meltzer also strongly values the broad role of the IMF. A recent serious source of concern is smaller willingness of the IMF to provide emergency financing in times of crises, for example, in Argentina.

The main lessons from recent crises are, indeed: (1) that as a preventive measure, wider use should be made of both private and official contingency credit lines that are agreed on during periods of adequate access to capital markets following the (partly successful) experiences of some "emerging" economies; (2) that large-scale funding may be required, though not all of it (and maybe even none of it) needs to be disbursed if support programs rapidly restore market confidence; (3) that funds should be made available *before*—rather than after—international reserves reach critically low levels; and (4) that, due to strong contagion effects, contingency financing may be required even by countries that do not exhibit fundamental disequilibria. Positive measures have been adopted in this area, including a significant expansion of IMF resources through a quota increase and the New Arrangements to Borrow, which finally went into effect in late 1998; the launching of a new window in December 1997 to finance exceptional borrowing requirements during crises; and the creation of the Contingency Credit Line in April 1999 to provide financing to countries facing contagion and its redesign in September 2000; however, unfortunately this letter facility has not yet been used.

The major controversies relate to inadequate funding, the design of some specific credit lines, and the broadening scope of conditionality. With respect to the first issue, bilateral financing and contributions to the IMF will continue to be scarce during crises. This might reduce the stabilizing effects of rescue packages if the market decides that the intervening authorities (the IMF plus additional bilateral support) are unable or unwilling to supply funds in the quantities required. As bilateral financing and contributions to the IMF will continue to be scarce and unreliable in crises, the best solution may be to allow additional issues of SDRs during episodes of world financial stress; these funds could be destroyed once financial conditions normalize.[7] This procedure would create an anticyclical element in world liquidity management and would give SDRs an enhanced role in world finance, a principle that developing countries have advocated in the past and should continue to endorse in the future. Second-best alternatives are to make a more active use of central bank swap arrangements under IMF or BIS leadership and/or to allow the IMF to raise the resources needed in the market.

It is useful to put the discussion on the second issue in the broader context of the functions that IMF facilities have to perform in today's world. In this regard, there are, first of all, the traditional needs of emergency financing to face balance of payments crises due to two sets of causes or a mixture of both: (1) inconsistent macroeconomic policy, and (2) traditional external shocks such as deterioration in the terms of trade, increased interest rates in developed countries, and/or a slowdown in developed countries' growth. The Standby Arrangement (SBA), the Extended Fund Facility (EFF), and the recently modified Compensatory Financing Facility (CFF) have for some time dealt with these traditional needs.

Second, there are the new needs, linked to "twenty-first-century-style" currency and financial crises, that are mainly caused by the interaction of volatile capital flows and domestic financial fragilities and can spread via contagion among countries (including, as we have noted, those with fairly sound macroeconomic fundamentals). The challenges here are both improved crisis prevention and better crisis management if these crises do occur. Recent crises have led to the creation of the Supplemental Reserve Facility (SRF) and the mentioned Contingency Credit Line (CCL). While these facilities reflect the clear new need for significantly enhanced public liquidity provisions in a globalized world, where the risk of crises has significantly increased, they do not go as far as may be desirable and necessary in the provision of official liquidity financing.

There are, finally, the special needs to provide to low-income countries and to strengthen in a sustainable way their balance of payments position while supporting growth and poverty reduction. In 1999, the traditional facility in this area was transformed into the Poverty Reduction and Growth Facility (PRGF).

This broad menu is essential to respond to the call by the G-24 for the

Bretton Woods institutions in their annual statement to the IMF, in September 2001 to "maintain a range of instruments to address the needs of their diverse membership." It should also be added that in the first two cases, but also possibly in the third, IMF lending should be perceived as "a bridge to and from private sector lending" (Summers 2000).

Some facilities seem to function fairly well, with regard to the scale of financing they provide and the circumstances under which they are used, though the nature and the scope of the conditionality should be narrower, as will be argued. The facilities that function reasonably well to meet current needs include the Standby Arrangement, which it is agreed will remain the Fund's main instrument, and the Extended Fund Facility, though some observers have challenged its value, in spite of its importance to developing countries, because it allows longer periods of adjustment to balance of payments disequilibria of a structural character. The simplified CFF can also perform a useful function in helping primary-producing countries cope with exogenously determined terms of trade shocks. However, the CFF should be expanded to cover the full extent of export shortfalls and its conditionality reduced, given the fact that the cause of the problem is international. The fairly recently created Supplemental Reserve Facility, which was designed to provide exceptional financing during crises, has also worked well, even though resource limitations cause it to fall short of what would be desirable in today's world.

The CCL was created as "a precautionary line of defence readily available against future balance of payments problems that might arise from international financial contagion" (IMF 1999). The philosophy of the IMF in moving more strongly into precautionary lending that would reduce the chances of countries being caught by contagion and would give leverage to the IMF to encourage countries to pursue policies that would make crises less likely is clearly the right one. However, the fact that the CCL had not been used at the time of writing since its creation in April 1999 reflects design problems that were only partly corrected in the 2000 redesign of this facility. These include: (1) the limited scale of the facility; (2) the lack of automatic triggering in the original design, which was partially corrected by making "activation" a fairly automatic process, though still requiring a "postactivation" review that would result in a conditional adjustment program; (3) the "two-phase or double conditionality" that characterizes such design; and (4) the fear of countries that private lenders and investors might see the use of the CCL as "the ambulance outside the door," which could contribute to rather than deter a speculative attack or withdrawal of flows.

To overcome problems of the CCL and the reluctance of countries to use it, in spite of its modification, a further change could make it more effective. This would imply that any country that had been very successfully evaluated during its Article IV consultation and that continued to perform well during the next three months could automatically get a CCL. Should a crisis linked to contagion hit such a country, the CCL could be disbursed automatically for a relatively short period. As pointed out earlier, if the CCL is to be made more effective and easier to disburse it must be accompanied by better regulation to avoid problems of excessive moral hazard. Debt standstills and orderly debt workouts would also help reduce the excessive cost borne by debtor countries in crises under present arrangements (for detailed discussions, see UNCTAD 1998 and United Nations Task Force 1999). However, as mentioned earlier, care must be taken in designing such measures so they do not excessively discourage private flows to developing countries or significantly increase their cost (Soros 2000).

With regard to Fund conditionality, it is now accepted that it should be streamlined, refocusing on the IMF's central competencies (see IMF 2000a), thus reversing the trend toward increase in its areas and scope over the past two decades. Furthermore, while conditionality is clearly valuable when domestic policies are the source of macroeconomic disequilibria that lead to balance of payments and financial difficulties, its relevance is unclear when difficulties are generated due to external shocks such as contagion.

As Rodrik (1999) clearly warned in relation to the recent widening of conditionality, "An unappreciated irony is that conditionality on developing countries is being ratcheted up at precisely the moment when our comprehension of how the global economy works and what small countries need to do to prosper within it has been revealed to be strongly lacking. . . . The reality is that our prescriptions often go considerably beyond what can be supported by careful theoretical reasoning or empirical demonstration" (13). Conditionality should thus be carefully tailored to the specific circumstances of the particular problem faced.

The Fund's core competence has traditionally been in macroeconomic policy and has rightly been expanding into financial vulnerabilities, as its interactions with the macroeconomy are strong. The new emphasis on growth and poverty reduction as a key aim for Fund programs and on countries' macroeconomic policies, especially in low-income countries, is clearly welcome, as is its greater collaboration with the World Bank on these issues. However, this should not lead the Fund into involvement in detailed poverty-related conditionality. Similarly, great care must be taken that in both middle-income and low-income countries the large number of standards and codes of conduct that have arisen since the Asian crisis, however useful they may be individually, do not collectively pose an excessive burden (via IMF conditionality) on countries' administration and policy making. Indeed, it seems best if, as argued by the G-24, implementation of such standards remain voluntary. On the other hand, to ensure that Fund conditionality truly contributes to growth, automatic rules could be included in Fund agreements with countries to ease the restrictions of the adjustment program should evidence of overkill become clear.

Finally, but most importantly, the principle of ownership of policies should be respected, not just in rhetoric but in actual practice, and should cover all areas of policy, including short- and long-term macroeconomic policies and poverty-reduction strategies. This can only be possible if policy alternatives suggested by the authorities are actually discussed, even if they contradict the traditional preferences of IMF and World Bank programs. Indeed, the principle of ownership can only be effectively pursued in the context of a broad policy discussion, in which these and many other institutions, including those in the developing world, can go beyond the narrow range of alternatives that have been the focus of both macroeconomic and structural conditionality over the past two decades.

NOTES

1. An excellent and constantly updated source for the debate on international financial architecture is the Roubini Web site <http://www.stern.nyu.edu/~nroubini/asia/AsiaHomePage.htm>. Our modest recent contributions can be found at <http://www.ids.ac.uk/ids/global/finance/intfin2.html> and <http://www.eclac.cl>.

2. We thank Hans Tietmeier, former governor of the German Central Bank, for insightful comments on this.

3. Remarks by Alan Greenspan before the thirty-fourth annual conference of the Federal Reserve Bank of Chicago, May 7, 1998.

4. Other estimates were somewhat lower but still showed major increases in spreads for borrowers below investment grade.

5. We thank Andrew Crockett for his suggestive remarks on this point.

6. This important distinction is made by Helleiner (1999). For a fuller discussion of this issue and its relation to IMF access to adequate resources, see Mohammed 1999.

7. See United Nations Task Force 1999, Council on Foreign Relations 1999, Group of 24 2000, and Camdessus 2000. See also Griffith-Jones and Kimmis 2001.

REFERENCES

Ahluwalia, M. 2001. "The future of the IMF and the World Bank." In *Developing countries and the global financial system.* Ed. S. Griffith-Jones and A. Bhattacharya. London: Commonwealth Secretariat.

Aizenman, Joshua, and Stephen J. Turnovsky. 1999. "Reserve requirements on sovereign debt in the presence of moral hazards: On debtors or creditors?" Working Paper 7004, NBER.

Basle Committee (2001). Consultative document on proposal for a new Basle Capital Accord. January. www.bis.org.

Basle Committee on Banking Supervision. January 2001. The New Basle Capital Accord (Consultative Document), Basle. http://www.bis.org.

BIS (Bank for International Settlements). 1997. *Core principles for effective banking supervision.* Basle Committee Publications No. 30 (September 1997).

———. Bank for International Settlements (2001), *Annual Report.*

Camdessus, Michel. 2000. "An agenda for the IMF at the start of the twenty-first century." Remarks at the Council on Foreign Relations, New York, February.

Cornford, A. 2000. "The Basle Committee's proposals for revised capital standards: Rationale, design, and possible incidence." Paper presented at the meeting of the Technical Committee of the Intergovernmental Group of 24, Lima, Peru, March 1–3.

Council on Foreign Relations Task Force Report. 1999. *Safeguarding prosperity in a global financial system: The future international financial architecture,* by Carla A. Hills, Peter G. Peterson, and Morris Goldstein. Washington, DC: Institute for International Economics.

D'Arista, Jane, and Stephany Griffith-Jones. 2000. "The boom of portfolio flows to emerging markets and its regulatory implications." In *Short-term capital flows and economic crises,* ed. S. Griffith-Jones, M. Montes, and A. Nasution.

De Gregorio, Jose, Barry Eichengreen, Takatoshi Ito, and Charles Wyplosz. 1999. *An Independent and Accountable IMF: Geneva Reports on the World Economy 1.* CEPR: London.

Eatwell, J., and E. Taylor. 2000. "Global finance at risk: The case for international regulation." New York: New York Press.

ECLAC (Economic Commission for Latin America and the Caribbean). 1998. "The fiscal covenant: Strengths, weaknesses, challenges." LC/G.1997/Rev.1. Santiago, Chile, April.

———. 2000. ECLAC, *Equity, Development, and Citizenship.* LC/G.2071(SES.28/3). Santiago, Chile.

Eichengreen, Barry, and Richard Portes. 1995. "Crisis? What crisis? Orderly workouts for sovereign debtors." Centre for Economic Policy Research, London.

The Eminent Non-G7 Report. 2001. "Financial instability in the third world." Ford Foundation, New York.

FSF (Financial Stability Forum). 2000a. "Working group report on highly leveraged institutions." Basle.

———. 2000b. "Working Group Report on Offshore Centers."

Goldstein, M., G. Kaminsky, and C. Reinhart. 2000. "Assessing financial vulnerability: An early warning system for emerging markets." Institute for International Economics, Washington, DC, June.

Greenspan, Alan. 1998. Remarks before the thirty-fourth annual conference of the Federal Reserve Bank of Chicago, May 7.

Greenwald, B., J. Stiglitz, and A. Weiss. 1984. "Informational imperfections in the capital market and macroeconomic fluctuations." *American Economic Review* 74, no. 2:194–99.

Griffith-Jones, Stephany. 1998. *Global capital flows: Should they be regulated?* London: Macmillan.

———. 2001. "An international financial architecture for crises prevention." In *Finan-*

cial crises in "successful" emerging economies, ed. Ricardo Ffrench-Davis. Brookings: Washington, D.C.

Griffith-Jones, S., and J. Kimmis. 2001. "The reform of global financial governance arrangements." Report prepared for the Commonwealth Secretariat, London.

Griffith-Jones, Stephany, and José Antonio Ocampo, with Jacques Cailloux. 1999. "The poorest countries and the emerging international financial architecture." Expert Group on Development Issues (EGDI), Stockholm.

Griffith-Jones, S., and S. Spratt. 2001. "The Pro-Cyclical Effects of the New Basle Accord," in J. J. Teunissen, ed. *New challenges of crisis prevention.* FONDAD: The Hague.

Group of 7. 1998. "Declaration of G-7 finance ministers and central bank governors," October 30.

Group of 24. 2000. *Communiqué.* Washington, DC: September 23.

———. 2000. *Communiqué.* Washington, DC, April 15.

Helleiner, G. 1999. "Financial markets, crises and contagion: Issues for smaller countries in the FTAA and post-Lomé IV negotiations." Paper prepared for the Caribbean Regional Negotiating Machinery, Kingston, Jamaica, January.

IFIAC (International Financial Institution Advisory Commission). 2000. "The International Financial Institution Advisory Commission on the future roles of seven international financial institutions." March. Available at <http://phantom-x.gsia.cmu.edu/IFIAC/Report.htm>.

IMF (International Monetary Fund). 1998. "Toward a framework for financial stability." IMF, Washington, DC.

———. 1999. "Report of the acting managing director to the Interim Committee on Progress in Strengthening the Architecture of the International Financial System" IMF, Washington, DC, September.

———. 2000a. "Report of the acting managing director to the International Monetary and Financial Committee on Progress in Reforming the IMF and Strengthening the Architecture of the International Financial System." IMF, Washington, DC, April.

———. 2000b. "Report of the acting managing director to the International Monetary and Financial Committee on Progress in Strengthening the Architecture of the International Financial System and Reform of the IMF." IMF, Washington, DC, September.

IMF International Monetary and Financial Committee. 2000. Communiqué, September 24.

IOSCO (International Organization of Securities Commissions). 1998. "Causes, effects, and regulatory implications of financial and economic turbulence in emerging markets." IOSCO, September.

J. P. Morgan. 1998. *World Financial Markets.* New York: J. P. Morgan.

Kaminsky, G., S. Schmukler, and R. Lyon. 1999. "Managers, investors, and crises: mutual fund strategies in emerging markets." Mimeo, World Bank, Washington, DC.

Meltzer, Allan H. 2000. "Report to the U.S. Congress of the International Financial Advisory Commission." IFAC, March.

Mohammed, Ariz Ali. 1999. "Adequacy of international liquidity in the current financial environment." In UNCTAD, *International Monetary and Financial Issues for the 1990s,* Vol. XI. United Nations publication, sales no.E.99.II.D.25. New York and Geneva.

Montek, Ahluwalia. 2000. *Reforming the Global Financial Architecture.* Commonwealth Secretariat: London.

Reisen, H. 2001. "Will Basel II Contribute to Convergence in International Capital Flows? Mimeo, OECD Development Centre, Paris.

Rodrik, Dani. 1999. "The new global economy and developing countries: Making openness work." Policy Essay 24. Overseas Development Council, Washington, DC.

Short-Term Capital Flows and Economic Crises. Ed. Stephany Griffith-Jones, Manuel F. Montes, and Anwar Nasution. Oxford University Press.

Soros, George. 2000. *Open society: Reforming global capitalism.* New York: Public Affairs.

Summers, Larry. 2000. "International financial crises: Causes, prevention, and cures." *American Economic Review* 90, no. 2 (May): 1–16.

Turner, Philip. 2001. "Procyclicality of regulatory ratios?" In *Global financial regulation,* ed. John Eatwell and Lance Taylor. New York: Oxford University Press.

UNCTAD (United Nations Conference on Trade and Development). 1998. *Trade and Development Report, 1998.* UNCTAD/TDR/1998. Geneva: UNCTAD.

———. 1999. *Trade and Development Report, 1999.* UNCTAD/TDR/1999. Geneva: UNCTAD.

United Nations Task Force of the Executive Committee of Economic and Social Affairs. 1999. "Towards a new international financial architecture: Report of the Task Force of the United Nations Executive Committee of Economic and Social Affairs." LC/G.2054. Economic Commission for Latin America and the Caribbean (ECLAC), Santiago, Chile, March.

Williamson, John. 2001. "The role of the IMF: A guide to the reports." In *Developing countries and the global financial system,* ed. S. Griffith-Jones and A. Bhattacharya. London: Commonwealth Secretariat. 97–124.

World Bank. 1998. "Global economic prospects and the developing countries, 1998–99." World Bank, Washington, DC, December.

———. 1999. "Global development finance, 1999," World Bank, Washington, DC, March.

———. 2000. "Global development finance, 2000," World Bank, Washington, DC, April.

Wyplosz, C. 2001. "How risky is financial liberalization in the developing countries?" Paper presented at the seventh Conference on Current Issues in Emerging Market Economies, Dubrovnik, June 28–29.

Zedillo, E., et al. 2001. "Technical report of the High-Level Panel on Financing for Development." Report commissioned by the secretary-general of the United Nations, June.

Contributors

Jacques Cailloux Economist, Barclays Capital; former Fellow of IDS.

Stephany Griffith-Jones Professorial Fellow of IDS; former Deputy Director of the Commonwealth Secretariat. Professor Griffith-Jones has published many books and articles on international finance and macroeconomic policy issues. She has advised many international organizations, including the World Bank and the European Commission, and several national governments, including the Czech Central Bank and the Brazilian Presidency.

Ammar Siamwalla Director, Thailand Development Research Institute; Senior Advisor to the President.

Yos Vajragupta Senior Researcher, Thailand Development Research Institute.

Pakorn Vichyanond Researcher, Thaliand Development Research Institute.

Jomo K. S. Professor of Economics, University of Malaya, Malaysia.

Anwar Nasution Dean and Professor of Economics, Faculty of Economics University of Indonesia; former Senior Deputy and Acting Governor of Bank Indonesia.

Yung Chul Park Professor, Department of Economics, Korea University; Ambassador on Financial Matters for Korea.

Innwon Park Associate Professor, Graduate School of International Studies, Korea University. Has research interests in Trade Liberalisation and Regional Economic Integration (APEC; EAEC; Northeast Asia; and ASEAN); Foreign Direct Investment and Development in Development Countries. Has published widely on issues such as financial reforms, trade arrangements, and regional integration.

Oldrich Dedek Member of the Monetary Board and Deputy Governor of the Czech National Bank; former Economics Advisor to the Governor of the Czech National Bank, and Deputy Director of the Economics Institute of the Czech National Bank.

Ilan Goldfajn Director of the Economic Policy Department, Central Bank of Brazil; ex-Professor of PUC-Rio, and former IMF Staff Member; Consultant of various international organizations (e.g., World Bank, IMF, UN), and of international banks and domestic banks.

Ricardo Gottschalk Fellow of IDS; former Economic Advisor to the Planning Secretary of Sao Paulo State Government, Brazil; Reseacher of Fundap, Brazil.

José Antonio Ocampo Executive Secretary of the Economic Commission for Latin America and the Caribbean (ECLAC); former Minister of Finance and Public Credit, and of Agriculture and Social Development, Colombia; member of the Board of Directors of FEDESARROLLO.

Index